Modern America

MODERN AMERICA

WALTER T. K. NUGENT
Indiana University

HOUGHTON MIFFLIN COMPANY
BOSTON

Atlanta   Dallas   Geneva, Illinois   Hopewell, New Jersey   Palo Alto

Printed in the U.S.A.

Library of Congress Catalog Card Number: 72-85905

ISBN: 0-395-14051-X

Preface

During the several years when I was working on this book, colleagues and students would often ask, "What are you up to these days?" I would answer, "Writing a textbook on recent American history." Their normal reaction was to raise their eyebrows, or even roll their eyeballs, and after a few seconds of trying to think of something polite to say, they would usually come up with "Yes, but what are you doing that's *original?*" or "I thought there already was a textbook," or most succinctly, "Who needs it?" At that point I would launch into an explanation, beginning with my belief that existing books had not said everything that today's college students want to know about the recent American past, and that indeed there was plenty of room for a different kind of book, and that I hoped I was writing it. Specifically, I told them that the differences between this book and other texts came down to two main points.

First, this text is briefer than others. It was planned that way, so that instructors could use it as a core of information and interpretation (yet not a "reference work" that would be fact-crammed and unreadable), build a list of paperback readings around it, and argue with it as they wished. Many of us who have been teaching American history have become disenchanted with the big, fat "blockbuster" textbook that prevailed through the 1950s and into the 1960s. On the other hand, when we tried to ignore a text entirely, and asked students to read a stack of paperbacks, it often happened that the course became amorphous or even invertebrate. My own view of what was needed was a relatively short "corebook," rather than a "textbook," and here it is.

Second, this book takes a broader view than other texts of what is worth knowing about in history. History is indeed past politics and foreign affairs, but it is also, in my opinion, past demography, past economic developments, past ideas, past works of art and science, and past popular attitudes. We want to know what happened to society and the people in it, not just what political leaders did. In fact, politics and foreign policy are better understood after we gain a firm idea of social, economic, and cultural patterns, since these patterns underlie political behavior and actions. Consequently, about 60 percent of this book—a much larger proportion than in other texts on recent American history—deals directly with demographic, economic, and cultural changes. And the chapters on those changes usually precede the chapters on politics and diplomacy for the same period. Thus we will be looking at such events as the movement of white and black people, changes in status, business cycles, popular attitudes (what I call "folkthemes"), minority groups of various kinds, age structures and life expectancy, and other nonpolitical matters in some detail. What we have here, then, is a "corebook" that emphasizes social change in America over the last several decades.

Many people have helped me greatly in the preparation of this book, and I must thank several of them in particular; they are not responsible for the results, but they preserved me from error on many occasions: Robert F. Byrnes and Robert D. Cross, who were there from the start and for much of the way; Arthur S. Link and James T. Patterson, who provided invaluable readings of the manuscript and confirmed me in the conviction that a strong emphasis on demography was needed in a text on recent history; and Gerard F. McCauley, Cliff K. Travis, Peter Curtis, and Glanville Downey, for essential help. I also thank my wife and children for putting up with my more mercurial moments during the research and writing process.

WALTER T. K. NUGENT

Bloomington, Indiana

Contents

Maps and Graphs

Victorian America: a family outing around 1900. (Culver Pictures, Inc.)

1

THE ECLIPSE OF THE OLD AMERICA, 1865-1897

Since the late 1960s—when the Vietnam War was at its peak, universities were most uproarious, ghetto riots seemed unending, and the general public began to take notice of something called the "drug culture"—the notion has become almost commonplace that American society is going through a crisis in values. The future, through the final third of the twentieth century, seems to have no clear shape (except for the frustrating persistence of problems such as overpopulation, environmental pollution, and the lurking threat of atomic war). At the same time, the experience of the past is not, in some people's view, providing very many helpful lessons. Traditional lines of authority—in the home, in education, in politics, even in the military—appear to be loosening. Established patterns of social behavior, from dress to consumption to sex to race relations, are eroding under rivers of criticism, sometimes rational, sometimes emotional.

As American society begins its careening path through the last decades of the twentieth century, it presents the picture of a people enormously wealthy, on the average, but too often, in individual cases, poverty-stricken; of a nation immensely powerful, but with a government, especially the executive branch, increasingly distrusted by the people; and, overall, of a society not at peace with itself, forgetful of its own revolutionary origins of 200 years ago. America looks in many respects fat and middle-aged, her spiritual arteries hardening, without a clearly defined purpose except her self-preservation. To many individual Americans, that is not enough. Much evidence suggests that America is undergoing, or is about to undergo, some profound changes as the 1970s begin. But it is hazardous even to guess what this country will be like twenty or thirty years hence, after the changes take place.

The Late Nineteenth
Century Parallel

Although the present may be an uncertain time, and the future mysterious and possibly dangerous, the past presents some consolations. Whatever else may be said about it, society at least survived it, even though what is now past was once a present and a future. Moreover, to the people who once faced those other presents and futures, their problems and their crises of values and their uncertainties about what was to come were, from time to time, as baffling as those American society now confronts. The stresses and changes which beset America in the late nineteenth century were in all specific respects different from those of the late twentieth, but they were just as severe. And it is not likely that the response of late twentieth-century Americans to their problems could be as lame, groping, and sadly unsuccessful as the response of late nineteenth-century Americans was to theirs.

From the end of the Civil War to the close of the 1890s, the contours of American society probably changed more than in any period of comparable length in its history. The America of 1860 would have been recognizable in many important ways to a revisiting Founding Father. Not so, the America of the late nineties. The biggest differences between America in 1860 and in 1890—a people no longer predominantly farmers, now effectively occupying the whole area between the Atlantic and the Pacific, operating a national, industrialized economy rather than a localized, agricultural-mercantile one, and increasingly active in world affairs—were already becoming visible by the time of the Centennial Exposition in 1876. But the magnitude and profundity of those and other changes were not clearly realized until much later. Consequently the late nineteenth century in the United States, the time of the first large-scale confrontations with industrial and urban conditions, deserves to be looked at briefly both as a backdrop to the history of America in the twentieth century, and as an example of a society enjoying and producing changes which it understood so poorly that it unwittingly provoked within itself a deep "crisis of values" by the turn of the century.

Centrifugal Forces:
The Movement of People

American institutions, wrote the British observer James Lord Bryce in 1887, "represent an experiment in the rule of the multitudes, tried on a scale unprecedentedly vast, and the results of which every one is concerned to watch. . . . Thoughtful Europeans have begun to realize, whether with satisfaction or regret, the enormous and daily-increasing influence of the United States, and the splendour of the part reserved for them in the development of civilization." Bryce was not the only onlooker impressed with American development in the "Gilded Age"; indeed, it was impossible to miss. Most concretely and visibly, development occurred in two great areas of life: the physical expansion of the population and the increased size and complexity of the economy.

In 1865 the land area and natural resources of the United States were much as they are today but were largely unspoiled, waiting to be exploited. The boundaries of the continental United States did not change after Gadsden's Purchase in 1853, and no significant nonadjacent areas were added between the Civil War and the late 1890s, except for Alaska in 1867 and part of Samoa in 1889. "Manifest Destiny" was not a keynote of the Gilded Age, as it was during the 1840s and again in the late 1890s; the imperialist urge was unusually quiescent. Instead of pushing beyond their borders, as they did into Texas, Oregon, and California in the 1840s and into the Caribbean and the Pacific in 1898 and after, the American people busied themselves with occupying the land they already had. The population roughly doubled between 1865 and 1897, growing from about 35.7 million to 72.2 million. This increase was not evenly spread, however. Virtually all of the population changes of the period fell under three headings: (1) the "westward movement," the internal migration which made the population west of the Mississippi and Missouri Rivers increase at a much more rapid rate than the population to the east, and which ended the "American frontier" before 1900; (2) urbanization, or the continual increase in the proportion of city-dwellers to total population because of the formation of new cities or the growth of existing ones; (3) immigration from abroad, mostly Europe. Some people participated in none of the three movements; others in one, two, or all three.

Since the time of Leif Ericsson's voyages in A.D. 1000, America had been a magnetic "frontier," and in 1865 the unoccupied West included over a million square miles. But by 1890, despite inconveniences such as the 600 flat and semi-arid miles of the Great Plains, the huge herds of buffalo, and the Plains Indians who depended on them for life and resented the white man's destruction of them in the seventies, the frontier line of settlement had disappeared, leaving only a few pockets of uninhabited territory. The population of the trans-Mississippi West almost quadrupled, rising from 4.5 million to 16.8 million people, most of them in the Great Plains states. Despite the melodramatic imagery handed down from the time of dime novels to television, the typical experience of post–Civil War western settlement involved plains more than mountains or desert, farms more than towns, sod-busting more than gold mining or cattle drives, barbed wire more than open range, railroads more than stage coaches, backbreaking work more than saloons and sporting houses, and a scarcity of water more than a scarcity of Long Branch whiskey.

There was, to be sure, a "mining frontier." From the first California gold strikes in '49, through Nevada and the Dakotas in the sixties and seventies, to Cripple Creek and the Yukon in the late nineties, hardy (and greedy) souls tried to get rich quick by sifting gold and silver from western mountainsides. A handful did strike it rich. Mackay and Fair found a quarter of a billion pre-income-tax dollars in silver when they reopened Nevada's Comstock Lode in 1873. More often the story was as Mark Twain described in *Roughing It*: "We had not less than thirty thousand 'feet' apiece in the 'richest mines on earth,' as the frenzied cant phrased it—and were in debt to the butcher. We were stark mad with excitement—drunk with happiness—smothered under mountains of prospective wealth—arrogantly compassionate toward the plodding millions who knew not our marvelous canyon—but our credit was not good at the grocer's." The lonely prospector was already giving way to the mining company with the capital to employ modern technology.

There was also, certainly, a "cattleman's frontier," which brought wealth for a short time to a few stout folk who drove thousands of half-wild cattle from south Texas to railheads in Missouri and Kansas from 1866 until 1873 when the railroad reached Texas, and again after 1880 in order to stock the northern Great Plains.

But railroads also made possible a much more significant frontier, in terms of numbers and permanence: the last frontier of the farmer. With railroads in the vanguard, Americans pushed relentlessly across the notorious "Great American Desert," impelled by idealism and opportunism, courage and brutality. Within a decade or so after Appomattox, they destroyed several million buffalo. By 1890, they had "pacified" the Plains Indians, the seminomadic tribes of whom the largest were the Sioux in the north and the Comanche, Kiowa, and Apache in the central and southern plains— people who doggedly, then despairingly, resisted the expropriation of their country. Sitting Bull, the great chief of the Sioux, lamented the Indians' plight in 1877: "I never made war on the United States government. I never stood in the white man's country. I never committed any depredations in the white man's country. I never made the white man's heart bleed. The white man came on to my land and followed me. The white man made me fight for my hunting grounds. The white man made me kill him or he would kill my friends, my women, and my children." Dependent upon the buffalo, less "civilized" (i.e., agricultural and mechanical) than southeastern tribes, such as the Cherokee or Seminoles who had been pushed westward before the Civil War into present day Oklahoma, the Plains Indians were herded onto reservations, made "wards of the government" by act of Congress in 1887, and deprived both of American citizenship and of their tribal culture.

Americans, while hostile toward the Indians, were simply ignorant of the problems of people attempting to turn the Plains into farms. The Homestead Act and other federal legislation dividing up the public domain provided farmers with nothing but acres, and often too few of them to produce a living in semi-arid regions. Settlers needed from $1,000 to $1,500 in cash or credit, which they often obtained partly through borrowing and partly from selling farmland they owned farther east, in order to move to Kansas, Nebraska, or Texas, break the sod, fence the land, drill a well, build a house, plant crops and buy livestock, and survive for several months until the first crops came in. Homestead Act land amounted to only about one-tenth of the newly-farmed area; better land could be had from railroads, to which the government gave large tracts as an endowment to help pay construction costs, or out of public domain, which the government retained for direct sale.

The settlers of the Plains were consequently farmers whose capital resources were small but not nonexistent. Some went west in order to "make it"; others migrated because they had failed elsewhere. The average settler was neither a landless migrant nor a landed baron, but a lower middle-class American who had grown up on a farm in a nearby state. Most were native-born, but considerable numbers were immigrants, of whom the non-English speaking (Germans, Swedes, Russian Mennonites, Bohemians, and others) often settled in colonies, making the ethnic composition of the trans-Missouri states more diverse than the rural areas of older states like Ohio or Kentucky. By the mid-nineties, the trans-Missouri West was dotted with a mixture of millions of people, achieving mixed economic results and substantial frustration. By then the area was boiling with bitter political protest.

While the tide of settlers drove the frontier line westward and into history, even greater numbers swelled the Middle Atlantic and East North Central states, chiefly in cities. The American population not only doubled between the Civil War and 1900, but the proportion of city-dwellers was doubling—one-fifth in 1860, two-fifths in 1900. Six cities had populations of 100,000 or more in 1860; thirty-nine in 1900. The first American million-plus metropolis, New York, reached that size (as yet without Brooklyn) in the seventies, while two others, Chicago and Philadelphia, did so by 1890. With large-scale urbanism came large and unprecedented problems, which were mostly unsolved by 1900. By then, some experience with urban living was widespread in the United States. Some of the new smaller metropolises (i.e., cities of 100,000 to 500,000) were mainly appendages of the giants, satellite overflows from an already thriving center; examples were Newark and Jersey City. More often they were the first major cities in a whole region, growing up like San Francisco or Cleveland basically from fresh or salt-water commerce, or like Kansas City, Denver, or Indianapolis, because of railroad connections and the gradual build-up of the surrounding area, or hinterland, with agriculture or mining. In the Great Plains, regional metropolises appeared regularly in census returns twenty to thirty years after the first heavy influx of commercial farmers, indicating the function of these cities as hubs of trade, finance, and culture for their hinterlands, and as primary processing centers (milling, meat packing) for staple products raised

THE EMERGING METROPOLISES, 1860–1900

Each two-digit number represents a city. The first digit indicates the year of the federal census in which the city first had a 100,000+ population. The second digit indicates the chief reason why it reached that size.

First Digit

6 = Existing 100,000+ Cities in 1860
7 = City Reached 100,000+ by 1870
8 = City Reached 100,000+ by 1880
9 = City Reached 100,000+ by 1890
0 = City Reached 100,000+ by 1900

Second Digit

1 = Growth Based on Shipping and Commerce
2 = Satellite City
3 = Primary Processing Center and/or Regional Metropolis
4 = National Market Manufacturing Center
5 = Growth Based on Other or Mixed Reasons

Example: 71 = Shipping City Reaching Metropolitan Size by 1870
93 = Primary Processing Center Emergent by 1890
04 = Manufacturing Town Emergent by 1900

Names of Cities:

61 New York	71 San Francisco	81 Cleveland	93 Minneapolis	01 Los Angeles
61 Philadelphia	71 Buffalo	81 Detroit	93 St Paul	01 Memphis
61 Brooklyn	71 Louisville	81 Milwaukee	93 Omaha	02 Worcester
61 St Louis	72 Newark	82 Jersey City	93 Kansas City	02 Paterson
61 Chicago	75 Washington, D. C.	85 Pittsburgh	93 Denver	03 St Joseph
61 Baltimore		85 Providence	93 Indianapolis	03 Scranton
61 Boston			94 Rochester	04 Syracuse
61 Cincinnati				04 Fall River
61 New Orleans				05 New Haven

nearby. Generalizing broadly, one can say that rural areas and regions east of the Mississippi grew in population very quickly through the period, but urban areas and the West grew at even faster rates. Meanwhile, immigration from abroad boosted cities and rural areas, East and West alike.

Immigrants had been arriving on the Eastern seaboard for 250 years before the Civil War, but with few exceptions, mainly a few hundred thousand Irish and Germans, they were homogeneous in being English-speaking, Protestant, and ethnically British. Post–Civil War immigration was significantly different, not only because of its large size but also because of its "foreignness" in language, religion, and ethnicity. Old-stock Americans were often puzzled by it, blamed it for some knotty problems such as "corruption" in city government, and by the end of the century were often anxious to prohibit it by federal law. The immigrants, on the other hand, had virtually nothing in common except the fact of their birth somewhere else and the suspicions directed at them by the native-born. Even within groups, or what seemed to outsiders to be groups, deep splits existed; between German reform Jews and Russian orthodox Jews, northern and southern Italians, Lutheran and Catholic Germans, relations were no closer than between the immigrants and the natives. The term *immigrant* covered scores of peoples, disparate in language, origin, culture, religion, or economic position.

They came in quantity—more than 12.5 million between 1865 and 1897, mostly Europeans plus some Canadians and, until Congress excluded them by law in 1882, Chinese. Less than a million arrived in the late seventies, which were depression years in America and Europe, but over three million came in the prosperous early eighties. The sources of immigration shifted slowly at first, then more rapidly from the mid-eighties on. Ireland, Germany, and Scandinavia sent over half of all immigrants between 1865 and 1885. But by the late nineties, these relatively "familiar" people were outnumbered three to one by Southern and Eastern Europeans. In 1896, for the first time—in a year of labor trouble, agrarian revolt, depression, and a bitter election—Russian and Italian immigrants outnumbered the combined Irish, Germans, and Scandinavians.

THE OLD AND THE NEW IMMIGRATION, 1866–1900

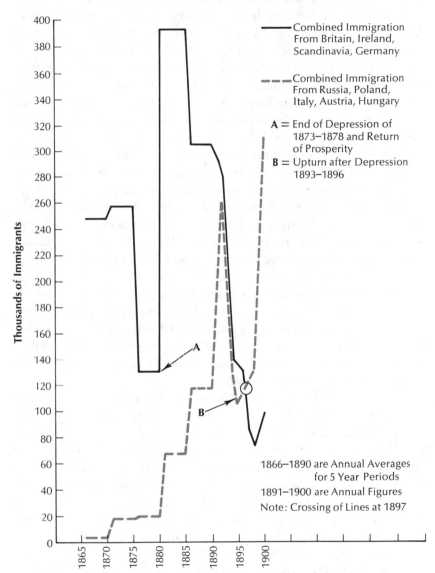

━━━ Combined Immigration
From Britain, Ireland,
Scandinavia, Germany

━ ━ ━ Combined Immigration
From Russia, Poland,
Italy, Austria, Hungary

A = End of Depression of
1873–1878 and Return
of Prosperity

B = Upturn after Depression
1893–1896

1866–1890 are Annual Averages
for 5 Year Periods
1891–1900 are Annual Figures
Note: Crossing of Lines at 1897

Note points A and B: Immigration rose steeply at the end of the depressions of the 1870s and the 1890s. In about 1897, "new" immigrants began to outnumber "old" ones.

The "older immigrants" arrived just as the Great Plains were being settled, and many of them became prairie farmers alongside native Americans, sharing the same successes and problems and ultimately, in the nineties, joining them in Populist protest. The "newer immigrants" arriving in the nineties came too late to people the Plains, and seldom had the capital to do so anyway; much more often they stayed in the large cities where they had disembarked, swelling the ranks of the urban poor as well as the fears of native Americans about the evils of great cities.

Sometimes people became immigrants for religious reasons, such as Russian Mennonites escaping conscription into the Czar's army in the seventies, or Eastern European Jews fleeing pogroms later on. Others, such as some of the Irish and many of the subject nationalities in the Austro-Hungarian Empire, were escaping a political climate stifling to their nationalist ardor. But more often, economic reasons both pushed people out of Europe and pulled them toward the United States or other parts of the New World such as Argentina and Brazil. To European peasants tilling small plots of nearly exhausted land, to laborers who heard of comparatively high American wages, to all who read steamship advertisements or glowing letters from townsmen or relatives already in America, the republic across the sea seemed a golden dream that could come true for the meager price of steerage passage.

But the physical and psychological shocks of immigration began at that point. The twelve- to fourteen-day steerage trip did cost as little as ten or fifteen dollars, but it was miserably overcrowded and primitive; steerages were "floating stockyards," in the words of one Navy doctor in 1880. The wrench of leaving an ancestral home and of arriving at entry points like New York's Castle Garden or Ellis Island, then to be tossed into a brawling foreign city, compounded the disorientation. But many people did it, with the result that despite great increases in the native population, the foreign-born population kept pace, at 13.8 percent of the total in 1870, 13.4 percent in 1900, while the proportion of foreign-born together with their children rose from one in four to one in three.

As the population grew more "racially mixed" through the eighties and nineties, the attitudes of native Americans grew less friendly. No matter how foreign the Irish Catholic or the Polish Jew or the Chinese tradesman or the Bohemian farmer were to each other, they were all "outsiders" to the native Americans. To many natives, the Irish and Poles had the wrong religion, Jews ate weird food and wore weird clothes, the Chinese were an inferior race, and southern Europeans were dirty, lazy, illiterate, and unable to comprehend democratic institutions. Not surprisingly, the post–Civil War generation that failed miserably to protect or provide for the millions of emancipated slaves also made the first attempts to exclude specific immigrant groups on racist grounds. By no means all, not even a majority, of Americans felt this way; many agreed with Congressman William D. "Pig-Iron" Kelley of Pennsylvania, who called for laws "to aid the poor and oppressed laborers of other lands to escape from a diet of 'rye and potatoes,' to a land of free schools and liberal wages, in which the fare of the family will be wheat, mutton, beef, or pork, with the vegetables and the fruits of all the States of our broad, and then assuredly prosperous, country." But nativism lurked in many hearts. Immigration was a moral and social problem for native Americans, and their response to it was ambiguous.

The net effect of the three great population movements of the late nineteenth century—to the West, to cities, and from abroad—was to diversify, often to fragment, the American people. By 1897, in contrast to 1865, a population twice as large occupied nearly twice the land area. Urban-dwelling was twice as common, but the novelty of metropolitan life and the foreignness of millions who lived there did little to allay the traditional American suspicion of cities, handed down since the days of Thomas Jefferson. If old-stock Americans found their trans-Missouri West a new, strange experience, they found great cities even more so, and the tide of immigration strangest of all.

The society was not without binding elements, however, which helped to counteract the centrifugal forces. A single federal government, never again internally threatened after 1865, bound the country politically; the 1787 Constitution capped a common legal system; the English language was customary everywhere except (temporarily, it was assumed) among certain immigrants. Society was also united to an extent by a developing system of communications, particularly daily newspapers, whose circulation increased sixfold, a growing periodical press, and a book and pamphlet industry which more than doubled between 1865 and 1890. The Associated Press began to syndicate news nationally. The network of railroads, which crossed the continent several times by the nineties, served to transport not only goods but people as well, and the social effects of the railroad in moving people far beyond their birthplaces to new farms or metropolises helped to homogenize the population somewhat. But transportation and communications technology did not remotely knit together a society that was changing so fast, in terms of simple demography alone during the seventies, eighties, and nineties, that it could hardly describe its own problems, much less solve them.

The Wonders and Woes of Industrialism

Economic developments between the Civil War and the late nineties also mixed successes and problems; there was much to be proud of, much that was personally painful. Although there were clear signs before 1860 that the United States was passing through an Industrial Revolution similar to the one being experienced in Britain and western Europe during the nineteenth century, the most visible, fast-moving phase of American industrialization happened after 1860. By 1900 it had outstripped the industrial production of Britain, and the chances that the United States could ever revert to a predominantly agricultural economy were about zero. America's emergence as a world political power around 1900 took place, not coincidentally, when it possessed a large, urban population and an industrial economy comparable to that of any other power.

Between the mid-sixties and the late nineties, the real output of the economy expanded at a rate about twice as fast as the growth of the population. Every sector of the economy grew substantially. Agricultural output more than doubled in quantity, as farmers moved west and brought the Great Plains under staple-crop cultivation, and as mechanization, the plant and animal sciences, and the ability to reach distant markets made farm output more efficient per man-hour of input. But agricultural production increased only

slightly faster than population, whereas the most striking development was in manufacturing, where production grew three times as
fast as population. In the 1870s, for the first time in American experience, farmers dropped below a majority of the labor force, as
workers in the other sectors (such as manufacturing, trade, finance,
and transportation) began to outnumber them. Despite substantial
increases in the farm labor force, as a consequence of western settlement, the real driveshaft of the economy in the late sixties and early
seventies was railroad building, not only across the plains and
mountains to the Pacific, but also in the industrializing Northeast
quarter of the country. Manufacturing of rails, locomotives, and
other steel products prospered on the demand that the railroads created. Steel, petroleum, and electrical equipment, and more railroads, sparked further growth in the eighties.

The American economy, with its abundant coal and ore deposits,
resources for steam and electrical power, and a labor force being
swelled by foreign immigration, was endowed from the eighties onward with one further critical element: an inventive business leadership that found ways to operate efficiently and profitably what
were then very large enterprises. By the late nineties, "big business," in the recognizably modern form of the multi-million-dollar
corporation, was an entrenched part of American life, and apparently a necessary one from the standpoint of continued economic
development. By then it was very debatable whether big business,
in the long run, could survive the social dislocations, such as maldis-
tributed profits and labor violence, that it seemed almost inevitably
to carry with it.

The great expansion of manufacturing, together with the physical tie of the railroad network and the less visible ties of large corporate managements, made interdependence as much of a keynote as
growth was. American railroads, with 35,000 miles of operating
track in 1865, grew to 70,000 miles in 1873, doubled again by the
late eighties, and by 1897 stretched over 183,000 miles, not counting another 160,000 miles in doubled track, switching yards, and
sidings. The spectacular achievement of four transcontinental lines
—a single one had been the dream of the fifties and sixties—was
dwarfed in everyday usefulness by the growing network connecting
the trunk lines, criss-crossing densely populated industrial districts
in the Northeast, and carrying people to and from work in and
around large cities. In two great waves of railroad-building, from

1868 to 1873 and from 1880 to 1893, the transcontinentals reduced travel time from Kansas City to the Pacific by 90 percent to less than a week, and enabled people or goods to move hundreds of miles a day instead of fifteen or twenty. Ships and wagons could never have permitted Omahans or Californians to use Pittsburgh steel in quantity, or allowed oil refined in Cleveland to light lamps in New York, or put the Kansas wheat farmer in competition with another farmer hundreds of miles distant. The railroads were the prime initial factor in helping to create an interdependent, national economy.

Interstate commerce began to play a major role, and interstate, unified corporate managements were being devised. From the fifties to the seventies, railroad entrepreneurs such as Commodore Cornelius Vanderbilt of the New York Central and J. Edgar Thomson of the Pennsylvania began tying together assortments of small, local roads into interstate companies of which long-distance trunk lines were the core. These made possible freight shipments over hundreds of miles without costly transfers. Farmers and other users of the roads consistently denounced high freight rates, but the economist Edward Atkinson expressed a popular view when he praised Vanderbilt for having "abolished distance," and said that "his fortune was but a trifling share of the labor that the men of Massachusetts and other Eastern States have been saved by the application of that single piece of capital, the railway which he controlled, to the mere mechanical work of distributing the products of the Great West."

The railroads greatly stimulated manufacturing, directly through their demand for steel and other goods needed to build and operate the roads, and indirectly by making distant markets accessible. The manufacture of perishable goods, such as foodstuffs, rose dramatically, no doubt in large part because the expanding city population had to buy more processed food, since they could not raise it as farmers did. Output of liquor and other beverages rose fourfold between 1879 and 1899, bakery goods and processed sugar increased from five to sevenfold. But production of semidurables, such as clothing and shoes, and consumer durables, such as furniture and vehicles, increased only slightly faster than population. The big boom was in producer durables—heavy goods used to make other goods—such as industrial machines, farm equipment, electrical equipment, or locomotives. Office and factory equipment quadrupled; steel production shot from under twenty thousand tons in

1867 to over seven million tons in 1897 despite two technological revolutions in steel-making, the Bessemer process in the seventies and the open-hearth method in the eighties and nineties; petroleum refining and the manufacture of electrical equipment were practically unknown as the period opened, but they were giant industries when it closed.

The availability of raw materials, a labor force, technology, transportation, and markets were each essential to the manufacturing outburst of the time, but business leadership was required to capitalize on them, and one of the peculiarities of the age was the energy, ruthlessness, and managerial skill of a relatively small number of industrial leaders in an exceptionally competitive situation. The most famous of these men were Andrew Carnegie in steel, Cornelius Vanderbilt, James J. Hill, E. H. Harriman, and Jay Gould in railroading, and above all John D. Rockefeller of the Standard Oil Company and J. Pierpont Morgan in investment banking. They ingeniously built small companies into vast empires, using new technology to create "economies of scale," developing legal devices such as the corporation and the trusteeship to gain control over collections of companies, and cultivating the admiration of a populace imbued with the myth of the self-made man and the moral goodness of worldly acquisitiveness. They were personally responsible for much of the interdependence, in the form of business consolidations, between manufacturing, finance, and transportation, and thus for the nationalization of the economy.

Rockefeller, Morgan, Carnegie and other captains of industry were amply rewarded for their skills by the accumulation of personal fortunes sometimes reaching several hundred million dollars. For a much larger number of other people actively involved in the growth and interdependence of the economy, namely the workers in factories or mines or on railroads or farms, the benefits were less tangible, and in fact often very dubious. The rhetoric of interdependence did not include them. In 1878, the *Bankers' Magazine* proclaimed that "for success in industrial production capital now has to move in larger masses than formerly. The principle of association gathers together in banks and in corporations for manufacturing and distributing commodities vast sums, which are expended in constructing and working steam engines, railroads, telegraphs and a multitude of labor-saving inventions which employ millions of operatives. . . . We might as well quarrel with the law of gravitation, as with this equally resistless law of organization of capital." But the same editorial refused to apply the same principle to labor unions, wherein "ambitious men, greedy of power . . . taught their ignorant and credulous followers to believe that war was the normal relation between the masters[!] and their men." When labor attempted to organize, as it did in the short-lived and "radical" National Labor Union of 1866–73 or the loosely-organized and impractically idealistic Knights of Labor, which flourished in the eighties, it ran into a stacked deck.

Employers and much of the press damned unionists as communists, anarchists, and socialists; the courts refused to uphold the right to strike, boycott, or bargain collectively; union leaders could be held personally responsible for any property damage resulting from the strikes they had called, regardless of the actual cause. Yet employers could blacklist a man suspected of being a labor organizer, without redress; they could fire strikers *en masse* and replace them with hungry immigrants unaware, or too hungry to care, that they were being made "scabs"; and they could and did use spies and private armies to break unions. Public armed forces often were sent to "uphold law and order" against strikers, as when state militia came to Pittsburgh at the time of the "Great Railroad Strike" of 1877, and nervously fired into the crowd. More than fifty were killed in that first nationwide eruption of labor strife, which spread from Pennsylvania to California. In 1894, President Cleveland sent federal troops to "protect the mails," and break the strike, at the Pullman Company near Chicago. The public and the authorities did not yet understand industrial conditions, and could not comprehend labor militance.

The general condition of skilled workers was, in certain senses, not bad; the average of dollar wages for this group rose slightly through the period, while the cost of living declined, and thus real wages rose. However, too many workers did not share in this rise, and improvements in real wages did not nearly match rises in output or wealth. The average annual cash income of all nonfarm wage earners in 1890 was $486. For this they could feed, house, heat, clothe, and sometimes entertain themselves and their families, but they could save little, acquire little property, nor protect themselves against disasters in a day before health or accident insurance, workmen's compensation, or pensions. Fatal accidents to railroad workers alone averaged more than 2,000 a year during the nineties.

The "Great Railroad Strike" of 1877 spread across the country from Pennsylvania to California; the troops and the crowd committed mutual mayhem. (Vigo County Historical Society, Terre Haute, Indiana)

Work stoppages or layoffs, of which there were over a thousand per year after 1880, meant wages irrevocably lost. Child labor was common in mines and textile factories, brutalizing children and depriving adults of jobs. Women worked a ten- to twelve-hour day for less than a dollar. Peonage and contract labor forced immigrants into virtual involuntary servitude. The poorly-skilled worker, in an industrial situation, had lost much of the bargaining power and freedom of job choice that he had had in an economy dominated, as it was in pre–Civil War days, by small shops, craft work, and local-market farms. Collective employment replaced individual employment, but collective bargaining did not replace individual bargaining. As a result, the growing power of the economy was accompanied by the decreasing power and increasing frustration of its workers. By the nineties, America's "labor question" was dangerous and baffling.

Farmers seldom experienced the brutalities that marred the history of industrial labor, but as a property-owning lower middle class that had formerly been the backbone of the labor force and the economy, they were increasingly deprived and degraded. Agriculture, as a sector of the economy, did well; the average farmer, as an individual, did not. Between 1860 and 1900, American farms tripled in number, doubled in acreage, rose two and a half times in total value, produced far more crops and livestock, and occupied 50 percent more workers. But compared to manufacturing and other sectors, agriculture fell behind. Crop prices, the return to the individual farmer for his effort, declined: corn brought 78 cents a bushel in 1867, 26 cents in 1897; wheat brought $2.01 in 1867, 81 cents in 1897—low, but still better than the 49 cents of 1894, a year, not surprisingly, of widespread agrarian political unrest. Railroad freight rates also declined, but as farmers moved farther west across the Plains, their total freight charges remained high. Mechanization was expensive, but essential for competition: first barbed-wire fencing and windmills, then tractors and cultivators, became necessities for western farmers. In the South, small farmers, black and white alike, chopped cotton for miserable returns and lived a life of poverty as grinding as anywhere in the country. Debt was a chronic problem for farmers in both of the capital-poor areas, the South and the West. Farming was becoming less a way of life and more a small business, with many thousands of unaffiliated small units forced to compete with each other for a share of an increasingly national, even international, market. Tenancy often resulted: in 1880, only one farm in six, outside the South, was operated by a tenant, but by 1900, one in four; in the South the proportion rose from one in four to one in three.

Many farmers were acutely aware of their problems, and on two major occasions in the post–Civil War years, they organized on a broad scale for their self-protection. In the late sixties and early seventies, the Grange (officially, the Patrons of Husbandry) spread swiftly across much of the country, and was strong enough in the staple-crop upper–Mississippi Valley states to elect sympathetic majorities in state legislatures. A handful of people, controlling terminal elevators or setting railroad freight rates, were fixing returns received by thousands of farmers for their labor. This situation was intolerable to the farmers and to some urban businessmen whom the monopoly also hurt, and the state governments responded in their favor. Granger legislatures in several states, heeding farmers' and businessmen's pleas to combat monopolies in railroads and terminal warehouses, helped lower transport and storage costs by asserting the regulatory authority of state governments over private enterprises within the states. State and federal courts upheld the principle of state police power over private enterprises, which affected the general welfare, especially in the "Granger cases" (notably *Munn* v. *Illinois* and *Peik* v. *Chicago and Northwestern Railway*) that the United States Supreme Court decided in 1877.

Farmers were in trouble again a decade later. First, the regulatory effect of the Granger laws was largely nullified by another Supreme Court decision, the Wabash case of 1886, that denied state regulatory power over interstate commerce, which by that time involved a large share of farm product. More disastrous, a farm depression struck the West and South from late 1887 until late 1896. Farmers responded to extremely low crop prices, heavy freight costs, crushing mortgage indebtedness, and lack of circulating currency by organizing into Farmers' Alliances, which quickly devolved into a political party in Kansas in 1890 and nationally in 1891: the People's party, or Populists. By then, farmers' problems as they defined them—especially the demand for more abundant currency—were solvable only at the national level, and despite the Populists' success in many state elections in the early nineties, their failure to capture the presidency and the Congress demonstrated among other things that it was no longer possible in the United States to equate "farmers" with "the people."

Farmers had become one economic group among many, and they had become more dependent on nonfarm sectors such as transportation, finance, and manufacturing. They were producing surpluses in excess of existing domestic markets, and selling their products on world markets while buying finished goods on higher-priced, protected, domestic markets. They were too efficient for their own good. Efficiency created surpluses, which brought lower prices and drove marginal farmers into tenancy or into deep and frustrating debt or completely out of farming. Unable to effect consolidations parallel to those that so enriched the big businessman, the farmer became a casualty of economic forces that he believed should have benefited him.

The impotence of the farmers was another example, along with the dehumanizing of industrial labor and the concentration of capital into unresponsible monopolies, of the frictions, impediments, and inefficiencies that developed within the late nineteenth century economy. Growth and interdependence, remarkable though they were at that time, might ideally have been much more beneficial socially and even more profitable economically had they been rationally governed.

Government, rather than intervening actively to correct concentrating wealth and inadequate rewards for farmers and industrial workers, as it would do in the twentieth century, was expected to remain aloof. A labor spokesman claimed as early as 1869 that "as labor is the foundation and cause of national prosperity, it is both the duty and interest of government to foster and protect it." Farmers in the 1890s repeated that idea. But it was a minority view. Federal receipts and expenditures crept slowly upward throughout the period, but no faster than the general economy, remaining at 2 to 3 percent of the gross national product. Revenue came mostly from customs duties on imports (tariffs) and excise taxes on liquor and tobacco, while the money was spent in the seventies mainly to pay the Civil War debt, in the late eighties and nineties for veterans' pensions, and in general to maintain the post office, equip military garrisons in Indian areas, and pay for a minuscule bureaucracy.

The federal government did stimulate economic activity in a number of ways, such as selective tariffs on foreign-made goods, ship-building subsidies, donations of enormous tracts of the public domain to support railroad-building, navigation aids along coasts, and improvements of rivers and harbors. Also, the federal government did begin to regulate private enterprise in a very tentative fashion with the passage of the Interstate Commerce Act in 1887, which controlled railroads, and the Sherman Anti-Trust Act in 1890, which set restraints on certain other businesses. But neither act was stringently enforced. Governments, federal and state, were not inactive—the period was not, as often reputed, one of thoroughgoing *laissez faire*—but their regulatory actions were few.

Flaws in the economy retarded growth itself. A world-wide deflationary trend lasted from 1873 to 1897. It meant that prices declined and dollars bought more (the cost of living in 1897 was 73 percent of the 1866 level) but those valuable dollars, especially for farmers—the largest part of the population and the labor force—

were harder to come by. Capital investment in new factories or other enterprises might well have been greater if dollars had been more plentiful. But the deflationary prospect encouraged builders to wait for lower prices, and people with capital tended to put their funds into bonds or other investments with a fixed dollar return. The resulting high rate of savings did provide funds for banks and other businesses to invest in new factories or railroads, and foreign investors lent large amounts of working capital to Americans. But capital markets were loosely organized, and the banking system had no central regulating mechanism. The result of this major flaw was the intensification of money shortages, causing periodic panics, and the heating up of speculation when money was plentiful. Investment capital was often either overabundant or too scarce, so that recessions and speculative periods, rather than stability, were chronic.

The business cycle was consequently very irregular throughout the period. Two major depressions struck the country, the first from 1873 through 1878, and the second from 1893 until 1897. Spotty slowdowns and recessions occurred at other times, most notably the farm depression which lasted for nearly a decade after 1887. The late nineteenth century American economy was a perplexing mixture of great overall growth, amidst few periods of even two or three consecutive years that could be called truly prosperous for the mass of farmers, workers, or businessmen.

Folkthemes: The Gilded Age Mind

Much that hindsight regards as stupid, even shocking, about late nineteenth century American society becomes understandable, if not excusable, when the prevailing values and ideas of the time are taken into account. The concentration of wealth, the inequitable distribution of it, the inactivity of government, the imperialism of the closing years of the century, the decimating of the Indians and disregard for the emancipated slaves did not occur primarily as the result of malice or even, as a Briton said of his own country's imperialism, from a fit of absent-mindedness. They seemed either inevitable, or at least worth the cost, in view of the beneficial social and economic development taking place.

The "Indian Menace" personified: Geronimo of the Apaches. (Brown Brothers)

Furthermore, the Americans of that time were not a race of free-booters bent on social and economic piracy. Many of them respected ideas and learning, and intellectual achievement of a high order took place often. American inventors harnessed electricity and helped make daily newspapers and automobiles practical. Scientists included J. Willard Gibbs, whose "rule of phase" helped make complex chemical reactions predictable, and Albert A. Michelson, who began measuring stellar distances and the speed of light in the late seventies. Artists and other professional people demonstrated a high order of intellectual creativity—architects such as Richard Morris Hunt, who built mansions for the Vanderbilts and other plutocrats, and William LeBaron Jenney, who built the first steel-frame skyscraper; writers such as Mark Twain, William Dean Howells, and Henry James; social scientists such as the economist Richard T. Ely or the sociologist Lester Frank Ward; and the psychologist-philosopher William James, who developed C. S. Peirce's ideas into the peculiarly American philosophy called pragmatism. Graduate education, particularly in the form of the German-style Ph.D., began at a number of public and private universities. Far-reaching changes occurred at the lower end of the educational ladder. A widespread desire for literacy and for the fulfillment of the social and job needs of an increasingly city-dwelling population generated a rise in school enrollment from under 7 million in 1870 to nearly 15 million in 1897, a rise in the proportion of school-age population from 57 to 72 percent. By 1900, thirty-two states had legally compulsory "common school" systems, and though daily attendance was about two-thirds the enrollment and the school year was often only half its present length, an eighth-grade education was becoming a normal expectation, if not always a reality. Parochial schools began appearing in some numbers after the Catholic bishops mandated them wherever possible in 1884. Secondary schools, though enrolling fewer than 10 percent of the appropriate age group by 1897, had an assured future; and teacher training began seriously as most states created one- or two-year "normal schools" before 1900. Paralleling urbanization and economic industrialization, the educational system was taking on twentieth-century shapes.

The churches, the schools, and the press, as institutions in a society undergoing rapid social and economic changes, attempted in various ways to come to grips with those changes. Ministers who founded institutional (i.e., social action) churches, scholars critical of *laissez-faire* economic doctrines, writers of protest novels or exposés of big business were all trying to rectify the aspects of socioeconomic changes in the eighties and nineties that were harmful to major social groups and to social order itself. These people were harbingers of the crusade for "reform" that became widespread after 1900. In the late nineteenth century, however, both opinion leaders and the general church-going or magazine-reading public clung to folk-themes formulated in an earlier age and reinforced by semi-academic popularizations. The effect of these themes was to justify, rather than to analyze and criticize, the socioeconomic changes taking place. At that time, the popular impact of these themes and ideas, and the frequency with which they appeared in essays, sermons, editorials, lectures, and political speeches, made them much more significant, much more widely known and held, than the insights of a William James or a Lester Ward, or the social commentary of a Twain or a Howells.

Classical economic doctrines, as simplified and filtered through the commonly-used textbooks of political economy, helped justify resistance to governmental activity in the economy and to changes in the relation between laborers and capitalists. Adam Smith's concept of an "invisible hand" beneficently regulating the collectivity of individual economic effort was taken as a prohibition of government regulation and of labor organizations. David Ricardo's "wages fund theory"—which many people took to mean that a fixed amount of capital existed in society and that siphoning off too much into wages rather than into investment (or profits) weakened the economy for all—seemed to justify low wages. Examples abounded of the employment of theories developed by Smith, Ricardo, John Stuart Mill, and others to justify the unbridled accumulation of wealth and the resistance to unions and government action. Orthodox political economists regarded classical theory as a set of laws, scientifically determined, as binding and universal as Newton's laws of physics. On occasion, writers added a religious and moral underpinning; since economic laws were universal, like gravity, and since God was the designer of the universe, it was immoral as well as unwise to contravene them. Francis Bowen's popular text of 1870, *American Political Economy*, put it neatly: ". . . the economical laws of human nature (i.e. the principles of Political

Economy), through their general effects upon the well-being of society, manifest the contrivance, the wisdom and beneficence, of the Deity, just as clearly as do the marvellous arrangements of the material universe, or the natural means provided for the enforcement of the moral law and the punishment of crime."

In the eighties and nineties, views like Bowen's were beginning to come under attack from younger social scientists such as Ely and Ward and social-gospel ministers such as Washington Gladden, men troubled by labor strife, unsavory urban conditions, and unregulated big business. Yet the adherents of "social Darwinism," the "Gospel of Wealth," and orthodox economics remained popular. Firmly convinced that the universe operated according to unchanging natural laws, they expressed a genuine sincerity that was a huge stumbling block impeding ideological change. The widening gap between social change and the people's understanding of it was engendering blind stubbornness on one side, utopian dreams and rage on the other.

It is difficult to recapture the popular mind of past periods, but certain attitudes or popular beliefs appear so often in the writings or speeches of people of the time that we can assume they appeared in the thoughts and dreams of the general public as well. Nationalism, natural law, the virtue of producers, puritan morality, individualism, and democracy; these were folkthemes that the mass of Americans held and through which they interpreted their society. Not every American held all of them in exactly the same ways all of the time, but in one form or another they were common notions that tumbled down through time from the eighteenth century Enlightenment, from Jefferson and Jackson, and from the collective national experience of Revolution, nation-building, and Civil War.

American nationalism, like other nationalisms, reflected a belief that one's own culture and folkways were innately superior to those of other people and had something special to offer the rest of the world. This belief, though itself culturally-derived, was held to be self-evident, like Jefferson's "life, liberty, and the pursuit of happiness." In the United States after the Civil War, many retained their prewar notion that the American Revolution created a society unique in the world: "a nation," as Lincoln said, "dedicated to the proposition that all men are created equal," a place more free and less corrupt than despotic and slum-ridden Europe; in another phrase of Lincoln's, a "last, best hope of earth," to which struggling men could look for solace and hope. Such a society could not have developed without divine guidance, and indeed the long-term development of America, as the historian George Bancroft asserted, manifested the special working of Providence. America had been ordained providentially to lead the world. But how? By good example only, or by vigorous action? The preservation of the Union, by the northern victory in the Civil War, seemed to many a further proof of providential protection. To some it was also an invitation to spread the blessings of liberty to others—sometimes whether they wanted them or not. American nationalism in the late nineteenth century often assumed a benign form, in which the conviction that American society and government were superior to others led to the welcoming of immigrants who wished to become citizens, and also led to the peaceful encouraging of other nations to adopt American institutions.

More vigorous nationalists, however, began in the eighties and nineties to seek the exclusion of "undesirable and unadaptable" immigrants, as their nationalism shaded over into racial superiority, and the annexation of Pacific and Caribbean territories became a sign of a new "manifest destiny." Nationalism was a heady elixir, and like other intoxicants, its effects were unpredictable and sometimes violent.

Natural law, a second pervasive theme, affected many areas of thought. "Life, liberty, and the pursuit of happiness" continued to be "natural rights," American superiority was "natural." The final work of the great Philadelphia political economist Henry Charles Carey bore the title *The Unity of Law: as Exhibited in the Relations of Physical, Social, Mental, and Moral Science* (1872). Nothing was more insistently dubbed "natural" than political economy; as the *North American Review* stated in 1870, ". . . the laws of finance, like those of other sciences, are universal and invariable in their operation; that however they may be for a time artificially counteracted, they will ultimately assert themselves; that the mills of God, though they may grind slowly, grind exceeding small." Some interpretations of "natural law" left room for change and development; "progress" was itself supposed to be natural, and many accorded Darwinian evolution the rank of a "natural law" though, at first, an inflexible and deterministic one.

But even in these cases, and especially when natural laws were considered fixed and inexorable like the movements of the stars and planets, the popular attachment to the "natural law" notion functioned as an ideological force buttressing resistance to change, especially change in government monetary policy or in labor relations, since change involved interfering with some "natural" law. The force of the "natural law" theme began to wane by the nineties, but it was strong even then.

A third folktheme was the belief that people who in one way or another "produced" wealth were superior to those who did not. A hangover from the predominantly agricultural past, this belief rested on Adam Smith's theory that labor was the source of all wealth, and on the occupational experience of a society of farmers and craftsmen. Farmers were most prone to believe it, but expressions of "producer superiority" were also common among manufacturers into the eighties and among industrial workers into the nineties. The *Workingman's Advocate* of Chicago defined producers broadly in 1872: "In our definition of workingmen we embrace all who are engaged in productive industry; all who are in good faith obeying the Divine decree by eating bread in the sweat of their own faces, and not living upon the honest earnings of others. Not those only who open up and cultivate farms, build cities, construct railroads, and toil in workshops, but those also, who, by intellectual labor, extract the principles of science from the great arcana of nature. . . . In short, EVERY HUMAN BEING, who by physical or intellectual labor, contributes to the substantial wealth of the nation."

Producerism and the natural law theme fit together closely. "The productions of the earth," declared the constitution of the National Grange, the leading farmers' organization of the seventies, "are subject to the influence of natural laws, invariable and indisputable. . . . The ultimate object of this organization is for mutual instruction and protection, to lighten labor by diffusing a knowledge of its aims and purposes, expand the mind by tracing the beautiful laws the great Creator has established in the Universe, and to enlarge our views of Creative wisdom and power." Since producerism tried to confer moral superiority upon one economic function over others, it obscured economic understanding and slowed the comprehension of many economic changes taking place at the time. But it was deeply rooted in many minds, and its foundations only just began to shake during the closing years of the century.

"Puritanical" morality also affected the outlook of the majority upon politics, economic life, and personal relations. Though Puritan theology had long since fossilized or become softened in the "liberal" Protestant denominations, the majority of native-born Americans, as well as North European Protestant (and in some ways also, Catholic Irish) immigrants followed a code of behavior deemed to be "puritan." References to the Deity and quotations from the Bible were common and widely understood. Home and school tried to inculcate prudence, temperance, and justice. In the aftermath of the Civil War, editorialists condemned "speculation" as sinful, and the public was shocked at revelations of "gross public immorality" in Washington and city governments in the seventies. The ethic of hard work and honest accumulation—"work hard and you will get ahead"—had moral force. In personal affairs, Americans shared the buttoned-up views of their Victorian contemporaries regarding sexual conduct. The society, like any other, had its speculators, lazy people, and sexual activists, but they were uncelebrated and outside the pale. America was still very much a Protestant country. Protestant morality in its "puritan" form (shared in many ways by Irish or German Catholics and "Victorians" generally) was not easily distinguishable from the national moral code.

Individualism, the conviction that an individual should be able to act politically, economically, or in other ways without interference from society, seemed to lie at the very heart of the American creed. Free speech, a free press, freedom of worship, the right to vote, all manifested a belief in individualism, which in economic life meant the right to accumulate, possess, and use property without hindrance. But if America was a free country, freedom was not total. For example, anyone could vote—if he was male, twenty-one or over, white (except for some states where Negroes could freely vote), not an idiot or a felon. Individual freedom in economic behavior traditionally had fewer limits. The theme took many forms, the most popular of which was the "rags to riches" myth. According to that long-lived pipedream, poor but honest boys left school at a tender age to do something more productive than to sit in a class; they worked doggedly and eventually became millionaires. That this actually happened to almost no one did not hinder the wide acceptance of the idea, nor did the fact that the very wealthiest (J. P. Morgan or the Vanderbilts, for example) usually started life with silver, if not gold, spoons in their mouths. John D. Rockefeller and Andrew Carnegie were odd exceptions. But popular novelists such as Horatio Alger sold millions of copies of practically indistinguishable success stories to practically indistinguishable young clerks and apprentices. These men and women presumably cast themselves in the roles of Alger's heroes, in the belief that sweeping office floors, blacking boots, or delivering telegrams would lead, somehow, to a silk hat and a fat wallet.

Unfortunately a tradition of untrammelled individual freedom to seek wealth blocked comprehension of the changing shape of society, as did the other folkthemes. In earlier days, when the economy consisted of small units (farmers, merchants, craftsmen), individualism seemed to have worked. But what was to be thought about economic individualism when it enabled a few men, like John D. Rockefeller, to accumulate so much wealth and power that they encroached upon the economic freedom of others? When a handful of grain elevator owners in Chicago, through that kind of economic individualism, came to control markets into which thousands of farmers poured their grain, what happened to the economic freedom of the farmers? The economic growth and interdependence of the late nineteenth century fertilized economic individualism so successfully that, like plants in a dense jungle, individualism was choking itself to death. One of the most baffling questions of the age was whether this overgrowth could be cut away without destroying the plant entirely. Could restriction and regulation be made compatible with individualism, even to save individual opportunity?

Popular belief in democracy made an answer to this problem seem especially urgent. Representative government was not in question; by that time in American history, political democracy—the right of a person to take part in the governing process, then to acquiesce in the majority will—was secure (again, except for women, Negroes, those under twenty-one, and others). But economic democracy, the right of a person to equal opportunity in the economic process, was seriously threatened. Most Americans believed, with Adam Smith, that labor was the source of wealth. They assumed further that labor should bring rewards. If the rewards were not commensurate with the labor, if people did not receive an equitable share of the general wealth, economic democracy was not functioning as it should. To many people, the concentration of wealth in a few hands was just such a perversion of economic democracy, a denial of equal opportunity. At that time, as in earlier days, one of the dirtier words in the American language was "monopoly." If regulation by state or even federal law was the only way to curb monopoly and preserve economic democracy, then, said many, let it come.

The industrializing, urbanizing society of the late nineteenth century sharpened the latent conflicts among these several folkthemes, which had coexisted in a simpler age. To preserve individualism for the many, and to preserve economic democracy, the individualism of some people had to be restricted. As Lester Ward pointed out, perfectly free competition ultimately destroys itself. But to restrict it seemed socialistic, not individualistic. Furthermore, government regulation of enterprise seemed to require interference with the "natural laws" of economics. To protect the positions of certain producers, such as farmers and laborers, other producers, such as manufacturers, needed to be restrained.

The conflicts between these traditional folkthemes increased after the labor troubles of the seventies, the continuing emergence of large business units in the eighties and after, and the agricultural depression in the last nine years of the period. Reinterpreting and reconciling these folkthemes was no simple task. Those who had benefited most from the social and economic changes of the time, not only the *nouveaux riches* multimillionaires but also many lesser men who had gained in wealth and status, often refused to see that the task existed. However, others—farmers, workers, protest writers, and some politicians, professors, and churchmen—began to see in the eighties that many recent changes were undemocratic, antisocial, or un-American. Just before the Panic of 1873 ruptured the surface tranquillity of American life, a steelmakers' journal, *Iron Age*, gave the opinion that "while we are still far from the establishment of perfectly harmonious relations between labor and capital, there is much less apparent danger here than in any other of the great producing countries of the world, of a conflict of classes. Indeed, it may be said that society here is so homogeneous that no distinctive class divisions are possible, except in the sense of broad and general distinctions between rich and poor, producers and distributors, or educated and uneducated." The prophecy was poor; these distinctions became more, not less, marked.

Politics: Much Shooting, Wrong Targets

Late nineteenth-century American politics, at the federal, state, and local levels alike, are generally remembered for having reached unparalleled levels of corruption and complacency. The scandals of the Grant administration and the boodling of New York City's Boss

Tweed and the "Grey Wolves" of the Chicago City Council, the election campaigns fought on dead-and-buried issues such as the tariff or the money question, all support the accusations. But these claims are largely unhistorical. For every Tweed or pilfering federal place-holder there were a hundred honest politicians and administrators. The very meaning of "corruption" was not yet spelled out in a twentieth-century sense by either law or custom; large governmental and business units were too new. In every election campaign, emotions rose and hot words flowed because people believed deeply that tariff levels and currency policy meant something real to them, regardless of how meaningless they seem now. It is unfortunate that so much energy was spent on peripheral problems; in fact, the real criticism to be leveled at the politics of the Gilded Age was its failure to recognize, tackle, and solve the most fundamental problems engendered by the profound social and economic changes taking place. City growth, the treatment of the Indians and the ex-slaves, the assimilation of immigrants, disputes between labor and capital, the precarious position of farmers, the dips and jolts in the business cycle, the maldistribution of wealth: these were increasingly defined as problems that American society faced, but relatively few defined them further as problems that politics and government should attempt to ameliorate. Governments were not idle, but the positive conviction prevailed that their functions should be strictly limited. That attitude was a major stumbling block preventing social and economic problems from becoming defined as political issues, until farmers and intellectuals at first, and then others, realized that there was no other path to "reform."

The extremely close voting balance nationally between the Republican and Democratic parties from the early seventies to the mid-nineties also hindered effective political action. The result of this balance was the unwillingness of either major party to risk "unorthodox" positions on existing issues or to define fresh ones, until the Democrats did so in 1896 with disastrous electoral results for themselves. Similarly, "great" leaders—who might disturb known voting coalitions and thus do more harm than good for their parties—were almost never nominated (again, before 1896). The more usual choice of candidates was that of 1888, between Grover Cleveland, the Democrats' pudgy nay-sayer, and the G.O.P.'s Benjamin Harrison, who according to one of his sympathizers had a personality "like a dripping cave." Third parties, devoted to pushing a few "radical" issues which were too hot for the major parties

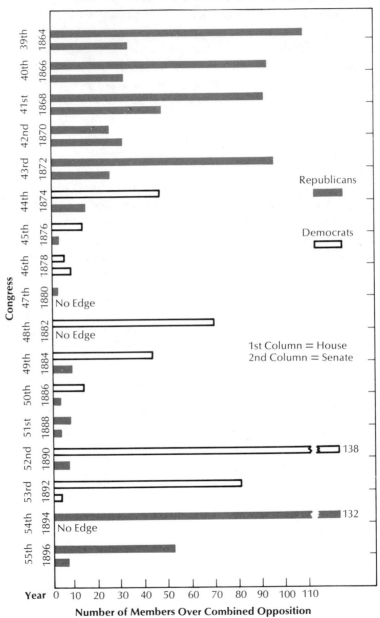

CONGRESSIONAL MAJORITIES, 1864–1896 ELECTIONS

to handle, flourished in consequence; but they never came close to capturing electoral majorities, as indeed third parties never have in the United States, except for the Republicans in the 1850s.

Yet Lord Bryce was not accurate when he stated in the eighties that the differences between the Republicans and the Democrats were like those between Tweedledum and Tweedledee. The sectional, social, and economic group coalitions that comprised each of the major parties were different. The Republicans could depend upon most of New England, the Middle Atlantic states outside the largest cities, the upper Mississippi Valley and the northern Plains states, and the South during Reconstruction but not afterward. The backbone of Republicanism everywhere was the growing number of small towns and cities across the country, except in the South; the G.O.P. was the party of Main Street, more than of Wall Street or the countryside. It included nearly all of the newly-rich multimillionaires, but much more numerous within it were the "better sort of people" in many communities, the elements whose status was secure or rising, who actively sought affluence, even if in small-town terms; it was the party, in short, of the rising middle class. Purporting to be the party of progress, more aggressively nationalistic than the Democratic party, it portrayed itself for years after Appomattox as the instrument of the Union's salvation, wrapping itself in Old Glory and damning the Democrats as the party of secession, and in the nineties it officially supported imperial expansion. The "bloody shirt" was a standby of Republican campaigns, and no Republican speakers' platform was complete without a contingent, preferably on crutches, from the Grand Army of the Republic, the Union

---

The Republican party enjoyed substantial majorities during the Reconstruction era (through 1872). Democratic-Republican equilibrium prevailed from 1876 through 1888. A Democratic landslide occurred in 1890, largely because of opposition to Republican identification in the Midwest with moralistic issues such as prohibition and anti-ethnic public school laws, together with the rise of Populism. But in 1894, a Republican landslide resulted, most of all because of the widespread depression that began in 1893, which was blamed on the Democratic Cleveland administration, and because of the internal split in the Democratic party over the money question.

veterans' organization. The ethnic and religious coloration of the Republican party was native-stock and Protestant, and a few strongly Protestant immigrant groups such as Scandinavians, British, and evangelical Germans. Relatively homogeneous in its group makeup and attitudes, the Republican party conveyed successfully the image of the party of the future, the party most receptive to young and aggressive leadership.

The Democratic party, in contrast, was less attuned to acquisitive expansiveness, and more representative of low-key government and pre-industrial economics. Strong in the border states (Maryland, Delaware, Kentucky, and Missouri) and in several large cities, the basic Democratic stronghold was the post-Reconstruction South, which by 1880 had become the "solid South" and remained so for seventy-five years. The Democratic party had indeed been sympathetic to white southern positions since the fifties, and the very fact of its electoral success in the South lent credibility to the Republican denunciation that it had been soft on slavery, soft on secession, and later, soft on segregation. Another handicap to Democratic unity was the party's peculiar mixing of social opposites. Northeastern patricians such as the Hudson River Delanos and Roosevelts and the Bayards of Delaware; southern conservatives like Alexander Stephens of Georgia, the former vice-president of the Confederacy; southern demagogues like "Pitchfork Ben" Tillman of South Carolina; and western agrarians and laborites were all Democrats. The one Democratic president during the period, Grover Cleveland, and the one almost-president, Samuel J. Tilden, were New Yorkers of recognized status and minimal-government economic views, men of a type which dominated Democratic leadership until the mid-nineties. Then the party shifted suddenly and with a conspicuous lack of success to its western and non-aristocratic wing, led then by the one-time Illinois farm boy, William Jennings Bryan of Nebraska.

The Democrats were not only more diverse socially and economically than the Republicans, but ethnically and religiously as well. With a few notable exceptions, the Democratic party was the party of the immigrant, as it had been since the Irish influx of the 1840s and as it would remain well into the twentieth century. Catholic and Jewish immigrants were repelled by the Republicans' apparent proclivity for Sunday closing laws, prohibition of drink, and evangelical Protestantism. But the greater social, sectional, and economic diversity within the Democratic party made it much harder to lead and to unify on issues than the Republican party. By the mid-nineties, the more homogeneous, bourgeois Republicans were in a better position to take the political initiative, in the sense of creating new programs and determining electoral issues. Before then, from the end of Reconstruction to 1893, sociocultural issues and state party organizations were much more important than national organizations, issues, or leaders in motivating Democratic or Republican votes.

Despite these many differences, the Republican and Democratic coalitions added up to virtually the same number of votes in each national election from just after the Panic of 1873 until just after the Panic of 1893. Democrats depended on the South, Republicans on New England and much of the Midwest. The states that decided elections were the fast-growing, industrializing states not firmly committed to either party—the "swing states" of the Middle Atlantic and eastern Midwest, especially New York, Pennsylvania, Indiana, Ohio, and Illinois. Of the twelve men who ran for President on major party tickets from 1868 through 1896, four were New Yorkers (Seymour, Greeley, Tilden, and Cleveland, all Democrats) and three were from Ohio (Hayes, Garfield, and McKinley, all Republicans). Since neither major party felt it could afford to stray very far from the middle of the road, it remained for third parties to make the first calls for "unorthodox" changes such as free trade, civil service reform, prohibition, and above all, currency expansion by means of greenbacks or silver coinage, and then to thrust these issues on the major parties. Deeper attempts to define social and economic problems as political issues—the "single tax" or socialism —gained relatively little electoral support anywhere.

The national political issues of the Gilded Age were Reconstruction and the future of the freedmen, in the late sixties; the "money question," especially the resumption of specie payments and the nature of the coinage, in the middle and late seventies; civil service reform and tariffs, in the eighties; and the "money question" again—bimetallism or the gold standard?—in the mid-nineties.

Reconstruction involved the restoration of the secessionary Confederate states to the Union and the rebuilding of some kind of stable life for the emancipated slaves. The first objective was accomplished between the late sixties and 1877, though not without a monumental battle between the president and Congress over the method, and a serious and permanent revision of the relationship between the states and the federal government through the Fourteenth Amendment to the Constitution, which defined federal supremacy. The second objective was achieved temporarily from 1867 through the next several years by army-backed state governments created by Radical Republicans in Congress. Freedmen participated in these governments and received legal rights, supposedly for all time. But in the seventies the Radical state governments were replaced by "redeemer" governments led by southern whites, whereupon the freedmen's rights were gradually eroded. A new life did develop for the freedmen, but through the late nineteenth century (especially 1890–1906) it involved the gradual replacement of slavery with Jim Crow laws and economic subservience.

The two longest-lasting effects of the Reconstruction era were ironic jokes played on the idealism of the best-intentioned Radical Republicans. First, they passed the Fourteenth Amendment in an attempt to protect the civil rights of the freedmen, but through the rest of the century and well into the next, court decisions restricted its application to individual civil rights and widened the function of the amendment to make it a protector of business corporations against state regulation. Second, the Reconstruction governments involved and protected the freedmen only temporarily, and in doing so, they engendered sufficient racial hatred and hysteria about "Negro rule" among native white southerners that Reconstruction hopes for the freedmen had no faint hope of permanence.

Between 1870 and 1877, a number of developments took place that cleared the way for reaction: the end of the Freedmen's Bureau (the federal welfare agency for the freedmen), the failure of the Radical state governments to provide the ex-slaves with economic security, the gradual removal of federal troops (never more than 20,000 anyway), and the organized intimidation of freedmen by the Ku Klux Klan and other white vigilante groups. Congress' amnesty to ex-Confederates in 1872 and the subservient economic and social position of the freedmen ended the Radical governments. "Home rule" came to the southern states when duly elected native whites, called "redeemers" or "conservatives," replaced the Radical Republican governments with Democratic ones. The redeemers, in many cases wealthy ex-planters, were dedicated to white supremacy with regard to office-holding but felt no economic or social threat from the freedmen and therefore did not disfranchise them. Only gradually, as the redeemers were themselves displaced in the eighties and nineties by Negro-hating white Democrats of lower social and economic positions did Jim Crow laws, disfranchisement, and lynchings become common. By then, Radical Reconstruction was long since over, and American Negroes, nine-tenths of whom then lived in the South, had become forgotten, invisible men.

Another political issue began to develop during the Reconstruction years and became much more widely discussed for the next thirty years than the future of the freedmen. This issue—the money question—first arose just after the end of the Civil War. The Union government had accumulated a towering $2.7 billion in war debts, in the form of either short-term, high-interest bonds or paper currency, called "greenbacks." The greenbacks were not backed by gold, which was generally assumed at that time to be the only "intrinsically valuable" form of money, into which all other forms of money had to be in some way convertible. How to pay the war debt was an enormous and real problem. The method arrived at involved (1) issuing new government bonds, at lower interest rates and longer terms, to replace those sold during the war emergency (this process began in earnest in 1870) and (2) assuring potential buyers that their investment would be protected against currency inflation by stabilizing the greenback currency (achieved for the most part in 1870) and by abolishing silver as a monetary standard, in 1873, despite its traditional use as such. In taking these steps, the goal of Ohio's Senator John Sherman and other Republican policy-makers was the laudable, indeed necessary, one of protecting the public credit. To do so, policy-makers also had to see to it that the monetary system of the country would return to the gold standard, suspended since 1861, within a reasonable time.

But though the goal was admirable, the means chosen to reach it undoubtedly benefited bondholders and other people who already owned some capital and who gained from its appreciation in value as a result of what came to be; in fact, currency deflation. Demonetizing the silver dollar and clamping a lid on paper currency did stabilize the dollar amount of currency in circulation, but in the context of expanding population and expanding business needs, the actual result was deflation. Businessmen in search of dollars to invest in expanding enterprises, laborers seeking higher wages, farmers wanting better crop prices, all found themselves hemmed in. Beginning in the late sixties, spokesmen for industrial labor complained, correctly from their point of view, that the greenback currency ought to be expanded, rather than stabilized. From 1876 to 1878, agrarians and others smarting from the harsh depression of those years awoke to the fact that the silver dollar had been demonetized, and they argued vigorously for its restoration as a legitimate means, far more traditional than greenbacks, of re-inflating the currency. Silver was partially restored by the Bland-Allison Act of 1878, and in 1879 the banks and the Treasury resumed the pre-1861 practice of "specie payments," whereby banks paid gold coin to the bearer of a paper bank note on demand. A measure of prosperity also returned in 1879. As a result of these nearly simultaneous events, the money question died down for a time as a political issue. A moderate re-inflation of the currency had taken place, but with it an immoderate inflation of political conflict and theorizing about monetary policy. The argument was centered around such questions as which groups in society and in the economy were benefiting and which ones were hurting, and whether government policy ought to allow the rich to become richer or whether it should distribute economic gains more equitably to all of "the producers."

In the 1880s, the absence of an economic crisis like that of the seventies allowed national politics to revolve around factional fights such as the Republican split in 1880 between "Half-Breeds" and "Stalwarts," the enactment of the first federal civil service reform in the Pendleton Act of 1883 after more than a decade of arguing by certain Republicans and Democrats alike that the "merit system" would end or reduce inefficient and corrupt government, and in 1888 a controversy between Democrats advocating tariff reduction and Republicans advocating maintenance of high protective levels. The tariff issue touched many pocketbooks directly or indirectly, and as a consequence, many heartstrings. But it never acquired the theoretical and moral superstructure of the money question. Almost dormant during the 1880s, when vocal but small minorities continued to clamor for greenbackism or free silver coinage, the money question returned to the center of the political stage after the 1893–97 depression began.

By that time several other "reform" efforts had met with spotty success, particularly the briefly popular "single tax" proposal advanced by Henry George after 1879, which almost elected him mayor of New York in 1887, and the concept of "nationalism," a variety of non-Marxian socialism, advanced by Edward Bellamy in his utopian novel, *Looking Backward, 2000–1887*. The deteriorating

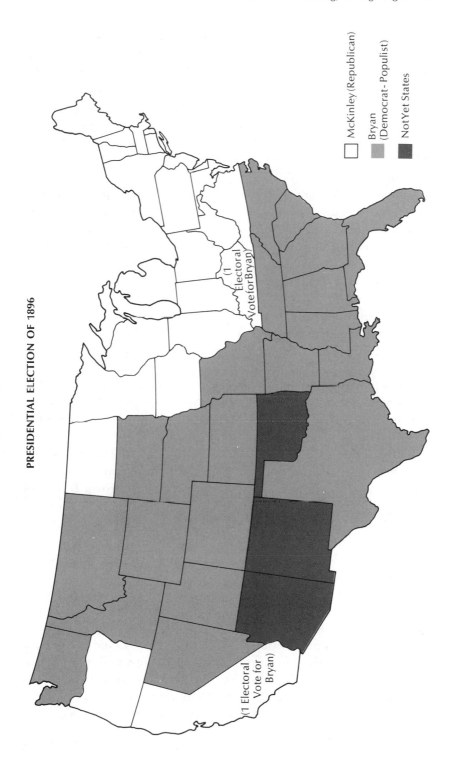

PRESIDENTIAL ELECTION OF 1896

McKinley (Republican)

Bryan
(Democrat- Populist)

Not Yet States

(1 Electoral
Vote for Bryan)

(1 Electoral
Vote for
Bryan)

and often violent relations between labor and capitalists during the eighties disturbed more and more people, and the beginning of the post-1887 farm depression jolted the dozing giant body of midwestern and southern farmers into vocal demands, politically expressed, for a more equitable economic order. In 1889, western and southern farmers organized thousands of local chapters of Farmers' Alliances and shortly after that formed the People's party, which in 1890 and 1892 won dozens of seats in Congress and hundreds of state and county offices.

From 1893 through 1896, financial panic, unemployment, the Pullman strike, the repeal of governmental silver purchases by President Cleveland and the resulting furore among pro-silver Democrats, vigorous third-party activity, and the frustration of reformers, all brought to the political scene a turbulence unmatched since early Reconstruction. Despite huge Democratic victories in the congressional elections of 1890 and 1892, a chaotic split on the money question rent the Democrats nationally, and Republicans took control of Congress in 1894 (over one and a half million people voted Populist). The G.O.P. began a period of national political domination lasting until 1930. Free-silver and pro-labor sympathies gained ground among many Democrats, especially in the West. The 1896 Republican convention nominated Ohio's "apostle of protection," William McKinley, for president, on a platform that attempted to soft-pedal its gold-standard position on money and to stress economic recovery, or as McKinley called it, the "full dinner pail." The Democratic convention, meeting shortly afterward, was dominated by western and southern pro-silverites. Bowled over by one of the most dramatic speeches in the history of American politics, when William Jennings Bryan warned the "goldbugs" not to "crucify mankind upon a cross of gold," the convention nominated the thirty-six-year-old Nebraska ex-Congressman for the presidency. The People's party followed suit.

The campaign aroused intense emotions. Both candidates were attractive personalities. Each represented contending sides of the money question that had divided the country since the Civil War. To the Democrats and Populists, McKinley represented the hateful plutocracy, the anti-farmer and anti-labor nabobs and monopolists who had fattened on the labor of others for twenty-five years. To the Republicans and many eastern Democrats, the Bryanites were dangerous radicals whose free-silverism threatened to wreck any hope of economic stability. It was indeed an election that presented the voters with a "real choice."

They chose McKinley. Bryan carried the solid South and most of the Plains and Mountain states, but McKinley swept the northeastern quarter of the country, with its concentration of cities and industry. Bryan's appeal to the "producing classes" failed to win

Not everybody loved the "Great Commoner" in 1896. (Culver Pictures, Inc.)

him support from industrial workers or small businessmen. Producerism and Bryan's whole approach were by 1896 too narrowly agrarian to command a majority. The loss for agrarianism was, moreover, not just for one election. On the first occasion since the Civil War when a major party espoused a reform issue in an attempt to deal with recent social changes, that party suffered its worst defeat in seven presidential elections. Clearly, no matter how necessary reforms seemed to be, the majority of the voters agreed that the Populist-Bryanite answer was not the right one. Free silver was not the panacea, nor was agrarian producerism the social ideal that would end injustice and inequality. But, at the close of 1896, a better answer was not yet agreed upon.

The Next Step: A Third American Revolution?

What had changed in American civilization between 1865 and 1897? An editorial writer in the Philadelphia *American*, in the early summer of 1897, thought he knew. "Are human rights, liberty, to be crushed to earth, that property rights, a moneyed oligarchy, may be enthroned? This is the all-important question before the American people. . . . [To ignore it] is to open the way to the enslavement of our industrial classes, [and] the undermining of the Republic. . . . A generation ago, the nation, in bloody strife, overthrew one oligarchy, the slave-holding oligarchy of the South, an oligarchy as detrimental to master as to slave. At the same time the seeds of a new and more far-reaching oligarchy were sown. The War called into being a new class . . . caring less for country than for self, caring naught for the sufferings of humanity." The comment was neither unique nor idle. Three immense population movements had peopled much of the West, doubled the proportion of city-dwellers, and brought over 12 million immigrants, many of origins unfamiliar to Americans, to cities and countrysides. The economy reflected these shifts, not only because wheat, corn, cotton, cattle, and other products poured out of the West, Midwest, and South in overabundance, but even more because of the burst of railroading and manufacturing that by 1897 had brought the United States the economic leadership of the world. Only thirty-two years before, a population half as large collectively produced one-fourth as much, lived almost entirely in the eastern half of the country, worked mainly as farmers, knew nothing of streetcars, electric lights, or naturalistic novels, and had just abolished human slavery.

But Americans in 1865 also knew little or nothing about vast slums, widespread poverty, degrading labor conditions, farmers pushed off the land, monopolistic corporations in manufacturing, banking, transportation, and elsewhere, or city governments riddled with graft. Political protest movements had flourished since the late sixties. But the demand of the National Labor Union and the Greenback party for an expansion of paper currency, the demands of the Liberal Republicans and the Mugwumps for civil service reform, an end to corruption, and lower tariffs, and the Populists' call for a wide range of reforms, resulted at best in piecemeal legislation and at worst in dismissal as the ravings of cranks and crackpots. Henry George and Edward Bellamy attracted a considerable following for their "single tax" and "nationalism" proposals, but a following not nearly large enough to effect their schemes. In 1896, as the nominee of the Populist and Democratic parties, William Jennings Bryan carried the banner of "reform" to the country, but his reform program was essentially limited to currency expansion by free silver coinage. Even thus limited, the American people rejected Bryan and free silver by the widest margin of defeat that a major-party candidate for president had suffered in twenty-four years. The country had serious problems, but did not want to face them, and had not arrived at any consensus on how to solve those problems if it did.

One of the earliest systematic discussions of social conditions among American poor appeared in 1904, when Robert Hunter published his book, *Poverty*. Hunter's report was chilling. "We have not made even a beginning in finding out the extent of poverty in America," he wrote; "it would seem fair to estimate that certainly not less than 14 percent of the people, in prosperous times (1903), and probably not less than 20 percent in bad times (1897), are in distress. The estimate is a conservative one. . . ." Using federal census figures, Hunter showed that 15 percent of the working force was unemployed during part of 1890, 22 percent during part of 1900, and that two out of every five persons partially unemployed "were idle from four to six months of the year. These figures are for the country as a whole . . . including agriculture." Unemployment and consequent poverty were worse in manufacturing and in the Northeast. McKinley had obviously not brought the "full dinner pail" to millions of families.

Unrestrained individual accumulation and observance of the "natural laws of Political Economy" had undergirded an enormous economic expansion in thirty-odd years. But they had also helped bring about a remarkable change in the structure, as well as the size, of the economy, taking it from an assortment of businessmen, farmers, and firms large in number, small in size, and independent from each other in ownership to an economy headed by a group of "trusts" small in number, large in size, and closely interconnected. John Moody's book, *The Truth About the Trusts*, which appeared in the same year as Hunter's *Poverty*, described the existence of interdependence and consolidation across the industrial spectrum. Not only did single companies fail to compete, said Moody, but the monopolies themselves did not compete with each other. They cooperated, because many of them were related to the two "supertrusts," the industrial empires headed by J. P. Morgan and John D. Rockefeller. Morgan, sitting in the office of his investment bank on Wall Street, directed a vast operation whose cornerstones were the United States Steel combine and several large railroads, which branched out into shipping, electrical equipment, rubber, commercial banks, and life insurance companies. Rockefeller, based at Standard Oil, also controlled his banks and railroads, and had interests in copper, tobacco, steel, public utilities, and life insurance. The Morgan and Rockefeller interests worked together. "These two mammoth groups jointly (for, as pointed out, they may really be regarded as one)," Moody wrote, "constitute the heart of the business and commercial life of the nation, the others all being the arteries which permeate in a thousand ways our whole national life, making their influence felt in every home and hamlet. . . ."

By 1900, many critics of the American scene blamed the "trusts" for poverty, insecurity of employment, and maldistribution of wealth. The economy produced more and more wealth, but who received it? Farmers did not; their products brought lower prices the more they produced. Industrial workers, city-dwellers, and immigrants did not. Figures on the distribution of income and wealth were imprecise at the turn of the century, but John Graham Brooks'

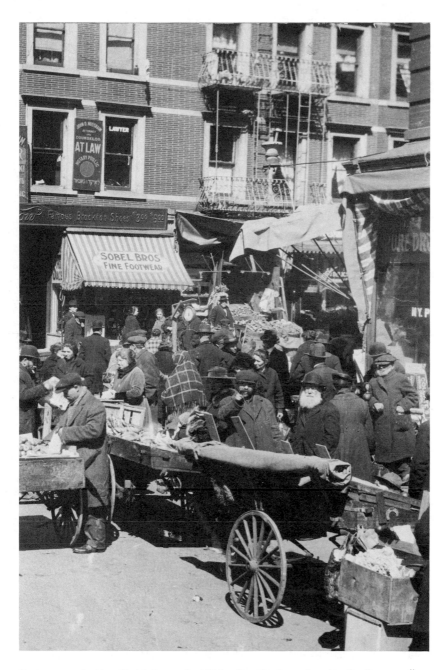

Street scene in New York's Lower East Side after the "new immigration" was well under way. (Freelance Photographers Guild)

estimate, which was often cited, figured that the richest 1 percent of the American population owned 55 percent of aggregate wealth, and the "very poor" *50* percent of the population owned none of the wealth. The very poorest were often "new immigrants" in north-eastern and midwestern cities, and Negroes in the South.

Hunter's summary of problems requiring "social reform" was frightening: "There are probably in fairly prosperous years no less than 10,000,000 persons in poverty; that is to say, underfed, under-clothed, and poorly housed. Of these about 4,000,000 persons are public paupers. Over 2,000,000 working-men are unemployed from four to six months in the year. About 500,000 male immigrants ar-rive yearly and seek work in the very districts where unemployment is greatest. Nearly half of the families in the country are property-less. Over 1,700,000 little children are forced to become wage-earners when they should still be in school. About 5,000,000 women find it necessary to work and about 2,000,000 are employed in fac-tories, mills, etc. Probably no less than 1,000,000 workers are in-jured or killed each year while doing their work, and about 10,000,000 of the persons now living will . . . die of . . . tuberculo-sis." This he found in a society that prided itself on equality of op-portunity, political democracy, world economic leadership, even providentially-directed manifest destiny.

These very real problems developed in the post–Civil War years while Americans moved about, worked at making a living, prayed, went to school, and voted for or against political candidates who, when they did espouse "reform," meant a civil service law or tariff revision or the money question. The political system, and behind it, the people's ideas about what politics and society should be, had not come to grips, in the late nineteenth century, with the social and economic problems that social and economic change had brought. Many questioned whether "the system" could be made to work again to produce any measurable good for the greatest number. An Adams of Massachusetts wrote of the "degradation of the demo-cratic dogma." Eminent sociologists noted "the decay of republican institutions." Many despairing Populists opted for socialism and the wholesale replacement of the "system." Labor leaders, lacking even legal status as such, entertained little hope of success through "the system" when the core of it seemed to be the immense entrenched power of Morgan and Rockefeller. What would the twentieth cen-tury bring? Class war and revolution, as a few hoped and many feared at the end of the nineties? Or a reform movement that would achieve support (as none had yet) in order to preserve the many satisfying features of late nineteenth century American development while, miraculously, divesting the country of its bad features?

Small-town America (specifically, Catskill, New York) in the twenties, after the automobile era began. (Culver Pictures, Inc.)

2

DEMOGRAPHY, 1897-1930: A TRULY CONTINENTAL SOCIETY

Despite the growing awareness of severe social problems in their midst, Americans retained an optimistic belief in their own progress and a pride in the continuing achievements of their time. Between 1897 and 1933 they moved about the land as much as ever, seeking new opportunities, wealth, and status, and were aided, especially after 1915, by a new means toward horizontal mobility, the automobile. Immigrants arrived, more numerous than before, sometimes more than a million of them a year. The "westward movement" continued, but to urban areas rather than to Great Plains farms. American Negroes trudged out of the South for the first time in significant numbers. Parts of the country that had grown rapidly in the late nineteenth century stabilized in population, while the urban-industrial belt from Illinois to the Atlantic became more than ever the demographic and economic heartland of the country. Over half the American people had become city-dwellers by 1920, and whether despite that fact or because of it, they were healthier and lived longer. The mass-produced automobile helped people move across space in all of these directions, causing social change of much more than just a locational kind; and Americans, as they moved across space, tried to move up the ladder of status, and found that kind of movement more difficult. Each of these demographic changes deserves some comment.

Census Regions: Which Gained, and Why?

An overview of the census returns shows clearly that migration patterns closely mirrored the availability of economic opportunity and the related processes of urbanization and industrialization. The total United States population grew 63 percent between 1900 and 1930, more slowly than the 91 percent increase of 1870–1900. But the post-1900 growth involved more people, as numbers rose from

76 million to 123 million. New England's overall growth was slow, except for large immigrant influxes into Massachusetts before the twenties and considerable native and immigrant increases in Connecticut, which benefited from its strategic position between New York and Boston. In the Middle Atlantic states, New York gained over a million foreign-born between 1900 and 1910, a gain slightly less than California's explosive native-born gain in the twenties but larger than any other immigrant increase in a single state in one decade before or since. New York City became the largest or near-largest Italian city, Jewish city, and Irish city in the world. It became unique not only for its size but also for its heterogeneity in America and in the world. All three of the Middle Atlantic states also gained in Negro population. Although Pennsylvania lost many of its native-born, New Jersey gained considerably in native whites, Negroes, and immigrants, and thrived on the great metropolises of New York and Philadelphia on either side of it.

In the Midwest, the major gainers were Ohio, Michigan, and Illinois—the states with new growth industries and emerging large cities. Ohio enjoyed a great native-born increase in the teens, as did Michigan in the twenties when automobile manufacturing and related industries boomed. Illinois suffered a net outflow of native-born until the twenties, but except for that loss, these three most urbanized and industrialized of the East North Central states gained in native whites, foreign-born, and Negroes throughout the period. Indiana and Wisconsin, while many of their native-born whites departed, received relatively modest Negro and immigrant increases. Meanwhile, the West North Central states, the booming "farmers' last frontier" of the late nineteenth century, nearly stagnated. Little good land was left to be taken up, except in the Dakotas, which attracted some native whites between 1900 and 1910, and as yet the Plains states were not urbanizing or industrializing rapidly enough to bring in large numbers of southern Negroes or foreign-born. The government patented more land under the Homestead Act between 1900 and 1911 than in the whole late nineteenth century, and by 1930 the United States had more farms, more acres under cultivation, and a much higher dollar value per acre of farm land than in 1900. But the number of farm households remained almost stable. Farmers who owned the land they operated decreased in number, while tenants increased by over a third. The owner-operated "family farm" was in relative decline as a way of life, as was farming as a way of making a living. Though the total *number* of farmers and farms continued to grow, the *rate* of increase in the rural population was only about one-fourth that of the general population.

As for the South, immigrants entered that culturally and economically inhospitable region in very small numbers, while more Negroes and native-born whites left than entered. Except for Florida, whose land boom and general development in the twenties did attract native whites, Negroes, and some foreign-born, the only "southern" area which gained more people in all three categories than it lost was the District of Columbia together with Maryland and Delaware, as the economies of those states became less agricultural and as the Washington bureaucracy began to expand. Meanwhile, Negroes fled nearly every southern state in large numbers. South Carolina and Virginia were the major losers between 1900 and 1910, South Carolina, Georgia, and Mississippi in the teens, and Georgia, South Carolina, and Virginia (in descending order) in the twenties.

California was the spectacular gainer in the West, although nearly all western states attracted native whites, Negroes, and immigrants throughout the period. Census figures show that the great boom in California's population, often associated with the years after 1945, really started in the twenties and was temporarily interrupted during the depressed thirties. Nearly 500,000 foreign-born and 1,250,000 native whites settled in California, particularly southern California, in the twenties, comprising a new and typically twentieth-century "westward movement." This movement, together with the migration of Negroes from the South and the arrival of millions of immigrants in the Northeast, was one of the three most important population trends of the 1897–1930 period.

The Northeast, meaning New England and the Middle Atlantic states, grew at a faster rate than any other part of the country except the Far West, and eastern growth involved more people than anywhere else. The chief reasons were the relative attractiveness of northeastern large cities and jobs to immigrants and, especially from World War I onward, to southern Negroes.

Almost 20 million people immigrated into the United States between 1897 and 1930, most of them before 1915, and two-thirds came from Central Europe, Russia, and Italy. After 1914, World War I and federal immigration restriction laws reduced the influx very substantially. The peak year for immigration throughout the

THE ERA OF MASS IMMIGRATION, 1890–1933 (1)

Immigrants Per Year in Thousands

THE ERA OF MASS IMMIGRATION, 1890–1933 (2)

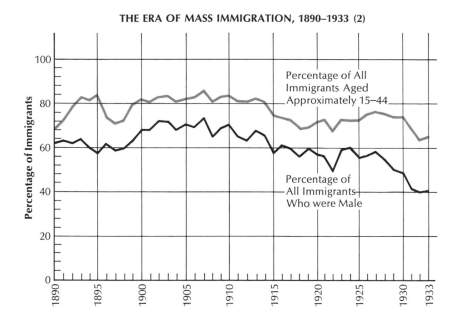

(1) In the graph on the opposite page, "immigrants" include only those who arrived and declared their intention of staying, while departures include any non-citizens —immigrants who changed their minds, plus "birds of passage"—who left. Even so, the *net* immigration was considerably smaller than the raw figures on immigrants indicate.

(2) The graph above shows that, during most of the era of mass immigration, and especially in the peak years of 1902–1907 before World War I, the bulk of immigrants were young males who could enter the labor force, very often taking up unskilled or semi-skilled jobs. During World War I, and notably in 1921 and 1928–1933, wives, parents, and people over 45 immigrated a little more frequently.

whole of American history was 1907, when 1.3 million arrived. The next highest peak year was 1914 with 1.2 million. Few countries could have absorbed such an invasion, and the United States handled it only with difficulty. The great bulk of the post-1897 immigrants were laborers (farm and otherwise), domestics, or people without any definite occupation—an unskilled, or at best a semiskilled, mass. Those with capital or craft were proportionately much fewer than among nineteenth century immigrants. Unfamiliar with the American language or American customs, they depended at first almost entirely upon countrymen or townsmen who had preceded them for assistance in getting settled, getting work, and getting the minimum necessities of life. Fewer by far settled on western farming land than had been the case in the late nineteenth century; many lacked the means or the knowledge to move beyond the port at which they entered (often New York).

A considerable proportion of the people who came never intended to stay, but rather hoped to accumulate enough cash or goods to return to a better situation at home. In 1908, the year following the peak year for arrivals, 400,000 people voluntarily left the United States. How many of these were genuine "birds of passage," people who came to seek their fortune and take it back home, or were seasonal migrants, and how many were forced back because they could find no place in America will never be known. Many others came before World War I, particularly young men with families left at home, intending to save enough to bring their families later. Some succeeded in this effort, through great sacrifice and hardship, but others never quite made it, and were, in effect, marooned in an unfamiliar and frustrating country. Nearly three-fourths of the immigrants who arrived in the peak year of 1907 were male, young men trying to better themselves or their families. Of them, a large number found more brass than gold in the American streets.

So many immigrants returned each year—20 to 40 percent of the previous year's arrivals—that despite the entry of nearly 20 million immigrants throughout the period, the total number of foreign-born in the country was only 14 million in 1930, as compared with the more than 10 million in 1900, a rate of increase about half that of the native-born population. The country was becoming a "nation of immigrants" much less rapidly than nationalistic Americans feared.

Even in the Northeast, where most of the new arrivals went, the proportion of foreign-born dropped from about one in four in 1910 to about one in five in 1930.

The children of the immigrants, however, increased at about the same rate as the general population. The character of the second generation, of course, changed over time. In 1900 the vast majority were German, Irish, British, or Canadian, but by 1930 second generation Italians outnumbered all but the Germans, while second generation Irish ranked third, Poles fourth, Britons fifth, Russians sixth, and Canadians seventh. Still, the worry of many native Americans that the United States would be overwhelmed by an immigrant horde was not borne out by the facts. Even when the numbers of foreign-born are combined with their sons and daughters of mixed or foreign stock, the whole group of immigrants, including the second generation, decreased between 1900 and 1930 to a little less than one in three. As usual, however, such facts made less impression on nervous old-stock Americans than their strange languages, strange names, strange ways, their tendency to live in large cities, which many Americans still distrusted deeply, and their suspected "radical" and "subversive" social ideas.

The Negro
Moves North

Another migration that began in earnest during this period and increased later was the trek of hundreds of thousands of southern Negroes to the Northeast and the Midwest. About 90 percent of the 8.8 million black Americans lived in the South in 1900, but in 1930 the number had declined to about 78 percent of the 11.9 million. Blacks actually declined as a proportion of the total population of the country during those three decades, from 11.6 to 9.7 percent, and their rate of increase was only a little more than half that of the population in general. But their numbers rose by 50 percent, proportionately, in the West; by 300 percent in the Northeast; and by 350 percent in the North Central region. In the South, however, the Negro increase was only one-third the general regional rate. So considerable was the black exodus from Dixie that the increase of blacks in the Northeast during the twenties alone was about equal to the whole northeastern Negro population in 1910.

Still, no region had a large Negro population by 1930 except the South. Even then, the proportion of blacks to the total population was only about one in twenty-five in the Northeast, one in thirty in the Midwest, one in a hundred in the West. Meanwhile, the South dropped from being one-third black in 1900 to one-fourth in 1930. The Northeast, the region most heavily settled by recent immigrants, was 20 to 25 percent foreign-born, but only 2 to 4 percent Negro. In the South the figures were almost exactly reversed: from 24 to 32 percent Negro, but only 2 percent foreign-born. However, this great contrast was beginning to dissolve in the twenties and would keep changing as the twentieth century wore on. Blacks and immigrants were undergoing certain parallel trends that would have great significance for the homogenization of the American population. Both groups were decreasing proportionately to the total population; both were growing at rates only a little more than half that of the population as a whole. But both groups were also dispersing much more widely around the country.

Reasons for the black exodus were clear. As southern state governments passed from the hands of the paternalistic "redeemers" who followed the Reconstruction period to the lower-status whites who competed with Negroes more directly, the southern race climate became more hostile. Disfranchisement through poll taxes and literacy tests, accompanied by "grandfather clauses" to let poorer whites continue to vote, began in Mississippi about 1890. All southern states except Tennessee had disfranchised Negroes by 1907. Laws and court decisions hardened Jim Crow patterns, lynchings and riots multiplied, and rural poverty persisted. The South was becoming less, rather than more, hospitable to the 90 percent of American Negroes who lived there.

One approach to racial peace (or survival) was gradual progress through practical education. Booker T. Washington, the most famous Negro leader of the late nineteenth century, advocated such an approach in a speech at the Atlanta Cotton States Exposition in 1895, and in many other speeches and writings. Washington's "Atlanta Compromise" foresaw the Negro achieving an equal place in southern society by becoming a better-trained farmer or industrial worker, a struggle which Washington frankly realized might

The "Great Migration": a Harlem street about the time of World War I. (Brown Brothers)

take fifty years. Voting and other rights, he said, "will come to the Negro . . . by beginning at the bottom and gradually working up to the highest possibilities of his nature." Washington thought that migration from the United States, or even to northern cities, was not a solution to the black man's problems; instead, he should be "identifying himself more closely with the interests of the South." The Negro's real chance was to "make himself of such indispensable service to his neighbour and the community that no one can fill his place better in the body politic." Washington acted as well as talked. He founded Tuskegee Institute in 1881 to provide vocational training to Negroes and was convinced that practical education, rather than letters and mathematics, fitted the needs of the southern black.

But violence continued, and Washington's view that riots and lynchings could "only be stopped by mutual confidence" did not receive a fair test. In 1905, two other Negro leaders, William E. B. Du Bois and William Monroe Trotters, at a meeting at Niagara Falls, Ontario, urged that Negroes should fight vigorously for their rights. "Was there ever a nation on God's fair earth civilized from the bottom up? Never . . . ," declared the Harvard educated Du Bois. The object of education, he said in direct contrast to Washington, was "not to make men carpenters, [but] to make carpenters men." The Niagara Movement, which developed out of the 1905 meeting, sought political and economic equality for the Negro without delay. But antiblack race riots continued, at Evansville in 1903, Atlanta in 1906, and with exceptional brutality at Springfield, Illinois, in 1908. The Springfield riot shocked white reformers such as Jane Addams, John Dewey, and Moorfield Storey into cooperating with Du Bois, Walter White, and other Negroes to call a National Negro Conference in 1909, which led to the founding of the National Association for the Advancement of Colored People in 1910. The NAACP advocated "full enjoyment of [Negroes'] rights as citizens, justice in all courts, and equality of opportunity." It promoted education, fought segregation practices and lynching, and with Du Bois as editor of its publications, received interracial support.

By 1910 the Negro exodus was well under way. Seeking economic opportunity and voting with their feet against their treatment in the South, Negroes from the Gulf states read the Chicago *Defender* and took the Illinois Central northward to Chicago, while Negroes from the Atlantic Coast states immigrated to Washington, Philadelphia, and New York, despite attempts by white police and other officials to prevent their departure. The exodus "out of the house of bondage" swelled greatly after 1915, when World War I cut off the immigration tide from Europe. But violence and segregation followed the migrants. In Chicago and New York, they found increasingly segregated neighborhoods, labor unions, and schools. Housing was costlier for blacks than for whites; in addition, blacks received hostility from white property-owners; and exceptional violence broke out in 1919, a year of twenty-five race riots, when Negro and white veterans returned from the War and competed for the same scarce jobs.

In the South, whites and blacks cooperated to form a Commission on Interracial Cooperation in 1919, to end lynchings and help provide economic opportunities, but the Commission's successes depended on avoiding a frontal attack on the prevailing segregation patterns. Marcus Garvey, who founded the Universal Negro Improvement Association in 1914 and claimed several million followers among American Negroes in the early twenties, proclaimed that the only answer to black problems was a return to Africa. But neither southern "cooperation" nor "back to Africa" movements provided Negroes with an answer as popular as the exodus to northern cities, despite the grim realities of New York's Harlem, Brooklyn's Bedford-Stuyvesant, and Chicago's South Side. Despair in the rural South could not compete with the lure of the big city, which afforded a life apart, even the pursuit of "black culture," and at least the possibility of economic improvement.

The New Urban
Majority

For whites, living in cities became the rule by 1920, instead of the exception. The proportion of city-dwellers in the general population rose rather steadily through those three prosperous decades, from about two in five in 1900 to about four in seven by 1930. Substantial cities, moreover, were no longer found principally in the Northeast and some parts of the Midwest; instead, they emerged everywhere, including the South, the Great Plains, and the West.

Yet the quality of urban life differed vastly from section to section and place to place. To live in a village of a few thousand was obviously different from living in New York or Chicago, or indeed a middle-sized manufacturing city. The reasons, moreover, for the emergence of cities of considerable size—100,000 or more—also varied greatly, depending on sectional or regional characteristics. The million-plus metropolises of New York, Chicago, and Philadelphia (and also Detroit and Los Angeles by 1930) were studies in complexity. Most were based on solid nineteenth-century growth (though not Los Angeles), highly mixed economies (except Detroit, the offspring of the emerging automobile industry), location, immigration (usually), and other factors. These places grew very fast; in terms of numbers of people affected, metropolitan urbanism expanded at almost twice the rate of small-town (2,500–10,000) urbanism, and intermediate cities, between 100,000 and a million, grew fastest of all.

These middle-sized cities, of which there were thirty-five in 1900 and eighty-eight in 1930, were chiefly of three types. Some, like Jersey City, developed as satellites of established metropolises. The satellites did not serve the nearby metropolises as dormitories, as the residential suburbs of a later day would do, but as partially dependent economic entities benefiting from the financial strength of the metropolis, serving as a market for its products, and supplying its industries with producer durables and its population with consumer goods such as processed food.

Another group of middle-sized cities developed independently of, and usually at substantial distances from, established metropolises. These "regional cities" usually grew up for one of two economic reasons: either as primary processing centers for the extractive industries (farming, mining, oil drilling) of the hinterland around it or as cities usually concentrating on a single national-market manufactured product, such as automobile tires, furniture, or appliances.

The regional cities based on the extractive industry of an agricultural or mining hinterland often reached the hundred-thousand-plus size about three decades after its hinterland had been extensively settled. Several cities in the Missouri Valley had reached metropolitan status for this reason by the end of the eighties. After that, however, because of the depression of the nineties and the saturation of agricultural areas, very few new metropolises emerged because they were primary processing centers for an agricultural

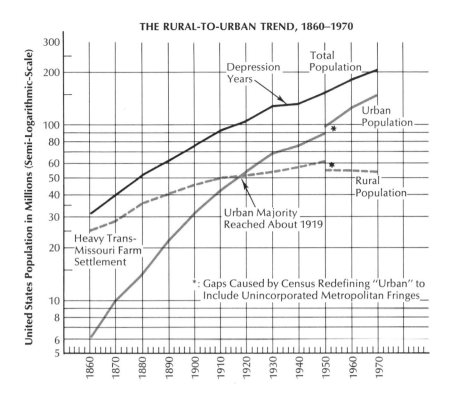

THE RURAL-TO-URBAN TREND, 1860–1970

Y-axis: United States Population in Millions (Semi-Logarithmic Scale)

Depression Years

Total Population

Urban Population

Rural Population

Urban Majority Reached About 1919

Heavy Trans-Missouri Farm Settlement

*: Gaps Caused by Census Redefining "Urban" to Include Unincorporated Metropolitan Fringes

Urban population rose faster than total population in every decade, even in the depression years of the 1930s. Rural population rose in absolute numbers until 1950, but has fallen off since then.

hinterland. Spokane, which passed the hundred-thousand mark in the census of 1910, and Salt Lake City, which did so in the census of 1920, were virtually the only examples.

Instead, new regional cities emerged because they benefited from the maturation of other kinds of extractive industries or because they held a strategic commercial-transportational position or because they had become the homes of new growth industries. The clearest example of the extractive industry metropolis occurred in Texas, where four cities—Dallas, Fort Worth, San Antonio, and Houston (which reached one million in the late 1960s)—reached the one-hundred-thousand-plus size during the same decade as the opening of the Texas oil fields (1910–20). At about the same time, Dayton, Grand Rapids, and Akron reached metropolitan status, but for the very different reason that they became the centers of newly-important, technologically-advanced manufacturing industries. And for all these reasons, the Far West and the South (quite aside from Texas) saw a flock of new metropolises emerge in the early twentieth century. The South had contained only one such city, New Orleans, which reached that size in the 1840s; for the rest of the century the delta seaport, commercial center, and provincial capital was solitary in her eminent size within the whole region. By the census of 1900, however, Memphis passed the hundred-thousand mark. While the growth of Memphis was explainable in large part by her strategic location for commerce and transportation on the Mississippi, more modern forms of economic activity, including heavy industry, clearly had much to do with the achievement of metropolitan size by Atlanta, Birmingham, Nashville, and Richmond by 1910, and other southern cities thereafter.

After 1930, urbanization in America was characterized by suburban sprawl and the stagnation of central cities. In the early twentieth century, however, the dominant trend was the emergence of new metropolises all across the land, many of them heavily committed to advanced manufacturing, even in the once-empty West and the decreasingly rural South.

Life-styles varied tremendously in the cities. More than in the nineteenth century, social distance flouted the fact of geographical proximity, as in extreme cases such as the few blocks between Park Avenue and Hell's Kitchen in New York, or the Gold Coast and the Ghetto on Chicago's Near North Side. In newer, more medium-sized cities—particularly in the Midwest or West where there was space to expand and relatively small numbers of ethnic out-groups such as blacks or immigrants—miles of city streets, often laid out in a tiresome grid pattern, became lined with stucco or frame duplexes or single-family bungalows, especially after 1915.

Cities gradually looked better, as overhead electrical and telephone wires began to go under the ground and as street paving commonly replaced mud or gravel. Cities also smelled better, as electricity replaced sooty steam engines on elevated and street railways, and motor vehicles substituted exhaust fumes for the several fragrances of the horse. The acrid smoke of steelmills in Pittsburgh or the stench of the slaughterhouses in Kansas City were an inconvenience, but smog and sulfur concentrations were a long way from reaching danger levels.

The common experience of the successful city-dwelling immigrant—not counting those who never managed to gain an economic foothold or who were killed or injured on railroads or in factories as they made the attempt—was to arrive in a large manufacturing city in the Northeast in the early years of the century and immediately seek, through sheer necessity of language, the blocks of tenements where members of his own ethnic group already lived. The first stop for young men arriving alone, as so many immigrants were in those years, was often a boarding house; for families it was often the home of kinsmen or perhaps a back room in the synagogue until they found their own tenement flat. Social life was not a major problem; twelve to sixteen hour workdays, often for both husband and wife, left few hours idle. Ethnic fraternal and benevolent organizations provided occasional relaxation, and occasional practicality since many functioned as cooperative burial societies. Among certain ethnic groups the neighborhood saloon supported a male social life, the front porches brought talkative women together, and street gangs gave a kind of practical education to pubescent males. Church organizations abounded; at the turn of the century one large Polish church in Chicago, St. Stanislaus Kostka, had over five dozen parish societies, which promoted everything from piety to card-parties.

The experience of the black migrant from the rural South to Harlem or to the South Side of Chicago was not fundamentally different in many basic aspects of social and economic behavior. Like the immigrant, he lived in a tenement, sought recreation where he could find it with his ethnic group, and depended on word-of-mouth, the help of friends, or the ward politician when he looked for a job. While some neighborhoods became Italian or Polish or Jewish, others became "colored." One difference was that when the Italian or Pole or Jew, after some years of desperate work, wanted to "move uptown," he did so, while the black migrant discovered that the door to his ghetto was closed, and residential segregation by race increased from 1900 onward.

At the other end of the urban social spectrum, the upper-middle-class family experienced its own kinds of segregation and social life, self-imposed ones that took the family from shady, spacious side-streets to a summer watering-place somewhere between Long Island and Newport, or Lake Geneva and the Rockies, depending on how "upper" the family was. Golf, tennis, even polo, and in sedentary moments auction bridge, until contract bridge became the rage in the twenties, satisfied the recreational urge instead of the baseball, boxing, and bowling of the urban masses. And, for both the wealthy and the wanting, the streets of the cities were in most ways safer than they became later in the century.

Birth Rates, Health, and Happiness

The American people were, to a significant degree, a collection of minority groups. Throughout the period, the foreign-born, together with people born in America of one or two immigrant parents, together with Negroes, made up between 42 and 45 percent of the population. Add to these the many whose grandparents had been foreign-born and who, although of the "third generation," still maintained ethnic identity, and the several hundred thousand American Indians, and the term *old stock majority* ceased to be statistically true.

But the term certainly had meaning in every other way. As in earlier periods, minority groups almost always lacked a collective identity. With nothing in common except a feeling that they were not fully part of the "mainstream," members of the minority groups ranged in their relations to the "general society" from the status of outcasts to that of skilled apprentices in the American way. Few of the ethnic or racial minority groups approached the "old stock" in income, education, living conditions, status, or even in life expectancy.

It helped a great deal to have been born white. Despite a higher birth rate among nonwhites, especially Negroes, throughout the period (the figures were 20 live births per thousand white women, 27.5 per thousand nonwhite women, in 1930), the Negro population increased much less rapidly than the population as a whole. One reason for this was the great difference in white and nonwhite life expectancy. Life expectancy for nonwhites, though it increased by nearly 50 percent (i.e., half a lifetime) between 1900 and 1930, was consistently thirteen or fourteen years less than for whites. Nonwhite infant mortality, mortality of mothers, and overall death rates were a third to a half again higher than for whites. Disease, malnutrition, and inferior medical care underlay those statistics both in the rural South and in northern cities. Illness and early death combined with educational and occupational disadvantages to hinder the advancement of American Negroes. Still, the nonwhite life expectancy improved very greatly, as did the white; the gap between white and nonwhite school attendance continued to close, as it had since the end of slavery; and nonwhite illiteracy was little more than a third in 1930 of what it had been at the turn of the century.

In addition, the whole population was healthier. Although the proportion of physicians in the population did not increase, those who were practicing were much better trained. Ill-organized and quack-ridden in 1900, American medicine took itself in hand in the years just before World War I, partly in response to devastating criticisms made by Abraham Flexner in his widely disseminated report on the shocking state of medical education. The American Medical Association became a vigorous professional organization, setting and enforcing standards of medical education and practice. At the same time, hospitals—particularly those operated by federal and state governments—increased greatly in number and competence, becoming not so much places to die in as places in which to be born and to get well.

The results of these changes in medical and hospital practices were reflected in changes in the causes of death across the population. Several of the diseases now regarded as easily curable, or even nonexistent, were major killers in 1900. During the first three decades of the twentieth century, the deaths per 100,000 from influenza and pneumonia dropped by half; the tuberculosis death rate by two-thirds; stomach and intestinal diseases to less than one-fifth; typhoid and paratyphoid fever to about one-eighth; diphtheria to one-tenth. All of these had been very common causes of death. On the other hand, the control of epidemics and contagion was still relatively primitive, and public health facilities were still inadequate. Occasional epidemics could strike and spread almost as unchecked as a medieval plague. The most famous of these disasters was the "flu" epidemic of 1918, which carried off many thousands with very little warning (588,000 died of flu or pneumonia that year, three times the 1917 number). Less calamitous yet serious epidemics occurred of polio in 1916, smallpox in 1920 and 1921, diphtheria in 1921. Control over diphtheria became adequate only late in the twenties, and widespread smallpox inoculation did not occur

LIFE EXPECTANCY AT BIRTH, 1900–1968

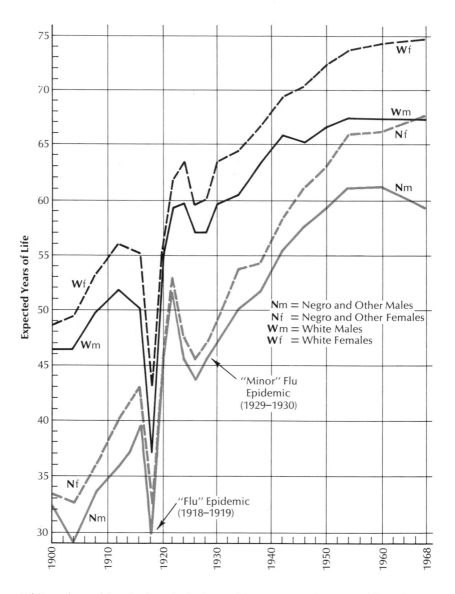

White males and females have had a longer life expectancy than non-white males and females, but in the late 1960s non-white females passed white males. The ravages of the 1918–1919 influenza epidemic were greater than those of World War I. Epidemics of "flu" and other diseases struck hard during the late 1920s, but medical advances and vast improvements in medical care and nutrition for Negroes (partly a result of their urban migration) in the 1930s and 1940s prevented such disasters later.

until the thirties. In the meantime, the more typically "modern" killers became even more usual, as in the case of heart disease (the leading cause of death throughout the period, except in 1918), or spread gradually to become one of the two or three leading causes, as with various forms of cancer. Americans became slightly more suicide-prone, and with the arrival of the automobile, they discovered a whole new method of ending their lives.

It seems to us today that the quality of American life has changed most radically in the very recent past, with the advent of mass air travel, suburbias, television, computers, "the bomb," and "the pill." But the changes that occurred between 1897 and 1929 were revolutionary. Some of the most frequently mentioned aspects of the "American way of life" did not become common until the early twentieth century, especially in the twenties. Anyone who has ever lived in a house or an apartment building constructed before World War I or, still more visibly, before 1900 remembers that "modern" conveniences—central heating, electrical outlets and wiring, flush toilets and other plumbing—were usually and obviously appended well after the original construction. Not until after World War I did outhouses cease to be the rule in most of the country (the rural South and Appalachia are still exceptions), or did the electric vacuum cleaner begin to replace the broom, or did furnaces and gas stoves replace kitchen coal-burners. Electric refrigerators appeared only at the very end of the period, making possible extensive changes in the national diet and driving from front windows the card with 25-50-75-100 in the corners, to tell the iceman how large a block to carry in from his truck. But the device that changed living patterns most profoundly, spawning whole new industries and smashing local traditions, was the automobile.

Automobiles:
Agents of Social Change

A new form of transportation, the mass-produced and mass-consumed automobile, revolutionized early twentieth-century living. Henry Ford's Model "T" and other motor vehicles were as fundamental to the transformation of American society in the first half of the century as the railroad had been in the late nineteenth century. The economic effects were prodigious. The automobile industry spurred not only the expansion of Detroit from a quiet, small metropolis to a booming large one, but also a number of other cities producing tires, plastics, shaped steel, and other automobile components. New industries were spawned, producing spare parts and fuel, and auto sales and service. A national system of paved highways, studded with service stations, tourist cabins, and billboards, developed from about 1915 onward.

The social effects of the automobile were equally profound. Millions of people, who otherwise would have shared the common pre-auto experience of never venturing out of their home county, drove themselves to places that their parents had only read about. People drove to work in cars, vacationed in them, were conceived and born in them, and died in them. They were still largely a rich man's toy through the first dozen years or so of the century, but through the teens, and definitely by the twenties, anyone who could shun a streetcar or shed a bicycle in favor of an automobile did so. Car sales climbed from 4,000 in 1900 to 181,000 in 1910 to nearly 2 million in 1920 to about 4.5 million in 1929. The exceptional attractions of motor cars as combinations of practical vehicles and status symbols put them in great demand, and remarkable inventions in production and distribution allowed manufacturers to satisfy the demand.

Before 1908 the auto was a largely hand-made, trouble-prone, expensive luxury. In that year Henry Ford, almost the last of the late-nineteenth-century inventor-tycoons, revolutionized auto production (and ultimately the production of many other items, too) by applying the newly-current idea of moving assembly lines, which efficiently divided workers' tasks into small operations in sequence, bringing the work to the worker as he stood at a point on the line. It took Ford several years to perfect the principle, but by 1914 his assembly line turned out over a thousand cars a day, all of them black, durable "Model T's." Ford has been laughed at for the statement that the consumer could have a car in any color so long as it was black; but he deserves credit for making it possible for millions to buy a car at all.

In 1914 he raised his workers' wages to five dollars a day, twice their previous level, on the grounds that a worker ought to be able to buy the thing he produced. Ford also lowered the price of the Model T over the years, from just under $1,000 in 1909 to $290 in

1926, the year before he replaced it with the "Model A." By then, 15 million Fords later, the "average man" was affluent enough to buy a Chevrolet, or even a Buick or a Chrysler, with more zip and frills than Ford's basic transportation. In less than twenty years, the irascible, efficiency-seeking Henry Ford had done more than most politicians and philosophers to relieve the social discontent so threatening at the turn of the century, and he made tens of millions in the process. Businessmen were exploiting the commercial possibilities of trucks, and a quarter-million were operating when the United States entered World War I, three and a half million in 1929. When ownership of cars became common in the twenties—one American in six owned one by 1929—localism broke down rapidly.

Both trucks and cars engendered a burst of highway-building, with happy effects on employment and on industries making road materials. The United States had only 154,000 miles of surfaced road in 1904, the first year for which figures were kept, but mileage quadrupled in the next twenty-five years. States and municipalities bore much of the cost, but the federal government spent between fifty and one hundred million dollars per year during the twenties, usually cooperating with the states, on new roads. Washington again served as a distributor of capital invested for social purposes, as it had when it underwrote the transcontinental railroads fifty years before, by subsidizing the network of "U.S." highways that became an all-weather car and truck network throughout the country. The harness maker, the hitching post, and the horse and buggy, all taken for granted in people's lives since early colonial days, began disappearing from the landscape.

The New Communications Media

The integration of the national society through communications devices, a process just beginning in the late nineteenth century, sped forward in the early twentieth with the advent of mass periodicals, the telephone, and the commercial radio. The United States had less than one telephone per hundred people in 1897, but one in ten by 1914, and about one in six by the end of the twenties. But this was far from post–World War II levels; Robert S. and Helen M. Lynd noted in *Middletown*, their social survey of Muncie, Indiana, in the mid-twenties, that operators only then were beginning to insist that people place calls by number instead of the name of the party they were calling. Dial phones and automatic exchanges were some distance off. Still, Americans made over 64 million calls per day by 1929. Telephone and telegraph rates declined; one could telephone London from New York for $10 per minute by 1930, and once more, localism and social isolation were giving way.

Publishers brought out two and a half times more books in 1929 than in 1897, the Post Office handled nearly four times as many pieces of mail, and newspapers sold four times as many copies. From the years just before World War I on through the twenties, publishing geniuses such as Horace Boni and Alfred A. Knopf helped change standards of taste in fiction and nonfiction, providing a forum for iconoclasts and social critics. Flamboyant journalistic techniques, pioneered by William Randolph Hearst and others, demolished the dull appearance of the nineteenth century newspaper with circus makeups, action photos, and banner headlines. The first syndicated comic strips, the early Broadway gossip columnists, and advice-to-the-lovelorn writers helped make fads and opinions the common property of newspaper readers across the country. The Black Sox scandal of 1919, Babe Ruth's sixty home runs, Lindbergh's solo flight to Paris, and the Scopes "monkey trial" hit city streets everywhere within hours.

Popular periodicals also reached and found a mass audience, and like the movies, they both shaped popular opinion and were shaped by it. American popular attitudes became cooler toward religion, warmer toward science and technology. Religious periodicals dropped from 4.5 percent of all magazine circulation in 1900 to 0.8 percent in 1930, while popular-science magazines rose from 1 percent to 4 percent. "Church interest" articles almost disappeared from the pages of women's magazines—one indication that much of American social history in the early twentieth century consisted of changes in the attitudes and actions of women. The expensive and genteel journals of the late nineteenth century either succumbed or conformed to the ways of new magazines such as *McClure's*, *Everybody's*, the *Saturday Evening Post*, and, in the twenties, *Time*—all of which succeeded in capturing a national popular market, both through their low prices and their often sensational content. "Muckraking" articles by journalists such as Lincoln Steffens, Ida Tarbell, and David Graham Phillips exposed corruption in city governments, national politics, and big business, and were interspersed in the pages of *McClure's* and *The American* along with uplifting fiction and biography. Muckraking subsided by 1910 or 1912, its trumpet blasts having awakened a popular mood for "reform," but mass journalism continued to expand, especially in the direction of satire, social criticism, and sexual frankness (though by no means explicitness) in the twenties. In those years, the modern advertising industry began, with syndicated display ads and attempts at creating consumer demand, as men like E. L. Bernays and Bruce Barton laid the practical and theoretical foundations for Madison Avenue.

An entirely new communications industry grew up in southern California with the development of the massive motion picture studios. From flickering nickelodeons in the nineties and the first "full length feature" narrative, *The Great Train Robbery*, which appeared in 1903, the movie industry moved from the New York area after 1911, and by 1919, 80 percent of the films made in the world came from Hollywood. Over-staged and over-acted vulgarities far outnumbered striking advances in "cinematic art," but that has always been true of stage and screen. Rapidly improving cinematic technique, the expanding city-dwelling audience, and the accurate feel of the big studios for an often not-very-refined public taste made Hollywood a glittering financial success. The opulent life-style of many screen stars may have been particularly gaudy examples of what Thorstein Veblen biliously called "conspicuous consumption," but such lavishness, especially in the twenties, sent many youthful hearts atwittering across the country. The nation laughed at Charlie Chaplin, Buster Keaton, Harold Lloyd and the Keystone Cops; emoted with the Gish girls, Gloria Swanson, and Greta Garbo; and thrilled at the melodramatic swashbuckling of Douglas Fairbanks. Whatever else could be said about them, the movies were more fun than quilting bees and tent meetings.

D. W. Griffith, the most innovative director of the time, brought out *The Birth of a Nation*—in praise of the Ku Klux Klan of Reconstruction days—in 1915, and he produced the first movie extravaganza, called *Intolerance*, in 1916. The biblical epic began its pseudopious life when Cecil B. DeMille discovered the box-office appeal of sex-plus-scripture and produced *The Ten Commandments* in 1923 and *King of Kings* in 1927. Americans paid millions to see silent films on themes of biblical religion, the glory and corruption of ancient Babylon and Rome, and the underdog poorboy-making-good fighting the rich and privileged. Gangsters and cowboys were, as always, staple fare. The movies unabashedly used racial stereotypes of Negroes, Mexicans, Chinese, and Japanese, almost always unfavorably or patronizingly; in this too they reflected popular attitudes. Stereotyping continued into the day of "talkies," when Warner Brothers brought out the first commercial sound film, *The Jazz Singer*, starring (in blackface) the Jewish crooner Al Jolson, in 1927.

By 1933, the movies were sufficiently established as a social institution to be surveyed by social scientists, and two studies published that year found that one-third of movie audiences were children and teenagers, who were not being shown a true reflection of "real life," according to an Ohio State psychologist. Half the characters were under thirty, and only 15 percent were married (as against 68 percent in real life). The movies showed no workers, except servants of the rich or cowboys in westerns; no manufacturing; no agriculture. Wealth and status, in amounts so great as to be unattainable to the viewers, were shown in abundance. Over a third of the heroes and heroines, and nearly two-thirds of the villains and villainesses, were portrayed as very rich, and formal dress appeared in 73 percent of the films, drinking in 66 percent, "intoxication" in 43 percent. One survey counted about three violent crimes per film. The other somewhat archly described the pernicious influence of movies on office girls with a quote: "Say, have you seen John Gilbert and Greta Garbo in love? Why, when he kissed her I almost passed out. Oh, for a man like that." The surveyors did not doubt that movies were a bad influence.

Radio developed from a scientist's toy to a national necessity. After the Italian inventor Guglielmo Marconi sent and received wireless signals in 1895, the American Lee DeForest invented the vacuum tube in 1906, and other inventors proved the practicality of radio in ocean and air navigation during World War I. The first commercial radio station, Pittsburgh's KDKA, broadcast the Harding-Cox presidential election returns in 1920, and boxing matches and major league baseball in 1921. By the following year, nearly a million receiving sets caught sports, politics, and news being broadcast by several hundred stations. In September 1926 the Radio Corporation of America opened the first national network, NBS, and others followed. In about twenty-five years, communications technology had taken on virtually its contemporary form, except for television, in the nationalizing of American popular culture.

Up and Down
the Status Ladder

Horizontal mobility—from east to west, from farms to towns, from Europe to the Northeast and Midwest, and for blacks, from South to North—continued to be a distinguishing feature of American society. Another kind of mobility, however, was less common: the movement of people up or down the social scale. The myth of the "self-made man" was seldom stronger than it was in the early twentieth century, when this hoary notion seemed to be validated by a lasting, if moderate, measure of prosperity and the millions of white-collar jobs that opened up. Some of the most brutal "survival of the fittest" situations, such as the sheer hazard of being a low-paid industrial or farm worker without social insurance, were ameliorated through a modicum of social legislation before World War I. But reform went only so far; it did not mean that America had become a classless society, or even a society where movement across status lines was frictionless.

How then was the American social hierarchy structured? How easy was it for a person to move from one to another level within a lifetime, or within the lifetimes of father and son? As far as we can tell, more vertical mobility existed in the early twentieth century than in the late nineteenth century, and considerably less than after 1945. Some people moved up or down the status ladder, but a majority probably held much the same position as that of their parents. Several devices were used to ascribe status (or the lack of it), and of these, race was the most determining; Negroes, almost without regard for education, occupation, or income, were assigned the low rung on the ladder. Almost as powerful as status determinants were religion and ethnicity. The recent immigrant, the Catholic, and the Jew found their opportunities and prestige circumscribed because of the way they worshipped or the places they came from or their traces of a foreign accent. The country's social hierarchy, in simplest terms, included a sizable group at the bottom, both urban and rural in residence, and disproportionately foreign-born or of foreign stock, non-Protestant, and Negro. Above this was a heterogeneous "middle class," increasing at a faster rate than the population as a whole, including farm owners, skilled workers, many businessmen, and white-collar workers. At the top was a small but visible and powerful upper-middle and upper-status group, highly prestigious and influential.

The farm laborers and blue-collar workers of the country were of low status occupationally. The difficulties confronting such persons who wanted to "better themselves" were considerable. If the worker was an immigrant or the child of an immigrant, he not only had to learn "American ways," i.e., middle-class values and behavior, but also forget the ways of his parents. If he were non-Protestant, he often faced anti-Semitic, anti-Catholic, or nativist discrimination when he sought to associate with the "majority" in churches, clubs, or other voluntary associations, or even when he looked for a job. If he were farm-bred, his route to higher status usually pointed to the city, a route that was hard on tender feet and that involved turning his back on familiar surroundings. If a boy's parents were unskilled or semiskilled workers, there were few ways, except luck, by which he could find the capital even to stay in school, much less to buy his own farm or business.

The insecurity of industrial workers, and hence of their families, was one of the root causes of lack of status mobility. As the Lynds pointed out in *Middletown*, industrial laborers had to start worrying at age forty about what would happen to them after age fifty, when many would be shelved, because pension plans were rare and job tenure and even unemployment insurance were practically nonexistent. As a consequence, many laborers could hold their jobs only two or three years, with obvious results such as low wages, inability to save, forced moves from place to place, and substantial shortening of their children's education. Their children commonly dropped out of school. Sometimes the reason was a "general dislike" of school, or a simple lack of academic ability, or economic stringency. Frequently, as the Lynds found, a person left school because he felt socially inferior, unable to compete in dress and casual expenditure, and hence unable to make the friends he wanted. Initial financial

The "Invisible Empire" extended far outside the South. Here, a Ku Klux Klan parade at Long Branch, New Jersey, on the Fourth of July, 1924. (Brown Brothers)

superiority, therefore, bred social superiority in the next generation, and since the dropout's economic chances in life were then, as now, much less than the diploma-holder's, social superiority bred financial superiority once more, in a vicious circle.

Yet education was then, as it has been generally throughout American history, the key to upward mobility. School attendance, especially high school attendance, rose dramatically during the early twentieth century. By the end of the period the high-school diploma had replaced the eighth-grade certificate as the "taken for granted" evidence of competence through formal education, even though a great many, especially nonwhites, did not get that far. For the urban-dwelling middle class and aspiring immigrants, it became the expected thing. The one *sine qua non* of upward status mobility present in all shifts from level to level, except into the elite, was education. Contrary to the "rags to riches" myth of the seventies and eighties, which insisted that schooling was a waste of time and money when a youngster could be out getting ahead in the world, the high school or college graduate had a definite advantage if he wanted to rise faster than his peers.

The middle class, which was very diverse occupationally but which included highly skilled workers, farm owners, small businessmen, some professionals such as teachers or clergy, and above all, those who wore white collars though they were not rich or powerful, was growing faster than either the industrial workers below or the elite above. The expansion of cities, the increasing size of businesses, the proliferation of small retail enterprises, as well as the marketing giants, created hundreds of thousands of respectable if often low-paying jobs—clerking, selling insurance, handling time payments, general office work—which carried a degree of status greater than that accorded a blue-collar worker. The holders of these jobs were becoming, instead of the formerly predominant farmers, the "great American average" in housing, use of consumer goods, attitudes, and life style.

Finally there were the envied few. The upper-level leaders of society, the wealthy and powerful, were a combination of several groups, who had in common the possession of white-haired or gray-haired money—i.e., they were not so much money-makers themselves as they were inheritors of wealth made one or more generations earlier. Black-haired money, the wealth of the self-made man, was not enough to confer elite status. Families that had possessed high status perhaps since colonial times, together with the beneficiaries of post–Civil War capitalism, formed this elite group, identifiable at their apex in the *Social Register* in various large cities. They were members of exclusive town and country clubs, often had prominent ancestors, and after 1900 especially, went to the "right schools," the eastern prep schools mostly founded in the nineties and the 1900s, to segregate them educationally from the mass. The exclusive academy led usually to one of the Ivy League universities or to an exclusive liberal-arts college, or for the girls a finishing school, and then entry into a not very cruel world.

My FRIEND, have you heard of the town of Nogood,
  On the banks of the River Slow,
Where blooms the Waitawhile flower fair,
Where the Sometimeorother scents the air,
  And the soft Goeasies grow?

It lies in the Valley of Whatstheuse,
  In the Province of Letterslide.
That Tiredfeeling is native there,
It's the home of the reckless Idontcare,
  Where the Giveitups abide.

It stands at the bottom of Lazyhill,
  And is easy to reach, I declare;
You've only to fold up your hands and glide
Down the slope of Weakwill's toboggan slide
  To be landed quickly there.

The town is as old as the human race
  And it grows with the flight of years.
It is wrapped in the fog of idlers' dreams,
Its streets are paved with discarded schemes,
  And sprinkled with useless tears.

It was easier, of course, to be born into a higher status level than to work one's way into one. Entry into the elite was extremely difficult except by marriage, because by definition personal achievement counted for less and prestige was ascribed by ancestry or inheritance. Entry into the professional or business leadership group was easier, especially if one worked his way up through an expanding corporation or other organization. As for movement from the lower class into the white-collar middle class, the critical factor that eased that path for many was the sheer increase in the number of those jobs. Quite possibly, if the occupational structure of the country had been stable and there had not been a large proportionate rise in white-collar, urban-located positions, there would have been more downward mobility than upward. After all, tenancy was increasing among farmers, and then status would have declined if many potential farmers had had no other opportunities.

Despite the considerable mobility that did exist, the road upward was steep, and climbing it demanded skill and doggedness. Most people still entered their fathers' occupations or other occupations on the same status level. Some fell, rather than rose. It was still very difficult for a lower-class person to become middle class, or for anyone to enter the elite, in both cases for reasons chiefly beyond the individual's control. Vertical mobility in the United States at that time was probably about as common as it has been in other countries at that stage of industrialization and modernization. The notion that the United States was a land of opportunity for emigrants from a class-ridden and static Europe was usually more myth than fact.

Ford's famous assembly line in 1924, still churning out the Model "T." (Courtesy of Ford Motor Company)

3

THE ECONOMY, 1897-1929:
THE SUNSHINE OF PROSPERITY

In four major ways, the American economy in the early twentieth century differed from that of the thirty years which immediately followed the Civil War. The new trends were (1) continuing prosperity instead of periodic panic and depression; (2) greater complexity and interdependence, especially in big business enterprise; (3) a widening gap between agriculture and manufacturing, and a marked increase in white-collar workers; and (4) a new emphasis, especially in the twenties, on mass production for consumers. Meanwhile, the "labor question" remained bloody and unanswered. These trends would probably not have developed without a growing population, increasingly urban and spread around the country, increasingly educated, and possessing some hope of vertical mobility.

Bulging Growth and
the Booming Business Cycle

The American economy grew mightily in the late nineteenth century, with its long-term deflation from 1873 through 1896, but it also grew during the early twentieth century, a time marked by gradual inflation from 1897 through 1929. Perhaps the deflationary character of the earlier period made investment and expansion more solid, even though more cautious, during that time. However, the inflationary post-1897 period probably hastened expansion more, with its greater promise of some kind of quick return on investment and with the accumulating optimism that was feverish by the end of the twenties, which encouraged businessmen to take risks. And for regularly employed skilled workers, wages and salaries rose more than fast enough to offset inflating costs. Standards of living improved.

Prosperity was widespread and almost constantly expanding after 1897. No depressions marred the business cycle until after 1929, and the single substantial recession, the post–World War I adjustment of

1921–22, was neither a prolonged one nor a harbinger of depression. The single severe stock-market panic before 1929, which came in 1907, did not touch off a depression as had the panics of 1857, 1873, and 1893. When calamity struck, as it finally did in late 1929, the disastrous consequences were unparalleled in depth and duration. But for more than thirty years before, most economic indicators pushed upward. The cumulative growth produced a feeling of security and well-being, which in turn created the confidence necessary for investment, inventive marketing, and the exploiting of new products and processes. Growth also bred bland unconcern about "problem sectors," such as agriculture, and too much faith in prosperity continuing almost automatically; these attitudes made the crash of 1929 all the more surprising and severe.

Before then, however, there was much to be confident about. The gross national product nearly tripled in constant dollars in the thirty-two years after 1897, to over $100 billion in 1929. In per capita terms, the increase was a hefty 70 percent, from under $500 to over $850 per year, and though not all of the increase in productivity was reflected in increased personal income to workers, the boost in the standard of living of the average American was very pleasurable. Even in the five years after 1929, when the economy plunged from its historic peak to the depth of the Great Depression, the gross national product did not dip below 1920 levels, and the per capita gross national product went no lower than what it was in 1905. From the late nineties until 1916, the upward climb in national wealth and income followed a mildly ascending slope, and then the great jump in demand and output that always has come during wartime shoved an inflating GNP steeply upward, by 84 percent between 1917 and 1921. Prices and wages dropped severely during the recession of 1921 and 1922, but prosperity returned thereafter for another seven booming years.

While growing, the economy changed direction. Emphasis shifted, both in the job market and in the kind of goods produced, from agriculture or basic manufacturing toward services, trade, and personal finance (including installment buying), and output for consumers. Despite the continuing maldistribution of national wealth, real income rose sufficiently to allow large masses of people to buy automobiles and home appliances, and to create insurance, advertising, financing, and marketing industries substantially larger than in the past. Changes in manufacturing output were not only

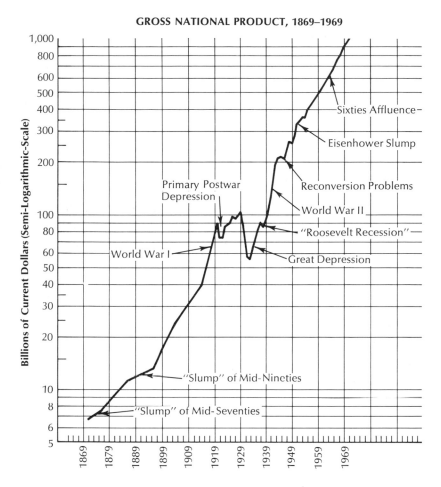

GROSS NATIONAL PRODUCT, 1869–1969

Figures are in current dollars, i.e., actual dollars as counted in a given year, rather than in "constant" dollars, i.e., corrected for inflation or deflation. Note that the rise in GNP was steeper during the 1960s (a time of quite mild inflation, by the way) than at practically any other time except World War II.

sizable—value rose from $5.4 billion in 1897 to $37.8 billion in 1929—but occurred most dramatically in consumer items such as home furnishings (up 1,200 percent), electrical appliances (from $2 million to $177 million), and of course all items relating to automobiles (from $4 million in 1899 to $2½ billion in 1929). Producer durables such as industrial machinery and office equipment increased ten times in value of annual output during 1899–1929, and industrial electrical equipment rose even faster. A single commodity, the family car, accounted for much of the rise in consumer durables, and also stimulated producer durables, since auto makers needed more machinery and semifinished products. Car-making also contributed to the rising value of services, the fastest growing sector of the economy, as service stations and other auto-related service industries (retail accessory stores, body shops, insurance agencies, highway police) dotted the land.

The rise in services was more than just a response to the demands of new car owners. It reflected something more basic about the economy—its increasingly complex interrelationships. Millions of producers and consumers required more transportation, more communication, more merchandising services, more banking and insurance, more office staffing, more public employees. Numbers of workers in service jobs such as transportation, finance, trade, education, government, and real estate tripled between 1900 and 1930, multiplying faster than the numbers of workers in manufacturing, much faster than those in agriculture or mining. The structure of output and labor was moving more and more away from the rural, relatively self-sufficient and isolated economic units of the nineteenth century.

Productivity also rose. The output of workers per man-hour doubled between 1897 and 1930, except in agriculture; the prime reasons were improved technology, the immensely greater application of manufactured energy (by electricity or petroleum products), and more efficient economic organization. For example, while white-collar jobs proliferated, the output of each white-collar worker rose substantially as offices came to include typewriters, cash registers, and calculating machines as standard equipment. Here the economic benefits from society's investment in public education were plain; greater and greater numbers of high-school-educated people, with the skills to hold down office jobs, were becoming available.

In such ways, American economic growth continued to be an interdependent process. The auto industry, becoming one of the mainsprings of the economy, depended on finding oil and refining it, which in turn required engineers. The number of engineers in the country rose sixfold between 1900 and 1930. Mass demand for cars, on the other hand, required a large pool of Americans with rising incomes, themselves the product of a growing economy. Such a pool of consumers required a high average level of skills, which the schools did much to provide. No single cause or small set of causes explain the economic development of the early twentieth century; a large number of factors combined to produce a relatively modern level of development through a complex cause-and-effect chain of relationship.

The Transportation Sector

To an American of the 1970s, the texture of the economy by the end of the 1920s appears generally familiar and in many ways modern. The economy of 1900 would seem foreign and primitive in many respects. The difference resulted in large part from the rapid growth of three sectors between 1897 and 1929—transportation, government, and manufacturing—and the slow growth of small businesses and of agriculture.

The transportation boom was based on motor vehicles. By 1914, most of the country's railroads were already built. New track was being laid at a rate of two to four thousand miles a year from the late nineties to 1914, a rate close to that of the early 1870s or the 1880s. After 1914, however, except for one or two years, new railroad track never exceeded a thousand miles a year. In contrast, motor vehicle production in 1923 was more than twenty times what it was in 1910, and it stimulated all manner of other goods and services. The age of the railroad was by no means over in 1929; even at the depth of the depression, railroads carried hundreds of millions of ton-miles of freight. But the peak year in American history for numbers of train passengers was 1920, when there were over one and a quarter billion fares; the number declined thereafter. By 1915 the future domination of American transportation by cars and trucks was already predictable.

The motor-vehicle expansion of the teens and twenties paralleled in many ways the railroad expansion of fifty years earlier. Technology and demand coalesced in the 1850s and 1860s for the railroads, and around 1920 for motor vehicles, just at the times when the federal government proved willing to provide large subsidies for each—land grants for the railroads and a paved national highway system for cars and trucks. In 1904, only 154,000 miles of hard-surfaced roads existed in the United States, and much of that was recently-paved city streets. By 1924 that figure had tripled, and over three million miles of country roads provided the outlines of a national highway network.

Governments Expand

The share of local, state, and national governments in national income nearly doubled between 1900 and 1930—slowly until World War I and then very quickly, remaining at a relatively high plateau during the twenties. Federal expenditure rose, except for five years, slowly and steadily from about a half billion dollars per year around 1900 to about three billion in 1929. The exceptional years were 1917 through 1921, when World War I and postwar costs sent federal spending to what was then an astronomical level. The rise in federal spending by no means reflected the coming of a welfare state; the chief devourers of the tax dollar were the traditional ones of paying interest on the national debt, running the Post Office, and maintaining a defense force. In the twenties, new spending categories were highway construction and benefits for World War I veterans. Individual and corporate income taxes provided most of the newly-needed funds, though tax rates remained very low as compared with the rates in the thirties and forties (individuals began paying about 1 percent on an income of $4,000 in 1924–29).

State and local governments spent about twice what the federal government did, except for the war years. Much of the money, which was mostly raised by property and sales taxes, went for local schools and roads—the traditional functions of state and local governments. But the sums were not traditional: expenditure on schools rose by 800 percent, highway costs by about 100 percent, in each case to about two billion dollars annually, or about half of all state and local spending. As schools began to require shops, libraries, cafeterias, and gymnasiums, as employers sought skilled white-collar workers, and as the public demanded good roads for their new cars, states and municipalities responded. Spending for higher education (state colleges and universities especially) and for conservation of natural resources rose dramatically. The economy and the public wanted government to do more, and governments grew in turn.

Manufacturing: Big Business and the "New Era"

From 1897 to the 1930s, the number of workers in manufacturing nearly doubled, wages and salaries increased sevenfold, the value added to goods by the manufacturing process also rose sevenfold, and the horsepower of machinery by over one hundred times. Companies grew in size rather than number; the number of factories rose slowly from 205,000 in 1899 to about 270,000 in 1919 but declined again to fewer than 207,000 in 1929.

The trend toward consolidation was visible before 1897, but for about a half-dozen years just around the turn of the century, a great wave of consolidations created several companies that were monsters for that time. In 1901, J. P. Morgan and others engineered the creation of the first billion-dollar corporation, the United States Steel holding company. Morgan bought out the personal holdings of Andrew Carnegie, who wanted to retire, for about $450 million, and around the nucleus of the Carnegie empire, Morgan added other multi-million-dollar bits and pieces to create the new giant capitalized at $1.4 billion. Several hundred million dollars worth of the stock was "water," i.e., paper not supported by factories, ships, or other tangible assets, but the company was successful in absorbing all the water by accumulating solid assets before the Justice Department prosecuted it for antitrust violations ten years later. At that time the steel company's capital value was larger than the federal budget; when it was formed in 1901 it was about three times the size of the federal government's annual expenditure.

Also in 1901, Morgan superintended the formation of an enormous railroad monopoly, the Northern Securities Company, which tied together the Great Northern, the Northern Pacific, and the Burlington, all of the trunk lines in the northwest quarter of the country. The monopoly did not end there. The Northern Securities was the product of a ferocious competitive struggle between James J. Hill, owner of the northwestern roads, and E. H. Harriman, who already controlled the Illinois Central, the Union Pacific, and the

Southern Pacific. Hill, Harriman, and Morgan all had interests in the new holding company.

Many other less elephantine examples of business consolidation took place between 1897 and 1903, and they amounted to "monopoly," or "rationalization of business," depending on one's point of view. The point of view of the federal government, beginning in 1902 and continuing until World War I, was that many of the consolidations were in violation of the Sherman Anti-Trust Act of 1890. The Sherman Act was honored more in the breach than in the observance during the 1890s, when Presidents Harrison, Cleveland, and McKinley rarely called upon their Attorneys General to invoke the act against corporate engorgement. Also, the federal courts construed the act so narrowly that almost any corporate management could see its way around it. In 1902 the large investment bankers and other potentates of capitalism were stunned to learn that the Justice Department, prodded by the young (and apparently "unreliable") President Theodore Roosevelt, was bringing suit to break up the Northern Securities Company. Morgan and others rushed to Washington on one of their railroads and waited hats-in-hand in a White House anteroom to dissuade Roosevelt, but to no avail. In 1904 the Supreme Court upheld the government's case, in which Morgan and his friends had by that time acquiesced. Other consolidations continued after 1902, but other antitrust suits followed also, and the tide of trust-making receded. Roosevelt, then Taft, and then Woodrow Wilson supported antitrust prosecutions by their administrations, and the Justice Department, around 1910, successfully tackled such giants as Standard Oil, the American Tobacco Company, as well as the United States Steel holding company.

But the number of manufacturing, trade, and transportation companies continued to rise more slowly than economic sales or assets; consolidation continued, for several reasons. World War I accelerated the process of "rationalization," since the country required an unprecedented degree of coordination of resources for the war effort, and the federal government oversaw such coordination through the War Industries Board, the Railway Administration, and similar agencies. In the twenties, the Justice Departments of Harding and Coolidge took a much more benign view of consolidation than their prewar predecessors had done, and the trend toward consolidation regained the momentum that it had not had since the Northern Securities case twenty years earlier.

There were other reasons for business consolidations. The general strategy was to maximize profits and avoid if possible the cut-throat competition that made large ventures by individual companies risky. Larger firms were able to use new technology more effectively than smaller ones, and diversification of product lines minimized market risks. In the early twentieth century, technology encouraged consolidation; the wider use of assembly lines, the greater employment of electric power, and advances in communication and transportation enabled regional or national market industrial firms to operate more easily and to compete with smaller local units. It was often cheaper, for example, for a merchant hundreds of miles from Grand Rapids to buy Grand Rapids furniture rather than furniture made locally. With the expansion of chain stores and mail-order companies, themselves evidences of consolidation, manufacturing was further concentrated as the marketing giants contracted more items from fewer and larger manufacturers. Another advantage of size was the firm's ability to develop its own expansion capital. One of the peculiar characteristics of American economic expansion in the early twentieth century was the increasing tendency of firms, especially manufacturers, to generate their own capital instead of borrowing it from possibly conservative banks. Ford is a good example; he never borrowed any outside money except his initial few thousand. This characteristic led to the relative weakening of the role of investment banking in economic growth.

Urbanization also spurred consolidation, by providing a mass semiskilled labor pool in fairly compact areas and by allowing interdependent firms to locate close to each other, with resulting economies. Changes in consumption patterns helped, too; as more people had more money to spend beyond the bare necessities of food, clothing, and shelter, they were able to buy consumer durables such as home appliances and cars, the kind of goods more efficiently produced by larger rather than smaller firms.

No manufacturing industry developed as fast as auto-making, and none so fully demonstrated growth, consolidation, the use of new technology, and dependence on an expanding consumer market. Scores of small companies were making automobiles with electric, steam, or gasoline engines by 1900, but a leader began to emerge after the forty-year-old Detroit mechanic Henry Ford borrowed $28,000 and founded the Ford Motor Company in 1903. By 1907 Ford outsold all other cars, and rapidly increased his lead after he introduced the Model T in 1908. The assembly-line, the steadily dropping price, and the five-dollar minimum wage for an eight-hour day kept him there for years. But the economy was changing rapidly around World War I, and Ford stubbornly refused to change with it. His major competitor already was the General Motors Company, founded in 1908 when William Crapo Durant merged the Olds, Oakland, Cadillac, and Buick companies.

Durant, more a promoter-type than a practical engineer like Ford, retained control of General Motors only by borrowing fresh capital from the Du Pont chemical company in 1915, making General Motors an exception to the rule that the auto industry grew up through retained, self-developed capital, and without dependence on East Coast investors. Durant's free-wheeling methods did not survive the hard times of 1921, however, and a new group of corporate managers, led by Alfred P. Sloan, replaced Durant, decentralized the company for more efficient management, and started bringing out the Chevrolet as a low-cost car to compete with Ford's Model T. By the mid-twenties, General Motors permanently took over sales leadership from Ford, forcing the irascible baron of River Rouge to end nineteen years of production of the black Model T in 1927 and to bring out, in several models and colors, the Model A in 1928. In the meantime, Walter Chrysler founded his multimodel company in 1923 and started selling Plymouths in 1929 to vie with Chevrolets and Model A's for the low-priced market.

By the end of the twenties, the auto industry had become an example of the phenomenon called "oligopoly," the dominance of an industry not by a single monopolistic giant such as Standard Oil or the American Sugar Refining Company had been in the nineties, but by a handful of large firms making a widely-used product whose manufacture demanded planning, pricing, and production decisions a year or more in advance. These firms were guided only indirectly by competition and more directly by complex administrative decision-making. Before 1910, nearly 200 firms made cars in the United States, but less than a dozen survived the 1920s, and those were dominated by the "Big Three" of Ford, General Motors, and Chrysler, which is still the case.

From 1919 onward, the much-feared "trusts" that had proliferated in the 1897–1902 wave of consolidation, with their unitary managements operating whole industries through single dominant firms, were less in evidence. Administrative unwieldiness, as much as government prosecution, forced managerial change. The post–World War I years brought a continuation of consolidation, but through much more sophisticated managerial frameworks. Certain very large corporations such as Du Pont, General Motors, and Sears effected administrative reorganizations allowing a management to superintend very diverse and widespread operations flexibly and efficiently. The creation of these modern administrative systems avoided the likelihood that massive corporations would become dinosaurs, with too few brains for too much bulk, and instead allowed companies to continue increasing in size while functioning profitably and innovatively.

So successful were these administrative inventions, and so publicly satisfying was the continuing growth of big business and the rise in the average standard of living, that the twenties began to be hailed as a "New Era" in economic life. After 1922, production and purchasing swept along at a rate and with an efficiency only dreamed of ten years earlier. Business growth and the widespread enjoyment of material things would increase, so it seemed, automatically; businessmen did not need to worry about risks or profits, but could concern themselves with service to the community and the rational efficiency of the whole economic enterprise.

Business success took on religious and patriotic tones, as when President Coolidge proclaimed that "the business of America was business," and an advertising man named Bruce Barton wrote in his 1925 best-seller, *The Man Nobody Knows,* that Jesus Christ ought to be remembered as the super-salesman of all time. According to the "New Era" philosophy, efficient big businesses were to be increasingly organized into diversified companies and into trade associations working not only for maximum profits but for the good of society. Critics called the "New Era" trade association movement nothing more than monopoly and trust-building under elegant and pious names. But many Americans were entranced with "New Era" notions, and before 1929, the prosperous economy did not gainsay them.

The country was advancing in world leadership, having escaped the devastation of World War I, which greatly set back Germany, France, and Britain. The United States maintained a favorable trade balance, and largely as a result of World War I, when the Allies borrowed heavily from American sources, it replaced Britain as the leading financial power in the world. The United States led in management techniques as well as in productive power. Ninety percent of the value of nonfarm enterprise and nonfarm labor were in businesses organized in the form of corporations, especially large ones. Ownership often became separate from management; individually- or family-dominated large companies, such as Ford, became rarer, as corporate officers ran companies with decreasing supervision from their more and more scattered stockholders. Businessmen became enamored of "science" and "efficiency," and theorists of "scientific management," especially the engineer Frederick Winslow Taylor, were lionized like prophets of a new cult. The day of the individual entrepreneur was not over—witness Henry Ford, the new nabobs of Hollywood, and the first Texas oil millionaires. But in most basic industries it was waning, as symbolized by Ford's loss of leadership in the auto industry to the team-led, decentralized management of General Motors under Alfred Sloan and his associates. The corporation executive, faceless to the public, was replacing the Gould, Carnegie, or Morgan of an earlier day as the archetypal American big businessman.

Wholesalers, Retailers, and Advertisers

Commerce inevitably grew, as a product of population growth and the continuing manufacturing boom. The expansion of retail and wholesale trade was undramatic—the trading sector actually declined between 1900 and 1930 in its proportion of national income —but in one very important way it underwent a transformation. The large, national market trading firm was gradually replacing the corner grocer, the "dry goods and sundries" store, the independent shopkeeper.

The outstanding example of the trend was the development of Sears, Roebuck. In the mid-nineties, Sears was a small mail-order house. After the return of prosperity in 1897, the company diversified into a large number of product lines and began distributing them not only through a bigger mail-order operation but also through its own retail outlets. Local merchants were often hard-pressed to compete with Sears' low prices and long menu of consumer items. By the twenties, it had become a mercantile giant on a national scale, with an efficient, decentralized management. Nor

Fashion at popular prices in Sears, Roebuck's spring catalog for 1929. Wide lapels and the plumb-line crease from waist to shoetop were the style. (Sears, Roebuck and Company)

was Sears unique, except in size. The retail chain store, an invention of the late nineteenth century, became widespread in the early twentieth. Thirty-five multiproduct chain-store companies were operating in 1897; by 1930 there were 2,000. The national or regional retail firm often drove the small businessman off Main Street by underpricing the local merchant, possessing dependable sources of supply and standardized product lines, and benefiting from national advertising and "standard brands." The small shopkeeper could defend himself by becoming an "authorized representative" of a national brand of shoes or bicycles or men's clothes, but even then he had trouble competing with the convenience of the chain department store. The grocer or butcher in an immigrant neighborhood was secure as long as the chain supermarkets could not or would not stock "specialty" items like kosher meats or lasagna noodles. The neighborhood saloon flourished (until prohibition wiped it out, at least legally, after 1918), and many immigrant families prospered as Americans caught on to the delights of Cantonese or Italian restaurants. But these were exceptions to the gradual, relative decline of the small retail business in the total national economy.

Advertising became a billion-dollar industry by 1910, and more than tripled in volume between then and 1930. Early in 1898, a Midwestern metropolitan newspaper carried advertisements of local stores offering bath towels for five cents, black fleece-lined ladies' hose with white feet at seventeen cents a pair, black Astrakhan ladies' fur capes, satin-lined, for $7.50, men's worsted suits from $4.50 to $10.50, and four-year-old rye or bourbon whiskey for seventy-five cents a quart. Grocery and drug stores hardly advertised at all. Thirty-one years later, on the worst day of the 1929 stock market crash, the same paper carried display advertising of chain stores and large local department stores offering men's suits and topcoats from $18 to $26.50, console radios at $119.50 and up, national-brand coffee at thirty-two cents a pound, and cigarettes at $1.15 a carton. The Sears catalog for 1929 pictured bath towels from twenty-five cents, silk hose from $1.25, electric vacuums from $21.95, and electric washing machines from $69.50. The retail grocer of the late nineties bought flour, crackers (in cracker barrels), sugar, and similar staples in bulk, which he doled out by the pound to his customers; by the twenties, traditional bulk-buying of that kind was replaced by prepackaged national brand items, the first of which was the National Biscuit Company's "Uneeda" biscuit, introduced in 1899.

Installment purchases, estimated at less than one billion dollars in 1910, totaled seven billion dollars in 1929, almost 15 percent of all retail sales. Before World War I, people were using installment plans to buy pianos and sewing machines; in the twenties they bought, "on time," cars, radios, and electrical appliances. With more and more people living and working in cities, they increasingly bought canned and prepared foods, fresh fruits, and electrical ware. Silk and rayon replaced cotton in many ladies' wardrobes. Furniture purchases stabilized, except for living room furniture and manufactured mattresses, and outlay for radios, phonographs, and the movies replaced spending for pianos, reed organs, and other musical instruments that had provided entertainment in the home prior to World War I. The chain store and display advertising were nationalizing consumer behavior.

Banks, Wall Street, and the Federal Reserve

An adequate flow of money and credit was essential then, as now, to manufacturing, trade, transportation, and the rest of the economy. Banks, insurance companies, and other financial institutions grew in the first three decades of the twentieth century on an expanding flow of money and credit. As they did so, they too exhibited the trend toward the consolidation and increased average size of companies, which was happening in other sectors. But in the financial sector, unlike the others, power became somewhat diffused. Control of money and credit by the great Wall Street investment banking houses was at its tightest about 1910, but lessened in the twenties. Also, a measure of public regulation of money and credit began when the Federal Reserve System was founded in 1914.

Populists in the nineties and many progressive reformers in the first years of the new century complained bitterly at the formation of monopoly conditions in finance, and by 1910, the existence of what they called "the money trust." From 1911 to 1913, a committee of Congress chaired by a Louisiana Democrat named Arsène Pujo undertook a dramatic investigation of the "money trust," hauling J. P. Morgan and lesser financial luminaries to the witness stand to face a barrage of probing questions from the committee's counsel, Samuel Untermeyer. The Pujo Committee concluded that a money trust did indeed exist, if "money trust" meant "an established and well-defined identity and community of interest between a few leaders of finance which has been created and is held together through stock holdings, interlocking directorates, and other forms of domination over banks, trust companies, railroads, public-service and industrial corporations, and which has resulted in a vast and growing concentration of control of money and credit in the hands of a comparatively few men." The committee agreed that the members of the money trust had not violated any laws, "but that is rather because of the loose, intangible character of this recently developed community of interest and because the law has not yet properly safeguarded the community against this form of control." As was so often true, law lagged behind social and economic conditions; the public will, in the form of regulatory statutes, had not yet been defined.

In 1913 Congress made a crucial addition to the national statutes by passing the Federal Reserve Act, giving the United States a central banking system. The formerly unrelated national banks were required, and state-chartered banks were permitted, to join twelve regional reserve systems, each with its federal reserve bank. The number of national banks doubled between 1897 and 1914, then steadied through 1929, but their assets rose eightfold between 1897 and 1929. State banks actually decreased in number during the twenties because of failures and mergers, which also happened to insurance companies. The Federal Reserve System involved further centralization, but with public regulation. The twelve regional reserve banks were supervised (though very loosely before the 1930s) by a Federal Reserve Board in Washington. Member banks joined the system by buying stock of their regional reserve banks and depositing their own reserves in it. The members could draw on the central pool of reserves, and the reserve bank could add to a member bank's reserves by loaning it money in the form of "rediscounting," i.e., buying short-term securities from the member bank at a discount. The reserve bank, and later the Federal Reserve Board, could control the availability or scarcity of credit by raising or lowering the rediscount rate, which it charged members when they sought funds from it, making it harder or easier for a member to borrow from the reserve bank, and therefore making it harder or easier for a customer to borrow from the member bank. The reserve banks were thus "bankers' banks."

The reserve banks also controlled the supply of money and credit in another way, which was ultimately much more effective. This was their "open market operations": the reserve bank could buy government securities in the open market with its own funds. These securities then went into circulation and increased the loanable money available to banks. The reserve bank could also sell such securities, thus decreasing available loan money as its purchases soaked up that money from its member banks. In addition, the reserve banks issued currency, called "federal reserve notes," the number of which they could expand when money was scarce, and contract when money was abundant; thus they eliminated the decentralized inflexibility of the old national bank notes. The creation of the Federal Reserve System gave the banking sector, and the country's money and credit system, a degree of unity and rationality previously lacking, although the full potential of the "Fed" as a regulator of money and credit was not realized until it was more tightly centralized in 1935.

The creation of the Federal Reserve introduced an element of public regulation into American finance, and though it by no means ended the power of the great private bankers, it did help reduce the element of irresponsibility inherent in private monopolies. The power of the "money trust" was reduced after 1914 and through the twenties in another way. The proportion of national income that was generated in the financial sector slackened slightly between 1900 and 1930, in part because of the increasing ability of manufacturing firms (the auto makers, the oil companies, the steel and chemical producers) to develop their own capital for investment and expansion. As the manufacturing and trading sectors matured, the need for investment banking as a coordinator of investment activity and consolidations, and as a supplier of capital, diminished. Commercial banking and the insurance business developed, but at a rate just rapid enough to match general economic expansion.

The "Golden Age" in Agriculture

The least organized and consolidated of all the major sectors in the early twentieth century continued to be agriculture. Some consolidation did occur, as the rise in tenancy suggests, but none remotely matched manufacturing or communications consolidations like United States Steel or American Telephone and Telegraph. The number of farms in the country increased, but only very slowly after 1910, from 6.4 million farms in that year to 6.7 million in 1933. The average size of farms, however, increased faster, and the rise in the number of farms operated by tenants, managers, or part-owners was greater still. Steadily and unavoidably, farming became more commercialized. A farm had to be efficient in order to meet competition and to remain in operation, and many small owner-operated "family farms" could not survive. Tenancy increased by a third; in the South, among Negro farmers, tenants outnumbered owners three and one-half to one in 1900, five to one in 1930. A continually smaller fraction of the labor force was engaged in farming, and after reaching a peak of 13.6 million in 1916, the number of farm workers slowly declined. By 1929, one farmer in three worked at a second job.

Productivity of crops or livestock, the amount produced per man-hour of work, rose as a result of greater efficiency in production and marketing, new technology (especially mechanized tractors and other implements), and more widespread use of scientific fertilizing, breeding, and growing techniques. Agriculture continued to receive a smaller share of the national income, declining even more steeply than it did in the late nineteenth century, until less than one dollar in eight was a farm-produced dollar, compared to one in five in the decade following the Civil War. Little new land came under cultivation after 1910. The agricultural frontier of the late nineteenth century, though it persisted into the early 1900s, was effectively closed by World War I. For the next fifteen years, the number of farms stabilized at its all-time high, and then, from the mid-thirties on, began a decline that still continues.

Understandably, however, the individual farmer was concerned less with the decline in agriculture relative to the economy as a whole than he was with his own personal fortune, which was good through most of the period. The sun began to shine in 1897 for farmers, as for others, after several years of depression. From 1910 to 1914, farmers were so prosperous that for decades afterward those years were used as the "parity base" (the groundpoint or theoretical figure for crop-support or subsidy levels), which stated how much farmers ought to receive for their crops and livestock, as measured against what they had to pay for manufactured and other purchased goods. Parity was actually surpassed during World War I, when demand for agricultural products forced farm prices to record highs and the parity ratio to 120 (exact parity = 100). Even in the twenties, when farmers did not fully share in the general prosperity and many slid into tenancy, the overall parity ratio stayed reasonably high, generally around 90. But after 1929, farmers were hit hard by the depression.

Farmers were, as always, at a disadvantage compared to most other occupational groups because they could organize to protect themselves only with great difficulty. In an "oligopolistic" industry such as auto-making, where a handful of producers each made large numbers of units, production could be cut back, or prices

Farm workers declined steadily, and white collar workers increased steadily, throughout the century. Blue collar workers became relatively fewer after 1950 (and labor union membership also steadied in the 1950s and 1960s). Definitions: "white collar" includes professionals, managers, clerical and sales workers; "blue collar" includes manual workers *and* service workers of all kinds, except agricultural; service workers include domestic servants and a number of occupations such as barbers, porters, waiters, elevator operators, hospital workers, policemen, and so forth.

WHITE COLLAR, BLUE COLLAR, AND FARM WORKERS, 1900–1969

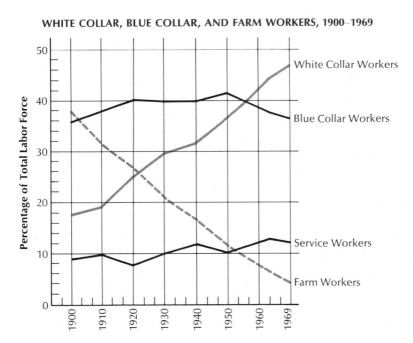

maintained, with some ease. But in farming, where several million small businesses each produced a tiny percentage of the total output, production and price controls were completely beyond the power of any single producer or even any organized group of producers. Farmers attempted in several ways, none very successful, to get around the problem. One way, an old one, was to elect candidates to public office who would support legislation to protect farmers. The Grange had done that around 1870. Another political solution was to form a farmers' political party, but the failure of the Populists in the 1890s taught the uselessness of that tactic.

Still another device was the political pressure group, and farmers sought to form such groups in the 1897–1929 period. Some of these pressure groups worked well for limited objectives. The Non-Partisan League, which came alive in the Northern Plains in 1915, captured the state government of North Dakota and elected a number of officials with strong agrarian sympathies. The League was a political power in the Northwest in the early twenties, when farmers were moved to protest the plummeting of prices that occurred in 1920–22 with the end of wartime demand. The League became one of the forces in a drive to elect a reform candidate to the presidency in 1924, but that drive failed, and the League's demands for a much stronger regulation of railroads and for outright state ownership of credit associations and grain elevators were not successful. Quieter but more effective than the Non-Partisan League was the group of midwestern Senators, led by Arthur Capper of Kansas, who formed a "Farm Bloc" in 1921 to promote agrarian legislation. The Farm Bloc secured some beneficial statutes, such as the Capper-Volstead Act of 1922, which provided a legal status to farm cooperatives. The number and size of marketing co-ops grew quickly through the twenties because of that law, and farmers valued the co-ops as an effective way of organizing to maintain prices.

But neither the Farm Bloc, the co-ops, nor the regulation of railroads and elevators succeeded in dealing with the central economic problem of small farmers then and later. The farmers overproduced beyond domestic needs and therefore received world-level prices for what they sold, while they had to buy manufactured goods on a protected domestic market. Manufacturers were insulated by protective tariffs and sometimes by oligopolistic price management, but farmers were unprotected. Growers of wheat, corn, cotton, and beef produced too efficiently for their own good. Here was a truly modern economic problem: production so efficient and so abundant that it threatened to impoverish or ruin the producers. It was unlikely that farming would ever be organized sufficiently by voluntary cooperation among farmers to control production and therefore prices; it was not in the nature of the enterprise. Where telephones or electric power seemed to tend naturally toward monopoly, or where manufactured products like cars or steel seemed to tend toward oligopoly, farming was anarchic. The instinct and tradition by which farmers sought political solutions to their problems was a sound one, but the right political devices eluded them. They needed legislation at the national level.

Some farm spokesmen proposed legislation in the twenties that was aimed at solving the problem of surpluses. George N. Peek of Illinois and Senator Charles McNary of Oregon wanted the federal government to support farm prices, and the two most discussed agricultural reforms of the twenties were the McNary-Haugen plan and the "export debenture" plan. These two plans would have segregated surpluses sold on low world markets from staples that were consumed domestically and that sold at higher prices, thus insulating the farmer from world markets as many manufacturers were insulated. But when Congress passed the McNary-Haugen bill in 1927 and again in 1928, President Coolidge, baffled by the incongruity of the bill, and the problem it tried to solve, with traditional free-market economics, vetoed it both times. Even if it had become law, it would not have solved the basic problem of overproduction, because it contained no provisions for crop or acreage controls and might even have stimulated still further overproduction. In 1929 Congress passed an Agricultural Marketing Act, and President Hoover signed it into law. It led to federal purchases of surpluses. But it did nothing to control production either, and by 1932 the federal government was overwhelmed by enormous inventories of surplus commodities. By then the parity ratio stood at 58. The problem of overproduction was ultimately attacked by federal crop and acreage controls and expensive subsidies, but before that happened, the "free market" so admired by Coolidge and many businessmen in the twenties, including many farmers, was running its predictable, natural course, and pushing thousands of farmers into tenancy or off the land.

Blue Collars and Anti-Unionism

The American labor force expanded from 29 million jobs in 1900 to about 49 million in 1930. While farm workers stayed at about the same 10.5 million in the twenties, receding from a high of 13.6 million before World War I, manual workers nearly doubled and white-collar workers nearly tripled. Twice as many women were working in 1930 than in 1900, and the biggest percentage increase in any job category, male or female, was in female clerical positions—over 2 million new jobs. Millions of clerking, clerical, stenographic, sales, and junior-executive positions were filled in towns and cities across the country, and the men and women who held them constituted a new middle class. The white-collar expansion also reflected the increased size of business organizations and the "emancipation of women," which characterized the period. The desire of many women to work outside the home went hand-in-hand with new opportunities to do so.

Nevertheless, prosperity, growth, and increasing complexity in business raised serious social problems, particularly the need to distribute more equitably the new wealth being created and to regulate the new economic mechanisms responsibly. Stronger labor unions might have helped by providing job guarantees and a better share of wealth to the growing mass of blue-collar workers. But employers, and many middle-class white-collar people, either opposed or distrusted unions, especially the "disruptive" ones. Thousands of editorials, feature articles, and politicians' speeches grappled with the "labor question" from the late nineties onward, claiming that the heart of the question was the need to make labor-capital relations equitable and harmonious—and to avoid violence. The new white-collar group was not much better off, in material terms, than blue-collar workers; both groups faced a problem of short rewards while the 5 or 10 percent of the population with the highest income took more than 50 percent of the national wealth. But status envy divided the workers more than class consciousness united them.

Workers actually improved their living standards substantially between the late nineties and 1929. The problem was that standards did not improve enough to avoid social and economic stresses. The average nonfarm worker earned well under $500 in 1897, while his annual income by 1929 was about $1,500. The average production worker in manufacturing made about twenty cents an

The Lawrence textile strike of 1912. Here, state militia drive strikers, led by the "Wobblies," away from the mills. (Courtesy of Lawrence Free Public Library, Lawrence, Massachusetts)

hour and worked a sixty-hour week in 1897; by the end of the twenties his workweek had decreased to fifty hours and his hourly wage had tripled. His costs as a consumer were higher, but laboring men and women generally enjoyed a rise in "real wages"—income rises after inflationary offsets have been accounted for—from the beginning of the period (slowly until 1914, faster thereafter) until the end of the twenties. Unionized manufacturing workers earned a handsome $46 a week, unionized building-trade workers a princely $58 a week, in 1926. Non-union manufacturing workers made about $25 per week in the same year.

There were several causes for the improvement. Unionization, though still weak, obviously helped. Membership in labor unions rose tenfold, from half a million to five million, between 1897 and 1920, particularly in the building trades, transportation and communication, and manufacturing of most kinds. After 1920, union membership slipped gradually to about three and a half million in 1929. Strikes and other work stoppages were very common, never fewer than a thousand a year involving several hundred thousand workers, rising to over 300,000 in each year from 1901 through 1903 and again from 1916 through 1920. After that, the prosperity of the twenties, and a hostile government and public, reduced work stoppages to a low of about 600 in 1928.

Many strikes were brief, local affairs, centering on lower hours and higher wages, or on demands that employers recognize unions. Others approached in scope the epic confrontations of the nineties at Homestead and Pullman. A two-month strike attempt by the old skilled-worker-oriented Amalgamated Association of Iron, Steel, and Tin Workers against the fledgling United States Steel Corporation in 1901, primarily over the issue of union recognition, was successfully broken by the Morgan interests. Without support from Samuel Gompers' American Federation of Labor, the Amalgamated came out of the strike with fewer union-organized mills than it had at the start, and a confident anti-union attitude settled upon the owners and managers of mass-manufacturing industries. The steel, auto, and other heavy industries were not successfully unionized until the 1930s. In 1902, the United Mine Workers under the young, dynamic John Mitchell led a strike of anthracite miners for better wages and working conditions and for recognition of the union as the miners' bargaining agent. Despite the relatively solid organization of the UMW, it gained some wage and conditions improvements, but not recognition, after several months of a bitter strike. The strike finally ended not so much because of union strength but because of the adverse public reaction to the mine-owners' arrogance—one of them, George F. Baer, had said that the miners were better off in the hands of "the Christian men to whom God, in His infinite wisdom, has given control of the property interests of the country"—and because President Theodore Roosevelt prevailed upon J. P. Morgan to "persuade" the owners to grant minimal demands to the workers and thus end a growing national coal emergency.

Other major strikes produced not even that much benefit for the workers, and violence marred many episodes. The United Mine Workers led a strike in the southern Colorado coal fields in 1913, seeking better wages and conditions, removal of armed company guards, workers' free choice of boarding houses, and union recognition. The strikers set up tent colonies near the companies' property. The local sheriff deputized private armed guards by the hundred. A striker was machine-gunned on October 17; three more were killed about ten days later. The governor sent in the National Guard. Four mine guards were killed in early November. The strike continued through the winter. In late April, a Guard detachment set on fire a tent colony near Ludlow; thirteen wives and children of miners died. Fourteen more miners and Guardsmen were shot to death in the ten days following the "Ludlow Massacre." The strike did not end until December, 1914, after intervention by President Wilson. The mineowners, led by John D. Rockefeller, Jr., granted few of the UMW objectives and instead set up a company union which left labor policy in the hands of management.

Radical unionism, in the form of the Industrial Workers of the World, understandably gained strength as many workers became convinced that only a class struggle, violent when necessary, would protect them against capitalist despotism. In 1912 the IWW led a strike of textile workers in Lawrence, Massachusetts. The mill operators and the town government adamantly refused to discuss the workers' demands for better wages; companies of militia were brought in, and within days 10,000 strikers and sympathizers opposed nearly two dozen armed militia companies. Two months later, after the picket line swelled to 20,000, the managements granted most of the workers' demands. Only one person, remarkably, had been killed. The IWW then turned to the textile mills of

A scene from the Ludlow massacre in Colorado, April, 1914: the strikers' tent colony after the authorities had burned it out. (Denver Public Library, Western History Department)

Paterson, New Jersey; after five months of striking, the workers returned to work without substantial progress. The IWW was a militant, class-conscious organization, aiming at the disruption of capitalism and the domination of the economy by workers, to be achieved by militant confrontations. It never, however, attracted more than about 50,000 members, and it lost most of its dwindling support when, like American socialists in general, it took an antiwar position in 1917 and 1918.

The more conservative unions limited their aims to a "market unionism" that concentrated on higher wages, shorter hours, better working conditions, and union recognition, instead of proletarian revolution. They did not enjoy any great success either. In 1919 massive strikes broke out in steel mills and coal mines. The steel strike involved over 300,000 workers, lasted effectively for nearly three months, brought about the eight-hour, three-shift day in the steel mills, and cost the lives of twenty people. It failed to gain union recognition. A general strike in Seattle, and a policemen's strike in Boston, also in 1919, frightened the increasingly antiradical general public more than any other of the 3,600 work stoppages that year.

Labor organizing was difficult for several reasons. One was the policy of Samuel Gompers of the AFL and other leaders of established unions of skilled workers against concentrating on the mass-production industries. Unskilled laborers were too easily replaced with "scabs," were divided by language barriers, and had too few resources to allow them to stay out on strike very long. Also, though the federal government no longer sent federal troops to intervene on the side of management as it had done in the nineties, formidable legal obstacles to union effectiveness remained. Major examples were the strike-breaking court injunction, the outlawing of boycotts in the Supreme Court's decisions in the Danbury Hatters' Case (1908) and in the Buck's Stove and Range Case (begun in 1906), and the continued liability of unions to antitrust prosecutions.

Even when labor gained a point, such as a New York law to limit bakery workers to a sixty-hour week and ten-hour day, the courts might strike it down, as the Supreme Court did to that law in 1905 in *Lochner* v. *New York.* Justice Peckham claimed that "the statute necessarily interferes with the right of contract between the employer and employees," and thus it violated "the liberty of the individual protected by the Fourteenth Amendment." Peckham's opinion was typical late-nineteenth-century liberalism, which no longer fit the facts of industrial life. Justice Oliver Wendell Holmes made a famous dissent in the Lochner case, declaring that "the Fourteenth Amendment does not enact Mr. Herbert Spencer's Social Statics. . . . A constitution is not intended to embody a particular economic theory, whether of paternalism . . . or of *laissez faire.*" But the New York law fell. The Supreme Court was not always unfriendly to labor; in the case of *Muller* v. *Oregon* in 1908 it upheld an Oregon statute limiting women workers to ten hours a day. It also upheld a number of other progressive state laws regarding child labor, daily hours, and workmen's compensation survived.

In the twenties, when union membership and work stoppages declined, managements often attempted to come to terms with labor problems by agreeing to pension plans, adopting the Ford idea of high wages to permit workers to become consumers, and instituting company unions. The public was more aware and more sympathetic to labor problems, and the euphoria of the "New Era" brought some gains for workers. Despite continued violence in mines and textile mills, which were often geographically and ideologically isolated, the twenties were a better time than industrial labor had seen as yet.

The national increase in productivity probably had more to do with the rise in real wages than unions did. Real wages in fact increased because of developments that were often not purely economic, such as the sharp upswing in compulsory school attendance, which reduced child labor, and the decline in immigration as a result of World War I and postwar restriction laws, which made green and hungry immigrants less available for strike-breaking or as competitors for very low wages. The condition of labor improved, but more because of social and economic trends beyond its control than because of the workers' own efforts, important though those were on occasion. The share of national income held by the wealthiest 1 percent of the population remained quite steady throughout the period, at around 14 percent. This was not the worst imbalance in the world, but it was enough to make many people, not just workers, question whether the economy was organized fairly. To many of them, the answer was no. Life was better in the twenties than in 1900 in many ways, but America was still far from being a paradise of abundance and leisure.

Two doughty battlers for women's suffrage, 1916. (The Bettmann Archive)

4

IDEAS AND ATTITUDES IN THE EARLY TWENTIETH CENTURY

The years between the late nineties and World War I have been labeled "the progressive era." Americans, pleased with much of the economic and technological change surrounding them, but increasingly aware that these changes brought problems for society, attacked those problems with a buoyant optimism—or at least the middle-class, old-stock majority did. World War I vitiated much of the optimism, but the progressive mood lingered on into the twenties, mixing with the money-getting of the "New Era," the hedonism of the "jazz age," the celebrated sexual abandon of "the flapper," and the bitter criticism of American society by some of its intellectuals.

The Progressive Movement

Progressivism involved so many ideas, notions, activities, and people that the movement almost defies collective definition. It was a reform movement, but one in which it seemed that almost everybody participated somehow. It had no focus on a single issue, as had the antislavery crusade of the 1850s, and it did not spring chiefly from one geographic and economic group, as Populism had. Progressivism meant, among other things, cleaning up slums, eliminating poverty and disease, extending and improving education and making it compulsory, establishing settlement houses to uplift and improve the lives of urban immigrants. It meant rousing popular indignation at corruption in business and government by means of "muckraking" journalism. It meant efforts by the clergy and the pious to effect the "Christian regeneration of society" through a movement called the Social Gospel. It meant "busting the trusts," or at least regulating them more effectively for the public interest. It meant changing the structure of government to make it less of a tool of "the interests" and the "bloated plutocrats," and more of a responsive agent of "the people." It meant a specific political party— "Progressivism" with a capital *P*—when Theodore Roosevelt walked out of the Republican convention in 1912 and took many "reformers" with him. But the movement was much larger and more diffuse than the party. To many, it was a kind of crusade with "the spirit of a religious revival," and after gathering strength during the first decade of the century, it captivated a sizable majority of the American people. By the time of the election of 1912, when two-thirds of the voters cast their ballots for either Woodrow Wilson or Theodore Roosevelt, the two "progressive" candidates, progressivism had swept the country.

The movement never managed to achieve the "Christian regeneration of society" or the elimination of social problems or the equitable distribution of wealth. But it did succeed in many ways in bringing about "safe" and "necessary" changes, in its optimistic heyday before World War I. Progressive common denominators are hard to find. None fit all of the progressives, but a few fit most of them. Many believed that a good part of the country's social problems rested in excessive concentrations of power unresponsive to "the people" (a term that often meant, as it had before and has since, one's own group). Such unresponsive concentrations included the trusts, ward bosses, and United States Senators who seemed to represent big businesses and political machines rather than "the people" of their states. Traditional American democracy, political or economic, had been obscured. To restore it, progressives sought to have the trusts "busted" and big business federally regulated and to replace powerful mayors and aldermen with commissions and city managers. Supposedly the latter were more "democratic" and "efficient"; often they simply represented different interest groups in the name of "the people." Progressives hoped to bypass "machines" through the initiative and referendum, to elect United States Senators by direct popular vote instead of by state legislatures, and to extend the franchise to women (though they seldom extended it to Negroes and even withdrew it from unnaturalized immigrants). The progressives redemocratized American politics and economics much less than they thought they had, but they genuinely valued democracy and believed they were reaffirming it.

The "crusade" aspect of progressivism, the strong urge of progressives to reaffirm what they saw as public morality, was another common denominator. Many progressives believed that corruption in government, business, and society had become all too evident in America since the Civil War, a too frequent accompaniment to economic, political, and social growth and diffusion. Struck by the "immorality" of manufacturers who made adulterated cereals or fake patent medicines, progressives sought pure food and drug legislation. To "immorality" in government, they responded with corrupt practices laws. To an absence or denial of social justice, they proposed wages and hours laws, workmen's compensation acts, child labor abolition, and other measures. To end the "liquor traffic," which appeared to many of them to be a major cause of poverty, they fought for a constitutional amendment prohibiting the sale of alcoholic beverages.

Progressives also believed in the desirability of "efficiency," the application of "science" to human affairs. Experts could solve urban problems and manage cities; "scientific management" could improve industrial output; nonpartisan commissions could oversee welfare programs, revise the tariff, investigate social and economic conditions, and recommend legislation to improve them. In one of his earliest books, *Drift and Mastery* (1914), Walter Lippmann wrote that science was essential to political democracy, because "the scientific spirit is the discipline of democracy, the escape from drift, the outlook of a free man." Many progressives besides Lippmann became convinced that the problems of their society could not be solved by appeals to traditional authority. Darwinism had weakened confidence in religious doctrine. Immigration had diversified the population and brought into it many people unfamiliar with American traditions. New scholarship in history, economics, political science, and sociology, often severely criticized social beliefs. To those whose confidence was shaken in these ways, the "hard facts" of "science" appeared to be the safest and most dependable base from which to examine and reform society.

With democracy and morality their aim, and science their tool, the progressives sought to reshape American society and reduce the tensions and fissures that they saw within it. In other words, many

of them were interested in social control. Herbert Croly, a social an-
alyst who later helped found the *New Republic* with Lippmann,
clearly stated this aspect of progressivism in his 1909 book, *The
Promise of American Life*. "The substance of our national Promise,"
Croly declared, "has consisted . . . of an improving popular economic condition, guaranteed by democratic political institutions,
and resulting in moral and social amelioration." In the past this
promise came about almost automatically "because it was based
upon a combination of self-interest and the natural goodness of
human nature." But America in the early twentieth century was
too complicated, too beset with concentrations of economic power,
for the "promise" to fulfill itself any longer without conscious direction. "The Promise of American life is to be fulfilled—not merely by
a maximum amount of economic freedom, but by a certain measure
of discipline; not merely by the abundant satisfaction of individual
desires, but by a large measure of individual subordination and self-
denial."

Croly was talking primarily about the antisocial effects of unregulated big business, but he and other progressives sought social control and social order in many ways: by campaigns to "American-
ize" the immigrants; by efforts to solve the "labor question" and
avoid the threat of "anarchy" or "socialism," which they thought
inherent in labor disputes; by cleaning up slums and corrupt city
governments; and by compelling children to attend school, where
they learned not only the "three R's," but just as important, the inspiring, patriotic glories of the national past and how to behave like
good American citizens. In short, the progressives sought to create
—or re-create—a more homogeneous, more orderly, society in
which middle class, native-stock values remained dominant.

The reestablishment of social order, and the scientific restoration
of "democracy" and "morality," required that Americans first become aware of social problems and then be willing to attack them
with organized instruments, especially the powers of government.
Progressive publishers, following the lead of Frank Munsey and
S. S. McClure, reached massive audiences with ten-cent monthlies
such as *Everybody's*, *Colliers*, *The American*, *Munsey's*, and *McClure's
Magazine*. In them, able journalists tore away a veil of genteel ignorance, which the more staid, expensive periodicals had helped create. In *McClure's* alone, in 1902 and 1903, several classic "muckrak-

ing" series appeared: Ida M. Tarbell's "History of the Standard Oil Company," exposing the ruthless practices that made the Rockefeller company a monopoly; Ray Stannard Baker on child labor and other labor abuses; and, most famous of all, the "lid-lifting" series by Lincoln Steffens on municipal graft, beginning with "Tweed Days in St. Louis" in the September, 1902, issue. Other muckrakers carried on the battle for democracy and morality for several more years; Samuel Hopkins Adams uncovered the frauds of the patent-medicine business, and David Graham Phillips lambasted the world's most exclusive rich-man's club in "The Treason of the Senate." The popular impact of the muckrakers was immense.

Progressive leadership was large and diverse, much too large to have had any set plan for social control or the manipulation of public opinion. As one of the movement's theoreticians, Walter Weyl, wrote in 1912, "Reform is piecemeal and yet rapid. It is carried along divergent lines of people holding separate interests, and yet it moves toward a common end. It combines into a general movement toward a new democracy." The progressive leaders—in journalism, social work, preaching, education, and politics—were linked occasionally by personal acquaintance, rarely by identical plans, but almost always by commonly-held values. The outstanding progressives in all fields were very heavily middle-class in occupation and status, native American, white (lily-white in the South), and, if they had a religious affiliation, it was Protestant. Many businessmen were progressive leaders, as were professionals including lawyers, clergy, college professors, editors of magazines, sometimes engineers or even stockbrokers. They lived in the small towns of the Midwest and South and in large cities all over the country—just the places where population was expanding fastest—and were usually people "of the better sort," community leaders whose words carried weight in their area. The followers of progressivism resembled the leaders but included people lower on the social and economic scales, people who thought the "better sort" were worth listening to. There were some progressives among Catholics, Jews, immigrants, labor leaders, and the very wealthy, but the main strength of the movement came not from those groups but from the nonfarming, native-born middle class.

In general, progressives disliked "radicalism." Some leaned leftward, as for instance the municipal government reformers who advocated "gas and water socialism"—the municipal ownership of gas works and water works—but hard-core, class-struggle socialism was not part of their ideology. They responded humanely to the "labor question" but deplored violent strikes, preferring the "market unionism" of the AFL or the company union movement, to the radicalism of the IWW. Sociologists like Robert Hunter and journalists like Jacob Riis made them aware of the sickening living conditions of immigrants in large cities, but many progressives favored immigration restriction, rather than tenement reform or welfare legislation, as a solution. They sought to extend democracy, but often in ways such as literacy tests or naturalization, which required minorities to conform to the native-stock, middle-class mean.

They were also patriotic and nationalistic. When World War I came along, a substantial minority opposed American entry out of religiously-grounded pacifism or the attitude that the United States was too good and pure to get involved in that bloody European mess. They also divided on the merits of overseas expansion and the use of force in the Caribbean and Central America. But the majority of them acquiesced in assertive diplomacy and entry into the War "to preserve democracy" and "to end all wars," and when the War was over, too many progressives of prewar days let their idealism slip into a generalized and sometimes hysterical fear of immigrants, "radicals," "labor agitators," and minority groups. It was a progressive, A. Mitchell Palmer, who as Wilson's Attorney General in 1919 and 1920 saw to the summary arrest of 6,000 people suspected of being "Bolsheviks" or "anarchists."

The progressives realized that the country needed reforming, but they abhorred the thought and feared the threat of "anarchy" or "social revolution" at least as much as they disliked the "resplendent plutocracy," as Weyl called it, the concentration of great wealth and corporate power. In the context of its time, progressivism in the fifteen years before 1917 was a liberal reform movement, much more broadly based and "respectable" than the agrarian reformers who comprised Populism in the nineties. But it was not radical. Indeed many progressives wanted reform to go only just as far as the point needed to avert violent social upheaval, and no farther—or, as the Socialist Party advocated, the collective ownership of transportation, communications, and distributive businesses peaceably arrived at through the ballot box.

"The White Man's Burden": Nationalism and Empire

By the nineties, practically everyone in the United States was nationalistic in some sense, except perhaps the most recent immigrants, but different methods existed for expressing pride of country. A benign form of nationalism welcomed immigrants, encouraged foreign trade but did not directly support it by gunboats and naval bases, and stressed America's "blessings of liberty" as an example for the rest of the world; but these blessings were not to be forced down others' throats. On the other hand, nationalism was sometimes expressed more directly and vigorously, such as in the urge to annex overseas territories, to create military and naval forces to protect them, and to maintain a standing army and navy of a size befitting a great power.

After 1897, vigorous expressions of national pride became more popular and more common. The United States went to war with Spain in 1898, many thought, to assist the Cuban people in their battle to throw off Spanish despotism. But whatever the initial motives, the "splendid little war" gave the United States the opportunity to govern or occupy temporarily large tracts of Central America and the Caribbean, and to annex Puerto Rico and the Philippine Islands outright. Annexation of noncontiguous lands was not novel; Alaska, Samoa, Midway, and other Pacific islands were earlier examples. Still, the Philippines were so distant and so large that annexing them was a new departure. Perhaps even more important, the United States, for the first time, was adding large new territories that from the beginning were not thought of as future states of the Union, as Texas or Oregon or even Alaska (which gained full territorial status in 1912) were intended to become, but rather, as dependent colonies like the colonies of European powers. This was indeed something new for the United States. Majorities in Congress supported it, and despite a strong anti-imperialist minority, many Americans thought the expansions of 1898 and after (including sovereignty over the isthmus of Panama, practical domination of the Caribbean, and a major voice in East Asian affairs) were entirely appropriate, something a great new country ought to be doing.

Imperialistic nationalism rested in part on the academically respectable views of the time that the "Anglo-Saxon peoples," which meant the British, the Germans, and the Americans, were morally and racially superior to other "races," especially to Latin Americans, Asians, and of course to Negroes. With this superiority went a "duty" (the English writer Rudyard Kipling called it "the white man's burden") that these superior races bring culture, Christianity, and civilization to the less able, whether they wanted it or not. The idea was widely accepted, and it provided a convenient rationalization for the vigorous version of American nationalism. Another academically respectable underpinning for American overseas ventures at that time was the theory of Alfred Thayer Mahan, a captain in the United States Navy, that control of adjacent oceans was essential to the security, and on occasion the expansion, of any great country. Mahan's ideas, explained at length in *The Influence of Sea Power on History*, found a hearty response after its publication in 1889, not only in the United States but also in those other expansionist and navy-minded nations, Britain and Germany. Mahan's views about naval security tied in nicely with the myth of Anglo-Saxon superiority as underpinnings for vigorous nationalism.

The Persistence of Racism

Racial prejudice continued too, sanctioned by custom and in some places by law. Racism directed against Negroes was more overt, violent, and powerfully institutionalized after 1900 than before; all over the South, Negroes were prevented by one legal device or another from exercising the right to vote, which Reconstruction leaders thought was guaranteed forever by the Fourteenth and Fifteenth Amendments. Patterns of segregation in public transportation, accommodations, schools, and churches were present in many northern states as well as in Dixie, and the Jim Crow railway car, the Jim Crow water fountain, the Jim Crow army unit in the World War were facts of life. In large cities, residential color lines became tighter and "mixed" neighborhoods became rarer. The federal civil service remained thoroughly segregated.

Lynchings of blacks not only continued but were openly justified as a moral necessity by Senator Ben Tillman of South Carolina on the floor of the United States Senate in 1907; how else, in extreme cases, to protect the virtue of white womanhood, Tillman asked. Reported lynchings did decline in number from a high of about one every three days in 1897 to one or two a month by 1930, but others went unreported, and lesser forms of physical intimidation were innumerable. The black man accused by an individual or a mob of some transgression, especially any kind of sexual advances to a white woman, was liable to be routed out of his home at night, condemned without trial by howling vigilantes, and then hanged or shot to death if he was lucky, burned alive if he was not. Before World War I many lynchings were done openly; in the twenties the intimidation of blacks went on with the relative refinement of Ku

D. C. Stephenson, the once-mighty leader of the KKK in Indiana, is shown in a Minneapolis jail years later on a parole violation. (Culver Pictures, Inc.)

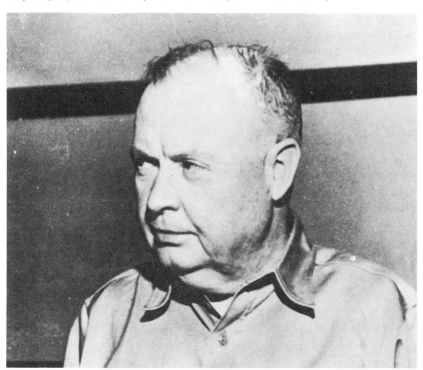

Klux Klan sheets and pillowcases to hide those who burned crosses or tarred and feathered the "transgressor." Race riots, mostly in northern cities, broke out like a rash in the first decade of the century, subsided for a decade, and then in 1919 exploded ferociously in nearly two dozen cities, most violently in Chicago where thirty-eight Negroes and whites were killed.

Anglo-Saxonism, that dandified form of racism, underlay the continued efforts to restrict immigration, especially of Asians and of Southern and Eastern Europeans. Anti-Semitic and anti-Catholic attitudes and restrictions still survived, although dwindling numbers of people (except for the Ku Klux Klan in the twenties) tried to justify them openly. Occasionally, however, they burst from beneath the surface into ugly incidents. A Jewish factory manager, Leo Frank, was lynched in Georgia in 1915 for allegedly molesting and killing a fourteen-year-old girl employee. Hundreds of aliens were deported and thousands of citizens arrested during Attorney General Palmer's "Red Scare" of 1919–20. In 1920, two Italian immigrants, Nicola Sacco and Bartolomeo Vanzetti, were accused of murdering two men during a payroll robbery near Boston, and they were convicted despite the lack of any hard evidence against them —only their admissions that they were sympathetic to "anarchism." Appeals from Felix Frankfurter, later a Supreme Court Justice, and other notables failed to keep Sacco and Vanzetti from the electric chair in 1927. The executions have since been considered by historians the most wretched example of judicial murder in American history since the Haymarket trials, which were also against "anarchy," in 1886.

Most middle-class progressives rejected the violent forms of racism and bigotry. But the pressure to conform did not necessarily require violence in order to succeed. A good many progressives were infected with the idea of Anglo-Saxon superiority, latent anti-Semitism, lingering suspicions that Catholics, with their strange rituals and segregated parochial schools, were indeed dominated by a foreign Pope, and the view—still respectable in "informed" circles— that some races were irretrievably better by nature than others. These notions were attitudinal bases for imperialist ventures, the drive to middle-class conformity, and immigration restriction. John R. Commons, a leading progressive reformer who was a professor of political economy at the University of Wisconsin, wrote in 1908 that "if in America our boasted freedom from the evils of social classes failed to be vindicated in the future, the reason will be found in the immigration of races and classes incompetent to share in our democratic opportunities."

The laws against "foreignness" multiplied. Many states before 1900 made no restriction against unnaturalized immigrants voting in elections, as long as the immigrant had filed his "first papers," declaring his intention to become a citizen. During the progressive period and World War I, alien suffrage was prohibited in state after state, and finally it disappeared. Powerful anti-German feeling during World War I squelched the teaching of the German language in many schools, produced such inanities as changing sauerkraut to "liberty cabbage," and provoked the tarring and feathering of German-Americans who were not sufficiently meek. A federal law passed in 1903 excluded anarchists from entering the country. Bills restricting immigration by means of literacy tests passed Congress in 1912 and 1914 and were vetoed by Presidents Taft and Wilson, but a literacy test bill passed over another Wilson veto in 1917.

In 1921 and 1924, federal laws ended the era of mass immigration, using quotas limiting the entry of people of certain nationalities as the restrictive device. The 1924 law limited the numbers to be admitted in one year to 2 percent of the number from a given country already in the United States in 1890. The 1890 date effectively shut off southern and eastern European immigration, since most of it came after 1890. When the Immigration Act of 1924, also called the National Origins Quota Act, became fully effective in 1929, it limited total immigration per year to 150,000 and severely restricted entry of the very nationalities pressing hardest to immigrate. In round numbers, the German quota was set at 51,000, the Polish at 6,000. Thirty-four thousand British could enter, but only 3,800 Italians; 29,000 Irish, but only 2,200 Russians. Asian and African countries were limited to a purely token 100 apiece per year. Only the countries of North and South America remained outside the quota system, and immigration from them (except Canada) and from the "old immigration" countries with the largest quotas was small. The persistent drive for immigration restriction was another manifestation of the compulsion of many progressives, and ex-progressives in the twenties, to find "social controls" that would homogenize society, they thought, once more.

The Progressive
as Politician

Though by no means all progressives favored it, imperialism was a logical extension of the progressive movement, especially progressivism's naïveté, self-righteousness, and paternalism. Progressivism at home also partook of these qualities, as well as less noxious qualities already described. Progressivism in domestic politics was a formidable force from 1900 until World War I, and it brought about reform at the local, state, and national levels. It aimed at moderating the power of groups thought to be too undemocratically powerful, especially big business combinations and machine governments; at improving the social position of groups thought to have too little power or share in the national life, such as workers, small businessmen, and women; and at further democratizing American society by political and economic changes.

Political progressivism burst forth on the state and local levels before it appeared in Washington. In local government, its manifestations were as varied as the cities in which they occurred. They ranged from the first establishment of the commission form of government in Galveston, Texas, after the chaos following a tidal wave in 1900 revealed the impotence of the existing government, to Mayor Carter H. Harrison's successful fight in Chicago to prevent the street-railway magnate Charles T. Yerkes from obtaining a fifty-year stranglehold on the public transportation of the city. Sometimes urban reform meant the passage of new city charters aimed at breaking the "machines"; sometimes it meant municipal-public ownership of public utilities; sometimes it simply meant concerted efforts to destroy links between police, criminals, and ward politicians. The common threads in urban reform were the cries that city government be restored to the people and that corruption and graft stop.

Pressure for urban reform especially in larger cities often came from upper-middle-class, native-stock professional and businessmen—so much so that a few historians have concluded that the reform impulse of that group stemmed from a desire to preserve its own high status and to prevent local political power from falling into (or remaining in) the hands of immigrant, lower class, or other groups unlike themselves. Progressive motives were not as cynical or self-seeking as this view suggests, but nevertheless such structural reforms as the commission or city-manager types of government frequently "restored democracy" to relatively few. Yet many progressives simply believed that urban (and other) governments could be cleaned up by throwing the rascals out of office and replacing them with "good men." (The ultimate answer to this notion came later from the Baltimore scribe H. L. Mencken; he said that such progressives thought that "the way to end prostitution was to fill the bawdy houses with virgins. [But] either they would jump out the windows, or they would cease to be virgins.")

Some urban problems such as the proliferation of slums and general lack of planning were visible but difficult to cure, partly because cities often had little self-governing power and had to seek authorization for change from nonreformist state legislatures. Still, much progressive reform did take place on the state level. A few highly-industrialized northeastern states, notably Massachusetts, instituted laws of the progressive type well before 1900. Beginning with an Australian (secret, less partisan) ballot law in 1888, Massachusetts reform proceeded in the nineties to secure regulatory and labor laws that other states quickly imitated. Midwestern state-level progressivism began in earnest in 1900. The most thoroughgoing case was Wisconsin under the governorship of Robert M. La Follette, who in three terms between 1900 and 1906 supervised laws substantially strengthening the state's railroad regulation commission, creating a direct primary, striking down corrupt practices in government, and taxing corporations and personal incomes. The La Follette measures became known as the "Wisconsin idea" and were widely emulated.

The new reform measures were diverse, but most of them fell into a few main categories: (1) antimonopoly laws, aimed especially at railroad freight rates and streetcar franchises; (2) attempts to democratize state and city government, by direct primaries, the initiative and referendum, women's suffrage (especially in western states), and tighter definitions of citizenship by the withdrawal of the suffrage from Negroes in the South and aliens generally; (3) laws aimed at various kinds of "corruption" or "immorality," from legislative lobbying to sale of alcohol to police graft to prostitution.

Instrumentalism and the Control of Complexity

Another "ism" that was closely tied to progressivism represented a crucial change of attitude from a pervasive nineteenth-century belief. The old assumption that social and economic ills resulted from "natural laws" of political economy, and could not be avoided by human action, was largely discarded. The typical progressive was an instrumentalist, not a determinist. He became convinced that it was right and good, necessary and proper, to use the instruments of government and private associations to better the conditions of life and to solve social problems.

In its most abstract, refined version, this new attitude was variously called "pragmatism" or "instrumentalism." The philosopher and educator John Dewey urged the instrumentalist case in books and articles, while the psychologist-philosopher William James raised pragmatism into a formal philosophical school. James defined pragmatism in 1907 as follows: "Rationalism sticks to logic and the empyrean. Empiricism sticks to the external senses. [But] pragmatism is willing to take anything, to follow either logic or the senses . . . [or even] mystical experiences if they have practical consequences. . . . 'Grant an idea or belief to be true,' it says, 'what concrete difference will its being true make in any one's actual life? . . . What, in short, is the truth's cash-value in experiential terms.' . . . The truth of an idea is not a stagnant property inherent in it. Truth *happens* to an idea. It *becomes* true, is *made* true by events." In other words, in a more modern idiom, James was glorifying "relevance" as a philosophical point of departure.

The pragmatism of James and the instrumentalism of Dewey (applied most concretely to educational reform in the progressive period) were refined versions of the "American practicality" admired in the days of Benjamin Franklin as well as in the 1970s. James' and Dewey's treatises erected the quest for practicality into metaphysical weapons that dealt mortal blows to nineteenth-century rationalism, and thus destroyed many people's inhibitions against positive social change. Most progressives learned their instrumentalism not from the pages of Dewey or James, but indirectly. It was in the air, a popular attitude, the product of the progressives' growing awareness that society needed changing and that there were respectable and idealistic and nonradical ways in which it could be changed. That nineteenth-century ideological bastion, natural law, fell before the onslaught of necessity (avoid revolution, improve society), the ability to communicate to the middle class that social ills did indeed exist (thanks to Theodore Roosevelt, the muckrakers, and other vocal reformers), and a willingness to use organizational means (government, business associations, churches, even labor unions) to achieve given ends. These end results were achieved in part, ironically, through imitating the organizational successes of big business monopolies.

At its most extreme, instrumentalism in expanding organizations led to the movement for scientific management and planned efficiency. Spearheaded by an industrial engineer named Frederick Winslow Taylor, the efficiency movement concentrated not on the productivity of industrial machines but on the productivity of the people who operated them. Taylor believed that society would benefit from the harnessing of vast numbers of man-hours lost because of wasted time and wasted motion. If machines could be organized to do more work, why not people? To this end, Taylor instituted "time and motion studies," measuring the physical motions and amount of time a worker used for a task and suggesting how time could be shortened and movement saved. Tasks were simplified, too. The results, where Taylor's methods were adopted, indeed included an increase in man-hour productivity, to the great satisfaction of managers who shared the progressive belief that human ingenuity could solve human problems and improve the general society. Critics of the Taylor system, however, were aggrieved by such side effects as the routinization of industrial work, the speeding up of assembly lines and the work pace without proper consideration for the stamina of workers, and, above all, the basic assumption that people ought to be treated like machines. The drive for efficiency exemplified progressivism's naïveté; "society in general," whatever that was, indeed could be improved, but at the cost of a degree of dehumanization and an eclipsing of the people and groups of which society was composed. Once workers and social commentators noticed these disagreeable side-effects, a measure of alienation and disenchantment set in which gave reform itself a suspect air.

Instrumentalism underlay not only the trend toward government action and away from private organizations, but even more significantly, the movement from small organizations to large ones. The mass manufacturing, distributing, or financial corporation and the large labor union were examples of that movement. Large size and complexity in public and private organizations became more and more accepted, if not universally beloved. With such acceptance came a new attention to how organizations might be run more efficiently. The managing of organizations became a very complicated skill, so much so that business administration became an academic profession by 1920. Managers could also switch from one business to another with some ease, because their knowledge of how to direct an organization was more important than a knowledge of how to make a particular product.

Progressive Education

The progressive mood was especially evident in education, that social institution with which more and more Americans were becoming familiar, and "progressive education" lingered on for decades after progressivism had vanished elsewhere. Progressive attitudes affected education at all levels, from elementary to professional schools. The leading prophet of progressive education before World War I was John Dewey, the philosopher of instrumentalism. Though Dewey was by no means the only progressive educator, and though he led and codified the movement rather than founded it, his name was inextricably associated with it after the publication of his widely-read *The School and Society* (1899) and his definitive statement, *Democracy and Education* (1916).

The school was to be another instrument of social progress. Its job, said Dewey, was to instill good moral habits such as the value of work and hygiene, tasks that the home was ceasing to perform in industrial and urban society; the school should function as a preserver of values. Dewey believed that schooling should be relevant. It ought to avoid useless subjects instilled by rote memory, and instead teach what students needed in order to function in society. Progressive education was supposed to humanize students by awakening them to human values and capabilities. To achieve this, the subject matter and teaching methods had to survive the pragmatic

SCHOOLING AND LITERACY, 1870–1970

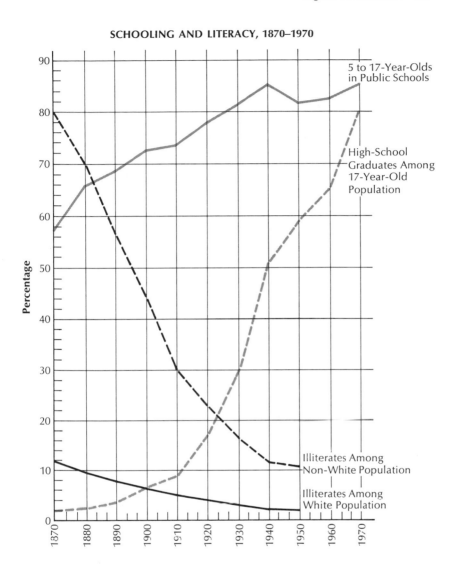

Note the steep decline of non-white illiteracy since the end of slavery. Illiteracy among all races continued to decline after 1950 toward an irreducible minimum. The decline in public school attendance in the 1940s was the result partly of the dislocations of World War II, partly of an artificially high rate during the jobless 1930s. Graduation from high school (not just high-school attendance) began to rise after 1910, and increased steeply during the 1930s and again during the 1960s.

test—were they useful?—and be subject to improvement by scientific investigation. In his 1916 work, Dewey explained that education was necessary in a democratic society not simply because citizen-voters had to make intelligent governmental choices, but also because a society with so much mobility and with such demands on the individual's own mental and moral resources had to provide popular education lest the individual be "overwhelmed" by society's complexity.

The roots of progressive education preceded Dewey. They went back to the work of late nineteenth-century psychologists such as G. Stanley Hall and William James, and late nineteenth-century pedagogical reformers such as William T. Harris of St. Louis and Francis Parker of Chicago. But it became widespread after Dewey published his statements. Columbia Teachers College became a research and training center for progressive educators after Dewey joined its faculty in 1905; the National Education Association became teacher-oriented about 1910; and the Progressive Education Association was founded in 1919. By the twenties, progressive education was orthodoxy among American educators. Its ideals were those of Dewey and the charter of the Progressive Education Association, which called for the schools to bring out the maximum capabilities of students according to scientific methods. Its concrete achievements included more flexible curricula, the classification of students according to IQ and achievement tests, less formality in the classroom, industrial and vocational training, and the inclusion of gymnasiums, laboratories, manual-arts shops, and art and music rooms in schools.

Other changes took place in education about this time. The motor vehicle revolution, influential in so many areas of American life, touched education, too. School buses made consolidated school districts possible in the twenties, allowing for richer curricula than were possible in small, isolated schools. Four-year teachers' colleges became common after World War I, replacing the two-year "normal school" common at the turn of the century. Separate schools of education emerged within large universities, public and private. Accrediting agencies for secondary and college-level education began to appear before World War I. State departments of public instruction and the United States Office of Education became much more "professional," publishing bulletins and other literature to inform teachers and school administrators of new educational research and practice. State laws not only required school attendance but prescribed educational standards and procedures much more precisely than before.

Curricular changes in secondary schools were extensive between 1900 and the early thirties, and most of these changes were in the direction of practicality, training for citizenship, and occupational preparation. From 400,000 students in 1897, the high schools accommodated over 5 million in 1932. Half of the students of 1900 took Latin; the proportion decreased to one in six by 1934. Thirty-eight percent took English in 1900; over 90 percent did so by the late twenties. Many subjects that did not even exist before 1910 or 1915 were soon being taught to large numbers: industrial subjects were being taught to one student in five by 1934; typing and home economics, one in six; shorthand and art, one in ten; physical education, one out of two; music, one out of four. Algebra and geometry lost ground to "general mathematics"; physiology, geology, and physics were partially supplanted by "general science" and "biology"; and civics and United States history became separate subjects.

Progressive education had its excesses, such as the extremely child-oriented schools, many established in the twenties, in which formal education was minimized to the vanishing point and any aberration was classified as healthy individual expression. But more commonly, American primary and secondary schools changed under the impact of the progressive education movement. It made the school, as the Lynds reported from Muncie in 1925, less an adjunct of the home, as it was in the late nineteenth century, and more an agent of social responsibility and conformity, and an instiller of proper social values; progressive education was indeed an aspect of progressivism in general. Extra-curricular activities, less classroom formality, more attractive textbooks and learning materials, and perhaps above all, better-trained teachers became permanent legacies of progressivism in education.

Universities were not exempt from the progressive drive. State universities, following the example of the University of Wisconsin under President Charles Van Hise, began to provide education "in the service of the state," producing useful citizens and useful research. Universities were bases of operation for many progressive activist-thinkers, such as Richard T. Ely, Thorstein Veblen, John R. Commons, and Simon Patten among economists, the sociologists

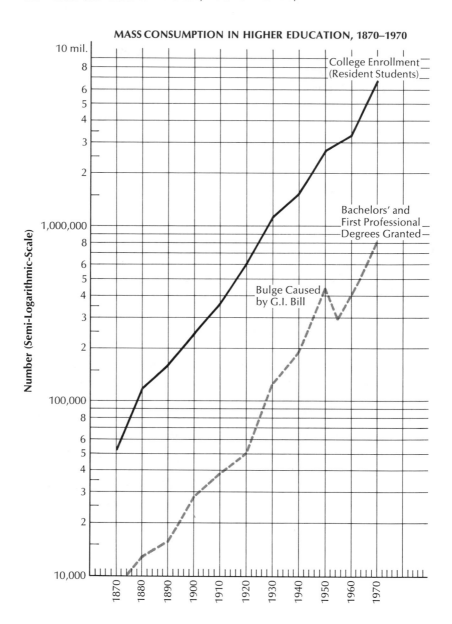

MASS CONSUMPTION IN HIGHER EDUCATION, 1870–1970

The steep rise in degrees granted in the late 1940s resulted in large part from the GI Bill; the momentary decline in the early 1950s, from the Korean War. Note that college enrollment roughly doubled—an increase of 3½ million—during the 1960s; while the rise in *rate* has been fairly steady for 100 years, the numbers involved were unprecedented in the 1960s.

Edward A. Ross and Albion Small, and the historians Frederick Jackson Turner, Carl Becker, Charles A. Beard, and James Harvey Robinson. Academic freedom and tenure were much less well protected than later in the twentieth century, and trustees or public pressure could easily cause discomfort or outright firing of professors who expressed publicly unpopular opinions. But as enrollment in colleges grew from less than a quarter of a million students in the late nineties to over a million by the early thirties, and from one-twentieth to one-eighth of the college-age population, and as college and university budgets rose from $35 million to almost a half-billion dollars between 1900 and 1930, American higher education took on most of its present structure, directions, and aims.

The Social Gospel and Fundamentalism

After 1897, religious groups responded strongly to two things: the changing condition of the urban population, especially immigrants and workers, and the challenge presented by Darwinian evolution and other scientific theories to traditional religious concepts. The first put the churches on the offensive, while the second put them on the defensive.

During the first decade of the century, some sizable church groups, particularly such well-established Protestant denominations as the Congregationalists, Presbyterians, Episcopalians, and Methodists, redefined their official primary goals from "faith and order" —doctrinal concerns—to "life and work"—social action. The shift reflected the growing success of the Social Gospel movement, which had its origins in the eighties and nineties. It quickly affected most Protestant denominations as well as many Reform Jews and Catholics. The Social Gospel was a frequently successful attempt to bring organized religion to grips with labor problems, poverty, vice, disease, corruption in urban life, and other blots on the social landscape. Churchmen preached, often from gilded pulpits, that labor as well as capital had rights; they went into urban slums to investigate and try to relieve conditions there; they founded "institutional churches" to provide the poor with social, recreational, and educational centers; they wrote theological treatises to provide a formal

rationale for their activity. After 1908, the year in which several
major denominations already committed to the Social Gospel supported the founding of the Federal Council of Churches of Christ in
America (later the National Council of Churches), the Social Gospel reached its high-water mark in American Protestantism. Social-
Gospel clergymen did much to change the emphasis in American
religion from the regeneration of individuals to the regeneration of
society, and they helped educate many middle-class Americans to
the basic notion that many of society's problems rested not on bad
or corrupt individuals but on a poorly structured system. It was the
social system that needed changing, they said, not just individuals;
the "kingdom of God on earth," which they sought, would be
achieved in the heart of society more than in the hearts of individual men. Regenerate society, and the regeneration of souls would
follow.

The movement's leading theologian, the Baptist minister Walter
Rauschenbusch, summed up its thrust in his *Christianity and the Social
Crisis*, published in 1907. Rauschenbusch declared that the purpose
of Christianity "was to transform human society into the kingdom
of God by regenerating all human relations and reconstituting them
in accordance with the will of God." "We must repent of the sins of
existing society," he exhorted, "cast off the spell of the lies protecting our social wrongs, have faith in a higher social order, and
realize in ourselves a new type of Christian manhood which seeks to
overcome the evil in the present world, not by withdrawing from
the world, but by revolutionizing it." Social Gospelers generally
agreed with Rauschenbusch that they were working toward the
"kingdom of God in America," thus echoing the old post-millennial
theme in American Protestantism, but their definition of the kingdom varied from a frankly Christian socialist commonwealth all the
way to a slightly more sanctified and smiling status quo. A modern-
day critic might say that the Social Gospel movement was just another example of the progressives' attempt to assert social controls
on behalf of the dominant middle-class majority and to avert radicalism. But the Social Gospelers themselves were consciously motivated by the fervent ideal that society could be bettered, even per-
fected (nearly), and that the instrument for achieving that goal was
social restructuring through organizational action. On the whole,
the Social Gospel movement functioned as the religious arm of the

progressive movement, and it shared in progressivism's broad assumptions. As pointed out by a leading historian of the Social Gospel, Charles H. Hopkins, it was principally concerned with socioeconomic problems in the flawed urban-industrial society of the time; it generally did not deal with imperialism or racism; it redefined "sin" as manifested in social structure rather than in individual souls; it used social science as well as preaching to attack problems; and it believed that man, if he worked at it, could progress—not only for his material welfare but in the sight of God.

Among Catholics and Jews, ideas and activities of the Social-Gospel type were less common. The two leading religious minorities, whose memberships consisted more and more of the immigrant urban poor, were concerned directly with labor unions and with the material and spiritual welfare of the Catholics and Jews who belonged to them. Catholic leaders were especially anxious that labor unions avoid socialism, which they viewed as inevitably atheistic, and perhaps official Catholic opposition to socialism was why socialism made little headway in the American Federation of Labor and other unions, whose membership was heavily Catholic. Cardinal James Gibbons of Baltimore, the leading bishop, worked successfully in 1887 to prevent the Vatican from condemning the Knights of Labor, partly on the ground that unions helped relieve economic problems, partly because a condemnation "would drive them [Catholic unionists] into the camp of revolution."

In an early progressive study of socialism, *The Social Unrest* (1903), John Graham Brooks noted the "virulent hostility" of Catholics to it, not so much on economic grounds as on moral and religious ones. "To save the workingmen," Brooks wrote, "the catholics [sic] have also started . . . scores of cooperative associations. They have opened halls, reading rooms, and lecture courses. At their congresses upon the social question . . . much of the programme has to do expressly with the material interests of labor." Catholic and Jewish welfare agencies proliferated in the early twentieth century, and some Catholic and Jewish leaders not only worked directly on social problems but also talked, like Protestant Social-Gospelers, of the need to regenerate society to get at the roots of problems—to strike, as the reforming Catholic priest John A. Ryan wrote in 1906, at "perverse individualism which prefers irrational liberty and industrial anarchy to a legal regime of order and justice." By World War

I, each of the three major religious groups had created service and welfare agencies (the Federal Council of Churches, the Jewish Welfare Board, the National Catholic War [later Welfare] Council), which on occasion worked together for common social aims.

Not all churchmen, even those who were theologically liberal, were caught up in the Social Gospel movement. While some "liberal" or "modernist" religious leaders had been coming to terms with the rather un-biblical hypothesis of Darwinian evolution and had been trying to channel the churches' activities in social-welfare directions, others had been thinking and working in other ways. To these non-modernists, the Darwinian tenet that *Homo sapiens* evolved from lower animals over millions of years seemed irreconcilable, despite the liberal theologians' explanations, with the biblical story of creation involving Adam and Eve, the Garden of Eden, and its occurrence, according to accepted biblical chronology, about 4000 B.C. Furthermore, said theologically conservative churchmen, the Social Gospel's emphasis on the affairs of this world diluted religion's proper concern with spiritual things.

The outstanding theological counterattack on the Social Gospel came with the publication in 1910 of a series of small volumes called *The Fundamentals*, each volume containing several essays, by well-lettered British as well as American authors, on the virgin birth and deity of Jesus, the deity of the Holy Spirit, the literal truth of Scripture and its divine inspiration, the bodily resurrection of Jesus, and refutations, by argument and evidence, of criticisms of the authenticity of the Bible. Fundamentalism received a hearty response among many Protestant clergy and laymen in various parts of the country. While recent research has shown it to have been less a continuation or reassertion of nineteenth-century Protestant orthodoxy than a stark reaction to "modernism"—i.e., the Social Gospel, liberal theology, and compromises with evolution   its adherents rejoiced in it as a reaffirmation of "old-time religion."

Evangelism also showed that the Social Gospel had not wholly captured American Protestantism. While fundamentalism re-stated traditional theological dogmas that had come under attack from modernists and evolutionists, evangelism urged the regeneration of individual souls. The long, rich tradition of religious revivals, a more direct continuation of eighteenth- and nineteenth-century religious practice than fundamentalism was, attracted hundreds of thousands. Around the turn of the century, many were swayed by

Billy Sunday, the hugely popular evangelist, at New York Tabernacle, 1917. (Brown Brothers)

the gospel songs and preaching of Dwight L. Moody and Ira Sankey. In the decade before World War I, the histrionics of Billy Sunday provided a slangy route to quick salvation for the crowds who attended his road-show revivals. Several revivalists made fortunes by going to sunny California and founding new religions, particularly in the twenties. The most successful, and to some people the most bizarre, example was the Four-Square Gospel Church founded by an emigrant Kansan, Aimee Semple McPherson. Thousands at a time crowded into Sister Aimee's Los Angeles temple to sing gospel songs, hear a long sermon laced with scriptural literalism and homely language, and, if the Spirit struck, hit the sawdust trail to rapid-fire conversion. Biting satire at such revivalism, most notably in Sinclair Lewis' 1927 novel, *Elmer Gantry*, ridiculing the commercialism and theological barrenness of it, failed to dissuade the faithful.

Controversies between fundamentalists and modernists, the former associated with "old-time religion" and the latter including most Social-Gospelers, split many Protestant denominations during the teens and twenties. Late in the twenties, neither fundamentalism nor modernism satisfied some theologically concerned Protestants. Formal theology, and pulpit oratory a little later, began to reveal the beginnings of a new movement critical especially of theological liberalism. Karl Barth in Europe and Reinhold Niebuhr in the United States were asserting a theology called "neo-orthodoxy," which rejected the modernists' optimistic, evolutionary belief in social progress—which was much less visible in the thirties than in the two decades before—and instead affirmed, as Niebuhr put it, that "the ultimate problem of human existence is the peril of sin and death." Unlike progressive and liberal theologians, Niebuhr, Barth, and company rejected the assumption that man was good, his nature sinless; they re-stressed the ancient doctrine of original sin. During the same years, Catholic seminaries and schools adopted and propagated "neo-scholasticism," a rationalistic theology based on the writings of the medieval theologian Thomas Aquinas. Conservative Judaism was providing a more ritualistic alternative to Reform. All three major religious groups, by 1930, were shedding some of the naïveté of the progressive period, seeking more reasoned theological moorings, and taking a hard look at the idea that churches were to be purely, or mostly, instruments of social betterment.

The bright hopes of the first years of the century, the liberal crusade called the Social Gospel, and its Catholic and Jewish counterparts, continued into the twenties. But by then its critics were many, and the crusade had dwindled to a plea. American religion had made a partial break with the nineteenth century. But the Social Gospel faded, along with progressivism itself, after World War I. In 1932 a presidential commission on social trends gazed at what was happening to the churches, and reported that "the wave of approval for sex freedom appears to have been closely associated with the decline of religious sanctions for sex conduct." Indeed, there was a decline of religious sanctions for most conduct.

The Armory and the Ashcan

American taste and creativity in the fine arts changed decisively in the early twentieth century. The classicism and realism of the 1890s lingered after 1900, but "modern art," naturalistic and abstract, arrived in force between 1905 and 1910. A new group of painters emerged, whose themes were often urban and commonplace, and whose techniques were independent of most European sources except the realistic cartoons of Daumier and a few others. Several of this group, in fact, came to painting from magazine and newspaper illustrating. George Luks, John Sloan, and George Bellows were the ablest members of this group, and their representations of the drabness of big-city streets, or the repressed violence of a boxing match at a private club filled with cigar smoke, earned them the name "the Ashcan School." Naturalism such as theirs was far removed from the seascapes of Winslow Homer or the portraits of James McNeill Whistler, as different in theme and technique from these talented American predecessors as the novels of Theodore Dreiser and Frank Norris were from those of William Dean Howells and Henry James.

The "Ashcan School" made its bumptious entrance on the staid American art scene at a New York exhibition in 1908, and from then on, found a substantial response. At that very time, however, a second change in American painting was already beginning. This was the introduction to America of European (primarily French) innovations including impressionism and early cubism—the great revolution against representational painting itself. Ironically, some of the leaders of the Ashcan School, together with Alfred Stieglitz, one of the first men in the world to raise photography to a fine art, brought the best of the new European nonrepresentational painting to America, although their own work did not imitate it. Stieglitz, who had a studio on lower Fifth Avenue in New York, brought a few of the paintings of the new French masters to the United States in the years around 1910. Then, with the aid of Bellows and other Ashcan leaders, he engineered the single most shocking event in American art history in February, 1913: a large exhibit at the 69th Regiment Armory in New York that included a comprehensive sampling of the new European painting. The Armory Show attracted tens of thousands of viewers in New York and other cities around the country. Many critics damned it, but much of the public loved it, and nonrepresentational painting was in America to stay.

The Armory Show, however, caused only moderate changes in the practice of American painting and other art forms. In the succeeding twenty years, descendants of the Ashcan School multiplied and their work was often of high quality, though not of the brilliance of Cezanne or Van Gogh. John Marin, Georgia O'Keeffe, and others blended American and French styles with considerable skill in the twenties. In sculpture, realistic representation remained more prevalent than in painting, perhaps in part because those who paid for public monuments or private portraits so preferred. Augustus St.-Gaudens and Daniel Chester French did some of their finest work in the early twentieth century, such as St.-Gaudens' statue of *Grief* for the tomb of Mrs. Henry Adams in Washington's Rock Creek Park. Later in the period Gutzon Borglum's vast carving of four presidents on Mount Rushmore in South Dakota, monuments by Lorado Taft, and portraiture by Jo Davidson continued to be representational. Some abstract treatment of forms appeared in the works of William Zorach and others. Painting and sculpture in the early twentieth century produced two results. A respectable indigenous group of American painters and sculptors had appeared, their best work was naturalistic and, less often, abstract. Second, the public began to appreciate "modern" art, as wealthy collectors and donors to public galleries brought examples of modern European masters to America, thus creating outstanding collections such as that of French impressionists now in the Chicago Art Institute.

American classical music still depended heavily on European performers and composers in the early twentieth century. The "golden age of opera" began when Giulio Gatti-Casazza came from Italy to manage the Metropolitan Opera in 1908, bringing Arturo Toscanini with him to conduct. But American operatic and instrumental performers appeared in greater numbers than before, especially after the Juilliard and Eastman schools of music opened in the early twenties. One American composer of exceptional merit, Charles Ives, wrote just after 1900, but his complex works were virtually unknown until almost mid-century. In the twenties, Henry Cowell made pioneering efforts in electronic music, and Aaron Copland, born of Russian-Jewish immigrants in New York in 1900 and trained in Paris under Nadia Boulanger, began in the twenties a career that soon made him one of the finest American composers of the century.

In the meantime, the greatest and most peculiarly American contribution to the history of music began spreading across the country, accompanying the Negro migration from the South. Jazz, in its earliest forms, emerged from plantation origins as ragtime from the late nineties onward and developed into "blues" music, exemplified by W. C. Handy's *Memphis Blues* (1909) and *St. Louis Blues* (1914). Sheet music, piano rolls, and the first phonograph records spread ragtime and later forms of jazz into many American homes after 1900. For those of "more refined" taste, light operas were common entertainment, whether European imports such as Rudolf Friml's *Rose Marie* (1924) or Sigmund Romberg's *Student Prince* (1924), or American products in the Viennese style by Reginald de Koven, John Philip Sousa, or, above all, Victor Herbert (*Babes in Toyland*, 1903; *Naughty Marietta*, 1910; *Indian Summer*, 1919, among others). George Gershwin's *Porgy and Bess*, a musical drama using very different themes, vibrantly treated urban black life, adapting to music the Negro playwright DuBose Hayward's successful play of 1927. Gershwin bridged the "popular" and "classical" gap in his own compositions, which included many "hit tunes" during the twenties, and also the classically-structured *Rhapsody in Blue* (1924) and *Concerto in F* (1925), which used thematic material inspired by jazz. But the originality and vigor of jazz continued to come from black America.

The most visible achievements in architecture during the early twentieth century were increasingly larger and higher office buildings of the steel frame type pioneered in 1885. Higher than any predecessor, the ornamented Woolworth Building rose fifty-five stories and 760 feet above lower Manhattan in 1909. Other tall buildings brought a vertical dimension to skylines in regional metropolises across the country in the teens and twenties. The expansive, acquisitive twenties witnessed a remarkable skyscraper boom, begun with the thirty-four-story, Gothic-topped Tribune Tower on Chicago's Michigan Avenue, and in the next eight years the boom nearly doubled office space in New York and Chicago. It culminated in the Empire State Building (1929–32), towering almost a quarter of a mile above mid-town Manhattan. The skyscrapers did not involve structural innovations, and they became increasingly devoid of decoration, increasingly reflective of the presumably "scientific" business affairs conducted within them. The boxy, antiseptic quality of office buildings (and later also of apartment buildings) resulted in part from the growing influence in America of the "International School," led by the Germans Walter Gropius and Ludwig Mies van der Rohe.

The most famous American architect of the early (and middle) twentieth century, however, expressed a very different, very romantic mood. Frank Lloyd Wright developed his "prairie style" in a number of private homes he built in Chicago, its suburbs (especially Oak Park), and elsewhere—long, low, multi-level houses that suggested a ship anchored in the flat expanse of the midwestern prairie. He also built churches, office buildings, and educational institutions that expressed a warmth quite absent from the unadorned, blocky products of the International School.

Writers:
Angry Craftsmen

In literature, the pattern of naturalistic revolt, followed in the twenties by alienation, was even clearer than in painting. Twain, James, and Howells lived into the twentieth century, but except perhaps for the dark sharpness of Twain's last writings, the old giants no longer set the pace. Howells' call for "realism" had already been more than answered well before 1912 by the tougher-minded school called "naturalism," which portrayed the grim and grimy side of American life, the despair of the masses, and the way

impersonal forces beyond people's control determined their unhappy lives and ends. The first naturalistic novels were Stephen
Crane's *Maggie: A Girl of the Streets* (1893), Frank Norris' *McTeague*
(1899), and above all, Theodore Dreiser's *Sister Carrie* (1900). In
that novel, Dreiser dealt so insistently and so powerfully with the
midwestern *demimonde,* and the theme of how to succeed in life
through semiprofessional prostitution, that social criticism became
not only possible but almost expected from novelists, despite Dreiser's near-inability to write with any grace. Later, in 1912 and
1914, Dreiser described the machinations of a big-business bucca-
neer with something close to admiration in *The Financier* and *The
Titan,* fictionalized versions of the life of Charles T. Yerkes. Here
Dreiser joined a group of muckraking novelists who had by 1912
become part of the progressive movement. Often more successful as
social critics than as literary artists, they were widely read and their
novels intensified the reform spirit. Frank Norris exposed California
railroad monopoly in *The Octopus* (1901) and the Chicago commodity market in *The Pit* (1903); Jack London published several
strongly socialist novels through the decade; Upton Sinclair described revolting conditions in the Chicago meat-packing industry
in *The Jungle* (1906) and aroused public support for the Pure Food
and Drug Act.

While Norris, London, Sinclair, and several other novelists were
bringing out their tracts for the times, more artistic though less socially conscious novels appeared that also owed something to the
naturalistic spirit. Some of the best regional novels were written by
women, notably a Virginian, Ellen Glasgow, whose *Barren Ground*
appeared in 1925, and a Nebraskan, Willa Cather, who published
her masterpiece *Death Comes to the Archbishop* in 1927. Both began
their careers as novelists in the years just before World War I. The
two finest novels about immigrant life were very different: Abraham Cahan's *The Rise of David Levinsky* (1917), which chronicled the
ruthless rise of a Russian-Jewish boy in New York through garment
manufacturing to millionaire status; and *Giants in the Earth* (1927)
by Ole Rolvaag, a gripping study of Norwegian farm life on the
northern Great Plains.

As migration brought more and more American Negroes out of
the South and into northern cities, a new climate developed for
Negro literature. The first major black writer of the period was the
dialect poet and novelist from Ohio, Paul Laurence Dunbar, who

came to New York in 1900 and died in 1906. After 1910, as Harlem became more and more of a Negro community, a separate cultural life grew up, large enough by the twenties to be called the "Harlem Renaissance." Its poets included Claude McKay, a Jamaican intrigued with his adopted country, whose novel, *Home to Harlem* (1928), won general acclaim; Countee Cullen, writer of wistful lyrics; and Langston Hughes, whose lovely, poignant verses (and forthright essays) portrayed many aspects of Negro life and the subtleties of the position of American Negroes in their own country. Alain Locke's *The New Negro* (1925), a landmark essay in Negro culture, explained how Sambo and Uncle Tom were dead, and that Harlem, the product of segregation, was in truth a great, vigorous mix of races and cultures from the United States, the West Indies, and Africa, and was becoming a "race capital." Locke was not a black separatist like his contemporary Marcus Garvey, but he celebrated the coming of race pride and solidarity exemplified in the Harlem Renaissance. By 1930, the movement had its own historian, James Weldon Johnson, who published *Black Manhattan*, a cultural history of the New York Negro community and of the entry of American Negroes into the Broadway theater and other areas of general American cultural life.

Despite the continuing tradition of literature by and about minorities and regions, the more dominant trend of the time in American writing led elsewhere. Dreiser and the naturalistic and muckraking novelists of the first decade of the century had made it possible, even desirable, for writers to criticize American bourgeois life and standards, to write of the region or the small town with disillusion, and to seek what they thought would be the cosmopolitan air of big cities, where they could find the company of other social protesters and literary radicals. The years just before World War I saw a trend toward the metropolitanization of American letters—the gravitation of the best new talents first to Chicago and then, more permanently, to New York. Chicago was the scene of a significant though short-lived "literary renaissance" around 1908–12. Its leaders were the young bohemian Floyd Dell, of Davenport; the ex-businessman from Ohio, Sherwood Anderson; Clarence Darrow's disgruntled former law partner, Edgar Lee Masters; and the poet Carl Sandburg. The Chicago writers expressed themselves in a succession of magazines: first the *Dial*, then *Poetry* in 1912, then in turn *The Little Review* in 1914. The "Chicago Renaissance" was a significant movement in American letters both because of the quality of the writings of its members and because its style, literary and personal, was "bohemian" for the first time in the modern sense in America. But even Chicago became confining and stale to them, and most of the best talents carried off their bohemianism and their typewriters to New York's Greenwich Village between 1912 and 1915.

The five years preceding World War I were the freshest and most originally creative in the long history of Greenwich Village as a haven of *avant-garde* literature. To the Village came Dell and other lights of the Chicago Renaissance; Dreiser lived there, as did the radical writer Max Eastman and the brilliant young poet Edna St. Vincent Millay. The Provincetown Players were founded then, pioneering off-Broadway theater and producing the first works of America's finest tragedian to date, Eugene O'Neill. The leaders of the Ashcan school in painting and sculpture worked nearby, as did the photographer Alfred Stieglitz, new young political thinkers such as Walter Lippmann, and progressive, searching young publishers. Even when the new writers and journals were bitingly critical of America and the intellectual vacuum they saw nearly everywhere, even at their gloomiest and most pessimistic, they exuded freshness and innocence and a crackling air of discovery.

World War I dispelled much of this. There was a limited but real congruence between literary and political radicalism, and when political radicalism was harshly dealt with during and just after the war, the bohemians were decimated and their naïveté dispelled. The result, in literary productivity during the twenties, was striking. It was as if the war had acted as a Bessemer converter on literary talent, forcing cold air through the molten raw mass, with some of the product emerging as the finest, most highly tempered literary art in American history, the sentimental remnants of the genteel tradition dropping like slag. The Village continued to attract would-be artists and writers after the war, but they produced little that was first-rate.

On the other hand, new masters of fiction appeared, in New York and elsewhere, including several eventual Nobel laureates in literature. Sinclair Lewis burst on the scene in 1920 with *Main Street*, a devastating indictment of the anti-intellectual atmosphere of the midwestern small town. In the same year, F. Scott Fitzgerald published *This Side of Paradise*, the first of his celebrations of the inner emptiness of the jazz age. Eugene O'Neill hit his stride as a playwright, and Dreiser produced what some critics consider his best work, *An American Tragedy*, in 1925. H. L. Mencken, the German-American journalist from Baltimore, probably the sharpest satirist of national illusions and mediocrity in American literary history, terrorized and titillated the reading public with his roars at the "booboisie" (to whom Sinclair Lewis' *Babbitt* [1922] was more than alliteratively related), the "Bible Belt," the "Sahara of the Bozart" —all of which included, as far as Mencken was concerned, most of the United States.

These villagers, ex-midwesterners, and other naturalistic critics oriented American fiction and drama toward the role of conscience to society. They stayed in America and dealt, if hostilely, with American experience. But several other American writers of the first magnitude began producing their best work during the twenties, and they dealt with peripheral, almost imaginary, locales and people. Others simply emigrated. T. S. Eliot, the finest American-born poet of the time, perhaps of any time, left his native St. Louis in 1905 and a few years later arrived in London, where he lived the rest of his life. Eliot was once on the fringe of the Chicago Renaissance, and one of his best early works, "The Love Song of J. Alfred Prufrock," appeared in Harriet Monroe's *Poetry* magazine. But even then, Eliot was about to become so integrated into British intellectual life that his poetry, including the monumental *Wasteland* (1922), became as much a part of English literature as of American. Another major twentieth-century poet, Ezra Pound, was American-born but also expatriated, living in France and Italy much of his life.

Pound and Eliot, severely alienated from America and the anti-intellectualism they felt there, were only carrying to an extreme a feeling common among American writers just after World War I. Few of these writers took up European residence permanently, but many, artists as well as writers, had a "Paris period" of at least a few years. Ernest Hemingway was the best talent among the expatriate novelists, and except for some fine early short stories set in Michigan, his novels, such as *The Sun Also Rises* (1926), about the "Lost Generation" in France and Spain, and *A Farewell to Arms*

The antagonists at the Scopes "monkey" trial, Dayton, Tennessee, 1925. At left, Clarence Darrow, the renowned Chicago trial lawyer who defended John Scopes, the teacher who violated Tennessee's statute against the teaching of Darwinian evolution in the schools. At right, William Jennings Bryan, who helped prosecute Scopes to protect the statute and the anti-evolution viewpoint. Nearly thirty years after he first ran for president, Bryan made this last stand for his kind of fundamentalism; he died shortly after the trial. (Brown Brothers)

(1929), on the brutality of World War I, dealt with the confrontation of Americans with foreign cultures and settings. The other first-rate American novelist who began publishing in the late twenties stayed home but created a fictional world of Mississippi life that few Americans could regard as personally familiar; certainly it was far from the main stream. This was William Faulkner, whose *The Sound and the Fury* (1929), *Light in August* (1932), and *Absalom, Absalom* (1932) launched what some critics regard as the finest literary talent in American history.

There was a vast artistic gap between the muckraking books of a Frank Norris or Jack London and the best work of Eliot, Hemingway, or Faulkner. But in nearly all of them, as well as the others mentioned here, criticism of American society was vigorously, if sometimes indirectly, expressed. Muckrakers hoped to speed reform in American life, naturalists from Dreiser through Lewis and Fitzgerald portrayed its flatness, and the expatriates shunned it. American literature was never more critical of America. It was ironic that a culture so supposedly vacuous could produce so many fine writers.

The changes in "permissible" literary taste between the first days of naturalism, around 1900, and the mid-twenties, were enormous. H. L. Mencken, finishing fifteen years as literary critic of the *Smart Set* magazine in 1923, remarked on the transformations. "What strikes me most forcibly is the great change and improvement in the situation of the American imaginative author—the novelist, poet, dramatist, and writer of short-stories. In 1908, strange as it may seem to the literary radicals who roar so safely in Greenwich Village today, the old tradition was still powerful, and the young man or woman who came to New York with a manuscript which violated in any way the pruderies and prejudices of the professors had a very hard time getting it printed. It was a day of complacency and conformity. . . . And when, in [1910], Dr. William Lyon Phelps printed a book of criticism in which he actually ranked Mark Twain alongside Emerson and Hawthorne, there was as great a stirring beneath the college elms as if a naked fancy woman had run across the campus. . . . [But a writer in 1923] is quite as free as he deserves to be. . . . *Babbitt* scored a victory . . . for its target was the double one of American business and American Christianity; it set the whole world laughing at two things that are far more venerated than the bodily chastity of women."

Social Scientists: Optimistic Critics

The theme of social criticism was much less overt in social thought and social science. Nonetheless, after 1900 jurisprudence, economics, history, political science, and sociology began bluntly questioning nineteenth-century assumptions, sometimes iconoclastically discarding long-held beliefs and myths, and searching for a dispassionate, "realistic" analysis of American society, often with a view toward reforming it. In these fields, discouragement and reaction against reform did not occur in the twenties as they did in literature. Throughout the period the mechanistic natural-law assumptions of the late nineteenth century were being eroded by a hard spray of social fact. In legal theory, Oliver Wendell Holmes and Roscoe Pound led the movement for "legal realism," the admission that society changes and that courts should be attentive to the statistical evidence of these changes. In 1908, the United States Supreme Court acted upon sociological evidence, rather than contenting itself with an exegesis of the Constitution, when Attorney Louis D. Brandeis argued in favor of the Oregon law limiting women to a ten-hour workday (*Muller* v. *Oregon*).

In economics, Wesley C. Mitchell raised monetary theory above the level of sloganeering, with his dispassionate and methodologically brilliant studies of the gold standard. Meanwhile, Thorstein Veblen, notably in his *Theory of the Leisure Class* (1899), railed against the materialism of the time by labeling "pecuniary emulation" and "conspicuous consumption," rather than Carnegie's self-acclaimed high moral purpose, the real motivators of wealth-seeking. In history, Frederick Jackson Turner and James Harvey Robinson concentrated less on the acts of statesmen and more on the lives of masses of people, while Charles A. Beard shocked pious readers by arguing, in *An Economic Interpretation of the Constitution* (1913), that the Constitution of 1787 had not been drawn up by demigods on some Olympus, but by very human men whose chief concern was to protect and expand their own property interests.

In political science, J. Allen Smith (*The Spirit of American Government*, 1907) and Arthur Fisher Bentley (*The Process of Government*, 1908) freed the whole field from arid studies of constitutions and reoriented it toward the study of class, group, and special interests in the formation of political decisions. Albion Small and other pioneering sociologists, like their counterparts in history and political science, moved their discipline toward the study of popular behavior, social organization in rural and urban settings, and mass trends. John Dewey's *Reconstruction in Philosophy* (1920) stated, in a pragmatic vein, that the task of philosophy was not to discuss metaphysical abstractions but to clarify and help solve social and moral problems, especially conflicts between "inherited institutions" and "incompatible contemporary tendencies."

These men were the vanguard of a legion of social scientists who, armed with the seminar method, nourished by the growth of college

Law and order in prohibition days: federal agents doing in a speakeasy. (Brown Brothers)

and graduate education, and supported by expanding popular interest in mass behavior, scrutinized American society as never before. Some of their results directly supported legislative change; some, like the writings of Veblen and Beard, aroused public controversy; some were buried on library shelves. All told, however, the success of the new social science revealed the growing willingness of Americans to regard social trends and processes as more than abstractions, individualism and natural law as inadequate explanations of what made society run, and change and reform as normal and desirable.

Developments in the natural sciences depended far more on the theoretical work of Europeans such as Albert Einstein than on social trends in America, but pathfinding work brought Nobel prizes to eight American scientists, including Albert Michelson, who worked on the speed of light, Harold Urey, who discovered "heavy hydrogen," and Thomas Hunt Morgan, who in 1911 discovered the linear arrangement of genes along chromosomes.

To most Americans, technology was more visible. Orville and Wilbur Wright, with their four manned heavier-than-air flights of December 17, 1903, and Henry Ford, with his assembly-line mass production of inexpensive automobiles, were among the last and most successful inventors in the individualistic nineteenth-century tradition. In the 1910s and 1920s, technological innovation began to demand skills and financing better found in research laboratories such as those of Thomas Edison, of General Motors under the direction of Charles F. Kettering, and of General Electric under Charles Proteus Steinmetz and the Nobel laureate Irving Langmuir. Marconi's wireless telegraphy expanded into commercial radio in the twenties. The gasoline tractor, chemical fertilizers, and plant hybrids continued to transform agriculture. Petroleum chemistry began producing synthetic fabrics such as rayon and many other products, while X-ray crystallography helped develop metal alloys for building construction and other uses. Industrial sociology, industrial engineering, and personnel administration were being employed in industry in the twenties. The celebrated "technological revolution" of American life was well under way by World War I.

From Greenwich Village to Los Angeles, from the professor to the man on the street, changes in ideas and attitudes had been pervasive in the progressive era and the twenties. A writer in 1932 who drew up a partial list of "social inventions" nonexistent in 1900 but present in 1930 included "Armistice day, Australian ballot, Auto tourist camp, Basket-ball, Bonus to wage earners, City-manager plan, Community chest, Company union, Correspondence school, Day nursery, Esperanto, Four-H Clubs, Group insurance, Intelligence tests, Installment selling, Junior College, Juvenile court, Ku Klux Klan, League of Nations, Legal-aid society, Lock-out, Matrimonial bureau, Minimum wage law, Mothers' pension, One-step, Passport, Psychological clinics, Research institute, Rotary club, Social settlement, Summer camp, Tag day." What to make of this? Mostly confusion, the same writer thought: "We have the anomalies of prohibition and easy divorce; strict censorship and risqué plays and literature; scientific research and laws forbidding the theory of evolution; contraceptive information legally outlawed but widely utilized." And all of this happened during a Republican era when voter participation dropped to the lowest before or since.

Ex-President Theodore Roosevelt at Chicago Hall, August 8, 1912, during the "Bull Moose" campaign. (Culver Pictures, Inc.)

5

POLITICS AND EMPIRE IN THE PROGRESSIVE PERIOD, 1897-1916

In the progressive period, the money question and the tariff, those great political issues of the Gilded Age, faded in importance as Americans became deeply concerned with the regulation of big business, the return of government to the people, the welfare of underprivileged groups, and the territorial extension and diplomatic influence of the United States in the world. Those four issues used up most of the political energy of the pre–World War I years.

The relative strength of the major parties also changed. Between 1874 and 1894 an extremely close electoral balance existed between the Republicans and the Democrats, while after 1930 the Democratic party won and kept a national electoral majority. In the early twentieth century, which in terms of national elections means the years from 1894 through 1929, the Republicans dominated. Third party activity, intense in the nineties, dwindled except for 1912 and 1924. The only Democrat elected to the White House within the period was Woodrow Wilson. He won in 1912 with a minority of the popular vote when the Republicans split into progressive and conservative factions, and he won again in 1916 with the closest of electoral vote margins. The only Democratic Congresses of the time either rode in with Wilson or, as in 1910, resulted from a Republican split. The rest of the time the Republicans were victorious, not only nationally but usually (outside the South) on state and local levels as well.

The Republican Era Begins

The root causes of the Republicans' success were, first, good leadership and the ability of that leadership to define and act upon popularly important issues; and second, the relative homogeneity of the groups that composed the Republican coalition, a homogeneity that the Republicans brought with them out of the nineteenth century.

These elements, together with the anti-Democratic effect deriving from the "hard times" that occurred during most of Cleveland's second administration, made the Republicans dominant in the late nineties, but that dominance disappeared about 1930 when both their leadership and their coalition fossilized, preventing the assimilation of new ideas, issues, and groups when the country faced "hard times" once more.

The Republicans were seldom without attractive presidential candidates well-matched to the popular mood of the electoral moment. William McKinley may today seem colorless compared to William Jennings Bryan, but to the voters of 1896 and 1900, McKinley appeared more stable, equally clean-cut, and in some ways more modern. After McKinley defeated Bryan in the emotion-ridden battle of 1896, he won again with relative ease in their rematch in 1900. By 1904, McKinley had been assassinated, but his successor, Theodore Roosevelt, had quickly established himself as the most vigorous and engaging Republican president since Lincoln. The Democratic candidate, a little-known New York judge named Alton B. Parker, did not begin to match Roosevelt in voter appeal.

The Democrats, having learned in 1904 that the Parker cure for Bryanism was worse than the disease, nominated the Nebraskan a third time in 1908. But Roosevelt's record and popularity were so great that his handpicked successor, William Howard Taft of Ohio, won easily, despite Taft's lack of magnetism. In 1912 and 1916, the voters thought Taft and Charles Evans Hughes compared unfavorably to Woodrow Wilson, but the Republican nominees of the twenties (Harding, Coolidge, and Hoover) appealed to the voters as more "livable" than the Democrats' James Cox, John W. Davis, and Alfred E. Smith. There was more to winning elections than the personalities of the candidates, however; a very low voter turnout between 1900 and 1930 was also a key factor. But personalities were imponderably important, and Republican ones had the edge.

The presidency itself became more significant in the political life of the country. One reason for this was Theodore Roosevelt's use of the office: a man of truly extraordinary vigor, magnetism, and popularity, Roosevelt like no president before him, except possibly Washington and Jackson, focused the political attention of the nation upon the chief executive. Another reason was that America's politics, like its social and economic life, were becoming national in

PRESIDENTIAL VOTING, 1888–1968

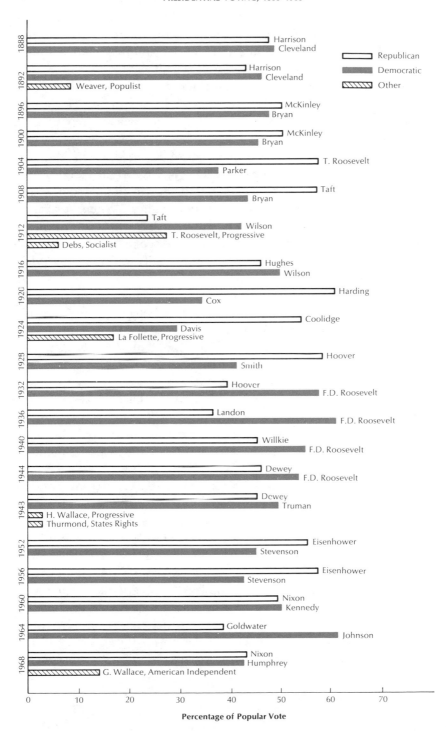

Percentage of Popular Vote

scope. National issues were taking on clearer shape as the president, more than Congress, formulated them. Complexity in so many aspects of American life seemed to demand a counterbalancing simplification in politics, by concentrating attention on what the president—especially T.R. and Wilson—said and did.

Theodore Roosevelt and a good many of the young, articulate Republicans who won governorships and seats in the House and Senate during the Roosevelt and Taft presidencies also had the handy knack of being able to speak to popular concerns and to state issues in such a way that the issues could be acted upon. Theodore Roosevelt seemed to millions to possess just the right blend of progressivism and conservatism, vigor and restraint in foreign affairs, derring-do and intellectualism in personality. When he talked about reform, he was able to state clearly what most Americans experienced as inarticulate fears or hopes; he spoke for the masses, yet he led them, from what he called his "bully pulpit," the White House.

The other great cause of Republican dominance in the early twentieth century, in addition to good leadership, was the constituent make-up of the party and the disunity of the Democratic opposition. From the mid-seventies to the early nineties, both parties minimized their party's inherent divisions over the issues, and searched for candidates acceptable to all wings. This strategy succeeded until Cleveland's second term. When Cleveland decided in 1893 that silver coinage had to cease, he thoroughly antagonized the western and less affluent Democrats, who captured the party leadership in 1896 and nominated Bryan. This, in turn, alienated the eastern Democrats.

Those events of the nineties formed the backdrop for national politics for some time to come. The split within the national Democratic party persisted for almost fifteen years after the election of 1896. Only after that did the Democrats absorb new issues and find new leaders. The sole dependable power base of the Democratic party at that time was the South, to which its presidential candidates or long-range programs had to be acceptable. Fortunately for the Democrats, whose electoral chances might otherwise have been nonexistent, progressivism not only was known in the South, but also specific parts of it were home-grown there. By 1910, any leader who hoped to carry the Democrats to national victory had to do the following: retain the western Bryanites, including former Populists, who had become by default perhaps the largest single element in the enfeebled Democratic coalition in the decade after 1896; retain the reservoir of southerners, many of whom were Bryanites, too, but also others who were more urbanized and "middle class" and who would respond to a progressive stance; make inroads on progressive independents or Republicans outside the South; and intensify the Democratic leanings of Catholic and Jewish ethnic groups in the Northeast and North Central states. Bryan was not the man for that job. Only in 1910 did the right man appear, even briefly, and in the thirteen Republican years before then, politics had become progressive and imperial.

McKinley and American Overseas Expansion

When William McKinley was inaugurated president in the spring of 1897, he found himself thrice blessed. First, the decisive Republican defeat of Bryan and his Populist-Democratic coalition had scattered the political opposition and reassured the many who quaked at the thought of the "anarchy" that Bryan might have loosed. Secondly, the depression following the Panic of 1893 was ending; in fact, the whole world-wide deflationary cycle that had prevailed since 1873 was giving way to the long prosperity cycle that ultimately lasted until 1929. McKinley's promise of a "full dinner pail" had a chance of coming true. The Ohioan's third blessing was substantial Republican control of both houses of Congress, assuring him support.

But McKinley had few programs and even less determination to push them through Congress. The last of the nineteenth-century presidents, McKinley expected to take his cues from the small, powerful band of Republican leaders in Congress. The McKinley administration produced little domestic legislation, and what there was, notably the high-protectionist Dingley Tariff of 1897 and the Gold Standard Act of 1900, affirmed long-standing Republican policy and was not innovative.

By far the most important events of McKinley's presidency occurred in foreign affairs. Between 1897 and 1901, the United States began to behave like a world power, dominating the Western Hemisphere, making heavy commitments in Asia and the Western Pacific, and playing a broker's role in European diplomacy. In those years the United States won a war against Spain, which was then ruled by an established if creaking European monarchy. As a result, the United States fell heir to much of Spain's world empire and assumed the "white man's burden" that such imperialism entailed.

The reasons for this emergence of the United States as a world power were a complex mixture of desire, readiness, opportunity, and historical accident. The desire and readiness were provided by notions of Anglo-Saxon superiority, Captain Mahan's treatise on naval power, the imperialism of Britain, Germany, and France, and the long-held hope of expanded commerce in the Western Hemisphere and across the Pacific. Opportunity and resulting accident arose from a popular uprising in Cuba, the last large fragment of the ancient Spanish Empire in the New World. The Cubans wanted independence and a republican form of government. Many Americans agreed, and by 1897, over two dozen American missions of arms and supplies had gone to Cuba. These were organized by private citizens, but the American government interfered little. By early 1898, the Cuban insurrectionaries had successfully propagandized their case in the United States, arguing that brutal Spanish repression was crushing the just cause of Cuban freedom, and likening Cuban anticolonialism to the American Revolution of 1776. Spanish hands were in fact far from clean, but in late 1897 the Spanish government did recall General Weyler, their military governor whom the American press had nicknamed "Butcher," and offered Cuba and Puerto Rico some measure of autonomy.

Spain acted too late. American opinion, strongly pro-Cuban, pressured Washington to intervene officially. Late in January 1898, McKinley sent a battleship, the U.S.S. *Maine*, to Havana harbor to increase the American presence in Cuba. Three weeks later, on February 15, the *Maine* exploded, killing 260 Americans, as a result of an underwater mine. No one ever discovered who set the mine; the Spanish were trying to avoid war with the United States and were very unlikely suspects. But the American public was already incensed by a New York *Journal* report on February 9 of a letter by Enrique Dupuy de Lôme, the Spanish minister in Washington, calling McKinley "weak and a bidder for the admiration of the crowd

. . . a would-be politician." Newspapers adopted the slogan "Remember the *Maine*" and added "to Hell with Spain." On March 9, Congress appropriated $50 million for defense, and McKinley responded to whoops from the pro-war "jingo" press by calling on Spain to withdraw from Cuba. By April 9, the Spanish government accepted most of the American terms, but McKinley asked Congress on April 11 for authority to send an American armed force to Cuba. Reluctant to stand up to the jingoes, and facing congressional threats to declare war without him, McKinley rejected the Spanish offer and jumped in front of the march of public opinion. On April 19, Congress passed a joint resolution affirming Cuba's independence and calling on the president to send a force to Cuba to insure it. The resolution also contained an amendment by Senator Henry Teller of Colorado, a silverite Republican, disclaiming any intention by the United States to annex Cuba. Humanitarian rather than imperialistic motives underlay Teller's amendment, as they did the attitude of many supporters of Cuban intervention, including, to some extent, McKinley himself.

The Spanish-American War began as an American attempt to help bring about the independence of the Cuban people. As such it was a kind of final chapter in the policy made explicit in the Monroe Doctrine in 1823 to support the independence of the Americas from European colonialism. But it quickly developed into the first chapter of modern-day American imperialism.

The war was brief and, for Spain, disastrous. Despite shocking disorganization and some outright corruption in the American army, the Spanish forces in Cuba rapidly capitulated. Puerto Rico fell with even less of a struggle. The United States Navy destroyed the main Spanish fleet almost ship by ship, while at the beginning of May, a small American squadron under Commodore George Dewey steamed from Hong Kong to Manila in the Philippines and wiped out the Spanish fleet there without losing a single American life. The fighting was effectively over in early August. The subsequent Treaty of Paris, signed in October and ratified in February, 1899, gave Puerto Rico, Guam, and the whole Philippine archipelago to the United States, while freeing Cuba. In July, 1898, during the height of the War, Congress annexed Hawaii by joint resolution.

The Treaty of Paris passed the Senate by only a one-vote margin, and Hawaii was annexed by resolution rather than treaty because the former required a simple rather than a two-thirds majority, which would have been unobtainable. Clearly there was strong anti-imperialist feeling in Congress and among the public. The anti-imperialists were an oddly assorted group: the majority of Democrats, many Populists and Silver Republicans, aging Liberal Republicans and Mugwumps (G.O.P. bolters) such as Carl Schurz; the conservative Republican House Speaker, Thomas B. Reed of Maine; educators, writers, and others. But they were still a minority, however illustrious. The mass of Republicans supported the annexations, including that of the Philippines, on ideological, missionary, and commercial grounds.

Thus by 1899, the United States governed island colonies in the Caribbean and across the Pacific to within a few hundred miles of the mainland of Asia. It had "come of age" as a great power. But the entanglements that imperialism demanded, particularly in the western Pacific and therefore necessarily in European power politics, only gradually became apparent. These entanglements were so serious that even as vigorous an imperialist as Theodore Roosevelt soon had second thoughts about the annexation of the Philippines. Indeed the chain of events was very direct from Dewey at Manila in 1898 to the Japanese Air Force at Pearl Harbor in 1941. American policy, unknown to anyone in 1898, was moving on a collision course with the Japanese Empire.

The motives of the anti-imperialists were progressive, just as were the motives of the imperialists. Battlers for social welfare and the extension of democracy within the United States could not accept the idea that a society based on democratic principles should rule colonies inhabited by second-class citizens, unprotected by the Bill of Rights. The United States Supreme Court disagreed in the Insular Cases of 1900 and later: the Constitution does not necessarily follow the flag, except as Congress permits. The Court's position seemed at odds with the "no taxation without representation" of 1776, or for that matter, with the humanitarian motives which prompted many to support American armed intervention in Cuba in 1898. Men with such anti-imperialist misgivings were doubly shocked by American official action in the Philippines after 1898, which pointed up the inconsistencies in so-called humanitarian motives. The Filipinos, happy to be rid of Spanish rule, expected to gain their independence as the Cubans had done. Instead, American armed forces after three bloody years succeeded in subjugating the

Emilio Aguinaldo, the leader of the Philippine "insurrection." (Brown Brothers)

Filipinos, who were ably led by a young nationalist warrior named Emilio Aguinaldo. The United States government simply decided that the Filipinos were not ready for self-government, and enforced its decision with the bayonet when the Filipinos disagreed. The ruthless stifling of Philippine independence was ignored by many Americans, who convinced themselves that stable government, American protection, Christian missionary work, and public education justified American domination. This was the first American attempt at third-world nation-building, and it was not pretty.

Theodore Roosevelt, the First Modern President

In the years between 1900 and the entry of the United States into World War I in 1917, government actions in both foreign and domestic affairs expanded to levels that were then unprecedented for peacetime. A key reason for that expansion was the enormous vigor of Theodore Roosevelt. "T.R.," one of the most remarkable personalities ever to occupy the presidency, did more to make progressivism a national movement than any other single person or force. Born into the Republican wing of the patrician Roosevelt family of New York, he had prodigious energies that drove him to excel in a dozen different ways. Poorly endowed by nature, he had miserable eyesight and, initially, the constitution of the proverbial ninety-eight pound weakling. He fiercely strove to correct his physical liabilities by rounding up cattle and riding broncos in the Dakota Territory. His devotion to "the strenuous life" extended throughout his life into bee-line hikes, bear hunts (one of which produced the "Teddy bear"), safaris, and an exploration of western Brazil that almost killed him. He was an able student, and his Harvard bachelor's thesis on the naval war of 1812 became a very respectable history book. He wrote several others in the years following. He loved nature study and achieved a substantial reputation as an amateur botanist.

But his real passion and profession was politics. Combining a patrician sense of *noblesse oblige* with a sure common touch, he moved rapidly up the political ladder in a day when other members of the "upper crust" disdained politics as vulgar and dirty. He was elected to the New York Assembly in 1884 and soon became the Police Commissioner of New York City. No radical, he jumped into the New York mayoralty race in 1887, when he was twenty-nine, to try to defeat Henry George, the single-tax advocate. Named a United States Civil Service Commissioner by President Harrison, he became Assistant Secretary of the Navy in the McKinley Administration. When sending Commodore Dewey to Manila Bay proved to be too tame a way to fight the Spaniards, Roosevelt resigned from the cabinet, accepted a Colonel's commission, and formed the "Rough Rider" regiment of whites, Negroes, cowboys, and gentlemen. Roosevelt led the Rough Riders' charge up San Juan Hill in

Cuba in 1898, and then rode directly through a hero's welcome in New York City into the Governor's Mansion in Albany.

Scarcely forty, he achieved a reformist, but not a radical, record in his two years as Governor of New York. He exposed corrupt links between big business, notably insurance companies, and state officials. He instituted tougher taxes on corporations and secured a rudimentary workmen's compensation law. These were popular measures, and as a vote-getter Roosevelt was a major asset to the Republicans. But he was no asset at all to the Republican state machine because of his incorrigible tendency to think and act on his own, and in 1900, Senator Thomas C. Platt, the "easy boss" of New York's Republicans, and Mark Hanna, the Republican national chairman, decided to relegate Roosevelt to political oblivion by giving him the vice-presidential slot on McKinley's reelection ticket. Roosevelt accepted with misgiving, was elected, and for months languished as president of the Senate. Then in September, 1901, came the gunshot by Leon Czolgosz, an American-born anarchist, that killed McKinley, and "that damned cowboy," as Mark Hanna called Roosevelt, was in the White House.

Two points are crucial to remember about the Roosevelt presidency. His development as a progressive reformer was gradual, so that his positions in 1912 were much more advanced than in 1901 or even 1905. Secondly, the concrete achievements, legislative or administrative, of his presidency were less significant than the change in presidential style that he created. He was the first modern president—a popular tribune of the people, an effective party leader, a world statesman. From Roosevelt onward, the President was expected to be the focus of national political life, instead of the Congress or the states, as was usually the case between Lincoln and McKinley.

When he took office, Roosevelt reassuringly stated that he would continue McKinley's policies and retain his cabinet. For his first three years in office, until after the 1904 election, he departed from that stance only three times. Generally Roosevelt cooperated with the conservative Republican leaders in Congress; he supported their currency policy; he refused to press for downward tariff revision, which progressives wanted. He reorganized, in the interests of efficiency, the Army general staff and the United States consular service. He supported the 1902 Newlands Act, which provided federal help for dam building and land reclamation in the West, and he regularized the American occupation of the Philippines. With these measures, much of the G.O.P. was happy. But the departures were another matter.

The first such departure was the Justice Department's suit, filed early in 1902, to break up the Northern Securities Company just created by Morgan, Harriman, Hill, and Rockefeller. Wall Street was shocked, but the popular reaction to this surprising enforcement of the Sherman Anti-Trust Act was favorable. Incipient progressives had begun to despair that any agency would effectively control the trusts, and were delighted when the president took the lead. Roosevelt's second departure was equally pleasing: his intervention in the 1902 anthracite strike, bringing mine owners and United Mine Worker officers to the White House. When the mine owners refused to compromise, Roosevelt began arranging with the governor of Pennsylvania to send federal troops to operate the mines, on the ground that the shortage of coal—with winter coming on—was a national emergency. J. P. Morgan persuaded the mine owners to accept an arbitration board to be appointed by Roosevelt, and to abide by its decision; the UMW quickly agreed, also. The workers went back to the mines, the threat of federal troop operation evaporated, and the flow of coal resumed. The arbitration board, to which Roosevelt had ingeniously appointed a labor leader in a slot provided for "an eminent sociologist," awarded the miners better wages and working conditions, though not union recognition. But again Roosevelt showed that the executive was ready to take decisive action to limit the power of capital. Roosevelt's third departure from Republican cooperation with the plutocrats was the establishment of a Bureau of Corporations in the Commerce Department in 1903. When the Standard Oil Company wired congressmen to vote down the bill that set up the bureau, Roosevelt publicized the Standard's attempt, whereupon the bill whisked through Congress on a wave of hostile public reaction. The bureau became the major federal fact-finding agency for providing the Justice Department with evidence to try antitrust suits.

The three departures of 1902–1903 shocked pro-business conservatives and pleased many people who had begun to think that the "trusts" were uncontrollable. Perspicacious Wall Streeters, however, realized that they had little basically to fear from Roosevelt. His intervention in the anthracite strike was in response to a critical national emergency, and not the result of any ardently pro-labor

"Hinky Dink" Kenna and "Bathhouse John" Coughlin, aldermen of Chicago's First Ward, a noted haven of pre-prohibition vice. (Courtesy of the Chicago Historical Society)

bias. His attitude toward capitalists was indeed different from that of his predecessors, but was not fundamentally hostile. He was simply trying to distinguish between big businesses that operated in the public interest and those that did not. Large size, either of companies or of unions, was not an evil in itself, in Roosevelt's view. He could not understand the blindness of arch-conservative Republicans to the threat of social upheaval, which might well break out if capital were not subjected to some kind of controls by a popularly responsible agency. While stand-pat Republicans thought that business ought to regulate itself, Roosevelt preferred to use the power of the federal government.

This cleavage between Roosevelt and the Republican "Old Guard," among whom were most of the leaders of Congress, was already opening in 1902–1903. But Roosevelt minimized it until after the election of 1904. In that presidential campaign, corporations and capitalists contributed heavily to the Republican effort, as they had in 1896 and 1900. After being elected in his own right, however, Roosevelt took a much more openly progressive stance. In 1905 he announced his "Square Deal" program, calling on Congress to pass a series of progressive measures of which the foremost was a thoroughgoing revision of the Interstate Commerce Act, to regulate the railroads more stringently. Congress did little in 1905, but Roosevelt, with great political skill, engineered in 1906 the passage of the most important law of his presidency, the Hepburn Act. This act empowered the Interstate Commerce Commission to lower established railroad rates on complaint of shippers who presented it with acceptable evidence that the rates were unfair or discriminatory; instead of making a shipper or the ICC prove that an existing rate was unfair, the Hepburn Act placed the burden of proof on the railroad that the rate was fair. The law had one major loophole—a rate change authorized by the ICC could be blocked by a court injunction—but the Hepburn Act was nonetheless a stout weapon for controlling transportation monopolies and a major step in the history of federal regulation of private enterprise.

Congress also passed in 1906 the Pure Food and Drug Act, including a provision for federal inspection of meat. This was not originally a "Square Deal" measure, but Roosevelt assumed leadership of it when widespread public pressure appeared after Upton Sinclair published *The Jungle*, his pungent muckraking novel about conditions in Chicago packing houses. By 1907, the progressive movement was reaching full force as a reform effort, and Roosevelt was fast becoming its national leader.

The progressive impulse, however, scarcely touched the United States Senate. In 1907 and 1908 Roosevelt's popularity soared, and he became increasingly committed to reform; but he achieved few results except in the single area of the conservation of natural resources, a drive supported by reformers and a few others. By administrative action, the government placed 200 million acres under protection from lumber, mining, and other private interests, and awakened the public to the importance of conservation for the first time. Just before he left office, Roosevelt sent Congress a message asking for more federal regulation of railroads and other big businesses, more welfare and labor legislation, and more impartiality by the federal courts, especially when they dealt with labor cases. Congress ignored it.

Taft, Insurgency, and the Bull Moose

Roosevelt's progressivism was almost fully developed by 1908, and his personal popularity was immense. The Republican congressional leaders, the chief of whom were Senator Nelson Aldrich of Rhode Island and House Speaker Joseph G. Cannon of Illinois, could block T.R.'s legislative requests but not his domination of the Republican convention. Roosevelt kept the promise he made after his 1904 election not to run in 1908, but he had little difficulty in naming William Howard Taft as his successor. Taft, formerly Governor-General of the Philippines and Secretary of War, took about 52 percent of the popular vote to Bryan's 43 percent, with the rest scattered among Socialist and other candidates. The most notable result of the 1908 election, aside from Taft's easy victory as Roosevelt's anointed successor, was the election of a substantial group of midwestern Republican progressives, shortly to be called "Insurgents," to the House and Senate. They, and Roosevelt, expected Taft to continue Roosevelt's policies and drive them into the statute books despite the opposition of Senator Aldrich, Speaker Cannon, and other "Old Guard" leaders.

Taft disappointed the Insurgents. The 1908 Republican platform had called for tariff revision, which was understood to mean revision downward, and the first major measure taken up under the new administration was a tariff bill. But the bill presented by the "Old Guard" revised the tariff *upward*. Insurgents, including Senators Robert La Follette of Wisconsin, Albert Beveridge of Indiana, Jonathan Dolliver and Albert Cummins of Iowa, Joseph Bristow of Kansas, and Moses Clapp of Minnesota, put on a tremendous struggle on the Senate floor to revise the bill. Taft, to their dismay, sided with the leadership, and when the high-protectionist Payne-Aldrich tariff bill of 1909 passed, he signed it. The Insurgents were disenchanted.

In 1910, House Insurgents led by George Norris, a young Nebraska congressman, believed that their first task as reformers was to curb the near-absolute powers of the Speaker, who called bills up for votes (or buried them) as he saw fit, appointed committees, recognized (or ignored) speakers, and otherwise ruled the House. The Insurgents neatly maneuvered to change the House rules to limit the Speaker's powers, but again Taft sided with the conservatives, and the Insurgents despaired. The final blow to their hopes was the unedifying Ballinger-Pinchot controversy, in which Chief Forester Gifford Pinchot, a friend and appointee of Roosevelt's, accused his superior, Secretary of the Interior Richard Ballinger, of collusion with private mining interests in transfers of public lands earmarked for conservation. Taft naturally supported his own cabinet officer and Pinchot was dismissed, but the Insurgents and much of the public were convinced that Taft had deliberately and fully rejected the Roosevelt conservation policy, and reform itself. By the beginning of 1910, the break between Taft and the Insurgents was practically complete.

Taft hoped to see many Insurgent Congressmen defeated in Republican primaries in 1910. But he was swimming against a progressive rip tide. Not only Republican Insurgents but also a great mass of progressive Democrats were nominated and elected. The Old Guard leadership in the Senate was swept out, replaced by progressive Democrats, and the great obstacle to Rooseveltian reform was gone. Taft's prestige in the Republican party wobbled; some Insurgents talked openly of dumping Taft for Roosevelt in 1912; Democratic contenders for 1912, such as the newly-elected governor of New Jersey, Woodrow Wilson, looked formidable. Senator La Follette began thinking of himself for the Republican nomination in 1912, and Roosevelt, returning from an African safari, which lasted through most of 1909 and well into 1910, listened sympathetically to Insurgent criticisms of Taft.

Ironically, in view of the Insurgents' disgruntlement, more reform legislation passed into law amid these turbulent political conditions than during Roosevelt's eight years in office. Antitrust prosecutions were twice as numerous under Taft as under Roosevelt the "trust-buster," and several major prosecutions that had been launched earlier, notably against Standard Oil and the American Tobacco Company, were decided in favor of the government by the Supreme Court. A Federal Children's Bureau, postal savings banks, extensions of federal civil service, and a substantial extension of railroad regulation (the Mann-Elkins Act, 1910) took place, as well as other reforms. Most important, Congress and the states passed two far-reaching Constitutional amendments, the Sixteenth, which made possible a federal graduated income tax—probably the most radical reform of the whole progressive era, at least potentially—and the Seventeenth, which made mandatory the growing practice by the states of direct election of senators. Taft was by no means responsible for all of these reforms, but he deserves considerable credit, together with congressmen who were often neither his partisans nor his sympathizers.

By the beginning of 1912, however, Taft was in political trouble. Senator La Follette actively began seeking the Republican presidential nomination, as the candidate of the Insurgent wing. Taft might well have crushed the Insurgents had they remained under La Follette's leadership, but luck deserted both Taft and La Follette. The Wisconsin Senator's pre-nomination campaign proved too strenuous even for that redoubtable man, and his health broke during a public speech on February 2. At that crucial point, Theodore Roosevelt announced that his hat was in the ring, and Taft's renomination bid was being challenged by the most popular and most aggressive man in American politics.

Yet the power of a president as party leader is great. Taft controlled a majority of the delegates to the Republican convention, many of them from "rotten boroughs" in the South where there were hardly any Republican voters, and he won the nomination. Galled, the Insurgent wing stalked out, and a few weeks later nominated Theodore Roosevelt for president on the "Progressive" ticket in 1912. Roosevelt, declaring that he felt like a "bull moose," accepted—"We stand at Armageddon, and we battle for the Lord," he had said in June—and the Republican party was split.

Progressivism had by no means totally overtaken the Democratic party. Although the Democratic nomination fight was less spectacular than the Republican, it was a battle. Only after forty-six ballots did Woodrow Wilson, with the support of Bryan and the key southern leader, Congressman Oscar Underwood of Alabama, defeat the Speaker of the House, "Champ" Clark of Missouri. Clark actually

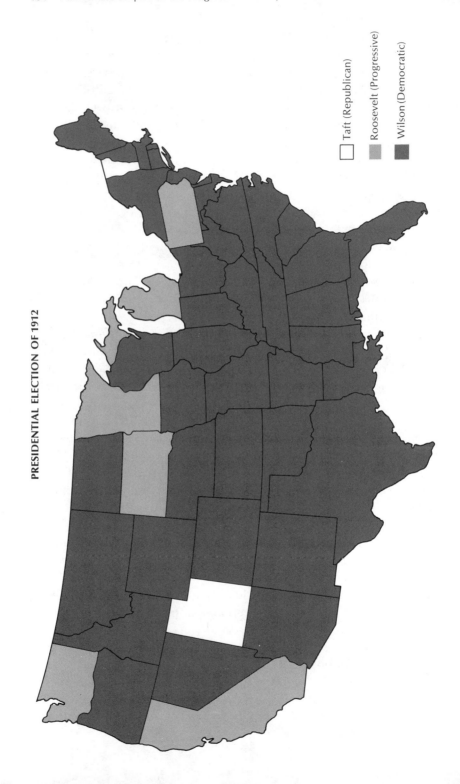

PRESIDENTIAL ELECTION OF 1912

☐ Taft (Republican)

▨ Roosevelt (Progressive)

■ Wilson (Democratic)

had a simple majority of the delegates at one point. But the Democrats' two-thirds rule, which gave the South a veto from Jackson's time until Franklin Roosevelt's, saved the day for Wilson. It also showed the strength of southern Democratic progressivism, and Wilson's debt to it.

The Socialist party nominated Eugene V. Debs, of Pullman strike and subsequent fame, and Debs' eventual capture of 900,000 votes—about 6 percent of the total and the highest proportion a Socialist candidate ever received—reflected a strong undercurrent of dissatisfaction even with progressivism as a solution to national problems. The 1912 election was truly a four-way battle, with only one of the four, Taft, representing more-or-less traditional positions against the radical Debs and the two progressives—an enormous change in national politics since the second Bryan-McKinley campaign in 1900.

It became obvious early in the campaign that Taft and Debs were out of the running, and that the real struggle was between Wilson and Roosevelt. Very different in personality, the New York Rough Rider and the Virginia-born college president differed also in party support: Roosevelt had little local organization and the Progressive party was almost all head and no body, while Wilson had the backing of Democratic organizations. Roosevelt called his program the "New Nationalism," and the two programs were agreed on fundamentals such as the need for expanded federal activity to protect the individual from oppressive corporate power, to eliminate corruption in government, and to end special privileges for big businesses. The differences stemmed from differences between the candidates' personalities and parties. Roosevelt had never assumed that business, because it was big, was necessarily bad, and hence he sought to regulate and channel corporate enterprise. Wilson, suspicious that any great corporation was likely to crush the individual, hoped to control them more stringently. Roosevelt wanted the federal government to act positively in providing welfare and labor legislation, while Wilson's attitude, a more negative one, was to take away special privileges from groups which possessed them unwarrantedly. As a consequence of these differences, the Progressive platform contained an impressive list of specific proposals for specific ends, including an array of regulatory commissions, while Wilson and the Democratic platform concentrated upon a few key evils which needed rectifying. But both called for reform, and both believed in expanded federal activity.

Woodrow Wilson's
New Freedom

With the Republicans completely split, Wilson won a majority of electoral votes and carried with him whopping Democratic majorities into both houses of Congress, so that the Democrats controlled House, Senate, and presidency for the first time since the forlorn and very unprogressive days of 1893. Democratic majorities did not mean Democratic unanimity, and Wilson had to exercise great skill with Congress. In 1913 he achieved two of the fundamental reforms he had promised in 1912. The first was a substantial downward revision of the tariff, for the first time since 1862. The Underwood-Simmons tariff of 1913 reversed the Republicans' policy of high protection. In laying low "the mother of trusts" (so-called by many progressives who were convinced that monopoly flourished behind high tariff walls), the Wilsonian progressives believed they had struck a great blow for individual freedom. Tariff levels dropped to an average of 25 percent, from the roughly 42 percent of Taft's 1909 Payne-Aldrich Act, and the new law also enacted the first federal income tax (its highest rate was 6 percent, for annual incomes of a million dollars) under the new Sixteenth Amendment.

Future Republican administrations would raise the tariff again, but the second Wilson measure of 1913 was to be permanent: the creation of the Federal Reserve System. It was also the greatest single achievement of his presidency. Bankers had wanted a privately-controlled central regulating mechanism since the Panic of 1907, but the revelations of the Pujo Committee about the "money trust" had awakened the drowsing hostility of many Bryanite Democrats toward bankers. The Democratic leadership in Congress responded in 1913 with a bill to create several publicly-owned regional reserve banks, issuing currency that would be entirely a public liability. The bankers' ideas seemed irreconcilable with the Democratic bill. President Wilson himself came up with a viable compromise, setting the regional reserve banks under a presidentially appointed Federal Reserve Board, while private member banks owned the reserve banks. Neither the Wall Street bankers nor the more dogmatic Democratic agrarians were happy with the compromise, but it passed Congress late in 1913.

Wilson had won his first two battles substantially according to plan. His third ended differently. One of his fondest campaign objectives in 1912 had been a new, comprehensive antitrust law which would explicitly set forth a list of monopoly practices, outlaw them, and thus strongly update and extend the Sherman Act of 1890. In 1914 the new Clayton antitrust bill came before Congress. There it languished. Too long and too specific, it evoked dissension rather than agreement from the Democratic majority, and after some months it seemed probable that the bill would not pass. At that point, Wilson, on the advice of Louis D. Brandeis, a leading progressive lawyer and Wilson aide, took a decisive step to save his antitrust program. The president stopped supporting the Clayton bill in its existing form, thus allowing Congress to remove many of the specifically outlawed practices. Wilson instead put his main weight behind a bill to create a Federal Trade Commission, a regulatory agency to supervise mergers and other trust practices. The control of big business by regulatory agency rather than by precise statute had a precedent in the Interstate Commerce Commission established in 1887 and resuscitated by Theodore Roosevelt, and it was much more a part of the 1912 Roosevelt platform than of Wilson's. Wilson's New Freedom was changing emphasis in a Rooseveltian direction. Wilson signed both the emasculated Clayton Anti-Trust Act and the Federal Trade Commission Act into law in the early fall of 1914.

From that point until just before American entry into World War I in early 1917, the New Freedom moved away from the somewhat negative thrust that was manifest in downward tariff revision, tightening the reins on the big private bankers, and the threats of prosecution of business implied in the original Clayton bill. The president began to advocate legislation and executive actions to benefit specific economic and social groups. Earlier he had insisted that these groups had no special claim on federal support and that special privilege of any kind, whether for corporations or for labor unions, ought to be abolished. Wilson's shift was first evident in the struggle over the Clayton bill, and although he neither supported nor actively opposed measures to benefit labor, farmers, woman suffragists, and child labor reformers even into 1915, he was moving in a more welfarish direction. Very likely he was spurred by the disquieting reduction of Democratic majorities in Congress in the 1914 election. Although the party in power historically lost seats in off-year elections, the 1914 losses were substantial, and Wilson, as a one-time political science professor, was certainly aware that the

Democrats were nationally the minority party at that time. To win again in 1916, he had to entice a good part of Roosevelt's 1912 "Bull Moose" vote into the Democratic column. He could hope to do that by urging enactment of parts of the Bull Moose platform.

In early 1916, Wilson moved emphatically toward social-welfare and regulatory measures. To open the year, he pleased many progressives by appointing Brandeis to the United States Supreme Court; Brandeis went on to a distinguished twenty-three-year career as a liberal justice. Three years earlier Wilson had shied away from appointing Brandeis to the potentially less critical post of Attorney General, because some thought him "radical"; he was also opposed, as the first Jewish Justice, by anti-Semites. Wilson also pressed Congress to the limit, for an election year, sponsoring a barrage of bills to benefit specific interest groups. The Federal Farm Loan Act provided credit for farmers. The Keating-Owen Act restricted the sale in interstate commerce of goods made by child labor. The Kern-McGillicuddy Act provided a federal workmen's compensation statute. Congress created, as many progressives had urged for years, a nonpartisan tariff commission, which was supposed to take the tariff issue out of politics and log-rolling. The Federal Highway Act, authorizing funds for a joint federal-state highway building program, had vast social and economic consequence. In September, 1916, Wilson signed the Adamson Act, granting railroad workers a maximum eight-hour day, and early in 1917 the Smith-Hughes Act provided federal aid for vocational training. In his administration, Wilson reaped a harvest of progressive legislation sown by Theodore Roosevelt and nurtured by Republican Insurgents and progressive Democrats alike.

The Democrats renominated their incumbent president in 1916. The Republicans, mindful of the need to present a "progressive," but unwilling to forgive Theodore Roosevelt for his 1912 walkout from the party, nominated Governor Charles Evans Hughes of New York, who had a good record as a reformer, if a rather starchy

During this period of Republican dominance, Democrats won control of the House of Representatives only when the Republicans were split from 1910 to 1914. After the economic downturn began in 1929, Democratic victories became customary.

CONGRESSIONAL MAJORITIES, 1898–1932 ELECTIONS

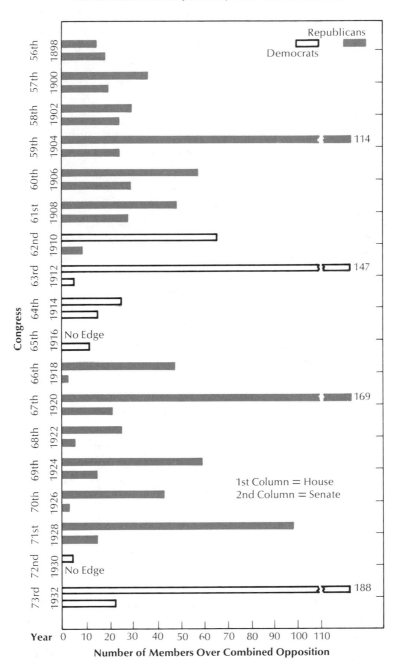

image. The remnants of Progressives offered Roosevelt a presidential nomination, but the tiring lion declined it. Many Roosevelt voters of 1912 swung to Wilson in 1916, and Wilson won reelection with many more popular votes than he received four years earlier. But he barely won a majority in the electoral college, going over the top only when the returns from California, the forty-eighth state to report, dribbled in. But Wilson did carry in Democratic majorities in Congress, and the New Freedom apparently still lived.

Yet the heyday of progressivism in domestic politics was nearly over, with one great exception—the Nineteenth Amendment giving women the vote. The only further progressive measures of magnitude on the federal level came from the movement's repressive side. Prohibitory legislation gained momentum in several states, and the Eighteenth Amendment, restricting people's alcoholic intake by forbidding liquor sales, was less than two years away. Immigration restriction, by means of a literacy test to keep out "undesirable races," urged in Congress since the nineties but fended off by the more generous progressives, passed Congress early in 1917 despite two vetoes by President Wilson. And unexpectedly, unintentionally, the progressive impulse was about to receive a mortal blow: the president whose party advertised him in the 1916 campaign as the man who "kept us out of war" was about to lead the United States into the First World War.

The net results of progressivism in domestic politics in the cities and states, and nationally during the presidencies of Roosevelt, Taft, and Wilson, were immensely impressive. Some progressive laws were struck down after 1918 by a reactionary majority on the Supreme Court; the *Hammer* v. *Dagenhart* case (1918), which invalidated the federal child labor law of 1916, was the main example. However, most of the progressive laws survived. Railroad regulation, the income tax, the Federal Reserve, state regulation of many kinds of businesses, and the democratization of government at all levels were permanent changes. So also was the concept of legislation to benefit specific underprivileged or deprived groups.

Yet progressive legislation by no means rectified all of society's problems. It certainly did not change in any drastic way the broad outlines of the American capitalist system, even though it did make some adjustments in the relations of social and economic groups within that system. Legislation had not basically dealt with "the labor question"; mass-production industries were years away from

unionization, and rising real wages and reasonably high employment, not new laws (except in the one area of workmen's compensation, which provided a modicum of security to workers), staved off
greater violence. The greatest abuses of uncontrolled wealth-getting
were moderated by antitrust prosecutions, regulatory commissions,
the conservation policies of Theodore Roosevelt (which were short-
lived and incomplete), and some other changes. But the federal
graduated income tax functioned in no significant way as an equal-
izer of wealth until thirty years later, and the Federal Reserve system was not utilized effectively as a regulator of the economy before
the New Deal.

Neither of the major political parties was reorganized as a continuing instrument of social and economic change. Wilson, for example, needed support too badly from southern white supremacists to
institute racial equality, even in the federal civil service, and the
growing split between the agrarian heirs of Bryan and the northern
city bosses was to shackle the Democrats in their attempts to develop any broad-gauged program, even on the scale of the New
Freedom of 1912. As for the G.O.P., although Insurgency, especially in the Midwest, was represented in Congress into the
twenties, the withdrawal of the Roosevelt Progressives from the
party in 1912, and the subsequent reluctance of party regulars to
admit the defectors to national leadership, left the party of Theodore Roosevelt and Robert La Follette unsympathetic to reformers,
congealing in an unresponsive pro-business conservatism.

The progressive years had also failed to educate the American
people in the realities of world politics and in the role of world leadership, which before many years became a major responsibility for
them. Wilson, when he became president, remarked how ironic it
would be if his administration became predominantly concerned
with foreign affairs. Yet that was exactly what happened.

6

PROGRESSIVE FOREIGN POLICIES, THE "GREAT WAR," AND THE TWENTIES

The humanitarian, democratizing, reforming character of the progressive movement seemed to crumble when it was exposed to foreign air, leaving only the moralistic side intact. Similar impulses governed American foreign policy in the early twentieth century as governed domestic policy, but the results were more fumblingly aggressive. Between 1815—the end of the Napoleonic Wars in Europe and the War of 1812 for the United States—and World War I, the United States had been generally free to ignore foreign affairs and to exploit its internal resources. Although an expansionist power, it could indulge its appetite for new territory without armed conflict with anyone stronger than Mexico or the western Indians because of the vastness of North America and its remoteness across the oceans from the great powers of Europe and Asia. When the country did enter world politics actively during and after the McKinley administration, it was far too big to be ground between any great-power millstones. Unfortunately it was also inexperienced.

The Caribbean and "Paramount Interest"

Most American diplomacy between 1898 and 1917 related to three areas: the Caribbean and Central America, East Asia, and Europe. The Spanish-American War confirmed what great-power diplomats had thought: the Caribbean was in fact dominated by the

Woodrow Wilson, not long before he left the White House. (Historical Pictures Service, Chicago)

United States and was not to be fruitfully entered into by another power such as Britain or Germany. It was the United States' "area of paramount interest," in the genteel diplomatic phrase, all the more so after the United States annexed Puerto Rico and occupied Cuba. Theodore Roosevelt, motivated less by ebullient expansionism than by a desire to impose order and strengthen American security, followed two lines of policy in the Caribbean. One was to create an American-operated canal across Central America, which would allow commercial and naval vessels to move easily between the Atlantic and the Pacific (and also multiply the mobility of the United States Navy). The other was to stabilize, if necessary by armed intervention, the internal affairs of the small republics of the area.

The idea of a Central American canal was an old one, but the events that made it a reality began only in 1899. At that time, Secretary of State John Hay negotiated with Britain a revision of the 1850 Clayton-Bulwer treaty, which had provided that any future isthmian canal would be a joint Anglo-American venture. After one false start, Hay secured British agreement to, and the Senate's confirmation of, the Hay-Pauncefote treaty, giving the United States complete control over a future canal. By then Roosevelt was president. He faced the choice between a canal across Panama or one across Nicaragua. The owners of some old French canal rights in Panama aggressively lobbied Roosevelt on the virtues of the Panamanian route. Panama happened to be a state within the Republic of Colombia, which would not agree to an American-controlled canal. A Panamanian revolt against Colombia erupted in November 1903; Roosevelt sent an American warship to the scene "to keep order," which in fact meant frightening the Colombians away from reasserting control, and he recognized the new Republic of Panama within hours. The new government of Panama granted the United States virtual sovereignty over a Canal Zone, and construction soon started. The Panama Canal opened in 1914 and became a cornerstone of American diplomatic and naval strategy. Roosevelt stoutly disclaimed having connived with the Panamanians during the revolution, but a few years later he blurted out, "I took Panama."

In the Caribbean, Roosevelt instituted a policy of "protectorates" over various "unstable" republics, meaning republics whose finances or foreign affairs or politics were sufficiently shaky to threaten American investments or to invite European intervention.

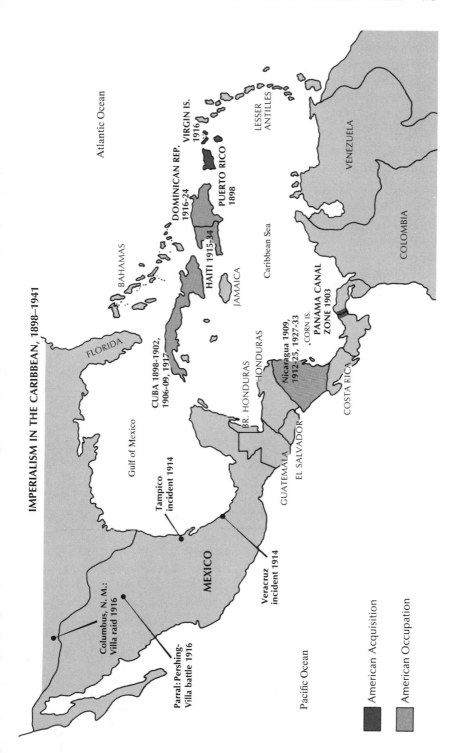

IMPERIALISM IN THE CARIBBEAN, 1898–1941

Atlantic Ocean

VENEZUELA

LESSER ANTILLES

VIRGIN IS. 1916

DOMINICAN REP. 1916–24

PUERTO RICO 1898

HAITI 1915–34

COLOMBIA

BAHAMAS

Caribbean Sea

JAMAICA

CUBA 1898–1902, 1906–09, 1917

FLORIDA

PANAMA CANAL ZONE 1903

CORN IS.

Nicaragua 1909, 1912–25, 1927–33

BR. HONDURAS

HONDURAS

COSTA RICA

Gulf of Mexico

Tampico incident 1914

GUATEMALA

EL SALVADOR

Veracruz incident 1914

MEXICO

Columbus, N. M.: Villa raid 1916

Parral: Pershing-Villa battle 1916

Pacific Ocean

American Acquisition

American Occupation

In 1904, he justified this policy on the "legal ground"—actually a unilateral American policy declaration—that it was the "duty" of a "civilized nation" to intervene in cases of "brutal wrongdoing, or an impotence which results in a general loosening of the ties of civilized society." This declaration, the "Roosevelt Corollary" or the "police-power corollary," was called an amendment to the 1823 Monroe Doctrine, but it was much more than that. Instead of waving European nations away from the area, the Roosevelt Corollary waved the United States in. It baldly assumed that the United States could decide which countries were "civilized" and which were not.

The pseudo-legal protectorate policy was followed not only by Roosevelt but also by Taft, Wilson, and later presidents until Franklin Roosevelt ended it in the thirties with his "Good Neighbor" policy. In the meantime, the United States kept troops in Cuba into 1902, sent them back from 1906 to 1909, and sent them in again in 1917 and again in 1922. These interventions were "legal," since the Cubans had been persuaded in 1901 to accept a treaty including the "Platt Amendment," which provided for United States control over Cuban foreign affairs and international debts, United States intervention to keep order, and a ninety-nine-year lease on Guantanamo Bay for a naval base. Cuba was an American "protectorate" from 1898 to 1934. Panama was a protectorate from 1903 to 1936; the Dominican Republic from 1905 to 1940 (as well as being in financial receivership to the United States from 1905 to 1941 and militarily occupied by the United States from 1916 to 1924); Nicaragua from 1911 to 1933 (with military occupations in 1909–10, 1912–25, 1926–33, and debt receivership in 1911–24); Haiti from 1915 to 1940 (with military occupation ending in 1934 and debt receivership in 1941). Not only were these republics "protected," militarily occupied, and financially controlled, but when such American activity ended, they normally fell under dictatorial regimes or military juntas. Roosevelt's policy looked advantageous in his own day. But it ultimately created such repressive governments in the name of stability that Castroism, by the late fifties, seemed logical and desirable to Cubans and to many other Central and South Americans.

Taft and Wilson continued Roosevelt's protectorate policy with little change. The only major novelty in Latin American relations was the responses of their administrations to revolution in Mexico from 1911 to 1917. Mexico had been governed since the 1870s by the dictatorship of Porfirio Díaz, and the United States had supported the Díaz regime until it was overthrown in 1911. Three Mexican governments then succeeded each other in a little over three years. The United States attempted to come to terms with each, but in ways that meant substantial American involvement in internal Mexican affairs—something each Mexican government naturally resented. American policy was tugged toward full-scale military and naval intervention in Mexico, especially by oil and railroad companies that had substantial Mexican properties and therefore felt threatened by the internal instability prevailing there. Mexico was in fact in a state of civil war through those years. Taft, and then Wilson, successfully resisted such business pressures, as well as pressures from many American Catholics who were outraged at the anticlerical activities of the revolutionaries.

Wilson developed a diplomatic doctrine of "constitutional legitimacy" as a requirement for diplomatic recognition of any Mexican government. This policy was moral and democratic in progressive terms; it demanded that a legitimate government had to have reached power by constitutional means rather than by force. But even so, it was a policy that necessarily involved Wilson in internal Mexican politics. The president soon found himself mixed in arms embargoes, recognition problems, secret missions, and disagreements with other powers (such as Britain) concerned about Mexico. Twice the policy almost resulted in war between Mexico and the United States. The first episode occurred in 1914, when American forces occupied Vera Cruz, killing 126 Mexicans, after Mexican authorities failed to apologize profusely enough, according to Wilson's thinking, for the momentary seizure of a United States Navy ship at Tampico. The second crisis came in 1916 and early 1917 after Pancho Villa, the leader of one of the contending factions in Mexico, stopped a train and later rode through a town in New Mexico, killing thirty-six *Yanquis* in the two raids. Wilson then sent a United States Army "Punitive Expedition," under General John J. Pershing, into northern Mexico. Pershing chased Villa for 300 miles without catching him. Mexican-American relations might have deteriorated further had not the problem of entry into the World War intervened. The key to a tranquil Latin-American policy had eluded the United States again. Moralistic constitutionalism in regard to Mexico, and the protectorate policy elsewhere, revealed the heavy-handedness of the "Colossus of the North." If Central

America and the Caribbean were America's area of "paramount interest," the United States was more than ever, for the people of those countries, their area of paramount resentment.

Asia, the Pacific, and the "Open Door"

In East Asia and the western Pacific, American policy also mixed moralism, commercial interest, and power politics. Americans had traditionally been intrigued with Japan and China as possible markets for American goods, and although Asia never absorbed more than a tiny fraction of American foreign trade, the idea persisted that the United States ought to do what it diplomatically could to protect an "open door" to Asian commerce. The "Open Door" idea was formalized just before Theodore Roosevelt became president. Secretary of State Hay asked the great powers concerned with China—they were Britain, France, Germany, and Russia—to agree that the "territorial integrity" of China ought to be preserved, or in other words that those powers would refrain from carving colonies or tightly-held spheres of influence out of the flabby Chinese Empire. The powers were also asked to adhere to the "open door" for trade. None of the governments committed themselves positively to the American idea, but the United States announced its adherence to the "open door," and Britain acquiesced. British and American aims in East Asia were nearly parallel, and this fact was recognized, especially after Roosevelt occupied the White House. Both countries wanted an open door for commerce, and both wanted diplomatic stability in China. Previous presidents had worried less about Asia, but Roosevelt was the first one who faced the need to govern and protect an American colony near the Asian continent. The man who had been instrumental in Commodore Dewey's fateful voyage to Manila in 1898 soon began to regard the Philippines as an albatross, a "heel of Achilles," because they made it impossible for the United States to ignore any longer what happened on the other side of the vast Pacific.

Before 1904, the great powers interested in East Asia had arrived at a reasonably stable balance there. American and British interests were running parallel. Britain had allied herself to Japan in a treaty of 1902. The French and the British were arriving at an "entente cordiale" uniting them loosely in European affairs and also in Asia. The potential troublemakers, Germany and Russia, were sufficiently checked by the opposing combination of powers to refrain from invading China's "territorial integrity." But the region was too attractive a power vacuum, and in 1904, Japan and Russia went to war over the issue of which would control the rich, semi-autonomous Chinese province of Manchuria. The Japanese, to the great amazement of Europeans and Asians alike, brought the Russian bear to his knees. For the first time, an Asian power had defeated a European one. But the cost to Japan was exhausting.

Theodore Roosevelt intervened to end the war, bringing Japanese and Russian diplomats together at a peace conference in Portsmouth, New Hampshire. The peace treaty, signed in September, 1905, restored Manchuria to China and carefully set out the rights of Russia and Japan in Manchuria. Japan was awarded suzerainty over Korea. The treaty did not award the Japanese a sought-for cash indemnity from Russia, a defect that, despite Roosevelt's real success as a mediator (which brought him the Nobel Prize for peace in 1906) earned him and the United States considerable resentment in Japan. Resentment was magnified in 1907 when Japanese immigration to the United States was cut off by "Gentlemen's Agreement."

Japan thus replaced Russia as the long-run threat to stability in East Asia, and hence to the Philippines. The trend of diplomacy in subsequent years was toward granting Japan more and more rights on the Asian mainland, especially in Korea and Manchuria, in return for Japanese recognition of the commercial "open door" in China and American control of the Philippines. Diplomatic swaps along these lines began with the Taft-Katsura memorandum of 1905 and continued in the Root-Takahira agreement of 1908. The balance of power was threatened in 1915 when the Japanese sought a vast extension of power with their "Twenty-One Demands" on China, but relations were somewhat restored in 1917 by the Lansing-Ishii agreement, which was favorable to Japan. Finally the United States recognized Japan's paramount naval strength in the western Pacific at the Washington Naval Conference of 1921–22. Ultimately, none of these negotiated expansions of Japanese power

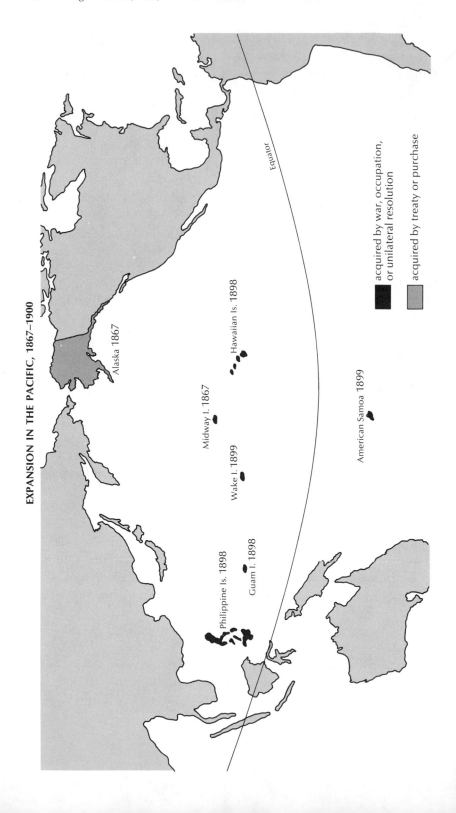

EXPANSION IN THE PACIFIC, 1867–1900

Alaska 1867

Midway I. 1867

Hawaiian Is. 1898

Wake I. 1899

American Samoa 1899

Philippine Is. 1898

Guam I. 1898

Equator

■ acquired by war, occupation, or unilateral resolution

▨ acquired by treaty or purchase

in Asia successfully maintained the power balance. In 1931 Japan invaded Manchuria, over protests from Secretary of State Henry Stimson that the Open Door was slamming shut, and once again American and Japanese policies regarding China were in direct conflict.

The main lines of American diplomatic policy both in the Americas and in Asia, as laid down by Theodore Roosevelt, were not changed by Taft or Wilson or their successors in the twenties. Under Taft, the quest for the Open Door in China and "paramount interest" in South America was undertaken with more blatant regard for American financial interests. Such "dollar diplomacy" involved, for example, the government's backing of a consortium of bankers who intended to build a major railway in Manchuria, under American control. The consortium's plan conflicted directly with Japanese interests, and American-Japanese relations worsened again. The Wilson administration, with William Jennings Bryan as Secretary of State, withdrew support from the consortium. Bryan and Wilson also pursued idealism in diplomacy by apologizing to Colombia for American interference in Panama a few years earlier and by paying $25 million to Colombia as indemnity. In addition, Bryan vigorously sought to build a structure for world peace by negotiating two dozen treaties of arbitration with other nations. But in the summer of 1914 peace disappeared beneath the quicksands of world war, and Wilson's idealistic diplomacy, after nearly three more years of thrashing to avoid the mire, also sank beneath it.

The United States in World War I

Europe was seldom a direct concern of American diplomats between 1900 and 1914. Except for a few forays by Theodore Roosevelt to help preserve the European power balance, the United States followed its traditional policy of isolation from European affairs. Roosevelt's major involvement in European affairs had been the Portsmouth Conference in 1905, which ended the Russo-Japanese War, and a conference at Algeciras in Spain in 1906 to mediate a dispute between France and Germany over naval rights in Morocco.

However, the European power balance collapsed in 1914, and the reverberations were so vast that the United States could not avoid involvement. Since the late nineteenth century, two opposing groups of great powers had gradually taken shape. The German Empire was linked with the Austro-Hungarian Empire and later with the Ottoman Empire to the south as the Central Powers. Counterbalancing them, France and the Russian Empire were joined by treaty, and Britain and France were associated by the less formal Entente Cordiale; this group came to be called the Allies. Italy, supposedly one of the Central Powers since 1882, signed a secret treaty with the Allies in 1915 and fought with them.

On June 28, 1914, a group of young Serbian conspirators assassinated the crown prince of Austria-Hungary, Franz Ferdinand, as he visited the town of Sarajevo in Bosnia-Herzegovina, part of the Austrian Empire. Austria, after securing the support of Germany, sent an ultimatum to Serbia amounting to an unacceptable infringement of sovereignty. The Serbs refused and called upon their fellow Slavs, the Russians, for support. The great powers looked down each other's cannon barrels. Within five weeks after the assassination, the massive European treaty system, laboriously constructed to keep the peace by making it unprofitable for any single power to make war on any other, made peace impossible. By early August, the two massive coalitions had declared war on each other. Germany struck eastward against Russia with tremendous effect, ultimately knocking Russia out of the war and so weakening the Czar's government that it was overthrown in the Russian revolutions of 1917. Moving westward with equal vigor in August, 1914, the Germans plunged into France and nearly captured Paris. A combined British and French army stopped them at the Marne River in September, and the German advance ended. But the Battle of the Marne ushered in a phase of indecisive and murderous trench warfare that characterized the western front for four more years. All of the combatant powers gradually exhausted themselves in a war that no government or people had demanded, and whose aims on either side were undefined. Germany, however, drained herself at a slightly faster rate than the Allies did, and rested her chances more and more on a novel and effective weapon against her island enemy, Britain: the submarine. In so doing, the Germans brought the United States into the war against them.

At the beginning of the war, Wilson formally proclaimed American neutrality and told the country that "the United States must be neutral in fact as well as in name. . . . We must be impartial in thought as well as in action. . . ." For two and a half years, neutrality was the government's avowed policy. But it was not in all respects the public fact. Americans as private citizens lent $2.3 billion to the Allies, which was almost a thousand dollars for every dollar they lent the Central Powers. The British and the Germans each attempted to prevent neutrals, including the United States, from shipping goods to their enemy. But the British and German methods of enforcing their policies against neutral shipping differed. Britain, with a powerful surface fleet, sequestered neutral vessels and impounded cargoes in port; by such actions, she violated neutral property rights. Germany's enforcement device was the submarine, which halted ships by the more conclusive means of blowing them out of the water. Submarines were not armed for surface combat or for leading neutral ships into German ports, nor did they have the space to carry rescued passengers or crews from torpedoed vessels. British curbs on American shipping involved loss of property, which might later be repaid; German curbs also involved loss of life, which could not be repaid. This difference was a solid reason for the much more vigorous American reaction to German anti-shipping measures than to British ones.

Several sinkings occurred in the Atlantic in early 1915. The most shocking came in May when a German U-boat sank the British liner *Lusitania*, killing 1,198. Of those, 128 were Americans. The German Embassy in the United States had run advertisements in the New York papers warning Americans that the *Lusitania* was fair game, and in fact the liner carried munitions as well as passengers. She was a legitimate target. But the United States government protested the sinking so vehemently that Secretary of State Bryan resigned from the cabinet rather than associate himself with a diplomatic protest that he believed would probably lead to war.

The Germans responded surprisingly to the *Lusitania* notes from Wilson: they pledged to cease unrestricted submarine warfare against passenger ships. The Germans could hardly be expected to stop using their best weapon indefinitely, but that was what Wilson was asking. Submarine warfare was not covered by international law. The law required a naval vessel to give warning before sinking enemy merchant or passenger ships, a rule that worked for surface vessels, but not for lightly-armed submarines. The U-boat was in mortal danger if it surfaced, either from escort vessels or from merchant ships themselves, since the British placed concealed guns on many of them. Wilson, however, felt impelled to treat the U-boat according to established law—that is, like a surface vessel.

Germany honored her pledge against unrestricted use of the U-boats through 1916. Wilson and the American government made several attempts from the time of the *Lusitania* sinking until then to bring about an armistice between the Allies and the Central Powers, but could work out no formula which was acceptable to both sides. The last peace-making effort failed in December, 1916. By then the enormous maw of the European war had consumed millions of lives. The German military high command convinced the Emperor that the only route to German victory was to suffocate Britain by a renewal of submarine warfare without restriction, sinking any ship, neutral or Allied, in the eastern Atlantic. They recognized that this would very likely trigger American entry on the Allied side, but they were willing to gamble that Britain would have to sue for peace before American force could be brought to bear effectively on the western front.

On January 22, 1917, Wilson spoke before the Senate about the war. He called for a negotiated settlement, an acceptance of "peace without victory" by both sides. But German policy was already set along opposite lines. On January 31, Germany announced that unrestricted U-boat warfare would resume the next day. On February 3, the United States broke diplomatic relations with Germany. Wilson still hoped for peace and an avoidance of American involvement, but three events in the following few weeks made American entry virtually certain. First, the Associated Press published the text of a note from the German Foreign Minister, Alfred Zimmermann, to the Mexican government. The Zimmermann note stated that if war broke out between Germany and the United States, and if Mexico assisted Germany, Mexico would regain the territory in the southwestern United States that she had lost in the Mexican War. The Zimmermann note infuriated many Americans, especially in the Southwest. The second event that removed the hesitation about entering into the war among important segments of the public was the overthrow of the Czar in mid-March. It had been difficult to

Pancho Villa (front and center) and aides. Wilson's and Pershing's preoccupation with Villa dwindled after the renewal of unrestricted submarine warfare by Germany early in 1917. (Culver Pictures, Inc.)

portray the Allied war effort as a struggle of democracy against despotism as long as Russia had the most autocratic government in Europe. The first Russian Revolution, replacing Czarist autocracy with a liberal parliamentary regime (which was itself overthrown seven months later by Lenin and the Bolsheviks), allowed many Americans to regard the Allies' war as a "clean" war, fought for democratic, moral ideals. The third event pushing the United States to the brink was the sinking of three American merchant ships by U-boats on March 18.

On April 2, speaking to Congress, Wilson denounced the U-boat campaign and asked for a declaration of war upon Germany; "the world," said the president, "must be made safe for democracy." Congress declared war on April 6. Fifty congressmen voted against the declaration, and pockets of pacifism remained scattered through the population. But a bellicose emotional commitment captivated the majority. American troops began arriving in France under General Pershing in late 1917 and made their presence felt far earlier than the Germans expected. The incredible carnage continued; the Germans made their last grand effort in the summer of 1918, and in the Somme offensive alone, 600,000 men died to move the battle line seven miles. The United States under Wilson's leadership might have stayed out of the "European civil war," as Dean Acheson called it years later. But after the events of February and March, Wilson, to do so, would have had to renounce the principle of freedom of the seas and the antisubmarine policy of two years. This, with majority support, he refused to do.

About 2 million American troops served in France during the war, and 53,000 died in battle. The American contribution was small in percentage terms—among all of the countries, Allied and Central Powers combined, that took part in World War I, 65 million men bore arms and 10 million were killed. But the effects on American government and society were great. The powerful economic upsurge between 1917 and 1920 has already been described. Centralization of governmental functions took place to a degree that would have been impossible twenty years earlier. The Wilson administration created a remarkably comprehensive set of agencies and regulations to mobilize all sections of the economy for the war effort. A War Industries Board, eventually headed by Bernard Baruch, mobilized industrial production and allocated priorities of materials for manufacturing. The Food Administration and the Fuel Administration coordinated agriculture and mining and the distribution of crops and coal. The Railway Administration in effect nationalized the railroads for the duration. The National War Labor Board arbitrated labor disputes and enforced a union pledge not to strike while the war was on. Treasury agencies hawked "Liberty Bonds" to raise money for the government. Wilson fully exploited the constitutional power of the president in wartime, and while the fighting went on, the government was practically a "Wilson dictatorship." But the mobilization measures were highly efficient by mid-1918, and surprisingly successful in centralizing the productive and distributive capacities of the country.

Withdrawal: America Spurns the League of Nations

As World War I drew to a close, Wilson became increasingly dedicated to the idea of a League of Nations to keep the peace that was soon to arrive. He had talked of a league since the spring of 1916, and in January, 1918, he presented Congress with a set of fourteen objectives that he considered the basis for a peace settlement. Several of these "Fourteen Points" were general principles about the conduct of international relations, such as freedom of the seas, impartial adjustment of colonial claims, and no more secret treaties. Others dealt specifically with parcels of European territory according to the principle that the national groups occupying them should be free to determine their own governments; these points led later to the formation of several independent "successor states"—Poland, Hungary, Czechoslovakia, Yugoslavia, and others—out of the ruins of the Czarist, Austro-Hungarian, and Ottoman empires. The fourteenth of Wilson's points was that "a general association of nations must be formed . . . for the purpose of affording mutual guarantees of political independence and territorial integrity to great and small states alike."

The response of other Allied leaders to the Fourteen Points was cool; Wilson's plans by no means meshed with everybody else's national goals and interests. By November, the Allied governments accepted the Fourteen Points as a basis for peace negotiations only under the pressure of an American threat to make a separate peace with Germany. During 1918, Wilson's dreams about the postwar world were also beginning to run into trouble at home. Indeed, from the fall of 1918 on, Wilson bewilderingly mixed idealistic efforts with political blunders. First he appealed to the public to elect a Democratic Congress in 1918 to support his war aims. Despite the fact that the Democratic congressional majorities elected in 1916 were not massive and that off-year elections normally reduced the strength of the party in power, Wilson tied his peace program to partisanship. The voters responded with a Republican victory—a small one, but enough to give control of Congress to the G.O.P. and to place a Massachusetts Republican, Henry Cabot Lodge, in the chair of the Senate Foreign Relations Committee, which would pass on a peace treaty in the first instance. Then, shortly after the November 11 armistice, Wilson announced that he would personally attend the peace conference in Paris. This move, marking the first time that an incumbent president had traveled outside the United States, was generally applauded in the United States and was overwhelmingly approved by the mass of Europeans. But he blundered again in naming not one prominent Republican to the American delegation to the Paris conference, despite the fact that he would need Republican votes to bring a peace treaty through the Senate.

After several weeks of negotiating at Paris, Wilson returned home in February, 1919, to discuss progress on the treaty with leading members of Congress. On March 4, just before Wilson left again for Paris, Senator Lodge secured a document called the "Round Robin" from thirty-nine of the Senators who would vote on the treaty; this group, many more than were needed to defeat ratification, would not approve the treaty as it was proposed. For several more months Wilson proceeded with tough negotiations with Britain's David Lloyd George, France's Georges Clemenceau, and Italy's Vittorio Orlando. Many of the Fourteen Points had to be modified to suit the national aims of the other Allies and the French passion for security against a resurgent Germany. Wilson agreed to these modifications while securing his overriding objective: acceptance of the League of Nations concept, and the imbedding of the charter of the League in the peace treaty, as its first section.

Wilson brought the treaty home in July. Two-thirds of the state legislatures and the state governors had declared their support of the League, and more than two-thirds of the Senate were willing to approve it—with some modifications. Senator Lodge adopted stalling tactics to allow public support to cool. The president began a whistle-stop tour around the country to mobilize popular support for passage. The public response was hugely favorable. But Wilson's health, precarious enough after the ordeal of the peace conference, broke in late September at Pueblo, Colorado, after he had given over three dozen speeches. He returned directly to Washington, and on October 2 suffered a stroke which partially paralyzed and nearly killed him.

Senator Lodge reported the treaty to the full Senate in early November with a series of reservations which stressed that the treaty and the League did not mean any impairment of American sovereignty and did not commit any American forces to keep the peace anywhere, unless Congress specifically approved. The treaty, with these reservations, would probably have commanded enough Democratic and Republican votes to assure passage. But Wilson, gravely ill and isolated in a sickroom, notified Senate Democrats that the reservations were unacceptable. Nearly all of the Senate Democrats then voted with the dozen or so Republican "irreconcilables"— those, including Robert La Follette and the California progressive Hiram Johnson, who refused to approve the League in any form— and the treaty was defeated on November 19. Public opinion would not let the League die; the Senate reconsidered the treaty late the next winter. But again, on March 19, 1920, the combination of Republican irreconcilables and Democrats who went along with Wilson's stubborn refusal to accept reservations killed the treaty for a second and final time. Had Wilson agreed to certain changes that surely would not have crippled the treaty, enough "reservationists" probably would have voted for the treaty to have allowed its approval. Senator Lodge became famous as the man who killed the treaty, Wilson as the man who forced it to the gallows because he would not compromise.

The Republican Era's Last Decade

When the Senate defeated the peace treaty and the League of Nations for the second time, the recluse President Wilson proclaimed that the 1920 election would be a "great and solemn referendum" on the question of American entry into the League. It was not to be. Despite the desires of many old progressives, Republican and Democratic alike, the mood of the electorate by late 1920 was no longer flushed with Wilsonian idealism. The bitter strikes of 1919 were over; the fear of anarchists and radicals and Bolsheviks were being satisfied by the Palmer raids; and the economy continued to roll on prodigiously. The desire to change the world in the progressive image waned; instead, the majority sought what the 1920 Republican presidential candidate, Warren G. Harding, called "normalcy." In 1920 and subsequent elections through the decade, "normalcy" meant continued prosperity, conformity to "New Era" business values, and, in foreign affairs, non-involvement in the rest of the world except in the area of expanded commerce. The Republican dominance of elections that began with McKinley and lasted until the Bull Moose split with the Old Guard in 1912 reasserted itself. Republican presidential candidates won easily in 1920, 1924, and 1928; in each congressional election from 1918 through 1928 the Republicans also captured both houses.

Progressivism lingered on, especially among midwestern Republicans who sought protective measures for their agrarian constituents and among the remnant of the New-Nationalist Republicans who continued to advocate expanded federal regulation. The farm bloc in the Senate secured the passage of some legislation helpful to farmers. But the chief aim of the bloc, which was the enactment of laws to protect farmers from low world prices just as tariffs protected manufacturers, failed with President Coolidge's vetoes of the McNary-Haugen bill. Regulatory-minded Republicans also gained some successes, notably in extending commission powers over railroads and other common carriers, especially in the Railway Labor Act of 1926. Other attempts by Republicans to extend progressive principles, such as the fight by Nebraska's Senator George Norris to save for federal development the government's large dam and nitrate plants at Muscle Shoals on the Tennessee River, succeeded only in drawing attention to the need for conservation; but they failed to bring it about.

Progressive efforts, particularly for more roads and schools, continued in the states and cities as well as in Washington, and government expenditure (federal, state, and local) throughout the country was substantially higher in the twenties than before the war. But the mood had changed, innovation was rare compared to the Roosevelt-Wilson days, and the politics of the Harding and Coolidge administrations are remembered far less for further reform than for a few laws much more generous to business, especially big business, than those of the prewar years. While Harding was president, the Republicans reverted to their traditional policy of high tariff protection by passing the Fordney-McCumber Act of 1922—at a time when war-poor European countries needed desperately to sell goods to the United States, not only to revivify their internal economies but also to raise cash to pay war debts and reparations demanded by the victors. Harding appointed several corrupt or incompetent subordinates, who proceeded to give away or sell for private gain some of the richest publicly-owned mineral lands. The resulting Teapot Dome scandal gained Harding's administration the reputation of being the most corrupt since Grant's.

President Calvin Coolidge, Mrs. Coolidge, and friend. (Brown Brothers)

When Harding died in 1923, he was succeeded by the dour vice-president, Calvin Coolidge, who won his place on the Republican ticket in 1920 because of his notoriety for helping break a policemen's strike in Boston the year before. If achievement of purpose is a measure of presidential greatness, Coolidge must be ranked high; he was dedicated to inactivity and achieved it almost totally. Coolidge vetoed the McNary-Haugen bills and the Norris Muscle Shoals bill, but approved tax cuts for the wealthy and the far-reaching restriction bill which ended the era of mass immigration.

Coolidge won handily in 1924, despite the fresh memory of the Teapot Dome scandal under his hapless predecessor. But the Democrats, who nominated a constitutional lawyer from West Virginia named John W. Davis, were crippled by a disastrous nominating convention, where Davis won on the 104th ballot after the party completely rent and spent itself arguing the merits of William G. McAdoo, Wilson's son-in-law and former Treasury Secretary, and Governor Alfred E. Smith of New York. McAdoo was "dry" and, though he repudiated it, had Klan support; Smith was "wringing wet" and a Catholic from New York City. The familiar story of a Democratic coalition whose groups were too disparate to hold together was repeated. The one interesting if forlorn element of the 1924 campaign was the candidacy of Senator Robert M. La Follette on a Progressive ticket. La Follette's program was indeed progressive, much like the one he probably would have advanced in 1912 if Roosevelt had not outdistanced him. It called for an end to monopolies, reduction of taxes and the tariff, protection for farmers and industrial workers, recall of judicial decisions, and a less mercenary foreign policy. But 1912 progressivism did not work in 1924, and La Follette received less than a third as many votes as Coolidge and 3 million fewer than the faceless Davis, the worst-beaten Democratic presidential candidate in history.

In 1928 Coolidge announced laconically, "I do not choose to run." The Republicans, however, were not displeased. Available to them was perhaps their most attractive candidate since Theodore Roosevelt, a self-made man, an Iowan who understood metropolitan life, a committed Republican who bore a nonpartisan image, a proven administrator in war relief work, and an extremely effective Secretary of Commerce, a man both businessmen and the rest of the people could trust: Herbert Hoover. Four years later, and for two decades thereafter, this paragon had become one of the most maligned men in American political history. The Democrats, still divided over prohibition and the Klan, faced the rural-urban split that the Smith-McAdoo fight in 1924 had revealed. In 1928, however, the donnybrook of the previous convention overrode even these mutual fears, and Governor Smith's careful line-up of big-city support brought him the nomination on the first ballot.

Two forces for change, although they did not visibly help Smith in the campaign, began to emerge in 1928, and they were shortly to reverse the thirty-year Republican domination of American party politics. One was the young man who placed Smith in nomination at the convention and who was himself to be the next Governor of New York, Franklin Delano Roosevelt. The other was the growing Democratic voting strength in northern urban areas. Demography years before had provided the raw material for a Republican majority; now it was beginning to help the Democrats. Smith, as a Democratic governor of New York during a Republican decade, supervised the passage of a series of social-welfare and labor measures that went beyond the welfarism of the prewar progressive period. In so doing, he and the Democrats in New York and in other heavily urban states were beginning to reap a harvest of votes from the immigrant and labor groups that the Democratic party had tended to attract for a long time, but who were becoming more numerous as voters in the twenties. Roosevelt's leadership during the depression of the thirties was going to reconstitute and vastly strengthen the Democratic party's group coalition, but signs of change were already becoming visible in 1928.

Roaring through the Twenties

American thought and folkways changed drastically in the first thirty years of the new century, as technology, the apparently unending prosperity cycle, and the increasing complexity of social and economic organization impressed new realities and new hopes on the American people. The years from the late nineties to about 1912, the early progressive period, were years of naïve optimism, restlessness, and dissatisfaction with social ills—years full of the hope and belief that progress and enlightenment were around the corner but fearful that class revolution would wreck society unless reforms came soon. From about 1912 to World War I the tentative explorations of the previous decade blossomed into abstract art, naturalistic writing, social and political criticism, and tracts demanding reform. At the same time more people realized that reform was not easy, that society was not going to change overnight, that progress was not inevitable, and that evil and ignorance were not to be eradicated by goodwill and shouting. The harsh reality of the World War, the wave of repression and forced conformity that followed it, and the brief recession of 1921–22 were followed by the seven star-spangled years of the "roaring twenties." During these years, the intellectuals expressed disillusion, the masses were apathetic to progressivism and tried frantically to grasp a now-reachable hedonism, writers bitterly criticized society, and many businessmen and politicians sympathized with reform if it was of the pro-business kind.

Certain aspects of progressive reform did last into the twenties, but the idealism of prewar days had vanished. If the prewar years were the time of "the end of American innocence" and the "revolt against formalism," to borrow the phrases of the historians Henry F. May and Morton White, the twenties were indeed "the jazz age" and the "New Era." The middle and late twenties were years of vigorous, sometimes violent, activity, when people threw themselves at life with great outward zest but, if they were like the characters in F. Scott Fitzgerald's novels, with deep inward confusion and emptiness about life's purposes. Fads came and sometimes went; flivvers, flappers, and mahjongg had a brief popular glory, but the new game of contract bridge survived, perhaps helped by a Kansas City jury's acquittal in 1929 of a woman who had shot her husband dead after he made a bad bid. Freud had already arrived; as H. L. Mencken lamented in 1918, "Hard upon the heels of the initiative and referendum, the Gary system, paper-bag cookery, the Montessori method, *vers libre* and the music of Igor Feodorovitch Stravinsky, psychoanalysis now comes to intrigue and harass the sedentary multipara who seeks refuge in the women's clubs from the horrible joys of home life."

Tens of millions "had never had it so good": a numerical majority lived in cities, and the urban life-style, its pleasures often still morally suspect, nevertheless began to dominate. Cars, cheap and efficient, were within reach of the many beneficiaries of the suddenly higher wage and salary levels from 1917 on. Money-getting was easier, and more people practiced the ancient art crassly. Would-be tycoons speculated frenziedly in Florida lots in the middle of the decade, buying more than their share of swamp and alligators. The stock market beckoned to the many who had a few extra hundred and thought they could gamble it into thousands. In 1928 and 1929, many of them were not disappointed. Speculation—in real estate, in securities, in dubious business enterprises—became a national mania, captivating people whose new affluence overcame the late-nineteenth-century moral scruples they had been brought up with. The complacent, materialistic small-town businessman, with his big cigar, round straw hat, and saddle shoes, did exist outside of the pages of Sinclair Lewis' *Babbitt.* Strikes were fewer, immigration was being cut off, race violence was less common; evidently the revolution feared by so many prior to World War I was not going to happen. The pressure for reform was off. Free enterprise, New Era–style, and the acquisition of status and riches were the order of the day; Coolidge was clearly a man for the season.

A major legacy bequeathed by the progressive era to the twenties was prohibition. Many progressives had identified the saloon and the "liquor traffic" as a root cause of city squalor, immigrant problems, and poverty; in state after state, between the late nineteenth century and World War I, the sale of alcoholic beverages was either left to local option or prohibited outright. By early 1919, Congress had passed, and the states ratified, the Eighteenth Amendment to the Constitution, providing that "the manufacture, sale, or transportation of intoxicating liquors within, the importation thereof into, or the exportation thereof from the United States . . . for beverage purposes is hereby prohibited." To enforce the amendment, Congress passed the Volstead Act in 1919 by large enough majorities to overcome President Wilson's veto, and the United States began the fourteen-year-long moral experiment known as "prohibition." Through the twenties, it was well-enforced and welcome in many parts of the country, where the moralistic side of progressivism lingered in an amalgam with evangelistic religious attitudes. In other places, particularly in large cities, prohibition became an almost unenforceable laughing-stock. It spawned frolicsome "speakeasies," where men and—something new to saloon life—women guzzled high-priced liquor under the titillating threat of raids by

A scene from the Jazz Age: the St. Valentine's Day Massacre, Chicago, February, 1929, a businessmen's disagreement over prohibition franchises. (Brown Brothers)

Treasury agents. Bath-tub gin became a byword, and smuggling from Canada became reasonably efficient, like an underground railway in reverse.

When prohibition was over, Mencken, as usual, had the last word. "Prohibition went into effect," the Baltimore sage said, "on January 16, 1920, and blew up at last on December 5, 1933—an elapsed time of twelve years, ten months, and nineteen days. It seems almost a geological epoch while it was going on, and the human suffering it entailed must have been a fair match for the Black Death or the Thirty Years' War. . . . I was, so far as I have been able to discover, the first man south of the Mason and Dixon line to brew a drinkable home brew. . . . This home-brew, when drinkable at all, was a striking proof of the indomitable spirit of man, but in the average case it was not much more." But then, Mencken was, in the words of his occasional imbibing companion, the poet Edgar Lee Masters, "a great eater and drinker of beer"; when repeal finally came, Mencken for once was on the side of the majority. Even a very dry social worker saw some golden bubbles in the repeal; though the pre-1920 saloons were often "unspeakably filthy," he wrote, prohibition hurt the really determined drinker even more. "Pre-Volstead liquor relaxed its victims; the bootleg of (prohibition) years poisoned those who used it and tied them up in knots. My former alcoholic acquaintances used to visit me, and I would find them stiffened into a kind of rigor mortis. . . . Each of these poisoned drinkers . . . insisted on sharing his infallible method for making bad liquor safe and palatable, such as straining it through an eighteen-inch loaf of rye bread, mixing it with milk," etc. Prohibition was like the Black Death whether one observed it or flouted it.

A wholly unintended result of the great moral experiment was the marked expansion of big-time gangsterism. Before prohibition, the major popular diversions that were illegal as well as immoral were prostitution and gambling. Both of these, considered strictly as economic enterprises, functioned very well as independent, small businesses. The entrepreneurs who ran "sporting houses" or gambling dens, like the legitimate small businessman around the corner on Main Street, had a local clientele, uncomplicated sources of supply, and only the local police or sheriff, who could be more or less cooperative, to worry about. Police graft, the links between ward politicians like Chicago's Bath-house John Coughlin and Hinky-Dink Kenna and the neighborhood police station, the protection, for a price, of the "criminal element" in the red-light district were all deplored by progressives but operated with a sleazy efficiency.

When national prohibition added liquor to the list of illegal taboos, the economic organization of American crime changed drastically, in the direction of regional or national syndicates. The speakeasy operator could no more brew his own liquor or beer, transport it from brewery to bar in large lots, or provide the financial and strong-arm protection required, than a blacksmith could make a Model T in his back room or the corner dry-goods merchant compete with Sears, Roebuck. Organized crime became a big business in the twenties, a kind of oligopoly where various mobs worked the liquor racket in their own broad territories. The public followed newspaper reports of gang wars like Chicago's St. Valentine's Day Massacre and the emergence of Al Capone as top gangster as avidly as they had read about the empire-building of Morgan, Harriman, or Rockefeller a few years before.

A sharp and sudden change in popular standards of behavior for women came out of World War I and demarcated the twenties from the progressive period. Signs were apparent before 1917; the increased numbers of women on the job market, the agitation for "women's rights," especially the right to vote, and the talk about the "new woman" had preceded the war. But after the war, changes in standards of behavior were more marked. To take the example of hemlines, what was daring in women's fashions was measured by inches above the ankle before the war, inches above the knee during the twenties. Parents who were themselves raised according to the Victorian code of the eighties and nineties watched in shocked disbelief as their daughters smoked cigarettes in public, donned backless swim suits, and began to explore the sexual possibilities of the motor car. The "flapper," the liberated little girl who smoked, drank bootleg liquor, and danced all night, was much rarer in fact than in fiction, but her very prominence as a social type represented a sharp break with the social customs of prewar days.

As skirts went up, morals, apparently, went down. Changes occurred in sexual behavior, especially the sexual behavior of women. Sex was much more openly discussed—in books, plays, films, magazines—and it was also more often practiced. Judging by the memories of Kinsey's interviewees, probably no more than 20 percent of the women and 50 percent of the men indulged in premarital intercourse even after the "sexual revolution" of the World War I years and the twenties. If so, however, that meant a sharp break with earlier patterns. Sexual activity remained close to late nineteenth-century levels until about World War I. Then, in less than a decade, it became more common and quickly stabilized at a level where it remained for about three decades, if not longer. Consequently, in terms of sexual behavior, too, the years between 1912 and 1917 marked "the end of American innocence," or at least the innocence of many American females. The progressive reform spirit had brought about the gradual closing of houses of prostitution; the fabled Everleigh House in Chicago was shut down in 1911, and in 1918 the last segregated red light district in America, New Orleans' Storyville, was eliminated. But we will never know exactly how often the amateur replaced the professional after that.

In a society where large organizations and increasingly complex social patterns were ending rural isolation in so many ways, the popular belief in individuality expressed itself in hero-worship, but a worship of heroes of the ephemeral sort rather than the epochal. Lacking Lincolns and Grants, the public fastened upon Dempseys and Tunneys. Crowds poured into stadiums to see the New York Yankees win five pennants and three World Series in the twenties. Babe Ruth became a national hero in 1927 by being the first baseball player to hit sixty home runs during a single season. Eclipsing even Ruth that year, the young Charles A. Lindbergh thrilled the United States and Europe when he flew a single-engine plane by himself from New York to Paris nonstop. It was the Knute Rockne era in Notre Dame football, when the memory of the prematurely deceased George Gipp, a fullback of 1920, presumably inspired the "Four Horsemen" to unparalleled backfield pyrotechnics in the next four years, only to be upstaged in popular admiration by Illinois' Red Grange in 1925. As individualism struggled for expression while the assembly line and scientific management threatened to reduce workers to cogs in the industrial process, the public sought out movie stars like Rudolph Valentino or Greta Garbo, or tennis champions like Bill Tilden and Helen Wills, or Gertrude Ederle, the first woman to swim the English Channel (1926), or Bobby Jones, whose 1930 grand slam of the United States and British Open and Amateur golf tournaments remains unique.

The twenties were a complex decade, crass, delightful, dry, prosperous. From Mack Sennett comedies to gang wars, from joyriding in Model A's to Klan marches, they had insistent tragicomic overtones, even in the stock market crash of 1929. But there was nothing funny about the depression of the thirties.

The Depression in Times Square: lining up for free coffee and a sandwich distributed by a New York newspaper, 1932. (Wide World Photos)

7

THE GREAT DEPRESSION, 1929-1940

The roaring twenties lasted about seven years, from the end of the postwar recession of 1921–22 until the autumn of 1929. Then, in about half that time, from late 1929 through February, 1933, the roars receded to a rueful mumble. The unthinkable happened: the country sank into an economic depression that was as severe as the one of 1893–96, but which lasted more than twice as long as any previous depression in American history. This depression was especially shocking because of the widespread expectation that the intoxicating prosperity of the twenties would go on indefinitely.

However, in the retrospect of thirty years, the Great Depression of 1929–1940 seems almost like a temporary interruption in the long trend of economic expansion from 1897 to the present. Beginning with the price crash on the New York Stock Exchange in October, 1929, economic indicators tumbled downward until early 1933, when many of them were lower than they had been since the late 1890s. The depression went on until 1940, the economy gradually struggling upward. After 1940, prosperity and expansion became the rule in American economic life, sparked first by the heavy-industry and military demands of World War II and later by broadly-based general growth from 1945 to the present. In the long view of history, the expansive trend since 1940 continued that of 1897–1929. Such a trend was a marked change from the nineteenth-century pattern of a financial panic followed by a four- or five-year depression every twenty years or so, as in 1819, 1837, 1857, 1873, and 1893. The first three decades of this century thus brought an end to what many people regarded as a natural law of cyclical prosperity and panic. But after thirty-two years of apparently broadly-distributed economic growth, the great American business civilization extolled by presidents and publicists failed utterly to prevent its own collapse after 1929.

For those who lived through it, the Great Depression was no interlude in a seventy-five-year expansive trend. The depression of 1929–40 was memorable not only because of its economic characteristics but also because it seared many Americans psychologically for a generation. The belief, which seemed so justifiable in the twenties, that businessmen were best equipped to run their affairs without interference and that government should function as a handmaiden to business never again commanded popular assent. For almost thirty years after the depression, the majority of the electorate voted their confidence in the philosophy that the federal government should be an activist government, regulating concentrations of private economic power and guaranteeing the welfare of less fortunate economic and social groups. Many of the political issues of 1945–70, and the confidence of people in federal activism during those years, had their roots in the general path taken by the federal government in the thirties to combat the depression. And, in contrast to the progressive era and the twenties, the majority of voters preferred to elect Democrats, who appeared to have done something about ending the depression, rather than Republicans, who had apparently failed to prevent it from starting. In these and other ways, the consequence of the Great Depression lingered on long after it was over, almost to the 1970s, when well over half of the population was born late enough to have no memory of it.

The Depression Experience

The stereotypical images still existing of the Great Depression, like all stereotypes, contain some truth. Some stockbrokers and stockholders did fling themselves from skyscraper windows on Wall Street or La Salle Street when the stock market first crashed in October, 1929, and others did so later, up to late 1932 when investment markets sank to their lowest points. Lines of unemployed men and hungry children did stretch for blocks along city streets, twisting up to temporary soup kitchens, which doled out to them enough basic sustenance to keep them going another day. Hobos hopped freight trains from town to town, looking for a handout or some work. The *Survey Graphic* described that problem: "Hat in hand, a weird-looking creature gasps to a half-startled householder, 'Believe me, sir, three days in a boxcar in zero weather, without water, sleep or food would make anybody look like a thug, but give me three days of heat and food, a razor, soap and a bed, and I will look just what I am, a graduate of the University of Chicago.' " (Twenty to thirty years later, Chicagoans complained that students at that institution, though well-fed by then, looked just the same.)

But the problem was real: roughly 30 percent of the college graduates of 1933 could find no jobs, and many who did worked as elevator operators, file clerks, gas station attendants, waiters, or other "dead-end jobs." One, according to a magazine story, was selling beauty preparations in New York suburbs. He analyzed them in his college laboratory and found them "useless or worse"; this bothered his conscience. In five weeks he made between 40 cents and $2.20 per day, and his costs were 25 cents a night "for a flop," 50 cents for food and cigarettes, 25 cents for streetcars, barbers, and incidentals. "And on the good days you've got to put aside something for the bad ones." Some graduates, whose lifelong career hopes were dashed and who were removed from the "shelter" of the classroom, ended up as mental cases; and graduate school enrollments went up, since there was nothing else to do. Once-prosperous businessmen with fur-collared greatcoats and receding paunches did resort to selling lead pencils and apples on streetcorners, occasionally consoling themselves with a nickel beer in newly-opened post-prohibition bars while grumbling jukeboxes played "Pennies from Heaven." Great Plains farmers whose topsoil had been blown two or three states eastward by "Dustbowl" storms did trek westward in shuddering Model A's to earn their daily bread as migrant workers in California, like the Joads in John Steinbeck's *The Grapes of Wrath.*

But these stereotypes reflect the depression experience of the relatively few, the almost picturesque. The more common experience was more drab and dispiriting, compounded daily over several years. The two basic economic facts that soured the lives of many millions were stark and simple: unemployment and the inability to sell goods and services. The man, white or black, who had migrated to a city in the 1910s or 1920s seeking better opportunity, and had found it, lost his position in the 1930s when his factory stopped making steel or cars or canned food because people lacked the wherewithal to buy these products. This man, especially if his skills were limited or highly specialized, might look for years for another job. The man who had built up a retail business in a city or a small town, a business perhaps struggling in the 1900s, safe in the 1910s, mildly prosperous in the 1920s, could find himself unable to replace his inventory, to pay his creditors, or to retain his store or even his house when customers, who were no better off than he was, simply did not cross his threshold except to commiserate. The small farmer, not very prosperous even in the 1920s because of technological and market changes, was beset by the old banes of mortgage debt, low crop prices, inflexible costs, and, in the Midwest and Southeast, the worst farming weather of the century. At least the farmer could usually subsist on his own scrawny chickens and potatoes, which was one major reason why fewer people left the poverty-stricken countryside for cities during that decade than in any other in modern American history.

Many who did have city jobs worked under pitifully primitive conditions. For the female blue-collar worker, for example, conditions had improved hardly at all in thirty years. Early in 1933, Frances Perkins—shortly to become the first woman cabinet member, as Roosevelt's Secretary of Labor—wrote a magazine article about the garment industry. A $4.95 dress is indeed a bargain, Miss Perkins said, but the sweatshop girl, not the buyer, paid for it. She quoted a letter from a worker: "I am working in _____ at _____. We have to be in at 7 A.M. work to 12 then 1 to 5 o'clock. . . . They also refuse to tell you the prices. When you receive your slip you are mark [sic] $2.75 for five days and a half. Some received $1.78. Some $.95. You never see your working slip. . . . I hope you be able to help the working girls of this place." And these women were not the only exploited and underpaid workers in the economy of those days.

Of course not everyone lost his job, his store, or his farm during the depression. People still required professional services and the professionals provided them, even though many were paid in produce or services rather than in cash. The white-collar manager and the schoolteacher usually kept their jobs, though they often took pay cuts or started careers at invisibly low rates (schoolteachers, including principals and supervisors, averaged about $100 per month in 1934, physicians less than $250 per month in 1935). Government workers under civil service were sheltered from job loss. A few areas of the country were not hit nearly as hard as were mining, staple farming, and mass-manufacturing areas. A very few localities scarcely noticed the depression, except in a newspaper photo or an

The Depression in Boston: a Greek immigrant fed the unemployed in order to pay his "debt" for American citizenship. (Wide World Photos)

occasional hobo passing through, and a few people actually prospered during the thirties. Yet when President Franklin Roosevelt stated that one-third of the American population was below the poverty line in food, clothing, and shelter, he was not exaggerating the problem, and he was using a standard of poverty lower than that of the 1970s.

All but the blindest economic conservatives knew that Roosevelt spoke the truth. Gross national product and personal income did not reach 1929 levels again until late 1940. Even in 1941, 5.6 million people, then about 10 percent of the labor force, were still without jobs. Real-estate values, high in the booming twenties, plummeted as farm and town properties languished for buyers. As demand for property, either real estate or securities, evaporated, those unlucky enough to have a supply of it had to lower their price, and their invested capital dwindled in value. Banks that had lent money in the twenties, taking land mortgages or securities as collateral, were themselves in desperate straits when the demand for land and the securities dropped. A shocking part of the depression experience for millions of steady and sober citizens, who had not been caught up at all in the real estate and stock market speculative fever of the late twenties, was the appalling tendency of banks to collapse. Savings that had been set aside for a rainy day, in accord with traditional admonitions about thrift and the moral virtue attached to it, disappeared when the economic cloudburst tore the banks themselves away from their foundations.

The depression was not simply a baffling economic event, whose length and severity seemed to defy solution. It was psychologically traumatic as well, striking down the provident and the prodigal alike with grim impartiality. Reformers had been saying since the first days of mass industrialization in the late nineteenth century that economic forces were essentially unrelated to personal goodness and morality. But it was not until the Great Depression brought the lesson home in a widespread, inescapable manner that part of the American middle class began to realize that unemployment or loss of hard-earned property could strike anyone, that hard work did not necessarily get one ahead, that a penny saved was not necessarily a penny earned but easily could be a penny washed away with the rest of some crumbling bank. The same problems afflicted other people in the world—the depression was virtually worldwide—but misery was not relieved by company, and the amoral impact of economic disaster, hitting many Americans for the first time, was a shock.

The economic slide ended in 1933. An upturn began in that year and in 1934 that was closely tied to the reinvigoration of the federal government just then. Franklin Roosevelt, the dynamic Democratic president who took office in March, 1933, not only provided the country with administrative and legislative action aimed at relief, recovery, and reform in dozens of economic and social areas. He also provided a symbol of confidence even more inspiring and contagious than the confidence that his cousin Theodore sprayed forth from the White House early in the progressive period. Franklin Roosevelt's "New Deal" did not solve the depression; the country was still groping its way out in 1940, two years after the last significant New Deal law was enacted. But some of the New Deal changes breathed life back into certain prostrate sectors, especially banking; some of them restored to people a measure of personal dignity and security, such as laws protecting bank deposits, insuring the right of industrial workers to organize and bargain collectively, and providing, through social security, the right to a decent old age. And Roosevelt's governmental activism itself helped restore the faith of masses of people in the country and its leadership.

Recovery began very slowly in the latter part of 1933, gaining some momentum until a real measure of improvement took place by early 1937. Then, for several reasons—a temporary drop in Roosevelt's personal popularity, because of political mistakes; a premature tightening of credit by the Federal Reserve; reduced federal spending; and the fact that some economic sectors were still too shaky to sustain recovery—the economy fell into a recession amidst the general depression. A new Buick straight-eight, F.O.B. Flint, cost only $765, and the biggest Packard 12-cylinder limousine only $3,420; but too few people had that kind of money. The slump of 1937–38, sometimes dubbed the "Roosevelt Recession," pulled the major indicators down again. But they never dipped to the disastrous levels of 1932 or 1933. A chastened but still hopeful economy began once more to climb the steep hill to recovery. By 1940, despite unemployment continuing at two and a half times the "normal" level, the end of the depression was definitely in sight.

Whether the depression was permanently at an end or only lying in wait for a repetition of the 1937–38 recession can never be known. At that point the brutal force of World War II intervened to wrench the economy toward prosperity levels with a momentum that has slackened only briefly and has never been lost, except for a few minor setbacks.

1929–1932: The Market Crash and the Slide into Depression

The debacle started in 1929. In October of that year, the get-rich-quick dreams of millions of people caught up in speculative fever were shattered as prices of securities plummeted on the New York Stock Exchange and other exchanges. Many people in the middle and late twenties had, or thought they had, more money than they needed for survival, for the first time in their lives. They could meet payments on their new Chevrolets or Model A's, careen around the country on the new network of paved highways, hearken to "New Era" propaganda, and hope to get in on the apparently effortless profits to be made in the rising securities markets. In 1925 and 1926 the hottest speculative item was Florida real estate. By 1928 and 1929, stocks and bonds were apparently an even better speculation. It took no great amount of cash to buy in; a few hundred dollars or less could put a man on the golden road of stock ownership.

Most of the price of a stock could be borrowed from a friendly broker, or even a bank, with the expectation that the rest of the price would easily be paid back from the rising value of the stock. The buyer only had to make a down payment, or "margin," of perhaps 10 percent, and his broker loaned him the rest. The only flaw in this happy arrangement was the possibility that the stock price might fall, rather than rise, whereupon the broker might call in his loan, require more margin from the buyer, and force him to scramble for cash—by selling off other stocks at the going price, mortgaging other assets, or in the worst of circumstances allowing his car to be repossessed. But through most of 1928 and 1929 prices were not falling; they were rising rapidly.

The securities markets in those days were normally quiet during the summer months, but 1929 was an exception. Stock prices kept going up through the summer and peaked on September 3, the day after Labor Day, when the then massive volume of 4.5 million shares were traded on the New York Stock Exchange. The *New York Times* index of industrials had risen more than 100 points over the summer. Margin buyers continued to come into the market, and the interest rate on brokers' loans climbed. Much of the buying was in the stock of investment trusts, as it had been throughout the bull market of the late twenties; these were stock-issuing companies whose assets were not physical properties but the stock of other companies, even other investment trusts, plus the presumed expertise of the managers of the investment trust who were supposedly able to pick high-profit securities for their company and its stockholders to own. On a rising market, the stock of an investment trust was extremely attractive because it skimmed the cream of fast-rising securities, and its price rose faster than the price of stocks of companies with solid physical assets. But if the market fell, the stock of the investment trust fell still faster. People who bought investment trust stock on small margin, with large broker's loans at high interest, were taking a high-risk gamble, the results of which would be either splendid or disastrous.

Through September and into October, the markets ceased to rise as they had over the summer. The collapse of a speculative company in England, the forbidding by the government of Massachusetts of another company's stock split, and a few scattered warnings from financial commentators apparently began to worry speculators. Confidence waned as the weeks went by and the bull market stabilized. In late October the markets weakened. On Thursday, October 24, 12.9 million shares changed hands on the New York Stock Exchange, and prices plunged. When that happened, brokers had to call loans to low-margin buyers, who were then forced into selling more and more assets to meet these loans. As they sold, more stock was thrown on the market, and prices dropped further; more low-margin speculators reached their margin limit and were forced to sell, speeding the downward cycle. So many transactions occurred so fast that the ticker-tape lagged over an hour behind, and by early afternoon speculators did not even know at what price they were being forced to sell. This chaos stopped late in the day, when a syndicate of the largest New York banks intervened in the market to buy millions of dollars' worth of key stocks in an attempt to stabilize the market.

The intervention restored confidence, and the markets closed on a firm note. On Friday and Saturday price levels held up reasonably well. Intervention by the big Wall Street banks was a tried-and-true stabilizing device, and it had worked successfully to put a stop to the Panic of 1907. But in October 1929 the banks were not as strong, and they were overwhelmed. Too many speculators, individual or corporate, were pushed to the wall too quickly, and over the weekend many discovered or decided that they had to sell. The market dropped on Monday, and then on Tuesday, October 29, came disaster. Over 16 million shares were traded on the New York Stock Exchange; the *New York Times* index dropped about forty points. The ticker tape fell far behind again, and this time the overwhelmed bankers' syndicate did not intervene. "Black Tuesday" was the worst day of the panic, but prices slid further downward to a low point in 1929 on November 13. On that day the *New York Times* index of leading stocks was 164; in mid-September it had been 312.

In the closing weeks of 1929, and for the first three months of 1930, the securities markets regained some of their lost ground. Popular magazines worried about rising unemployment, but there was no widespread talk of any depression. The country hoped that prosperity would survive, and newspapers pointed out correctly that the inflated securities markets did not reflect the solid strengths of the economy. After all, they said, stock panics had occurred in 1907 and other times without touching off a general depression. But the hope of recovery waned when the stock markets and other economic indicators continued to drop through 1930. Substantial numbers of banks failed, as loan collateral, in the form of securities and real estate, dwindled in value. The economies of European nations had never regained stability after World War I, and in 1931, several major European banks collapsed and Britain was forced off her sacred gold standard. The crisis of confidence over the disappearance of European investments further depressed the American economy. By 1932 the United States was in a full-scale depression.

By the beginning of 1933, goods would not sell, commodity and stock prices touched unremembered lows, bank failures multiplied, and the money and credit system of the United States threatened to grind to a complete halt. Almost every economic indicator showed a steady downward plunge from the heights of early 1929 to the deepest point of the depression in the winter of 1932–33. One and a half million people, or about 3 percent of the labor force, were out of work in 1929; the number rose over the next four years to 4 million, 8 million, 12 million, and to nearly 13 million in 1933, officially 24 percent of the labor force. The unofficial and real unemployment figure was probably closer to 33 percent. The average weekly earnings of factory workers, about $25 in 1929, fell to $17 in 1932, and total factory payrolls fell by more than a half, from $10.9 billion in 1929 to $6.7 billion in 1931 to $4.9 billion in 1933. An economy increasingly focused in the twenties on consumer durables, especially automobiles, rotted at the center, as the value of the output of consumer durables fell from $6.3 billion in 1929 to less than a third of that figure, $2.05 billion, in 1932, and installment debt for cars plunged from $1.38 billion at the end of 1929 to $356 million, about one-fourth as much, at the end of 1932. Paper values of common stocks evaporated to one-eighth the autumn 1929 level.

More frightening and destructive were three waves of bank failures, in late 1930 and early 1931, again in October, 1931, at the height of the European bank failures, and worst of all in the winter of 1932–33, when many large metropolitan banks across the country suspended payments. In 1929, 499 banks failed, most of them rural or small-town institutions, but over the next five years the number of failures rose to 659 in 1929, 1,352 in 1930, 2,294 in 1931, 1,456 in 1932, and finally 4,004 in 1933, while the progression of failures from small to large banks raised the total dollar value of failed banks' assets from $143 million in 1928 to $1.7 billion in 1931 to $3.6 billion, twenty-five times as high, in 1933. The impossible had happened; the nineteenth-century pattern of a stock or money panic followed by years of general depression had returned with a vengeance. The depression that began in 1929 was to become the longest and deepest of any in American history.

Why did the Great Depression become "great"—that is, so long and so deep? The main reason was that the gradual economic revolution of 1897–1929, the longest prosperity cycle in American history, had been incomplete in a very important sense: it had increasingly rested on stable, prosperous investment conditions and on the ability of consumers to consume. This fact was poorly understood in the late twenties. Instead of promoting stable investment, the economic system encouraged speculation. Instead of protecting the consumer, by protecting jobs, regulating credit, and preventing bank failures, the appropriate economic machinery did not act, or, often, did not exist. The stock market crash of October, 1929, did not by itself "cause" the depression; there were much more basic flaws in the economic structure before the crash took place. Growth was already leveling off before then: indexes of industrial production, factory payrolls, department store sales, and other signs of activity slackened from the early summer of 1929 onward; construction of new homes had peaked in 1925 and declined to 40 percent of that level in 1929.

But these basic economic activities might well have recovered. The stock market crash made recovery extremely difficult, not only by destroying many corporate and individual fortunes, but more importantly, by destroying the confidence and hopes of the country in its business economy. Thirty years of growth, reinforced by the pieties of the New Era, had lulled people into the belief that prosperity would never end. In actual fact, the economy as it had developed by 1929 was a growing young giant that was not yet immune to certain childhood diseases. One such disease was a speculative

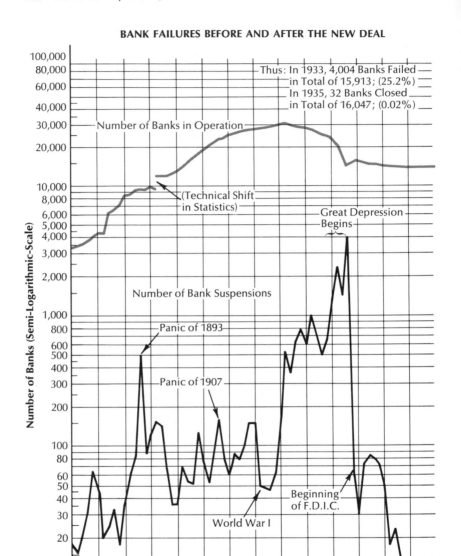

BANK FAILURES BEFORE AND AFTER THE NEW DEAL

Thus: In 1933, 4,004 Banks Failed — in Total of 15,913; (25.2%) — In 1935, 32 Banks Closed — in Total of 16,047; (0.02%) —

Number of Banks in Operation

(Technical Shift in Statistics)

Great Depression Begins

Number of Bank Suspensions

Panic of 1893

Panic of 1907

Beginning of F.D.I.C.

World War I

Number of Banks (Semi-Logarithmic-Scale)

Note the effect of panics and depressions, the calming effects of World War I upon banking, and later the quietude resulting from federal deposit insurance and World War II. Note also the instability of banking during the "prosperous" 1920s. Consolidation in banking is evident from the decline in the number of banks after 1923.

fever for which preventive medicine had not yet been applied; it was too easy to float stock, sell Florida swamp land, pyramid investment trusts built on paper assets, or play the stock market on margin. A willingness to invest was a good thing, necessary to economic growth, but a compulsion to speculate in such ways was a cancerous version of healthy investment. The roots of the degeneration from investment to compulsive speculation were manifold, but one, certainly, was the failure, in the economy and elsewhere, to prevent a disproportionate share of the national income from flowing into relatively few hands in an economy increasingly focused on consumption. With very high returns accruing to these relatively few wealthy people, and without statutory controls on speculative enterprises, the economy was forced to depend too heavily on luxury consumption and on people's willingness to save. But they preferred to speculate.

The economy was producing goods faster than people were able to buy them. Had income been distributed more equitably, allowing more people to buy cars, home appliances, and houses, it is likely that neither the crash nor the subsequent depression would have been so severe. Even though there was considerably more income to distribute to everybody by 1929 than there had been in 1900, and even though more people were indeed receiving it, the flow of income was still skewed toward the wealthy minority. At the same time the productive and distributive sectors were moving in the direction of consumer goods. But consumers could not consume without adequate income.

Economists have suggested other reasons for the crash and depression. Undoubtedly the banking structure was still too loose; despite the creation of the Federal Reserve System in 1914, the banks of the country were still too independent and panic-prone because the "Fed" did not use its statutory powers to regulate credit practices and the availability of money, especially in open-market operations at critical times. It even *raised* the rediscount rate during waves of bank failures, exacerbating the problems of banks. Also, the economies of European countries had never fully recovered from World War I, for many reasons, one of which was America's short-sighted policy of setting protective tariffs so high that Europeans had great difficulty selling goods in the United States. Europe's economic weakness meant too that American manufacturers had trouble selling goods abroad. It also meant that American investors in European business lost heavily after 1929, intensifying the American depression, when European enterprises collapsed and European currencies had to be devalued in order to "re-inflate" their economies—a step the United States took in 1933.

There are still further reasons. But in all probability, the most basic one was the national failure to give a growing number of potential consumers enough buying power to keep pace with a rapidly growing productive and distributive economy. That failure, as so often happens in similar tragic cases, did not happen because people *could* not do something about it, but rather, because people had the impression that they *should* not do something about it. The depression happened less because of deficient machines or modes of distribution, than because of deficient economic ideas and attitudes. That deficiency was evident, despite all good intentions, in the policies of the Treasury Department and of President Herbert Hoover.

Hoover Tries Individual Initiative

Prosperity and Hoover's progressive image were unbeatable in the election of 1928, and he easily defeated the Democratic candidate, Governor Alfred E. Smith of New York. Smith's Catholicism no doubt helped weaken him by splitting his own party, as did Klan opposition and the dry-wet issue—Smith was "wringing wet." But it would have taken a miracle for any Democrat to have defeated Hoover in that prosperous, excited year. Four years later it would have been miraculous if any Democrat had lost to him. The reason for this remarkable shift, which extended beyond the defeat of Hoover in 1932 to the eventual eclipse of the Republican party for four decades, was simple: Hoover's failure, and consequently the failure of the Republican party, in the view of the public, to respond adequately to the depression.

Very quickly after he was inaugurated, Hoover attempted to stabilize and improve conditions in agriculture, a problem sector during the twenties. In June, 1929, Congress passed and Hoover signed the Agricultural Marketing Act, the most extensive law to improve a major group's position since the Wilson legislation of 1914–17. Hoover's reputation as a social engineer and neo-progressive was apparently being justified.

But it is worth considering how the Agricultural Marketing Act worked, because it demonstrated Hoover's approach to government, its similarity to pre–World War I Wilsonian progressivism, and its dissimilarity to the farm policy of his successor, Franklin Roosevelt. The new act created a Federal Farm Board, made up of prominent representatives of various segments of agriculture, including leading implement manufacturers, and its benefits were weighted toward wealthier farmers. The board provided funds for national cooperative marketing associations to enable producers of a number of commodities to sell at more favorable times and prices. The act also provided for stabilization corporations to buy surplus grain and cotton to help maintain their prices. The Federal Farm Board, however, did not attack the problem of overproduction. It regarded as its primary policy, the national cooperatives, while the purchase of commodities was considered a reserve for emergencies. The board could encourage farmers to produce less and thus raise prices by cutting surpluses, but it could not compel them to reduce crops produced or acres cultivated. Nor did Hoover countenance such compulsion. The president was renowned, since he published a book called *American Individualism* in 1922, as the prophet of voluntary cooperation in economic life. He by no means believed that government should stay aloof from the economy, but instead he favored policies that helped create conditions of equal opportunity under which individual action, particularly by businessmen rather than industrial, farm, or white collar workers, could flourish. The voluntary nature of the agricultural legislation of 1929 applied that attitude directly. Government coercion, even expanded bureaucracy, was hostile to Hoover's kind of voluntary activity. Unfortunately, exhortation was not enough to conquer market realities, especially as the national cooperatives failed to prevent farm prices from dropping further after 1929, and as government purchases of surplus commodities overwhelmed the stabilization corporations by 1932.

If Hoover's farm law of 1929 did not solve the basic surplus problem, the other major measure passed early in his administration actually intensified economic difficulties. This was the Hawley-Smoot Tariff Act, passed in June, 1930. Originally a device to protect farmers, the bill in Congress degenerated into a general raising of protective rates. The harm of the act was not in its agricultural provisions, which again were simply unhelpful, but in its confirmation of United States economic policy along nationalistic lines. Higher

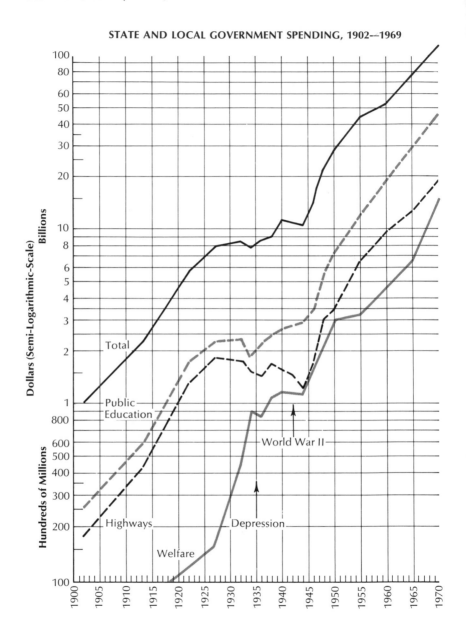

STATE AND LOCAL GOVERNMENT SPENDING, 1902––1969

Except for the depression and World War II years, state and local governments spent increasingly in the three major categories of education, roads, and welfare throughout the century, with the steepest rise in welfare.

tariffs made it harder for European sellers to reach American markets and earn dollars. European government debts were immense: the World War I peace treaty demanded from Germany billions of gold dollars in "reparations," especially to France and Britain, who in turn owed vast sums to wartime lenders, mostly American companies and individuals. The new tariff further reduced European liquidity, made German reparations and French and British war debts harder to pay and hastened the trend to general financial and economic failure in Europe. Though not entirely keen on Congress's tariff bill in 1930, Hoover had consistently been a protectionist, again in the belief that protection created a favorable climate for individual business energies. But there was seldom a worse time for upward tariff revision than 1930, because of the drooping world business cycle and the tendency of economically insecure countries to isolate their economies from the troubles of others. Hoover did declare a "moratorium" on war debts in June, 1931, helping to postpone the European financial collapse harmful to the United States, but America, like the countries of Europe, could find no real alternative to economic nationalism.

The economic slump following the October, 1929, stock-market crash was very serious, but still only a recession, well into 1930. Enough Americans were disenchanted with Hoover by then to vote the Democrats into control of the House of Representatives in the fall elections, for the first time in fourteen years. But there was still much ground for hope that recovery would begin shortly. In 1931, however, the depression began in earnest in the United States and in the developed world generally. From then on, Hoover's philosophy of fostering individual initiative proved insufficient to meet the deepening crisis, and his policies proved increasingly inadequate.

Yet Hoover's actions were a measure of how far the country, including what was in 1930 the more "conservative" (i.e., business-minded) of the two parties, had come since the days of McKinley. Hoover's response to the oncoming depression would have been unthinkably massive for the men who had presided over the last depression and recovery thirty-five years before. Hoover strongly exhorted state and local governments to assume the main burden of poor relief and welfare, and when these agencies became exhausted in 1932, he channeled federal funds to them. He called for a federally-supported, state-and-locally-operated, public works program larger than any that had gone before. He pleaded with business leaders to maintain employment as high as possible. Farm and home-loan banks expanded credit. Most significantly, in early 1932, Hoover brought federal resources to bear directly on the business slowdown by supporting the Glass-Steagall Act, which helped provide monetary expansion through the Federal Reserve System, and by creating the Reconstruction Finance Corporation, a semi-autonomous federal agency ready to loan funds at low interest rates to sound businesses in order to stimulate their recovery. This agency was retained and heavily depended upon by Franklin Roosevelt in future years. But the RFC did not help the thousands of migrant families who were seeking work and who got no food except by begging. When a large group of them camped on the Anacostia flats in Washington in the summer of 1932, demanding relief in the form of veterans' bonuses, Hoover sent army units (including tanks) to chase them away. The army burned the camp on July 29; two infants were killed in the melée.

In the last analysis, Hoover could not free himself from certain crippling economic dogmas: the necessity of a balanced budget, the fundamental requirement of the gold standard, and the conviction that compulsory federal control over economic behavior was wrong. Despite his many progressive views and policies, Hoover tragically failed to participate, in the crucial area of economic thought, in the overthrow of nineteenth-century concepts that had so affected America throughout the early twentieth century. The failure was not only Hoover's. Much of the nation shared it with him. But the penalties were assessed, or at least the political penalties, against Herbert Hoover and the Republican party.

Franklin Delano Roosevelt, a man not averse to shifts in economic dogmas or to the expansion of bureaucracy, thoroughly defeated Hoover in the presidential election of 1932, and a new age in American political history began.

The Democratic Roosevelt

Loved and hated like no president since Jackson, uniquely honored by four elections to the presidency, Franklin Delano Roosevelt changed the course of American life as perhaps no other individual did in modern times. During the depression and World War II, he

FEDERAL SPENDING AND INCOME, 1902–1971

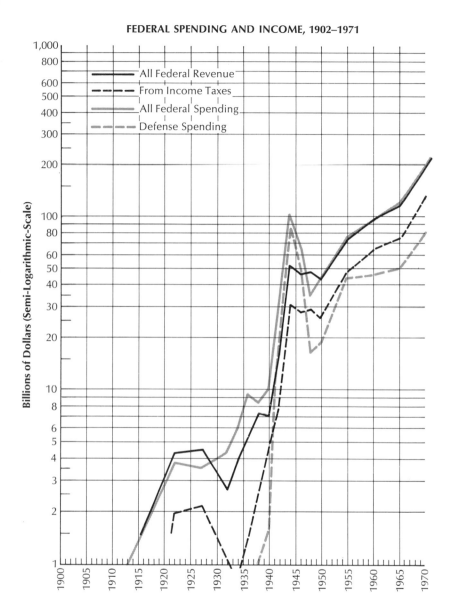

faced two challenges of an immediacy and magnitude unequaled since Lincoln confronted the armed rebellion of the South. Meeting the first challenge with the "New Deal," the collection of legislative and administrative measures that he superintended, he went beyond the immediate problem of the depression to permanent reforms that did much to bring American government in line with the social and economic changes of the preceding half-century. Meeting the second challenge with vigorous prosecution of the war against the Axis powers, he did not neglect the need to provide for postwar peace. He revitalized his Democratic party, restored confidence in the government and the economy, and oversaw the establishment of the federal government as the focus of national power responsive to national problems. Roosevelt did none of these things single-handedly, and still less did he plan them all, including much of the New Deal. But without F.D.R. as the central figure, the history of the thirties, forties, and later would have been very different.

Like almost every successful president, Franklin Roosevelt was a thoroughgoing politician, by career and instinct. In background, this future bane of businessmen and beloved of the masses was paradoxically an impeccable Establishment figure. A Hudson River landed gentleman of patroon lineage, he was a product of Groton School and Harvard; he attended Columbia Law School and was a descendant of Democrats of the Tilden-Cleveland type. Roosevelt won his first political office in 1910, when he was elected to the New York State Senate twenty-four years after his Republican cousin Theodore received his start in the State Assembly. Franklin quickly gained attention as a foe of Tammany Hall and as the leader of the pro-Wilson Democrats in New York. His qualifications as a big-state progressive Democrat helped him win appointment as Assistant Secretary of the Navy from Wilson (the job had been a stepping-stone for Theodore in the McKinley administration), and he performed well as a federal administrator. The 1920 Democratic convention chose him to be James M. Cox's vice-presidential running mate. At thirty-eight, Franklin's political career was moving even faster than that of the breathless Theodore, who was chosen to run with McKinley in 1900 at the age of forty-two.

But Cox and Roosevelt lost, and a year later, suddenly crippled by polio, Roosevelt appeared to be politically finished. Then, after initial despair followed by a courageous personal battle, he reestablished himself as a Democratic leader in New York, supported Governor Alfred E. Smith for the presidency in 1924 and 1928, and in the latter year was elected governor of New York himself while Smith lost the presidential election to Hoover. As a Democrat who could win an election in the "Republican year" of 1928, as the governor of the state with the largest bloc of electoral votes, and as an incumbent reelected in 1930 after establishing a progressive record on conservation and labor issues, Roosevelt was automatically a presidential contender in 1932. Despite Smith's rival candidacy and some coolness from other segments of the party, Roosevelt won the Democratic nomination for president in 1932 on the fourth ballot. His dramatic gifts for inspiring confidence immediately became manifest. Breaking with precedent and taking what many considered the huge risk of flying, he immediately brought his family to the Chicago convention in a Ford tri-motor plane to accept the nomination in person. From that point on, he eclipsed the tired and lackluster Hoover and won a substantial victory in November, carrying in solid congressional majorities.

Dogmas and theories bothered Roosevelt little during the campaign and after his inauguration. Practicalities did. They would have bothered anybody in March, 1933, the deepest point of the depression, when the angry silence of millions of unemployed workers and poverty-stricken farmers was broken only by the sound of the doors of the country's banks clanging shut. Roosevelt's inaugural address suggested hope—"the only thing we have to fear is fear itself"—and within hours the New Deal began.

The First Hundred Days, 1933

Roosevelt's initial attack on the depression, in the first three months after his inauguration, consisted of devising solutions to four large, pressing problems: the spreading shutdown of the country's banks, which had accelerated in February; the agricultural dilemmas of low prices, high mortgage payments and mounting surpluses, which were provoking farmer protests, especially in the Midwest; the stagnation of manufacturing and other industries at low levels of production; and the unemployment of a quarter to a third of the labor force. On March 4, very few people suspected what the New Deal might do about these obvious problems. F.D.R. had provided few inklings in the 1932 campaign, and at times, he even reminded his audiences of Grover Cleveland, when he talked of balanced budgets and retrenchment. Almost certainly, Roosevelt himself was unsure about what precise steps the federal government should take. In most areas the New Deal laws, which had been signed and sealed by the end of the summer of 1933, were the product of compromise, vigor, and the efforts of some very diverse people. Roosevelt's function was not so much to draw up specific measures and push them through Congress, as it was to bring together people who had in common, with each other and with the president, a desire for results rather than a particular set of proposals. As a result, the New Deal laws that were passed not only provided at least temporary solutions to the four problems mentioned above, but also dealt with the securities market, conservation of natural resources, and regional development.

The diversity of the early New Dealers and the vigor with which they worked and with which Roosevelt inspired them go far to explain why the legislation of the "first hundred days," from early March to mid-June, 1933, was so voluminous, so often innovative, sometimes contradictory, and so different in result. Some of it hardly worked at all, and some of it has lasted almost forty years. The president's close advisers were a collection of ideological opposites. They included his budget director, Lewis Douglas, who was devoted to balanced budgets; the monetarily conservative Treasury Undersecretary Dean Acheson; and the fiscally cautious Henry Morgenthau, Jr., an old Roosevelt friend who ran the Treasury Department after October. They also included Donald Richberg, Raymond Moley, and above all, Rexford G. Tugwell, advocates (in very different ways) of a governmentally-planned economy, in the tradition of Herbert Croly and the Theodore Roosevelt of 1912. They included Felix Frankfurter of Harvard Law School, an intellectual heir of the trust-busting progressivism of Justice Brandeis; the crotchety but humanitarian Chicago lawyer Harold Ickes; and the activist social worker–administrator Harry Hopkins. Democratic Senators as different in concern as the Oklahoma Bryanite Elmer Thomas and the industrial reformer Robert Wagner of New York placed their stamp on legislation. These and hundreds of other New Dealers honeycombed the federal bureaucracy and the Congress. Over them presided Roosevelt, whose key role was shown not only by the mass of laws and executive acts he signed, but also by the hundreds of other bills that he vetoed and the federal patronage and funds that he ruthlessly used to keep supporters in line and the New Deal moving.

Immediately after his inauguration, F.D.R. called Congress into a special session, which lasted until June 15. At the same time, March 5, he closed all banks not already shut down, to allow the banking system a respite from runs, and jovially called his action a "bank holiday." He also suspended transactions in gold. Three days later Congress passed the Emergency Banking Act of 1933, authorizing the issuance of more Federal Reserve notes and providing for bank reopenings after Treasury inspection. On the same day, Roosevelt outlined a quite conservative bill, which on March 20 became law as the Economy Act, to seek a balanced budget by cutting veterans' bonuses and the pay of federal workers (including congressmen); this very orthodox financial measure reflected the president's traditional economic beliefs as well as those of Lewis Douglas, the budget director. On Monday, March 13, the morning after F.D.R. delivered the first of his soothing "Fireside Chats" over national radio, many banks reopened, with deposits outrunning withdrawals, and the securities market moved upward. The financial crisis was ending after the administration's first week in office.

Next the New Deal tackled agriculture. By 1933, leaders of farm organizations, as well as the new secretary of agriculture, Henry A. Wallace of Iowa, agreed that the low-price and high-surplus problems would best be solved by limiting production. In March, these men hammered out a bill that went substantially beyond the Hoover farm program, and after some debate in the Congress, the Agricultural Adjustment Act of 1933 became law on May 12. It limited production by paying farmers, on the basis of parity prices, to leave acreage idle. Processors of crops paid a tax that financed the subsidies given to farmers. The secretary of agriculture was to reach acreage limitation agreements with local associations of farmers, who were expected voluntarily to enter the acreage limitation and subsidy plan. The act established an Agricultural Adjustment Agency in the Agriculture Department to carry out these and other support programs. In addition it included an Emergency Farm Mortgage Act to prevent foreclosures (and to reduce the possibility of violent strikes by the angry Farmers' Holiday Association in the Midwest). The "Triple A" began functioning immediately, and during that summer 10 million acres of cotton were plowed up and

5 million pigs slaughtered, in an effort to control surpluses. After 1933 the AAA's provisions worked so well that such drastic measures were unnecessary. The unrest of the Farmers' Holiday Association and the National Farmers' Union slackened. On June 16, another law created the Farm Credit Administration, which combined and expanded credit resources for farmers. In the following two years, the AAA did much to raise prices and reduce surpluses by using local committees of farmers and by encouraging individual farmers to participate in its plans.

The AAA was one of two cornerstones of the early New Deal's efforts toward economic recovery. The other was the National Industrial Recovery Act, which became law in June. Roosevelt did not even have plans for such a measure until early April, when the Senate passed a thirty-hour-a-week bill whose backers expected would create many more jobs. Then F.D.R. instigated the drafting of a much more comprehensive law, involving businessmen and bureaucrats in its design, which would provide for extensive federal planning of industrial activity. As passed, the act created a National Recovery Administration that was to negotiate codes of "fair competition" involving pricing and production with businessmen and labor representatives in given industries. The trade associations of the "New Era" of the twenties, blessed by the federal government by means of their agreements with the NRA, would plan and regulate their own industries. The act also provided that if the government discovered "destructive price or wage cutting" taking place in an industry, it could license well-behaved companies to do business, while keeping non-licensed companies out of interstate commerce. Section 7(a) of the act protected labor by requiring that all codes and licenses provide that workers "shall have the right to organize and bargain collectively through representatives of their own choosing" and that they shall not have to join company unions. Title II established a Public Works Administration with $3.3 billion to undertake heavy construction across the country, relieving unemployment and stimulating recovery. Always with an eye on political possibilities, Roosevelt signed an act containing something for big businesses, something for small businesses, something for labor, and quite a lot for the angry unemployed. The NRA, under Hugh Johnson of Illinois, set about negotiating codes in a raft of industries, and the PWA, under Harold Ickes, began works projects in cooperation with states and municipalities.

A WPA team building an overpass in Buffalo, 1936; a common type of WPA activity. (Wide World Photos)

The "first hundred days" of the New Deal brought many other measures. In early March, F.D.R. and Congress ended prohibition, first by permitting the sale of 3.2 beer (and raising funds by taxing it) and then by sending to the states the Twenty-First Amendment, repealing the Eighteenth. For the relief of the unemployed and destitute, the New Dealers provided not only Ickes' PWA, but also, in March, a Civilian Conservation Corps to produce jobs for hundreds of thousands of young men and at the same time to conserve natural resources. In May, the New Dealers passed the Federal Emergency Relief Act providing half a billion dollars, part of it on a matching basis with the states, to rescue the jobless. Later that year, when the PWA seemed to be moving too slowly, Roosevelt created a Civil Works Administration (CWA) under Harry Hopkins, which employed over 4 million workers by January, 1934, and saved many from want over the winter of 1933–34, until it was disbanded in the spring of 1934. In banking and finance, the New Dealers went well beyond the solution of the banking crisis in early March. In April, Roosevelt took the country off the gold standard, to the great dismay of many wealthy Democrats. In May and June, Congress passed the Truth-in-Securities Act, which required issuers of stock to reveal financial details; the Home Owners' Loan Act, which helped refinance home mortgages, thus protecting both borrowers and lenders; the Glass-Steagall Act, which separated investment and commercial banks, and established the Federal Deposit Insurance Corporation, protecting depositors and investors; and the Farm Credit act, which provided loans and the refinancing of loans to farmers. Another major act was passed in May, which created the Tennessee Valley Authority and provided for regional development and hydroelectric power under federal ownership on a scale well beyond the hopes of Senator George Norris and other defenders of Muscle Shoals in the twenties.

The New Deal Gets Results— And Opponents, 1934–1936

Congress adjourned in June, after passing these and other acts ranging in philosophy from the socialism of the TVA, to the New Nationalist regulation of the Glass-Steagall Act, to financial relief for middle-class home owners and farmers, to the NRA's government–big business cooperation. When Congress reconvened in January, 1934, Roosevelt added further ingredients to his "alphabet soup." Since October, Roosevelt and the Treasury had been buying gold in an effort to raise commodity prices and inflate the dollar. But the gold-buying failed to raise commodity prices, and in January, Roosevelt secured from Congress the Gold Reserve Act, empowering him to peg the gold value of the dollar at $35 per ounce, about 60 percent of its pre-1933 value. This massive devaluation cheapened exports, made imports more expensive (functioning like a high protective tariff), raised the dollar price of commodities sold abroad, and thus inflated the currency, which is what many farmers and businessmen wanted. By June, Congress tried to mitigate (without much success) some of the bad effects of devaluation on European economies when it passed, at Roosevelt's and Secretary of State Cordell Hull's urging, the Reciprocal Trade Agreements Act, allowing the executive to negotiate trade and tariff levels with other countries.

Other major measures of 1934 extended federal regulation and aided certain middle-class groups. The Securities Exchange Act created the Securities and Exchange Commission to supervise the stock markets. Another act established the Federal Communications Commission. Yet another created the Federal Housing Administration, which was to guarantee loans for home improvement and home building; not a public housing act for the poor, it was intended instead to aid home-owners and also to resuscitate the badly depressed construction industry. The Frazier-Lemke Farm Bankruptcy Act—more the brainchild of Louisiana's "radical" senator, Huey Long, than of the Democratic congressional leaders—helped farmers buy back foreclosed mortgages at better prices. The Railroad Retirement Act established pensions for railway workers. The Indian Reorganization Act strengthened tribal councils and reversed the "ward of the government" policy. The major land law of the New Deal, the Taylor Grazing Act, at once attacked the ecological problem of the dustbowl and benefited stock-raisers by allowing up to 80 million acres of public domain to be divided into grazing districts that would be supervised cooperatively by stockmen and government officials. Conservationists' howls were muted by the establishment of the Soil Conservation Service in 1935. In the meantime, the Reconstruction Finance Corporation, under Jesse Jones of Texas, expanded from its restricted role in the Hoover years to become the New Deal's most important recovery agency, loaning billions to banks, agribusinesses, railroads, and other private enterprises. Relief continued also, $2 billion of it by the end of 1934.

By mid-1934, the New Deal had attacked the depression with varied methods and uneven success. Virtually every New Deal measure was the product of compromise among different viewpoints and political pressures, and F.D.R. had proved himself an extremely capable politician in his many explorations of the limits of the possible. The paralysis of February and March of 1933 was recognized as the depression's low point; many economic indicators edged upwards in 1933 and 1934. Industrial recovery proceeded slowly. The NRA, not surprisingly, had difficulty writing workable codes for over 500 industries, and by mid-1934 businessmen and consumers alike complained about red tape, high prices, and domination by monopolies. The AAA worked much better, at least for middle-class farmers aided by its subsidies, though production limits pushed some tenants and sharecroppers out of farming. The tax and monetary policies of the Roosevelt administration did not redistribute wealth or end deflation to any marked degree. Nor did the New

Deal in general benefit the poverty-stricken, black or white, as much as it did the rural or urban middle class. It was a "new deal" for the middle class; but by the 1930s, unlike the 1900s, that group was a growing majority, and the New Dealers expanded the government's active definition of it to include farmers and union labor. Few New Deal measures directly aided the poorest and the propertyless, except through emergency relief, but the New Deal did reverse the situation of the twenties, when government catered primarily to big business. The New Deal did not abolish poverty or even social and economic inequity. But it tugged the country out of the quagmire of the depression. Beyond this, the New Deal should be credited with bringing hope and energy to millions. Although it did not nationalize various sectors of the economy, or institute far-reaching federal planning as urged by Tugwell and others, it restored faith and a measure of health in an economy beset with its greatest crisis in history.

The radical and reactionary nature, and the relatively small extent, of opposition to the New Deal in 1934–36 underscores how well Roosevelt walked a middle way. The American Liberty League, led by Alfred E. Smith and many wealthy anti-Roosevelt Democrats, railed at the New Deal's controls on businessmen. Communists opposed it because it was not revolutionary. In California, a physician named Francis Townsend won support from millions for his plan for economic recovery, which involved everyone over sixty retiring on a pension, thus opening jobs for younger people (who would be taxed to pay for the pensions). Upton Sinclair, the old socialist-progressive, announced his EPIC (End Poverty In California) plan in the fall of 1933, whereby the state would take over land and factories not in use, put the unemployed to work in them, and pay workers in scrip, which could be spent on the goods they produced. Sinclair almost won the governorship of California on the EPIC platform in 1934. Huey P. Long, Louisiana's "Kingfish," also wanted to go well beyond the New Deal. He generated strong support in the South, the Midwest, and California for his "Share Our Wealth" plan, which proposed to limit family incomes to one million dollars a year, set up old-age pensions, fund student scholarships and veterans' bonuses, and establish minimum wages and public works. The "Radio Priest" from Detroit, Father Charles Coughlin, whose antibanker and "social justice" addresses millions

Huey P. Long in a favorite role (haranguing the Louisiana legislature). Before Long was shot down in 1935, Roosevelt considered the "Kingfish" a major political threat. (Brown Brothers)

listened to weekly, was moving toward a public break with Roosevelt after initially supporting the New Deal.

But despite noisy opposition from right and from left, the New Deal received massive approval in the 1934 elections. Roosevelt commanded the great middle. Democratic majorities in Congress increased, a very rare result for an "off-year" election. For all his contradictions and for all the flaws (according to doctrinaire reform theories) in the New Deal, F.D.R. had won the support of the majority of Americans.

In his messages to Congress in early 1935, Roosevelt called for new measures to extend the New Deal in a generally more welfarish, regulatory direction. Probably influenced in part by the election returns of 1934, which reflected increased farmer and labor support for the Democratic party, in part by hostility from business (the United States Chamber of Commerce denounced the New Deal early in May), and by the first Supreme Court decisions overturning important New Deal laws, Roosevelt soon was backing an even more vigorous program than he had planned at the first of the year. In 1935, the New Deal brought new laws in the areas of social security, labor, banking, public utilities, taxation, farming, business regulation, and public works.

The Emergency Relief Appropriation Act authorized the establishment of the Works Progress Administration (WPA), which under Harry Hopkins' direction provided several million jobs over the next seven years at an expense of billions of dollars. The WPA became the administration's major unemployment and welfare agency, sponsoring projects as diverse as street repair, school and bridge construction, Federal Writers, Artists, and Theater Projects, a survey of historical records, and a National Youth Administration, which provided vocational training and 2 million part-time jobs to students. The Resettlement Administration, under Tugwell, struck at rural poverty, which the AAA did not do. A federal tax law, which F.D.R. initially said would "soak the rich," emerged as a much milder measure, but did raise estate, gift, and stock taxes, created an excess profits tax on businesses, and raised personal income tax rates at upper income levels. The Public Utilities Holding Company Act broke up large utilities combines and regulated the finances of others, while the concept of public exploitation or control of electric power was advanced further by expansion of the

TVA (though more as a power and fertilizer producer than as a regional development agency). Establishment of the Rural Electrification Administration brought electric lights and power to farms and hamlets, something private companies complained was beyond their means. The Banking Act of 1935 gave the Federal Reserve Board more rediscounting authority and approval power over officers of regional reserve banks, and established a centralized Open Market Committee to undertake its open-market securities operations.

Important as these measures were, the New Deal produced two others in 1935 of even greater long-run significance: the National Labor Relations Act, often called the "Wagner Act" after its chief designer, New York's Senator Wagner, and the Social Security Act. Social security took eight months getting through Congress, but when it became law it established the federal government as a guarantor, in principle at least, of personal security. The act left many people out, such as the older poor, and did nothing to provide medical insurance. Its financing, by means of employer-employee matching contributions, simply forced the worker to save and encouraged employers to pass the expense on to consumers. But despite these and other faults, the act provided a kind of personal security necessary in an urbanizing society.

The Wagner Act, which Roosevelt at first opposed, firmly guaranteed labor's right to organize and to bargain collectively. Replacing and expanding upon Section 7(a) of the 1933 recovery act, which the Supreme Court invalidated in May, 1935, the Wagner Act created a National Labor Relations Board to investigate and stop unfair labor practices, to supervise unionization elections, and to prevent management intimidation of workers and organizers. The act immediately became a charter for John L. Lewis and other CIO leaders to unionize the country's mass-production industries.

By the time the Wagner Act became law, the New Deal was under attack from a powerful quarter. The United States Supreme Court, which contained a few reform sympathizers such as Justices Brandeis and Cardozo but whose majority included Harding and Coolidge appointees of strict-constructionist views, began reviewing cases involving New Deal laws early in 1935. On "Black Monday," May 27, the Court unanimously—for even Brandeis opposed "centralization"—struck down the Frazier-Lemke Farm Bankruptcy

Act, and then the NRA itself. The National Recovery Administration had had serious problems of efficiency and enforcement, and had been severely criticized from several sides for over a year. But it was still the major industrial recovery program of the New Deal. The Court destroyed it in the case of *A.L.A. Schechter Corp. v. U.S.* (called the "sick chicken case" because the Schechter brothers, New Jersey poultry dealers, had been hauled up and convicted for selling diseased chickens, contrary to the NRA Live Poultry Code). The Court found that the NRA codes represented an illegal delegation of power by Congress to an executive body, and also, put the federal government out of bounds by regulating intrastate, not interstate, commerce. Other decisions in 1935 and 1936 invalidated the Railroad Retirement Act, the Guffey-Snyder Coal Conservation Act (an attempt to reestablish the NRA coal code after the Schechter case), and the Municipal Bankruptcy Act. Then, in *U.S. v. Butler* (January, 1936), the Court struck down by a 6–3 vote the second key recovery measure of the first hundred days, the Agricultural Adjustment Act. The Court said that government attempts to collect the AAA processing tax from the Hoosac Mills, a cotton manufacturer, were an improper use of Congress's taxing power and that, in any event, aid to agriculture was a state, not a federal, matter. Although the Court subsequently upheld the existence of the TVA, it seemed almost certain that the Wagner and Social Security acts would be invalidated as soon as cases involving them arrived before it.

F.D.R.'s Second Term

Few new laws appeared during the election year of 1936, except the Soil Conservation and Domestic Allotment Act, which replaced portions of the invalidated AAA. The PWA and the WPA continued to relieve unemployment by spending massively. The campaign and the election reflected the shift of the New Deal in 1935 toward regulation of big business and the welfare of farmers, laborers, and other "little people," and away from the recovery measures and government-business cooperation of 1933 and early 1934. The New Deal did not lack for vocal opponents; though Huey Long had been assassinated in September, 1935, some of his followers joined

Coughlin, Townsendites, and the Liberty Leaguers to fight Roosevelt through the presidential candidacy of William Lemke, a North Dakota congressman, on the Union ticket. The Republicans, facing a steeper uphill fight than they could remember, nominated Governor Alfred M. Landon of Kansas, a Republican of Bull Moose antecedents who had been reelected despite the Democratic landslide of 1934.

But F.D.R. was unbeatable. Renominated by acclamation at the Democratic convention, so well in command of his party that he was able to end the century-old two-thirds rule, which gave southerners a veto over the party's nominee, the president lambasted "economic royalists"—i.e., big businessmen—and promised a bigger-than-ever New Deal regulatory and welfare program. The people obviously listened. The Lemke ticket, whose supporters had had a falling-out before the election, polled 882,000 votes, many fewer than the New Dealers feared, while the Communist and Socialist candidates attracted only a fraction of their 1932 vote. The G.O.P. made its worst showing since it was founded, and Landon carried only Maine and Vermont. James A. Farley, the Democrats' chief political tactician, made the crack that the old Republican chant of "as Maine goes, so goes the nation," was revised to "as Maine goes, so goes Vermont." For the Republicans, only 89 representatives and 16 senators returned to Washington. The Democratic campaign was well-run and was financed heavily by labor, especially the CIO and the mine workers.

The second Roosevelt administration continued the New Deal, but at a much slower pace. There were several reasons why this was so, including the growing pressure of foreign emergencies in the late thirties and the simple fact that the New Deal had already passed so many acts. But one reason was that Roosevelt himself made a damaging political mistake in 1937 and another in 1938, mistakes that dissipated much of the tremendous reservoir of political support he enjoyed at the time of the 1936 election.

The first error was a poorly-executed plan to change the composition of the Supreme Court in order to tip it in a pro–New Deal direction. Two weeks after his second inauguration, the president asked Congress to pass a law enabling him to appoint a new federal judge whenever an incumbent judge did not retire at the age of seventy. Up to six new justices of the Supreme Court could have been appointed by this provision. Most of the measure's other sections were widely hailed, and the Supreme Court expansion, quickly dubbed "court-packing" by its opponents, might indeed have solved the constitutional impasse between the judiciary and executive. But instead of candidly citing the impasse as his main grounds, Roosevelt claimed that the federal courts had a huge backlog of undecided cases and needed more judges to clear it up (which was not the case) and that older judges could not work effectively or sympathetically toward reform (although Brandeis, the oldest Supreme Court justice at eighty, was usually the most liberal). Roosevelt also failed to discuss the proposal with Democratic congressional leaders, and consequently they refused to push it through. The court-packing battle raged furiously through the summer of 1937, sharing the headlines with the Spanish civil war, the CIO's fight to unionize steel, Amelia Earhart's disappearance over the Pacific, and the Japanese army's defeat of China at the Marco Polo bridge. At the same time, the Court upheld the Wagner Act, in *N.L.R.B.* v. *Jones and Laughlin Steel Corp.*, and one of the most conservative justices retired. The Supreme Court began to affirm state and federal reform legislation. The reversal made the court-packing plan unnecessary, and Roosevelt accepted a compromise limiting lower-court injunction powers but leaving the number of Supreme Court justices untouched. The judiciary erected few further roadblocks against the New Deal. But the high point of F.D.R.'s popularity had passed. There were limits beyond which even Roosevelt could not go.

His second mistake strengthened an anti–New Deal conservative coalition sparked by the court-packing controversy. The president attempted to "purge" a number of uncooperative Democratic members of Congress by openly opposing their reelection in the primaries and general elections of 1938. He failed in virtually every case, and the reelected members, most of them southern Democrats who thereafter obviously owed nothing at all to the president, often combined (and in fact continued to do so through the next three decades) with conservative Republicans to defeat reform measures and to reduce substantially the effectiveness of Democratic majorities in both houses.

New Deal measures kept coming, however, in 1937 and 1938. When the Federal Reserve Board and the Treasury helped cause recession in 1937 by too-cautious deflationary activities, Roosevelt was persuaded in 1938 to step up WPA work; Congress agreed, and economic indicators bent upward again. New laws included the Wagner-Steagall National Housing Act, a slum clearance and public-housing measure continuing the work of the PWA, and the Miller-Tydings Act legalizing "fair trade" retail price agreements helpful to small businessmen. The Guffey-Vinson Bituminous Coal Act assisted miners, and the Bankhead-Jones Farm Tenancy Act created a Farm Security Administration to provide cheap loans to tenants and to aid migrants. In 1938, the Civil Aeronautics Act created a regulatory commission for commercial and private aviation. A second Agricultural Adjustment Act replaced that of 1933 by reestablishing subsidies, allotments, and market quotas without the processing tax. The old trust-busting urge manifested itself in the Temporary National Economic Committee, which began a large-scale study of monopolies and trusts. Finally, in the last New Deal measure, the Fair Labor Standards Act of 1938, Congress established a federal minimum wage and maximum hours law.

Early in 1939, Roosevelt announced that foreign affairs had replaced relief, recovery, and reform as the administration's top priority. The New Deal was over. Experimental, helter-skelter, frequently unprecedented, and almost always controversial, the long list of New Deal acts had permanently changed the role of the federal government in American life. By 1939 the depression was not yet over, but economic and social conditions were immensely improved from the paralyzed months of early 1933. Some areas were hardly touched by the New Deal; it included no significant civil rights legislation (though Roosevelt, unlike Wilson, did integrate substantial parts of the executive branch); it seldom involved itself with educational aid except as an adjunct to recovery measures; and it did not nationalize industries, as some reformers wished. Nevertheless it dealt with virtually all of the well-formulated reform desires of the thirties, and it made reality of many dreams held by progressives since the opening days of the century.

In its overall content, the New Deal was scarcely radical; to the mass of voters in the mid-thirties, Huey Long's "Share Our Wealth" plan seemed much more so—and yet Long would have permitted million-dollar incomes and five-million-dollar maximum fortunes as long as every family was guaranteed an income of two or three thousand per year, a homestead, a car, and a few other things.

"Come along. We're going to the Trans-Lux to hiss Roosevelt."

Peter Arno in *The New Yorker*, 1936. (Drawing by Peter Arno; Copr. © 1936, 1964. The New Yorker Magazine, Inc.)

This was a long way from communism. But the New Dealers fought and feared Long for several reasons. His rabble-rousing style and wide support, had he lived, might have split the 1936 Democratic vote and thrown the election to the Republicans. Also, Long and Senator Joseph T. Robinson of Arkansas, the majority leader, were political enemies, and F.D.R. needed Robinson's help. Finally and simply, the Long program threatened the Roosevelt balancing act among interest groups.

Other contemporary opponents of the New Deal did consider it a radical departure from traditional ways. It certainly was, if one defined tradition as *laissez-faire* individualism. But the Great Depression itself was unprecedented, an untraditional situation. And if tradition meant the view—urged in different ways by Theodore Roosevelt and Woodrow Wilson—that the national government had a positive role to play in the social and economic life of the country, the New Deal depended on tradition and carried the tradition of government activism beyond the point to which the pre–World War I progressives had been able to go (though not beyond the point where many of them wished to go). The New Deal substantially expanded the job of the federal government. Roosevelt and the majority of his policy-making supporters did so in a way that was liberal, not radical: they preserved capitalism and did not intend that the government should own or operate the economy. Rather, they tried to make the government serve as the stimulator of individual initiative and, what is more, the guarantor of sufficient basic needs to prevent such initiative from being squashed by impersonal economic adversity. The New Dealers by no means succeeded in achieving this for all groups. But they did so for many, and in their fashion preserved the recognized fabric of American society well beyond the time of the provocative and dangerous depression itself.

Roosevelt and the New Deal also wrought long-term changes in the shape of American politics. Ever since the early nineteenth century, the relative strengths of the major parties prevailing at the onset of a depression had decisively changed, in that the party in power was severely weakened, the party out of power much augmented, until the next depression provoked a new alignment. The Great Depression was no exception. Republican dominance that had prevailed since the depression of 1893–97 ended, and the Democrats became the majority party from the congressional elections of

1930 onward. Except for rare Republican congressional victories, the two presidential victories of Dwight D. Eisenhower in the fifties, and the hairsbreadth victory of Richard M. Nixon in 1968, the Democrats constituted a majority of the country's registered voters and won White House and Congress from 1930 through 1970. Newer immigrant groups, whose second generation reached voting age during the twenties and thirties, not only found the Republican party uncongenial, as immigrant groups had often done in the past, but also were badly hit by the depression until New Deal relief and recovery measures helped them back on their feet. Italian, Polish, and Jewish voters remembered Roosevelt and the New Deal long after the thirties. Negroes suffered from the depression perhaps more than any other group; they were, proverbially, the last hired and the first fired. They too were recognized and in some ways aided by the New Deal, and the growing urban Negro vote shifted decisively to the Democratic party between 1932 and 1936 and has stayed there ever since. Union leaders such as John L. Lewis and Sidney Hillman came out for Roosevelt in 1936, and much of the labor vote, mindful of the Wagner Act and later the Fair Labor Standards Act, moved into the Democratic column.

The Democratic party had a rosy future; it was firmly based on immigrant, Negro, and labor votes; it dominated the crucial large cities and therefore many of the states with large blocs of electoral votes; and it could capitalize on its reform record and the charismatic personality of Roosevelt. Its coalition contained elements of instability, especially because of the inclusion of the urban Negroes and other ethnic groups under the same umbrella as the "Solid South." But the Democrats kept the coalition together on most occasions until after 1960, successfully capturing from the Republicans the image and record as the progressive, reform-minded party that the G.O.P. had held early in the century. From the New Deal into the seventies, the Democrats generally included leaders and programs that appealed to demographically dominant areas and groups. The Republicans' strongholds in most elections were small towns and rural areas outside the South, a hefty portion of suburbia, and when conditions permitted it in the sixties, parts of the South itself. Rarely were these elements sufficient to defeat the Democrats' New Deal coalition. The New Deal legacy included Democratic majorities and, until the late sixties, general acceptance of the practice of vigorous action by the federal government as an answer to most social and economic problems. It was not until thirty years after the end of the New Deal that the Democratic coalition showed signs of cracking, and that the notion of federal activism began seriously to be questioned by "liberals" and "progressives" themselves.

President Franklin D. Roosevelt at the Yalta Conference, February, 1945. At that time, two months before he died, F.D.R. bore little evidence of his robust vigor of 1933; such was the toll of twelve years of depression and war. Other notables pictured: Secretary of State Edward Stettinius (second from left); Soviet Foreign Minister V. M. Molotov (third from left); British Prime Minister Winston Churchill (at F.D.R.'s right). (Culver Pictures, Inc.)

8

WORLD WAR AND COLD WAR, 1938-1953

The foreign policies of the United States in the thirties were a curious mixture of noble ends—world peace and order—and passive means—isolation and appeasement. Prior to 1938 the means seemed to most policy-makers and to the American public to be the most likely way to achieve the end. From 1938 through 1941, however, the means were gradually discredited by aggressions in Europe and Asia, while the noble ends became unreachable.

"Isolation" has been used so often to describe America's policies and attitudes to the rest of the world in the twenties and thirties, and has been condemned as a failure so often since 1945, that its meaning has been oversimplified. In the sense of a complete abstention from international affairs, "isolation" never existed. Despite its refusal in 1919 to join the League of Nations, the United States had entered into agreements with other countries to limit and stabilize naval armaments, to solve the problem of war debts and reparations, to outlaw war, and to resist aggression. American corporations and investors played a vigorous economic role abroad. The State Department indeed had policies with regard to Asia, Latin America, and Europe, including multilateral moral suasion to shame aggressors. But "isolation," in the more precise sense of not intervening actively, with military, economic, or (with rare exceptions) diplomatic sanctions, in international disputes, did characterize American policy. Isolation in that sense was often realistic. It meant taking a passive role, in contrast to the unilateral or multilateral "internationalism" of World War II and since. And passivity was called "appeasement," which only became an opprobrious term after it failed in 1938 to stop Hitler. It would have been unrealistic—i.e., the available means would almost certainly have not achieved the desired ends—for the United States to have opposed Japanese expansion into China and Southeast Asia in 1931-40 by armed force, or Mussolini's invasion of Ethiopia in 1936, or Hitler's absorption of Czechoslovakia in 1938-39.

From Isolation to Collective Security

The role of America in world affairs between 1930 and 1938 was thus characterized by its ardent desire that peace continue and aggression stop; by State Department and (often) presidential employment of moral suasion mixed with impartial passivity, but nothing stronger, to achieve that goal; and public opinion hostile to international involvement and generally unsympathetic to even the very moderate activism of policy-makers. Different people were isolationist for different reasons, but some of the more common were the depression-based attitude that domestic problems were bad enough without worrying about foreign ones, too; generalized anti-foreign, restrictionist, anti-ethnic feelings; the apparent futility of the bloodbath of World War I; the tendency, popular in the thirties, to blame that war on a conspiracy of bondholders and munitions makers; and the desire to avoid another war at almost any price. Policy-makers tended to continue along paths set in the Wilsonian period and the twenties, which were to limit arms and negotiate problems by treaty rather than force and to use moral suasion to shame aggressors into "right" behavior. As it happened, the latter tactic was more successful in bringing domestic deviants into line with bourgeois mores than in restraining Japanese militarists or Nazi fanatics.

All of these factors produced a foreign policy and a widespread popular attitude about it that was not so much inactive as it was ineffectual. These underlying factors led in 1931 to the "Stimson Doctrine," whereby Secretary of State Henry Stimson and President Hoover attempted to dissuade Japan from encroaching upon Manchuria by convincing the "good" nations, through the League, to protect peace by refusing to recognize any Japanese gains. But Japan was not dissuaded, set up a puppet state called Manchukuo, and later proceeded to infiltrate China. Isolation and moral suasion also underlay Roosevelt's "Good Neighbor" policy, whereby the United States in 1933 renounced interventionism, abrogated the Platt Amendment of 1903, which "justified" it in Cuba, and gradually terminated its protectorates. But American economic imperialism continued.

Isolationism also underlay the Senate's Nye Committee investigations of 1934–35 into munitions makers' responsibility for World War I, and subsequently, several acts of Congress to legislate passive neutrality. The first Neutrality Act, passed in August, 1935, required the president to forbid the sale of armaments for six months to all countries involved in any armed conflict. Also, it called on the president to warn Americans not to travel on ships of belligerents, and it forbade the arming of American ships; Congress wanted no repetition of the 1915 *Lusitania* episode. A second Neutrality Act in 1936 extended those provisions and also made loans to warring powers illegal. A third, in 1937, extended the earlier ones "permanently" and required that any goods sold to belligerents had to be paid for in advance and transported on their ships—the "cash and carry" provision, to avoid war debt entanglements or sinkings of American merchant vessels. The Neutrality Acts marked the high tide of isolationism. They did not outlaw foreign relations; instead, they represented legislative attempts to keep the United States out of any wars by avoiding the mistakes of 1914–17. But they gave the president no discretion to throw American weight on one side or another in a future war, regardless of the foreseeable impact on American security or interest. His only option, as provided in the 1937 act, was to avoid invoking the cash-and-carry provision in certain circumstances.

By 1938, America's policies and attitudes had left the country unprepared to cope with situations in Europe and Asia that had already deteriorated in the direction of war to an almost irrecoverable degree. Between 1938 and the end of 1941, isolationism had to be painfully discarded by both policy-makers and public, and gradually replaced by the very different policy of collective security under American leadership, a policy that gathered strength during World War II and was followed during most of the postwar period.

The replacement of isolation with collective security seemed unlikely in 1938, however, when the mood of the neutrality legislation was upon the American public and "appeasement" still seemed, in the United States, France, and Britain, the most likely way to avoid war. Briefly stated, the international situation by that time was as follows.

In East Asia, a rapidly industrializing Japan continued to extend its control on the Asian mainland, as it had done ever since winning the Russo-Japanese War in 1905, and in 1931, Japan occupied Manchuria. The United States, committed since 1900 to the "Open Door" in China, responded with Stimson's "non-recognition" doctrine, but Japan, increasingly dominated by militarists, grew still more aggressive. In 1937, war erupted after Japanese and Chinese army units clashed at the Marco Polo bridge, near Peking. The United States deplored Japan's movement into North China but invoked no sanctions, even after Japanese planes (without Tokyo's approval) sank the U.S.S. *Panay* in December while the American gunboat was evacuating civilians from a war zone on the Yangtze. Japan did not want a fight with the United States at that time, but the China policies of the two countries remained on collision course.

In Europe, Benito Mussolini's Fascists seized control of Italy in 1922, and in January, 1933, Germany, which had never achieved economic or political stability after World War I, had a new chancellor: Adolf Hitler. In 1935, Mussolini invaded Ethiopia; in 1936, Hitler occupied the demilitarized Rhineland; and in Spain a military uprising touched off a civil war which lasted from 1936 to 1939 and ended with military dictatorship, under General Francisco Franco. In 1936, Germany and Italy formed the "Rome-Berlin Axis," and in 1937, Japan became associated with the Axis in an Anti-Comintern treaty. In March, 1938, Germany bloodlessly annexed Austria into the "Great German Reich." Hitler, encouraged by the British government's policy of appeasement, France's unwillingness to act without Britain, and American isolationism, next eyed the Sudetenland, the ethnically German part of Czechoslovakia. In September, 1938, the British and French prime ministers, Neville Chamberlain and Edouard Daladier, met with Hitler at Munich and agreed to German annexation of the Sudetenland in return for a promise to leave the rest of Czechoslovakia alone. Chamberlain returned to London claiming that the Munich agreement had won "peace in our time."

Up to that point Roosevelt and Secretary of State Cordell Hull had contented themselves with moral suasion and a general hands-off policy regarding Japan, and with following the British appeasement policy in Europe. Roosevelt did say, in a speech in Chicago in October, 1937, that aggressors ought to be "quarantined," but he neither defined his term nor prepared any definite plans to carry out a quarantine; in any case, the highly isolationist press and public objected to even that mild degree of official vigor. Roosevelt and most American diplomats were not at all unhappy about the Munich agreement, and they still hoped in late 1938 that appeasement would avoid war.

In 1939, however, the march of the dictators continued, and Roosevelt gradually and opportunistically began to lead the government and the public toward collective security. With Nazi provocation, Czechoslovakia split apart in March, with the Czech part becoming the German protectorate of Bohemia and Moravia, and in April, Mussolini took over Albania. American policy was not totally limited to appeasement; in December, 1938, the United States and all of the hemisphere republics signed the Declaration of Lima pledging collective resistance to a Nazi threat to hemisphere security, and from mid-1938 onward Roosevelt sought higher military and naval appropriations. Meanwhile, Britain and France attempted by more potent diplomacy to prevent Hitler from attacking his next target, Poland. Through the summer of 1939, they tried to secure from the Soviet Union a military guarantee of Polish independence, and thus surround Hitler with enemies on the east and the west if he struck at Poland. The negotiations lagged when the French and British balked at Stalin's demand for a "guarantee of Soviet security," which in effect meant Russian control of the three Baltic countries.

At that very time, Germany was also negotiating with the Soviets. Hitler would let Stalin have the Baltic states in return for Soviet neutrality if Germany attacked Poland. On August 24, 1939, to the profound shock of the Western powers, Germany and the Soviet Union signed the Nazi-Comintern Pact, providing for mutual non-aggression. Eight days later, with Russia neutralized, Germany invaded Poland. Two days after that, on September 3, 1939, Britain and France met their treaty obligations to defend Poland, and declared war on Germany. The Second World War, which twenty years of diplomacy since Versailles had sought to avoid, and which was eventually to kill more than 50 million people, had begun.

The outbreak of war in Europe dealt a strong blow to America's isolationism, but by no means a lethal one. Roosevelt with difficulty secured a fourth Neutrality Act from Congress late in 1939, ending the complete embargo of arms, but anti-war sentiment remained strong among Americans during the next several months of "phony war," when land fighting in Europe virtually ceased after Germany quickly overran Poland. However, in April, 1940, the German blitzkrieg swept Denmark and Norway into the Nazi net, and in a matter of weeks, in May and June, the Germans whipped France. The fall of France left Britain the sole bastion between Hitler's army and navy and the United States, and convinced many Americans that Britain had to be kept in the war by all possible means of aid except troops. Roosevelt got further appropriations from Congress for the army, still under-equipped and only a half-million strong. In September the president made his "destroyer deal" with Britain, swapping over-age destroyers for long-term leases on space for American bases on British possessions from Newfoundland to the Caribbean. Congressmen and the public approved with misgiving. At about the same time, Congress passed the Burke-Wadsworth Act, creating the selective service system.

Isolation was still strong. Although both candidates in the 1940 presidential election, Roosevelt and the Republicans' Wendell Willkie, were "internationalists," F.D.R. had to recognize the strength of isolationism, and before the campaign was over he promised that "your boys are not going to be sent into any foreign wars." Although he considered a direct attack on the United States not "foreign," he let the pro-isolationist effect of the statement stand. Campaigning on the record of the New Deal and benefiting from the new Democratic voting coalition, Roosevelt beat Willkie by 5 million votes.

After the German defeat of the Netherlands and France, Japan proceeded southward in Asia toward Indochina and the Dutch East Indies, and became a full Axis partner in September, 1940. The German Luftwaffe blitzed Britain with bombs, and a cross-channel invasion seemed imminent. Roosevelt and the growing body of internationalists saw the United States ringed by hostile Axis powers on the other sides of both the Atlantic and the Pacific. After Japan invaded Indochina in June, Roosevelt ordered an embargo on American shipments of scrap iron to Japan. But he allowed oil shipments to continue, in the fear that shutting them off would provoke the Japanese to invade the Dutch East Indies, rich in oil and rubber. The failure to embargo oil (which eventually came in July, 1941) smacked of the old appeasement policy, but American policy toward Germany certainly did not. In March, 1941, Congress agreed to all-out aid short of war by passing the Lend-Lease Act providing American loans to Britain in order to buy war goods. At the same time, the United States declared the Western Hemisphere, including Greenland and Iceland, off-limits to Axis warships, and American vessels began informing the British of the positions of German submarines. By November, 1941, American destroyers and German submarines were depth-bombing and torpedoing each other, American ships were convoying material to Britain and Russia, and Germany and the United States were carrying on an undeclared naval war in the Atlantic.

Were the American defense preparations unnecessary? Was Roosevelt leading the country into an unnecessary war? Some responsible senators and commentators thought so at the time, and their case would have been stronger had they known that Hitler in late 1941 had no intention of attacking the United States immediately. He had attacked the Soviet Union in June, and although the act of bringing the vast manpower and resources of Russia against Germany would ultimately have fatal consequences, he expected to win, and only then confront the United States. But the German navy, and the specter of German control of a captured British navy, was no phantom; the Atlantic coast was much more directly threatened by Nazi Germany than it had been by Imperial Germany in 1914–18. By November, public opinion and the Congress supported all-out aid, but not a flat declaration of war against Germany. Outside events changed that.

As Japan moved southward in Asia in 1940 and 1941, the United States continued to regard Axis Europe as its primary danger. Despite American discovery of eventual Japanese attack plans, after breaking a Japanese military code in January, 1941, no details were known (they were not yet decided by the Japanese), and it was assumed that Japan would concentrate its efforts on Asia. The United States formed joint Pacific defense plans with the British and Dutch, froze Japanese assets in the United States in mid-year, and in July, after Japan took southern Indochina, finally embargoed oil sales. The Japanese were infuriated; American—or Indonesian—oil was essential to them.

In August, Prince Konoye, the Japanese prime minister, tried to arrange a meeting with Roosevelt to negotiate Japanese-American differences. The main problem, in the final analysis, was China: Japan wanted American recognition of its penetration into China, while the United States wanted Japan to withdraw. Roosevelt, on

THE WESTERN PACIFIC, 1931–1945

U.S.S.R.

MONGOLIA

MANCHUKUO

Peiping

CHINA

KOREA

HONSHU

Hiroshima

JAPAN

Nagasaki

Atomic bomb,
Aug 6 & 9, 19.

"The Hump"

Chungking

Yangtze R.

Panay incident,
1937

RYUKYU IS.

Okinawa

BC

Burma Road

Canton

Okinawa,
Apr.–June 1945

Mandalay

FORMOSA

Hong Kong

Rangoon

HAINAN

THAILAND

FR. INDO-CHINA

Manila

PHILIPPINES

Saigon

Leyte Gulf,
Oct. 1944

Indian

Singapore

SUMATRA

New Guine
1942–44

BORNEO

CELEBES

NEW

Ocean

Batavia

NETHERLAND

JAVA

Java Sea,
Feb.–Mar. 1942

EAST INDIES

AUSTRALIA

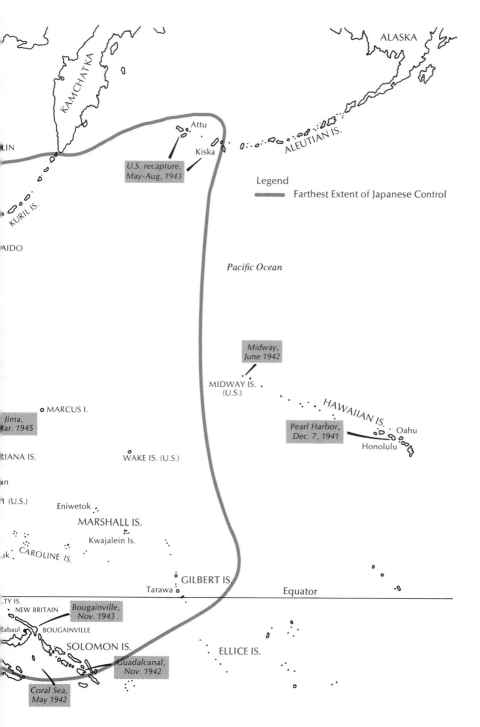

KAMCHATKA

ALASKA

LIN

Attu

Kiska

U.S. recapture,
May–Aug. 1943

ALEUTIAN IS.

Legend

━━━ Farthest Extent of Japanese Control

KURIL IS.

AIDO

Pacific Ocean

*Midway,
June 1942*

MIDWAY IS.
(U.S.)

HAWAIIAN IS.

○ MARCUS I.

*Jima,
Mar. 1945*

Pearl Harbor,
Dec. 7, 1941

Oahu

Honolulu

RIANA IS.

WAKE IS. (U.S.)

n

1 (U.S.)

Eniwetok

MARSHALL IS.

Kwajalein Is.

uk

CAROLINE IS.

GILBERT IS.

Equator

Tarawa

TY IS.

NEW BRITAIN

*Bougainville,
Nov. 1943*

Rabaul

BOUGAINVILLE

SOLOMON IS.

ELLICE IS.

*Guadalcanal,
Nov. 1942*

*Coral Sea,
May 1942*

Hull's urging, called on Konoye for commitments that the latter could not provide; the Americans feared that an inconclusive meeting might demoralize China, or even the Soviet Union. The meeting did not take place, and in October, Konoye's government was replaced by rabid militarists led by General Hideki Tojo. Diplomatic discussions had gone on in Washington for most of 1941. In early November, Japan even offered to withdraw from Indochina if the United States removed its embargoes on shipments to Japan and its support of Nationalist China. By then American diplomacy had achieved the important, if limited, objectives of stopping further Japanese aggression. But on November 26, a memorandum from Hull restated the much more moralistic American desire that Japan withdraw from China as well as Southeast Asia, a policy unattainable except by force or complete Japanese capitulation. This was interpreted by the Japanese as an ultimatum. They activated tactical war plans.

On the morning of December 7, nearly 200 carrier-based Japanese planes attacked the American naval base at Pearl Harbor, Hawaii. Communications mistakes abounded, in retrospect. The commanders there had received a general alert some days earlier that a Japanese attack somewhere was imminent, but they expected Malaya to be the target. An urgent warning from Washington specifically mobilizing Pearl Harbor did not arrive there until after the attack began. Except for aircraft carriers, nearly the entire American Pacific fleet was in port, and most of it went to the bottom. The raid killed more than 3,400 people. Franklin Roosevelt, speaking to Congress the next day, called December 7 "a date which will live in infamy," and Congress declared that a state of war existed with Japan. The Japanese began to attack the Philippines and other American islands in the Pacific. On December 11, Hitler and Mussolini, faithful to the Axis treaty and apparently believing that Russia could be conquered before American force would be felt in Europe, declared war on the United States. The shift in public opinion since 1938 away from isolationism and the policy of "all-out aid short of war" had made the country partially ready for hostilities. But the shock of Pearl Harbor catapulted the United States into full-scale military and naval participation, which it otherwise might still have avoided. The aggressiveness of Germany and Japan, together with a hardening of American will in the direction of protecting Britain and China, brought war. Allied with Britain and the

Soviet Union, and with then-prostrate France and China, the United States began its long, uphill struggle against the Axis.

From Pearl Harbor
to V-J Day

The "special relationship" between the United States and Britain marked World War II strategy from start to finish. Roosevelt and Prime Minister Winston Churchill first met in August, 1941, at Argentia Bay, off Newfoundland, and issued the somewhat Wilsonian "Atlantic Charter," important later as the first joint expression of intent to form the postwar United Nations. In December, a few days after Pearl Harbor, Churchill met Roosevelt in Washington, and that "Arcadia conference" set up a joint military high command and established the general strategy that the main American effort would be directed against Germany rather than Japan. Similar close coordination with the third great Allied power, the Soviet Union, was never achieved. Britain, through diplomacy, and the United States, through lend-lease shipments, endeavored to keep the Soviet Union in the war against Hitler. Russia, then reeling, fought back tenaciously and slowly stopped the Nazi tide late in 1942. In that year, the Axis powers reached the limits of their temporary empire in both Europe and the Pacific. The Germans pushed across Russia almost to the Caspian Sea and came halfway across Egypt toward the Suez Canal before the British stopped Erwin Rommel's Afrika Korps at El Alamein. Anglo-Canadian efforts to establish a beachhead in northern France failed. Japan controlled the Pacific eastward almost to Hawaii and southward into New Guinea.

Allied strategy was to leave the war in the Pacific to the Americans, who would "island hop" from the Solomon Islands northwest toward Japan; to push the Germans and Italians out of Africa and then invade Europe through Italy; to establish a "second front" in northwestern Europe as soon as possible (much too late, in the opinion of the beleaguered Russians); and to hold and reverse the German drive into Russia. All of these things happened, but slowly and at terrible cost. American force came to bear gradually. The Japanese, while conquering the Philippines, lost their first major naval battle to the United States, the Battle of the Coral Sea, in May,

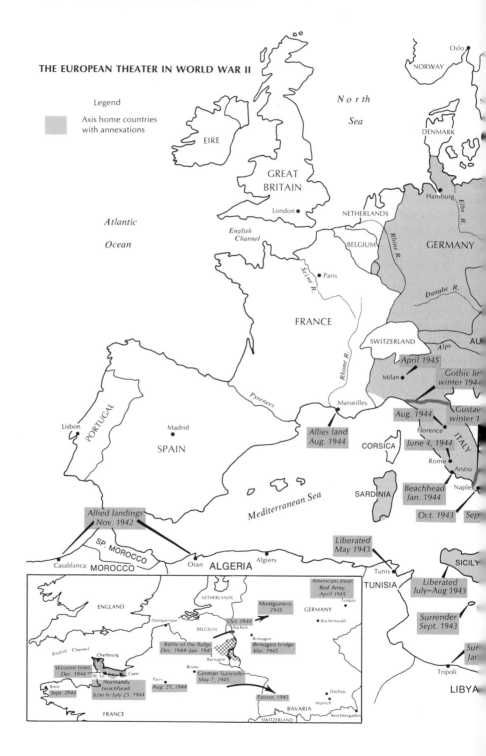

THE EUROPEAN THEATER IN WORLD WAR II

Legend

Axis home countries
with annexations

FINLAND

Stockholm

Leningrad

Volga R.

Moscow

U.S.S.R.

Farthest German eastern advance 1941–42

Army, y 1945

Vistula R.   Warsaw

POLAND

Kiev

Don R.   Stalingrad

Eastern front, early 1944

Curpathian Mts   UKRAINE

Red Army repulses Germans, winter 1942-43

SLOVAKIA

Budapest   Rostov

UNGRY

ROMANIA   CRIMEA

Bucharest   Sevastopol   Yalta

Belgrade

YUGOSLAVIA   B l a c k   S e a

Sofia

BULGARIA

ALBANIA

GREECE   TURKEY

Aegean

Sea

CYPRUS   SYRIA

CRETE

Fell Nov. 1942

British defeat Rommel Oct. 1942   PALESTINE

Alexandria

Benghazi   El Alamein

LIBYA   EGYPT

1942, and their second, the Battle of Midway, in June. In August, American forces invaded Guadalcanal in the Solomons and hopped from island to island for another three years. In November, after plans for an Allied invasion of northern France were dropped, to Stalin's dismay, United States forces joined the British in North Africa, and after early reverses, the Allies pushed the Germans into northern Tunisia and then off the African continent in May, 1943. During those early months, German submarines sank as much as 800,000 tons of war goods per month in the Atlantic, and the American people were preoccupied with the replacement of ships and material, lend-lease convoys to Britain and Russia, rebuilding of the Pacific fleet, and the mobilization of an armed force of over 10 million.

By the middle of 1943, the Axis was in slow retreat on all fronts. From Africa the British and Americans leaped to Sicily, took it in thirty-eight days, thanks in part to the vigor of the American general George S. Patton, and began inching up the Italian peninsula. The Red Army stemmed the German tide at Stalingrad in January, 1943. Mussolini's Fascist government collapsed in the summer of 1943, and its successor brought Italy out of the Axis into co-belligerent status with the Allies. The Germans resisted stiffly; General Mark Clark did not enter Rome until June 5, 1944. On the next day, however, the long-awaited Canadian-Anglo-American invasion of northern France began, and from the beaches of Normandy the Allies recovered most of France by the end of 1944. In the Pacific, American forces re-invaded the Philippines, after decimating the Japanese fleet in the Battle of Leyte Gulf.

Allied leaders held several conferences in 1943 to set joint war policy, and conferences in 1944 and 1945 became more and more concerned with the nature of the peace settlement. Roosevelt and Churchill met at Casablanca, Morocco, in January, 1943, and again at Quebec in August. By the time of their first meeting with Stalin, in late November at Tehran, Iran, Anglo-American cooperation was firm and Stalin's misgivings about a Western entente against Soviet interests were considerable. But Churchill and Roosevelt assured Stalin that the invasion of Western Europe, which Stalin had long demanded in order to relieve German pressure on Russia, would come in the spring of 1944; they also agreed to Soviet absorption of the Baltic states and much of eastern Poland, with Poland to be "compensated" with east German territory after the war.

In late 1944, Allied representatives agreed at the Dumbarton Oaks Conference in Washington to the American-inspired plan for a United Nations organization to keep the peace after the war ended, and the Bretton Woods economic conference of 1944 established the main outlines for postwar financial stability among nations. The last conference between Roosevelt, Churchill, and Stalin came in February, 1945, at Yalta in the Crimea. At that time, the Allied western-front advance had momentarily bogged down under a fierce, final German counteroffensive around Bastogne, Belgium. On the eastern front, in contrast, hundreds of Red Army divisions moved within a few dozen miles of Berlin itself and had long since occupied Poland and Rumania. Because of the momentary battlefield situation, the agreements at Yalta were more favorable to the Soviets than they might otherwise have been. Roosevelt in particular was bitterly criticized years later. At Yalta, Russia agreed to Anglo-American pleas to enter the war against Japan, if in return, the Russians would receive bases and territory south and east of Siberia. Stalin also was to recognize Nationalist China (ignoring the Maoists). Russia guaranteed free elections in the Eastern European countries (the Soviet and Western definitions of "free elections" later turned out to be very different). As decided at earlier conferences, Germany and Austria would be partitioned into occupation zones, with Berlin and Vienna likewise divided quadripartitely, although surrounded by the Soviet zone.

Two months after the Yalta conference, on April 12, 1945, Roosevelt, who had been reelected in 1944 for the fourth time, suddenly died. The sense of loss was great the world over; a sailor on Admiral Turner's flagship off Okinawa said it for everybody: "It's like somebody dying in your own family." The loss was perhaps nowhere greater than in the mind of Harry S. Truman. The vice-president was a Missourian whose chief claim to fame before F.D.R. dumped the wobbly Henry Wallace as a running-mate at the 1944 Democratic convention had been as chairman of a Senate committee investigating mobilization irregularities. Truman had never been briefed on significant problems, and consequently he began shakily to step into the huge shoes of his illustrious predecessor. But he proved to be a rapid learner. He ordered the United Nations conference, set for San Francisco in late April, to go on as planned, and the new international organization, with the Russians participating fully as they had promised at Yalta, became a reality.

"Fresh, spirited American troops, flushed with victory, are bringing in thousands of hungry, ragged, battle-weary prisoners . . ."
(News item)

Bill Mauldin, the GI's cartoonist, at about the time American forces entered Germany in 1945. (Drawing copyrighted 1944 by United Features Syndicate, Inc. Reproduced by courtesy of Bill Mauldin.)

German resistance, so fierce in the winter of 1945, was crumbling. In March and April, after the stunning (and accidental) capture of an undamaged bridge across the Rhine at Remagen, forces under British Field Marshal Bernard Montgomery nudged the Wehrmacht back across the plains of Holland and Saxony. Meanwhile, George Patton raced across Germany's midsection to link up with Red Army units at a place called Torgau, near the Czech-German border. Germany inflicted heavy casualties but lost tens of thousands of prisoners. The Berlin government decreed that, in view of domestic shortages, only two sizes of shrouds were to be manufactured, and no more linings for coffins. Robert Capa, a *Life* photographer, parachuted into Germany in March with the 17th Airborne, three cameras, and a canteen of scotch. Capa wrote, "It seems to me that the last days of the war were in the battle of Bastogne. Those kind of slow-moving businesses afterwards when we moved up the Rhine finished the German Army. And much as I hate to make primitive statements, the Germans are the meanest bastards. They are the meanest during an operation and afterwards they all have a cousin in Philadelphia. That is what I like about the French. They do not have cousins in Philadelphia." On May 8, Hitler's Third Reich, with 988 of its proclaimed 1,000 years unfulfilled, surrendered unconditionally. The Allied occupation of Germany began, and so did postwar problems among the Allies.

Some American army units were ordered to remain in Germany to supervise cleaning up the rubble, caring for masses of refugees and concentration camp victims, and restoring some semblance of civil order. G.I.'s were forbidden to "fraternize" with Germans, but the order became difficult to enforce when German girls emerged in summer costumes in June. "If you leave your hat on and don't smile, it's not fraternization," went the phrase. Other units, less fortunate, were ordered to the Pacific theater after thirty-day furloughs in the States. The war against Japan had reached its penultimate bloodbath, the battle for Okinawa; on that island in the summer of 1945, 6,990 Americans were killed or missing and another 30,000 wounded, while over 98,000 Japanese were killed. In June, General Joseph W. Stilwell, the veteran leader of the China-Burma campaign, warned that "a lot of people have the idea that this is a pushover. . . . It will take a long time—easily two years." But on July 16, the first atomic bomb was successfully tested at Los

The glory of war in the Pacific: United States Marines after defeating the Japanese at Eniwetok. (U.S. Coast Guard)

Alamos, New Mexico. The next day brought Truman, Stalin, and Churchill (replaced in mid-conference by the new prime minister, Clement Attlee) together at Potsdam, near Berlin. By then the Red Army firmly occupied Eastern Europe, and the two Western Allies could only hope that Soviet reaffirmation of "free elections" there would ensue. Russia finally seemed ready to enter the war against Japan, and did so on August 9. But the expectation, held by many (though by no means all) American military commanders, that Japan would not surrender until 1946, and at a cost of perhaps a million casualties, did not materialize. The atomic bomb, developed in a race with the Germans throughout the war, bludgeoned the Japanese into surrendering. President Truman stated ten years later in his memoirs that his decision to drop the atomic bomb on cities "of prime military importance" was taken on the advice of both his scientific and military advisers, who felt that a demonstration test would not be effective in ending the war. As for the obliteration of cities and tens of thousands of their populations, "conventional" weapons had done that already, in Hamburg and Tokyo and in Dresden (where in February, 1945, incendiary bombings killed between 65,000 and 130,000 in one night). Some military leaders, also commenting after the fact, believed Japan was ready to surrender anyway, and that the bomb was unnecessary. The military grounds for dropping the atomic bombs were arguable. But there were possibly diplomatic grounds also. Perhaps the president considered that the use of the bomb would bolster American post-war diplomacy and would end the war before the Russians could occupy large segments of East Asia, placing those areas beyond American influence, as had already happened in Eastern Europe. On August 6, American planes dropped an atomic bomb on Hiroshima, and on August 9 on Nagasaki, obliterating the two cities and killing uncounted Japanese, probably around 100,000. Emperor Hirohito convinced the Japanese high command that further resistance would be suicidal. Japan surrendered unconditionally on August 14, and the Second World War was over. But the Cold War was not far off, and the Atomic Age had already begun.

The winners: Americans at a San Francisco fountain, V-J day, August 14, 1945. (United Press International Photo)

The losers: Hiroshima after the atomic bomb, August 6, 1945. (Yosuke Yamahata, ©
Magnum Photos, Inc.)

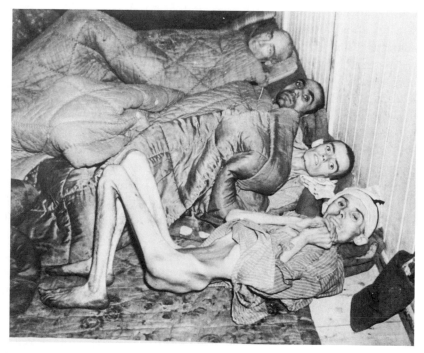

Survivors: Inmates of the Nazi concentration camp at Buchenwald after release by Allied troops, 1945. (United Press International Photo)

Truman and the Eightieth Congress

The victory of V-J Day was sweet. But what then? A return to depression? More New Deal? Or a new "normalcy" like the twenties? The intense concern with *winning*, which had preoccupied Americans for almost four years, relaxed. Different groups more openly sought their own private goals. Consumers, weary of wartime rationing and price controls, wanted food, houses, cars—without inflation. Labor, having abided by the wartime "no-strike" pledge, wanted higher wages and shorter hours, and was ready to go on strike for them. Businessmen wanted wartime profit levels to continue, price controls and priority restrictions to cease, labor to behave, and government to leave them alone. Northern Democrats wanted to win more elections, and thought that more New Deal farmer-labor-welfare policies would help them do so. Many Republicans and southern Democrats were as unsympathetic to those policies as they had been in the thirties. On a very few basics, the nation agreed: no more depression; no toleration of threats to national security, either from "internal subversion" or "outside aggression." Some desired a return to isolation, but a growing number were prepared, after the war experience, to cooperate with "allies" to resist evil in the world, and a new "evil aggressor" was quickly identified and labeled "world Communism." The United Nations charter sailed through the Senate. A few crackpots protested—one claimed that the United Nations was a plot to make the Duke of Windsor King of the world—but the opposition was nothing like that in 1919 against the League of Nations.

The new president was an unknown quantity. Truman contrasted with Roosevelt in nearly every way, a Missouri farm boy following the Hudson Valley squire, the self-educated midwesterner following the polished voice from Groton and Harvard, the "little guy" following F.D.R., the world figure. Democrats and many others despaired when their great leader during twelve violent years suddenly died on an April afternoon, to be succeeded by an apparent nobody. But Harry Truman, in his nearly eight years in the White House, surprised many people. He managed to preserve, and in some ways to extend, the welfare policies of the later New Deal, despite vigorous opposition from the congressional coalition of Republicans and southern Democrats that had developed in 1937–39. He oversaw, in foreign affairs, the economic and military revival of Western Europe. A Third World War, threatening constantly to erupt, never came. He had many critics, Democratic as well as Republican, and never enjoyed the popularity of Roosevelt or Eisenhower. But many "little guys" easily identified with him, even with the traits for which he was most criticized—excessive partisanship and excessive loyalty to friends and appointees whose activities had become dubious. Outspoken and vigorous, Truman kept on his White House desk a sign reading "The buck stops here." The accidental president who refused to pass the buck became, to admirers, "The Man of Independence," and to critics a narrow-gauge politician who nonetheless had to be reckoned with.

From August, 1945, until the election of 1948, the Truman administration and Congress concerned themselves, in domestic affairs, with three sets of issues: demobilization and peacetime re-adjustment; Truman's attempts to expand the welfare programs of the later New Deal against bipartisan congressional opposition; and reorganization of the federal executive branch of government. De-mobilization was an urgent problem in 1945 and 1946. There were no easy answers as to how, or how rapidly, to throw 12 million serv-icemen and women onto the labor market, to convert from wartime to peacetime production, and to relax price and wage controls, without sending the economy careening into either depression or wealth-destroying inflation. Congress had made some provision for discharged servicemen and women in June, 1944, when it passed a set of measures called the "G.I. Bill of Rights," establishing veter-ans' hospitals, homeowner's loans, educational subsidies, and the "52-20 Club," a dole of twenty dollars a week (up to a year) until a veteran could find a job. These measures smoothed demobilization, but the mustering-out process in 1945–46 was carried out too rap-idly to be tidy. Since an adamant public opinion forced Truman to reduce the armed forces much faster than he wanted to, the military services discharged over 9 million people in the first year of peace. The president did not get his way with price controls either: though the Office of Price Administration ended most rationing by early 1946, the president wanted some controls continued. When Con-gress sent Truman a bill in June, 1946, extending the OPA without some of the powers Truman wanted it to have, he vetoed the bill, thus abruptly ending price controls and setting off a rampant 25 percent price inflation lasting for two months until Congress pro-duced another OPA bill. The escalating postwar inflation was dif-ficult to stop, even without such bickering between Truman and Congress, and it continued to rise as OPA controls ended a few months later and as Congress passed a tax-reduction act, over Tru-man's veto, in March, 1948.

Industrial labor, hit hard by inflation and no longer bound after August, 1945, by the "no-strike" agreement, grew sullen. Electrical and auto workers struck in late 1945. When John L. Lewis' United Mine Workers struck in April, 1946, the government took over the mines, and the coal strike ended in the courts only in March, 1947. Railway workers also threatened to go out in 1946. Truman feder-alized the railroads and asked Congress for power to draft strikers. The unions settled reluctantly. More strikes occurred in 1946 than in any other year in American history, and the ensuing years were not much better. Labor troubles continued sporadically; finally, in 1952, Truman took over the country's steel mills in order to keep defense supplies moving toward Korea, and when the Supreme Court voided the action, the strike went on for almost two months. Truman sympathized with organized labor, but not enough to tolerate work stoppages in key sectors of the economy.

The majority of congressmen, and probably of the public, were even less sympathetic to labor than Truman was. The many work stoppages, the apparent dictatorial willfulness of certain labor leaders (particularly Lewis), and many businessmen's residual dislike of unions provided the context for sweeping revision of the Wagner Act. In June, 1947, the Republican-controlled Eightieth Congress passed its major achievement, the Taft-Hartley Act, over Truman's veto. It outlawed the closed shop and the secondary boycott, allowed employers to make their viewpoints known during union organization campaigns, and required, for NLRB certification, that unions file affidavits that their officers were not Communists. It also gave the president the power to invoke an eighty-day "cooling-off" period in strikes he deemed harmful to the national interest. Taft-Hartley did not repeal industry-wide collective bargaining, as some businessmen and congressmen wanted; union leaders nevertheless denounced it as a "slave labor law."

Taft-Hartley was only one example of Congress's resistance to presidential attempts to revive the welfarism of the mid-thirties and produce measures benefiting the farmers and workers in the Democratic coalition. In early September, 1945, days after the United States signed the armistice with Japan, Truman asked for legislation to insure full employment, national health insurance, broader social security and higher minimum wages, controlled demobilization, and governmental reorganization, among a twenty-one point program which he called his "Fair Deal." In the ensuing three years, few of these measures became law. The House even rejected a public housing act in 1948, though Truman and the Senate Republican leader Robert A. Taft of Ohio both supported it. The president and Congress disagreed about the proper way to demobilize, and Congress buried Truman's plan for national health insurance. After heavy infighting, Truman and Congress did agree to the Employment Act of 1946, which created the Council of Economic Advisers and committed the federal government in principle to maintaining a high level of employment.

Truman and Congress also cooperated in reorganizing the federal government in 1946 and 1947. The Atomic Energy Act of August, 1946, assured a government monopoly, under civilian rather than military control, of fissionable material. The Presidential Succession Act of 1947 placed the Speaker of the House and the president *pro tem* of the Senate ahead of cabinet secretaries in case the president and vice-president were disabled. In July, 1947, the National Security Act unified the armed services under the new Department of Defense, and also created the Central Intelligence Agency and the Joint Chiefs of Staff. Congress approved in 1947 the Twenty-Second Amendment to the Constitution, limiting presidents to two terms; a sufficient number of states ratified it by 1951. The Republican Congress thus assured that there would be no more four-term Democratic presidents like Roosevelt—and ironically, prevented their own winner, Eisenhower, from running a third time in 1960.

Taft Republicanism, the 1948 Upset, and the Fair Deal

The battles between Truman and the Eightieth Congress were in part the product of partisanship, the effusions of men who enjoyed the political fray. But they rested also on serious disagreements over the proper role of the federal government, the meaning of individualism and democracy, perceptions of changing social and economic patterns, and the nature of American world leadership. Republicans of mature age in the 1940s well remembered the time, only fifteen years before, when their party was, and had been for thirty-five years, the majority party. Many opposed the extent of the federal government's activity under Roosevelt and Truman. The exemplar of this Republican "conservatism" was the doughty Ohio Senator, Robert Taft. Taft was serious, articulate, and highly intelligent; Truman in his memoirs called him as "a highly ethical, straightforward, and honorable man." Taft distrusted the "welfare state" as a threat to individual initiative. In his view, a large bureaucracy oppressed people and stood in the way of their working out their personal destinies in a free society. Yet he was no hardhearted doctrinaire; when he saw a national need that would not be met by private business without federal stimulation, as in the case of housing, he supported federal activity. But he believed that federal interference should be minimized and, where it was necessary, controlled by Congress rather than by free-wheeling executive agencies. In foreign policy he was no less cautious about "entangling alliances"; he opposed NATO and Point Four, and only after solemn deliberation did he support the Marshall Plan, the decision to fight in Korea, and other activist foreign policies. With these views and personal qualities, Taft emerged as "Mr. Republican," the hero of many in the Midwest and West.

To almost everyone, 1948 shaped up as a "Republican Year." By-passing Taft as too outspoken to attract independent voters, the G.O.P. renominated their 1944 candidate, Governor Thomas E. Dewey of New York, who had lost to Roosevelt by only 3 million votes. The Democrats, meanwhile, split into no less than three tickets. Southerners opposed to Truman's federal activism, and his support of a fair employment practices law and racial desegregation in government and the armed forces, grouped around the States Rights, or "Dixiecrat," ticket, headed by Governor J. Strom Thurmond of South Carolina. On the left, disgruntled New Dealers and others unhappy with Truman's anti-Soviet foreign policies backed the Progressive ticket of former Vice-President Henry A. Wallace. The Democratic convention despairingly nominated Truman.

Contrary to the expectation of the Republicans, virtually every public opinion poll, and many Democrats, Truman upset Dewey and carried Democratic majorities into both houses of Congress. The Thurmond ticket carried thirty-nine electoral votes in the South, and the Wallace progressives won over a million votes, especially in big northern cities. But Truman showed that a Democrat could win without the "Solid South" or the socialist left. The lesson was not lost on future Democratic candidates.

The re-elected Truman called for a more comprehensive "Fair Deal" and had better luck in getting it from the new Congress than he had with the Eightieth. Congress balked at some Truman proposals, including national health insurance, a St. Lawrence Seaway, his farm subsidy plan, an anti-lynching law, and an anti-segregation "Fair Employment Practices" act. But it passed the Housing Act of 1949, providing slum clearance and over a million housing units over six years for low-income families. The federal minimum wage rose from forty to seventy-five cents an hour, social security benefits were raised and extended, the Displaced Persons Act of

1950 admitted 400,000 European war refugees. Truman appointed several blacks to high federal jobs and gradually integrated the armed forces and executive agencies. Thus the Fair Deal extended the New Deal, and in so doing solidified the Democratic voting coalition.

The Origins of the Cold War

In foreign policy, the Truman administration found a greater degree of consensus with Congress than in domestic policy. The isolationist spirit of pre–World War II days declined as events abroad continued to make headlines. Even Senator Arthur Vandenberg of Michigan, an impeccable midwestern isolationist before the war, converted fully, and with much effect on his senatorial colleagues, to the position that the administration ought to be supported in its international policies. The White House, the State Department, and the Senate frequently agreed on European and Soviet policy (less so regarding Asia) in the several years following the end of World War II, when America confronted an essentially new world situation. Most of Europe and China and Japan were prostrate; Britain and France, though "winners," had been badly damaged by the war, and their colonial empires (as well as those of Belgium and the Netherlands) were to last only a few more years. The Soviet Union, however, despite the ravages of the German war, emerged with a large and proven armed force, especially strong in ground troops, and with the Stalin regime committed to the diplomatic or military control of Eastern Europe. The United States emerged from the war with its continental territory unbombed and uninvaded, a massive economic capacity, and while its monopoly of atomic weapons lasted, greater military power than any other country. After 1945, in contrast to the pre-1939 world, Britain and France as well as the defeated Axis countries were markedly diminished in relative power, and the Soviet Union and the United States markedly augmented. Given these realities, the major fact of international politics after 1945 was rivalry between the United States and the Soviet Union.

The American-Soviet rivalry had four main dimensions. The first was political: the creation and enlargement of two great spheres of influence, which Americans became fond of calling "the free world" and "the Communist bloc," despite great differences among the countries and factions within each group. A second dimension was economic: Soviet-type socialism contrasted with more-or-less free-enterprise capitalism. A third was the ideological contrast between Marxism-Leninism and western-style liberal-democratic government with two or more political parties, based on the doctrine that the state is servant of the individual, not the instrument of the proletariat. The fourth dimension was the military confrontation of the two sides. To be sure, there were exceptions to these dichotomies: Yugoslavia, for instance, had a socialist economy but was not part of the Soviet political orbit after 1948; Nationalist China was politically aligned with the United States but was not a democratic regime in the western sense; India had a multi-party elected government and a semi-socialist economy, and was politically neutral. The rivalry between the "superpowers" was complex. It was not eased by the tendency of people and leaders on both sides to reduce the complexities to moralistic stereotypes such as "the world Communist conspiracy" or "the Yankee-dominated capitalist imperialists."

Sketched in its simplest terms, American-Soviet competition developed after 1945 in four stages. In the first, from the final months of World War II to the end of 1946, the Russians, British, French, and Americans established occupation administrations in defeated areas. Many leaders hoped that the "Grand Alliance" of wartime would continue more permanently through the United Nations, founded in June, 1945, to preserve world peace. However, as this first stage wore on, they saw that hope erode as American and Soviet leaders interpreted each others' actions, rightly or wrongly, as hostile. In the second stage, from early 1947 into mid-1953, the early Cold War, Americans and many others feared that war between the United States and the Soviet Union might break out at any time because of the "outward thrust of Soviet power" into countries weakened and confused by war. This period opened with the Soviet Union consolidating its control of eastern Europe, and American leaders enunciating the "containment" policy. It worsened in 1949 when the Russians exploded their first atomic bomb and mainland China fell under Communist rule. It climaxed in the Korean outbreak in 1950 and ended in 1953 with the death of Stalin, the end of the Korean War, and possession of hydrogen bombs by both the United States and the Soviet Union. The third phase, from mid-1953 to late 1962, was the later Cold War, characterized by "nuclear stalemate" or "balance of terror." It ended with the Cuban missile crisis, while "brush-fire" confrontations occurred in the Middle East, Africa, Southeast Asia, and the Caribbean. The fourth phase, from late 1962 into the seventies, brought the end of bipolarity, replaced by a mild and fluctuating *détente* between the two superpowers, as the Russians quarreled with their erstwhile Chinese ally, and the United States became increasingly mired down in Indochina.

By the end of the war with Germany, Churchill, Roosevelt, and Stalin had agreed upon occupation policy and zones at their conferences in Tehran and Yalta. The four allied powers (France included) established occupation administrations for their zones of Germany and Austria and cooperatively in the conquered capitals of Berlin and Vienna. UNRRA, the United Nations Relief and Rehabilitation Administration, began pouring billions of dollars in economic aid, much of it from the United States, into Europe. In these first months after the war, there were some signs that cooperation rather than competition might continue among the victors: the Soviet Union accepted multi-party republican regimes in Hungary, Austria, Finland, and Czechoslovakia, removed their troops from the latter, and seemed satisfied so long as eastern European countries were "friendly" to the U.S.S.R. The Soviets were not yet making those countries into Marxist satellites dominated politically by uncontested Communist parties. The victors cooperated also in prosecuting Nazi leaders in the Nuremberg war crimes trials from November, 1945, to October, 1946. The United States was still optimistic enough about preserving peace through allied cooperation, and confident enough that its atomic monopoly meant military and diplomatic superiority, that Secretary of State James F. Byrnes, in September and December of 1945, sought a twenty-five-year alliance of the United States, Britain, and the Soviet Union.

In early 1946, the Russians declined to enter such an alliance, and on March 5, 1946, in a speech at Fulton, Missouri, Winston Churchill declared that an "Iron Curtain" was clanging down around eastern Europe. The period of postwar cooperation between East and West was ending, and the Cold War was approaching. Why? There were many reasons, including the thirty-year-old fear

On the eve of victory and of the Cold War: members of American and Soviet Red Army troops as they linked up at Torgau, 1945. (U.S. Army Photograph)

and hatred in the West of "Bolshevism" and in the U.S.S.R. of "capitalist imperialism." But in terms of post-1945 power politics, it ended principally because the Russians wished, in the interest of their security, to have a sphere of influence in eastern Europe, and in the interest of their revolutionary ideology, to see Marxist-Leninist governments there; while the Americans and British desired "freely elected" governments in which the Communist parties would play whatever role their popular support merited. Above all, the Soviets were fearful of any resurrection of German power (World Wars I and II gave them reasons to be fearful), and they interpreted Anglo-American policy aimed at eventual restoration of Germany as hostile to Russia.

Germany was the crux. If she remained weak and divided, the Soviet Union needed eastern European satellites less for security reasons than as a possible magnetic base to draw western Europe into its orbit. If Germany recovered much of her former strength, even if divided, the satellites would serve not as a magnet but as a buffer zone against repetitions of 1914 and 1941. From the American and British standpoint, the reverse held true: Germany weak and divided would simply invite Soviet expansion to the west and increase the possibility of a Third World War. But Germany restored economically (not militarily), along with the rest of war-torn Europe, East or West, would help create stable economic and political conditions, which would make another war less likely.

The Soviet Union thus aimed at its own security (and at Communist expansion, where possible), while the Americans and British sought *their* security through world stability (and the instituting of non-Communist governments, where possible). These divergent aims came to a head over the treatment of defeated Germany and the nature of postwar governments in eastern Europe, and thus the conditions for the Cold War came into being.

By early 1947, the Soviet Union believed itself threatened by Anglo-American encirclement, while the British and Americans believed Stalin would pursue Soviet expansion by subversion or military force. In February of that year, the Western powers concluded a peace treaty with Italy, and the Soviet Union made treaties with Hungary, Rumania, and Bulgaria. In that same month, Britain informed the United States that she could no longer commit British military resources to fight Marxist insurgents in Greece. Without that help, Greece appeared liable to take-over by these revolutionaries, as Albania and Yugoslavia already had been. British withdrawal crystallized American policy. In March, the president announced the "Truman Doctrine": the United States would support "free peoples" against internal and external aggression. The first American act under the Truman Doctrine was to provide $400 million in military aid to Greece and Turkey. This aid, and the Greek and Turk resolution, helped keep the eastern Mediterranean out of the developing Soviet satellite system. During the same period Truman recognized the new state of Israel and backed United Nations efforts to preserve peace after the bitter Arab-Israeli War of 1948.

American policy for western and central Europe became clearer yet in June of 1947. Secretary of State George C. Marshall, in a speech at Harvard University on June 5, called for large-scale United States economic assistance to Europe. European recovery had not proceeded, Marshall said, at an adequate pace, and two years of occupying Germany and Austria had produced little more than discord between the West and the Russians. In early 1947, the United States still retained a waning hope of agreement in Europe with the Soviet Union, for Marshall invited the Soviet Union as well as the eastern European states to participate in this economic recovery program. The Soviets not only declined but also forced the satellites to withdraw. (Later, in October, they created the Cominform as a paradiplomatic agency to link the eastern European countries more closely to the Soviet Union.) The idea broached by the Secretary of State on June 5 was soon called the Marshall Plan, and it met with growing support in the United States and Europe. Later in June, an article signed "X" appeared in the American journal *Foreign Affairs*. The author was George F. Kennan, head of the newly-created Policy Planning Staff of the State Department, a career diplomat with unparalleled experience in Germany and Russia. Kennan's article, which had been in draft versions for several months, expressed the view that American policy toward Russia should be one of "containment" of the Soviet outward thrust at critical points. Kennan later explained that he had meant political, not military, containment of Soviet expansion, and in selected areas vital to the United States, such as Europe and Japan, rather than everywhere along the Soviet perimeter. But "containment" came to be interpreted, with the Truman Doctrine, as a global policy, military as well as political, and in such form was established as the basic American stance toward the U.S.S.R.

The United States reaffirmed and extended a much older American "doctrine," that of Monroe, in the Treaty of Rio in September, 1947, linking the Western Hemisphere in a mutual defense agreement. In May, 1948, the Pact of Bogotá set up the Organization of American States as a regional security mechanism under the United Nations charter. By that time, a Soviet-inspired coup had converted Czechoslovakia into a Russian satellite, while in Germany the British and Americans consolidated the administration of their occupation zones. These events, which took place in February, 1948, rapidly had consequences. Congress, shocked by the Czech coup and the threat that Italy might vote in a Communist government at its general elections in April, provided funds for the Marshall Plan, and the economic recovery of Europe began in earnest. The Soviets handed the United States a dramatic means to demonstrate its aid efforts when, in June, in response to the Anglo-American zone unification in Germany, they blockaded the access routes to Berlin set up at the late wartime conferences. The West responded with the Berlin airlift, by which a constant shuttle of air transport fed and supplied the isolated West Berliners from June, 1948, to May, 1949, when Stalin quietly ended the blockade.

Meanwhile, from late 1948 to September, 1949, the British, French, and Americans transformed their occupation zones into the German Federal Republic. They organized the Council of Europe, including the West Germans, as a consultative forum for Western European cooperation. Early in 1949, President Truman, in his inaugural address, recommended a four-point program for world peace. The first three points were not new, but the fourth called for a long-term economic and technical assistance program for underdeveloped areas which, as Truman said, "would enable them to help themselves to become growing, strong allies of freedom." "Point Four," which Congress approved and funded in 1950, was conceived at about the same time as the Marshall Plan and aid to Greece and Turkey, but it was to be more permanent than the former and lacked the military character of the latter. Its early implementations included public health measures, hydroelectric development, vocational training, and food-growing improvements in

South America and Asia. The other major policy step of 1949 was more directly military: the signing, in April, of the North Atlantic Treaty Organization defense pact among the United States, Canada, several Western European countries, and Greece and Turkey. When the Senate ratified the NATO treaty in July, by a vote of 82 to 13, it ended the traditional American policy of "no entangling alliances" of a permanent military character.

Undoubtedly the foreign policy of the Truman administration helped revitalize Western Europe, the area of the world (Latin America excepted) that the United States considered most vital to its own security. But the postwar peace was fragile. In the summer of 1949, the Soviet Union successfully tested an atomic bomb, ending the American nuclear monopoly and throwing further alarm into the minds of those Americans who already were saying that the United States was losing "every round" in the Cold War. The Soviet possession of atomic weapons was a serious strategic matter. When this development was coupled with events of 1949 in Asia, insecure and nervous citizens believed that, European successes notwithstanding, the "Communist tide" threatened before long to engulf them.

Asia:
An American Failure?

A successful policy for Asia eluded Truman. Probably no policy would have satisfied the expectations of many Americans that a friendly China would dominate the area. But to many accustomed to total war and total victory, the United States was supposed to "win," regardless of complexities. After V-J Day, the United States sought to reestablish a central government in China, parts of which had been occupied by the Japanese since the late thirties. General Marshall arrived in China in December, 1945, to seek the establishment of a coalition government, to be dominated by Chiang Kai-shek's Nationalists but to include the Marxist insurgents led by Mao Tse-tung. The United States was still emotionally attached to the Nationalists, as it was before World War II. During the war, Roosevelt had tried fruitlessly to wish great-power status on China by including Chiang in "Big Four" conferences and by arranging for China to have a permanent seat on the United Nations Security

Council. But the Nationalist government remained too corrupt and impotent to rule China. Marshall returned to the United States in January, 1947, abandoning his coalition-making efforts. The State Department advised that only an incredibly vast commitment of American funds and manpower could create a friendly and capable regime in China—a commitment of men and material on the Asian mainland that contravened traditional policy as well as prevailing conditions.

After Marshall departed, the struggle between the Nationalists and the Maoists widened. The Maoists overran large areas of China; popular confidence in Chiang dwindled accordingly; Truman and the State Department realized that no application of the Truman Doctrine and no Asian Marshall Plan could succeed. In October, 1949, the Maoists drove Chiang's remaining armies completely off the mainland to their island refuge on Formosa. China, the sentimental Asian favorite of Americans for over a century, the subject of the Open Door, and the key to American discord with Japan in the late thirties, was Communist. Although the connections between the Maoists and the Soviet Union were tenuous—Stalin had said that the Chinese were "not good Communists," and indeed Mao had fought the civil war in China largely without Soviet help—the two states were allied, and Americans looked at the new map of Eurasia and saw the same solid red color from Germany to the Pacific. Right-wing Republicans began blaming Truman and the Democrats for the "loss of China." Though the United States could hardly have lost something it never had, many believers in the myth of American omnipotence listened attentively. Deep disagreements between China and Russia were to become evident years later, but in 1949 and 1950, it seemed that America had suffered another major "defeat" in the Cold War.

The conquest of China by the Maoists and Russia's possession of atomic weapons were the backdrops for the Korean War. In early 1950, Americans believed themselves on the defensive in the Cold War. In response, Truman in January authorized the development of a hydrogen bomb. Secretary of State Dean Acheson clarified United States policy in Asia that same month by announcing that the United States considered occupied Japan and the Philippines to be areas it would defend in case of global conflict, while Korea, Formosa, and Southeast Asia could not be defended in such an eventuality. Korea had been under Japanese rule for decades until the end of World War II. As the war ended, Russia occupied the northern part of it, bordering Manchuria and the Soviet Union, and Americans occupied the part south of the thirty-eighth parallel. Under United Nations supervision, the southern zone became the Republic of Korea in 1948 under the presidency of an old Korean nationalist, Syngman Rhee. All American forces withdrew by mid-1949. Washington considered the Rhee government strong enough to protect itself against the "People's Republic" to the north. But the North Koreans, perhaps unaware that Acheson's policy by no means precluded American defense of South Korea in a local, as opposed to a global, conflict, were much stronger and more bellicose than American intelligence reports had estimated.

War
in Korea

Early in the morning of June 25, 1950, Korean time, after border skirmishes from both sides, the North Koreans threw their full force against the Republic of Korea, and in the following few days pushed southward with ease. The American response came that same week. Truman, Acheson, and their advisers regarded the North Korean action as a threat to American security because it endangered world peace and because it was a direct attack upon the peace-keeping role of the United Nations, which had supervised the establishment of the Republic of Korea. They decided to resist the North Korean invasion under authority of the United Nations, with the force necessary to repel the Northern army back across the thirty-eighth parallel. The United Nations Security Council met in emergency session and passed a resolution calling upon the North Koreans to withdraw, and asking United Nations members to provide all possible means to effect that withdrawal. Hours later, Truman authorized the deployment of American air and naval units as part of a United Nations force to give tactical aid to the South Korean army.

On the following day, the Security Council passed another resolution, calling for military sanctions against the North Korean invasion, thus fully backing the American action that had been taken after the first resolution and with the approval of most of the

Cold Warriors: Secretary of State Dean Acheson, President Truman, and Secretary of the Treasury John W. Snyder. (Brown Brothers)

Security Council delegates. The Soviet delegate was at that time boycotting the Security Council because it had refused to turn China's seat over to the Peking government, and therefore the U.S.S.R. was not on hand to veto either resolution. From the beginning, Truman and his advisers had acted through the United Nations, rather than unilaterally, in a successful effort to strengthen the United Nations, add international sanction to the American action, and avoid a direct American-Soviet confrontation. Later in the week, General Douglas MacArthur, the Allied Commander in occupied Japan who now directed the United Nations effort in Korea, visited the front. Appalled at the collapse of the South Korean forces, MacArthur asked Washington to commit American ground troops. Truman did so.

The response of Congress, the press, and the people to the American decision to resist the North Korean invasion was overwhelmingly favorable. A few congressmen criticized Truman for not consulting Congress in a formal way, but they fully approved the action itself. Taft and William F. Knowland of California, Republican leaders in the Senate, warmly applauded Truman's decision as "at last" showing American determination to wage the Cold War with vigor. Public and congressional opinion later soured as the Korean "police action" dragged on, but it was highly popular when it began.

In the first weeks of the war, the North Koreans almost pushed the United Nations forces (which were largely South Korean and American but included units from several other United Nations countries) off the peninsula. Then, as numbers of American and other troops increased, the defenders held at a perimeter around Pusan, in the southeast corner opposite Japan. In a successful tactical surprise, MacArthur established a beachhead at Inchon, on the west coast not far below the thirty-eighth parallel, and the United Nations forces began to push back the North Koreans. In September the United Nations recaptured Seoul, the capital, and cleared all the invaders from South Korea. At that point the original United Nations mission had been achieved. But MacArthur wanted to "liberate" North Korea, and despite a hint from Peking that the Red Chinese would intervene if United Nations forces invaded North Korea, Truman agreed to the move northward. In October, with United Nations approval, the army of Americans, South Koreans, and others crossed the thirty-eighth parallel and pushed the North Korean army toward the Manchurian-Soviet border. By November 20, MacArthur's forces had at one point reached the Yalu River, the Korean-Manchurian frontier. MacArthur had been directed to use only Korean troops in the border area, rather than Americans, to lessen the possibility of provoking a Chinese invasion. He did not. Washington had been anxious to confine the conflict to Korea, hoping against large-scale Chinese intervention through Manchuria, and possible Soviet tactical support of China. But on November 26, the Chinese moved in force across the Yalu, and pushed the United Nations army halfway back down the peninsula. The front stabilized not far from the thirty-eighth parallel, and bloody, indecisive battles continued for two more years.

The Chinese, supplied from Manchuria, had vast ground forces but were no match for the United States in the air. MacArthur, despite Washington's wish to avoid escalation, wanted to bomb Chinese bases north of the Yalu, and expressed this view in a letter to prominent Republican congressmen. The letter became public on April 5, 1951. A field commander, a very popular and almost legendary one, was publicly disagreeing with his Commander-in-

Chief. Truman responded with typical vigor: five days later he fired MacArthur from his command. General Matthew B. Ridgway succeeded MacArthur, and after the Soviet Union let out feelers for a peace settlement, Ridgway opened negotiations in July for a truce. Peace talks ground on for almost two more years, and the Korean War with them. The United States did not extricate itself until July, 1953, by which time the three-year effort had cost over 50,000 dead and over 100,000 wounded. But the Republic of Korea survived, through United Nations–sanctioned American efforts, without escalation into global and probably atomic war.

During the war the United States took other security measures in the Pacific. In August, 1951, it entered military alliances with Australia, New Zealand, and the Philippines, and a month later signed a peace treaty with Japan. The western Pacific had been defended in the interest of American security, as Europe and Latin America had previously been stabilized by defense treaties. The net effect of the Korean War on Americans was to chasten and exhaust Cold War belligerency. As far as they were concerned, a polar East-West conflict certainly existed; but so did the hope that it could be "waged" by treaties, not arms.

At Home, 1950–1952: McCarthy and the "Mess in Washington"

Truman's firing of General MacArthur added fuel to growing dissatisfaction with the administration's handling of the "Communist conspiracy." Despite the successes of postwar American policy in Europe, achieved through bipartisan efforts, and the overwhelming approval of the decision to resist the North Koreans in 1950, some congressmen and editorial writers accused the administration of being "soft on Communism," particularly in "giving China to the Reds" and in allowing Soviet spies and home-grown radicals to flourish within the United States itself. These were wild and unsubstantiated charges. The country hardly crawled with Russian agents. But some existed, and in the insecure mood prevailing in the early fifties, many people magnified their numbers. In January, 1950, a court convicted a former high State Department official named Alger Hiss of having perjured himself when he had earlier

denied any knowledge of passing government documents to a So-
viet-employed spy, Whittaker Chambers, in the late thirties. Chambers had confessed his activities to the House Un-American Activities Committee. The Hiss-Chambers affair occupied headlines
through much of 1948 and 1949. When Hiss was convicted, the real
losers were Secretary Acheson, who early in the episode had declared that Hiss was of good character as far as he knew, and Truman, who had called the Hiss trial a "red herring" designed to di-
vert attention from the inadequacies of the Eightieth Congress.
Other espionage trials in the United States and Britain shocked
Americans. One was the revelation that the Soviets' early success in
building an atomic bomb had been aided by a British physicist,
Klaus Fuchs, who worked at Los Alamos during the war and gave
the Russians full information concerning the American bomb. The
Truman administration itself helped feed the "Second Red Scare"
by stringent security measures in government in 1947–48 and by
prosecuting eleven leaders of the American Communist party in
1949 under the Smith Act of 1940 for advocating the violent overthrow of the government. By 1950, many people were extremely
nervous about "spies" and "subversives" and were becoming disturbed with a Democratic administration that seemed to harbor so
many of them.

The "Second Red Scare" accelerated in February, 1950, when an
obscure Republican Senator from Wisconsin, Joseph R. McCarthy,
claimed in a speech at Wheeling, West Virginia, that he had in
hand a list of 205 Communists in the State Department. McCarthy's list was borrowed, outdated, and had long since been acted
upon by the department. But he repeated the charge, changing the
number to 57 or 81, and he made headlines. When challenged,
McCarthy produced no names but counterattacked by accusing
Professor Owen Lattimore, an Asian expert at Johns Hopkins, of
being the leading Russian spy in the country. McCarthy said that
he would "stand or fall on this one," but when a Senate subcommit-
tee demolished the spy charge against Lattimore, McCarthy slung
mud all the harder. The popular mood of discontent caused by
Communist control of China and Eastern Europe combined with
conservatives' hostility to the Fair Deal. McCarthy and lesser
witch-hunters in the Senate and House enjoyed a wide audience.
McCarthyism became a term for the smear, the indiscriminate and
unproven charge, and the big lie. But the public was made insecure

by Soviet possession of atomic and hydrogen weapons, and supine officials in the State Department and other agencies who thought it best to "play ball" with McCarthy acquiesced in the dismissal of loyal employees who had been tarred by his brush, the removal of security clearance from some able and loyal scientists and Foreign Service officers, and the imposition of over-strict, repressive "security" regulations in government, education, and private corporations. Congress passed the McCarran Internal Security Act in 1950, over Truman's veto, imposing a jumbled set of "anti-subversive" statutes, and in June, 1952, the McCarran-Walter Immigration Act, again over Truman's veto, reaffirming the national origins

Senator Joseph R. McCarthy (R.-Wis.). (Eve Arnold, © Magnum Photos, Inc.)

quota system and providing for the non-admission or deportation of suspected "subversives."

As the 1952 election approached, the right wing viewed the Truman administration as suspiciously "soft on Communism," despite its anti-Soviet foreign policy and its substantial anti-subversive efforts. Further damage came in 1951 from revelations of corruption and improper use of influence in the Reconstruction Finance Corporation and the Internal Revenue Bureau, and by the Attorney General's refusal in the spring of 1952 to permit a thorough investigation of possible corruption in the Justice Department. Truman fired the Attorney General and continued clean-up efforts in the executive branch. But the public reaction to Truman's response to corruption charges was "too little, too late." The Republicans had captured an additional thirty seats in the House and five in the Senate in 1950, and sensed, correctly this time, that the G.O.P. would win in 1952. Their convention, meeting at Chicago in July, rejected the strong bid of Senator Taft for the nomination, and chose instead the most popular American of the day, General Dwight D. Eisenhower, who had commanded the Allied armies in Europe in World War II and subsequently headed NATO. Almost nothing was known about Eisenhower's political views—critics suggested he had none—but such a lack was undoubtedly an electoral advantage over Taft, with his conservative image. Eisenhower symbolized incorruptibility, American military strength, serenity, and anti-Communism—all of which the public worried most about in connection with Truman and the Democrats.

The Democratic convention nominated the governor of Illinois, Adlai E. Stevenson, who had not been associated with the Truman administration, and who proved, in 1952 and subsequently until he died in 1965, to have a strong appeal to liberal Democrats and intellectuals. An anonymous wag wrote the editor of the liberal *Reporter* in September:

> Between the Duff and the Dirksen,
>   When November's beginning to lower,
> Comes a pause in Republican thinking
>   That is known as the Eisenhower.

But most voters disagreed. Stevenson was "too much of an egghead." A Democratic precinct captain in Gary complained, "You know, Stevenson's probably the best man we ever put up, but he never comes across to the people." Steel workers remembered the good things that the New Deal and Fair Deal had brought them, but as a lathe operator said, "My wife crossed out my vote. I tried, but I couldn't keep her from voting for Eisenhower." Something, perhaps the knowledge that Stevenson had been divorced, caused millions of women to vote for Eisenhower. With over 55 percent of the popular vote, the general won in November.

The years of immediate postwar crisis were over. The accession of Eisenhower to the presidency in January, 1953, coupled with the death of Joseph Stalin in March and the end of the Korean War that summer, marked the conclusion of the early Cold War and early postwar period. The Republican party assumed power for the first time since Franklin Roosevelt succeeded the hapless Hoover in the deepest moment of the depression twenty years before. The Second World War and the acceptance of world leadership in the postwar years had changed the country dramatically between 1938 and 1953. These events and changes began to recede into the past, however, and the contemporary world began to assume clear shape.

9

DEMOGRAPHY, 1940-1971: YOUTH, SUBURBS, AND CIVIL RIGHTS

In superficial respects, the American population changed from the time of the Great Depression until the seventies in the same ways that it had been changing since George Washington's day: the population grew, kept urbanizing, shifted farther west, and contained minority groups whose assimilation was expedient but difficult. However, these traditional patterns continued in novel ways. Growth involved such contradictory elements as a population explosion and the future possibility of "ZPG," zero population growth; also, record-high increases in numbers but record-low birth rates. Urbanization affected the preponderant majority, not because of the growth of cities—central cities in general decayed and shrank—but because of the emergence everywhere of suburbs, a form of urban life that was relatively rare before 1940. The shift to the West was more accurately a shift to the Southwest and South. The minority groups whose struggles were most vivid were not the European and Asian immigrants who had fought for recognition earlier in the century, but rather the groups whose presence in America was most ancient: the American Negroes (since 1619), the Spanish-Americans (since the 1500s), and the American Indians.

This massive demographic ferment, which for years has involved moves by 20 percent of the American population annually, has been largely a post-1945 phenomenon. The depression decade of the thirties was demographically quiescent, with low birth rates, low geographic mobility, and the smallest percentage rise in urban

The variety of Americans—and their urban experience (in the sixties). (Arthur Furst)

proportion and in overall population in a century. Two eminent demographers declared in 1932, "It is even possible that the [United States] population will begin to decline after reaching approximately 146 million in 1970." Instead it reached 205 million and was still growing. The depression doldrums ended in the war years of the early forties, and great changes began to take place in the structure of the population, sometimes resuming interrupted trends already visible in the twenties, sometimes involving new configurations of people and groups. A distinctive postwar society began to take shape in the late forties, with the arrival of a "baby boom," the proliferation of suburbia, the gradual widening of affluence, and the continuing threat of atomic war. Through the fifties and sixties, population continued to grow, inflation and prosperity became nearly normal, and a domestic "revolution of rising expectations" was fulfilled for some and frustrated for others, especially minorities. The product of these postwar changes was a society that was very homogeneous and large but in many ways culturally and ideologically divided. "Contemporary America" came into being after 1945, and its differences from the past were nowhere clearer than in its demography.

Birth Rates and Age Structures

During the thirties, the national population increased slightly more than 7 percent, the slowest rise in any decade in United States history. The depression proved to be the most effective inhibitor of population growth yet known, except for famine, plague, and war, and the results have become apparent in the 1970s in the relative scarcity of people between the ages of thirty and forty. Conversely, the relative abundance in the 1970s of people between fifteen and thirty reflects the unusually high rate of population growth in the late forties and the fifties. To the injunction, "Don't trust anybody over thirty," a demographer in 1970 might have added, "because he remembers something about the depression and World War II."

Between the censuses of 1930 and 1940, the population grew by 9 million, an average annual increase of only 0.73 percent. The birth rate followed the business cycle: the increase of 740,000 in 1933 over 1932, the worst depression year, was the smallest since 1850, and in several other years in the thirties the increase was well under a million, smaller than it had been since the Civil War. In contrast, increases of about 3 million people per year were common in the 1950s. The war years of the early forties, when millions of young males were in North Africa, Europe, or the Pacific, but when the economy boomed, saw an annual increase of 1.20 percent, higher than in the thirties. Then, when the war ended, the "baby boom" and a dramatic rise in population growth rate occurred. The annual increase in the late forties jumped to 1.72 percent, and through the fifties to 1.85 percent. The addition of 28 million people to the American population in the 1950s constituted the largest numerical jump in any decade, and the percentage increase of 18.5 was the biggest since the days of mass immigration and improved medicine between 1900 and 1910.

In the late fifties birth rates began to drop. A dramatic reversal of recent population trends occurred in the sixties, when despite an increase of 24 million people, second only to the fifties for any decade, the percentage increase was 13.3, the lowest in history except for the depression years. The reasons for the drastically lower rate of increase were obviously very different from those that caused the low rates of the thirties; certainly depression had nothing to do with it, since the growth rate of the economy during the sixties was about five times as great as the rate of population increase.

The major reason for the wide fluctuations in population increase between the thirties and the seventies was a widely shifting birth rate. Logically, only two other trends could have accounted for population growth: immigration from outside the country or a decrease in the death rate. Neither factor operated. Immigration stabilized after World War II at around 300,000 per year, and death rates, while they dropped for nonwhites from 11.2 per thousand in 1950 to 9.5 per thousand in 1970, remained virtually constant at about 9.5 per thousand for the white majority. Population growth in the last few decades has in general been the result of massive changes in the decisions of Americans as to whether to have more children. In the thirties, they felt they could not afford it. In the sixties, a very affluent decade, they preferred not to. And in the years from 1945 to 1959, when they were in the process of creating an affluent society and expunging the economic traces of the depression, they had children by the tens of millions. Birth-rate statistics for the years since the depression fall very neatly into a pattern, as follows: unusually low—between 18.4 and 19.5 births per thousand women—from 1932 through 1940; then, during the war years, 1941 through 1945, a jump to between 20.3 and 22.7. During the "baby boom," from 1946 through the late fifties, the rate each year was between 24 and 27. Then it plunged in the sixties to well below 20 per thousand, reaching in 1968 the lowest American birth rate yet recorded, 17.5 per thousand. This meant a drastic drop in the number of children an American woman was likely to have in her lifetime. In 1957 the number of births per woman, over a lifetime, was 3.7. In the late sixties (1968 through 1970), the number fell to 2.5, a drop of about one-third. The birth rate of the late sixties was not very far from the life-time average of 2.1 children per woman estimated to bring about zero population growth and stabilize the American population at 275 million before the middle of the twenty-first century. However, birth rates began to drift upward again after 1968, when people born after 1945 began to reproduce in quantity, and they went down again in 1971–72. Consequently, stabilization for ZPG is by no means certain.

Changes in the birth rate meant changes not only in overall population growth but also in the age structure. With birth rates relatively high before 1930, low in the thirties, very high in the late forties and the fifties, and lower than ever in the middle and late sixties, great swings occurred in the proportion of the population classifiable as young, middle-aged, or old. These swings in turn had —and continue to have—enormous consequences for the economy (what kinds of jobs were available? were there too few or too many people to fill them? what kind of markets existed for cars or houses or stereos or cemeteries?), for education (how many people needed what kind of schools?), for popular culture, and for politics.

Note that in 1940 and 1950 the over-65s were less numerous than the 55–64 groups, but in 1960 and 1970 the over-65 groups outnumbered the 55–64 groups—the result of many more people living on into their seventies and eighties in 1960 and 1970. High birth rates in the periods 1916–1925, and even more in 1946–1955, are clearly evident, as are the low birth rates of the 1930s. Note that the youngest (0–4) group was smaller in 1970 than in 1960, despite the unusually large number of people of child-bearing age in 1970—evidence of the remarkably low birth rates of the late 1960s.

SHIFTING GENERATION GAPS, 1940–1970

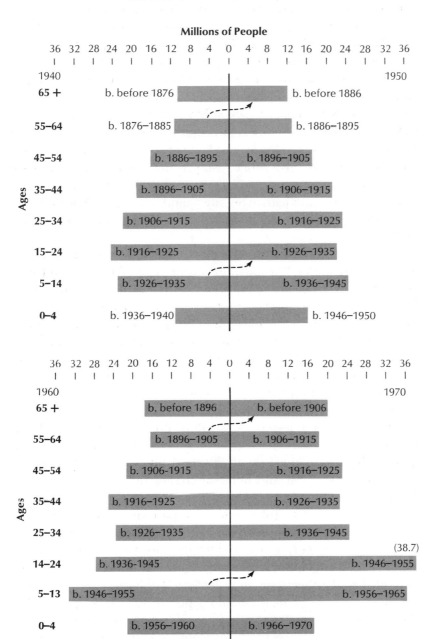

In the 1940s, the substantial number of people born before the depression had reached their twenties and early thirties, and were available to supply the massive manpower needs of the armed services during World War II. They also required greatly increased amounts of high-school and college education after the war. Marrying and forming families in large numbers, they steadily demanded cars, houses, appliances, and other consumer durables, and they constituted a sizable and reasonably well-trained labor force. At the same time, the small numbers of people between the ages of five and fifteen required a relatively small diversion of resources into elementary education and other needs of that usually nonproductive age group. Thus the simple facts of demography insured to a large degree that the American economy would not slip back into depression once the exceptional productive demands of war-making ended in 1945.

In the 1950s the age structure changed. There were more infants and children under fifteen, more people over forty-five and especially over sixty-five (a rise of over a third in the "senior citizen" group), and a drop in the number of people between twenty and thirty-five. For these young adults, the job market was favorable; for the middle-aged, especially with lower than average training or skills, it was not. The increase in the over-sixty-five group meant higher demand for retirement locations and for medical facilities, and the huge jump in the under-fifteen group meant an unprecedented demand for new elementary schools (and new teachers). The combination of fewer young adults but many more small children created an unusual need for "family-type" housing, and thus spurred the remarkable growth of suburbs during the fifties. This in turn kept the new-car and home-appliance industries producing at fluctuating but generally high levels.

The 1960s brought still another age pattern. Numbers of people over fifty-five, and especially over sixty-five, continued to increase substantially, furthering demand for the Florida condominium, the long-deferred trip to Europe, or the geriatric ward. The low birth rates of the 1930s were again reflected; at this point, they meant a stabilized number, and a declining proportion, of people in their thirties and early forties. As that group reached the normal age for entry into executive, tenured academic, and professional positions, it again benefited from the happy accident that it had relatively few members available to fill a relatively large number of well-paid, decision-making jobs. For Americans of young middle age in the

1960s, and into the 1970s, the facts of demography—or to be precise, the scarcity of births thirty to forty years earlier—produced a situation of relatively easy access to prosperity, and presumably to satisfaction with "the system." Born and brought up with some formative recollection of the close of the Great Depression and of the Second World War, often raised amid old ethnic animosities that lost strength in the 1960s, and comprising a group unusually small in number for the requirements of a "command generation," people who were over thirty and under forty-five in the 1960s and into the 1970s were fortunate. They were also, for those reasons, prone to accept the value system variously called the "work ethic," "middle-class values," or "the American way."

They were perhaps the last group so inclined. The demographic facts, and the personal experiences, of the next age group—those born between about 1945 and the late 1950s who were therefore in their teens or early twenties at the time of the 1970 census—were radically different. The much-talked-about "generation gap" that came to popular attention in the middle and late 1960s had a solid foundation in historical demography. For members of the "baby boom," personal recollections began politically with the decreasingly intense Cold War, and economically with increasingly prevalent affluence. They were the first body of citizens to grow up amid the homogenizing influence of television and other media, and the spirit of national "consensus" fostered by Eisenhower, Kennedy, and Johnson. And finally, they were a group unusually and forever large.

The census of 1970 recorded a considerable increase (around 15 percent) over 1960 of people aged 25 to 29, an increase of about 52 percent of those 20 to 24, and an increase of 44 percent of those 15 to 19. More than half of the total United States population growth in the 1960s occurred in the 15–29 age group. Among the consequences, all of them predictable, were an explosive rise in demand for high-school and college facilities (due not only to the much larger number of consumers of education but also to the fact that a rising proportion of the group went to high school and on to college), a rise in auto accidents, a rise in "juvenile delinquency" (through the sheer increase in numbers of "juveniles," not from an increased rate of crime among them), and a job market glutted with people with as yet few skills, producing a high rate of unemployment especially among people in their teens or early twenties. To drop out of high school, or even college, was to place oneself in an extremely risky employment situation. Job opportunities for minorities, especially blacks, improved markedly during the 1950s and 1960s, not only because of the success of "equal opportunities" efforts but also because of the undersupply and high demand for people in their late twenties and thirties, regardless of color. But in the late 1960s, and predictably into the 1970s, the minority-group teenager or young adult was disadvantaged both by color and by membership in a superabundant age group. Women, who likewise had poured into the people-hungry labor market of recent years, were finding through force of numbers that job opportunities were becoming scarcer in the late sixties.

They would continue to do so in the 1970s, in part because a stand-by job possibility for young women—elementary teaching—was becoming constricted as a result of the most remarkable fact about American age structure reflected in the census of 1970: a numerical drop of about one-sixth in the numbers of pre-school children, as compared with 1960. This drop was not quite offset by a rise of about one-seventh in the group aged five to fourteen. As the post-1958 decline in birth rates decreed, the size of the American population under the age of fifteen stabilized in the late 1960s. It is too risky to predict whether that stabilization will continue and whether, consequently, ZPG will be achieved in about the year 2040, as increasing numbers of people concerned with environmental problems from the mid-sixties on fervently hoped.

The immediate consequences of the stabilization of the under-fifteen population were clearer. Demand for more elementary schools and more teachers, a continuing fact of American life since 1945, was withering, and the same would happen to secondary schools later in the 1970s. Demand for new family housing, and durable goods to put in them, would decline, since the average size of families fell during the 1960s, partially offset by the rise already visible by 1970 in the numbers of late-teen and twenties people living alone, outside of family units. On the bright side, a smaller proportion of national resources would have to be devoted to the training and consumption needs of the nonproductive pre-fifteen-year-old age group, at the same time that numbers of taxpayers, people over twenty, were growing; some analysts of the 1970 census optimistically predicted that much more tax revenue could therefore be given over to solving urban and environmental problems.

Stabilization of the child-age population in the 1960s was a fact. Its causes were not so clear. Undoubtedly, however, one was the development and widespread marketing of reliable contraceptives, especially that consequential product of steroid chemistry, "the pill," the use of which obviated many births and also, incidentally, contributed to a doubling of the incidence of venereal disease, particularly gonorrhea, between 1965 and 1971. Increased availability of abortions also played some role in the lowered birth rate. But the drop in the birth rate first began in the late 1950s, before the new contraceptives (and long before legal abortions) became common. Very probably the most basic reason for the lowering in the birth rate and the stabilizing of the childhood population after about 1958 was not technological but psychological: a change in values, which induced people to choose against having children, or at least as many of them. "The pill" simply made it easier to effectuate that choice. Possible reasons in the late fifties for the drop in the national birth rate were the preference of working wives to continue to provide a second income for the family, even after relative affluence made it less necessary; the preference of unmarried women to pursue business or professional careers in which advancement was more likely than before; and the preference of families simply to opt for a second car or a better house rather than another child. In the 1960s, an additional reason emerged, as the mass media drove home the thesis that environmental problems were a by-product of population expansion, and that the retardation of birthrates was a moral duty. For whatever reasons, the concept of "ZPG" had become far more popular than that of the traditional large family.

Regional Changes and Ethnic Groups

Critical though the changes in age structure were in producing economic and cultural changes, other demographic trends were just as significant. The most outstanding of these were the redistribution of the population according to region; the declining importance of immigration and the lingering traces of "ethnicity"; the increase of metropolization; and the changed location and life-styles of the black minority.

Throughout the years from the depression to the 1970 census, the West grew at the fastest rate of the four census regions, the South second fastest (and had the largest numerical increases), and the Northeast and the North Central states grew more slowly than the other two regions, and at slower rates than earlier in the century. Rural population increased by 2.1 million in the fifty years between 1920 and 1970, but urban population increased by 94.7 million, forty-seven times faster. Those living on farms diminished from over 30 million as recently as 1940 to about 10 million in 1970, less than 5 percent of the total population. Seven million people left the land in the 1940s, another 10 million in the 1950s, and another 3.5 million in the 1960s. In both the fifties and sixties, the increase of over 50 million Americans was concentrated almost wholly in urban areas and in less than one-fourth of the nation's counties. Half of the counties lost population, especially those in a wide belt from southwestern Texas northward through central Kansas into western Nebraska and generally throughout the Dakotas and eastern Montana—the Great Plains area, where settlement had been heavy in the late nineteenth century. There, and in two smaller areas, the Appalachian mining district in eastern Kentucky, West Virginia, and western Virginia, and in the "black belt" of the Carolinas, Georgia, central Alabama, and Mississippi, small towns became depopulated, and theaters, hotels, stores, and even gas stations closed, as the young moved to better economic opportunities and the old to cemeteries or to sunshine. In contrast, the South Atlantic, Mountain, and (above all) the Pacific states increased in population much faster than the national average from the 1940s through the 1960s. In each of these divisions, one state with an agreeable climate spearheaded growth: Florida in the Southeast, Arizona in the Mountain states, and California, which passed New York in 1964 as the most populous state, in the West. Texas also grew rapidly. The old America of small towns and farms quickly withered away; the city-dwelling proportion rose from 56.5 percent in 1940 to 64 percent (including fringe areas) in 1950 to 69.9 percent in 1960 to 73.5 percent in 1970, when 69 percent of the entire population (i.e., all but 4.5 percent of the urban population) lived in large cities or their surrounding metropolitan areas.

Compared to the pre–World War I period or even the 1920s, foreign immigration contributed little to population growth. Annual totals seldom exceeded 300,000, even in the relatively peaceful and affluent years after 1945. Of these, the majority came from Canada, Mexico, the Caribbean, and Latin America, and also, after the immigration law of 1965 abolished the national-origins quota system, from the Philippines, Taiwan, Italy, and Greece. The immigration totals, however, did not include the numerically and culturally significant Puerto Ricans, who were not "foreign" in a legal sense, but who otherwise resembled past immigrants in clustering in New York's "Spanish Harlem" and other ghettoes, and in having lower-than-average occupational and educational levels. By 1970, Puerto Ricans and other Spanish Americans numbered over 9 million, or 5 percent of the population.

Except for the Puerto Ricans, however, immigrants since the late 1930s have been more influential than numerous. This was true of war refugees, especially Central and East European Jews, such as Albert Einstein, who began arriving in the mid-thirties fleeing Nazi persecutions. Other groups outside the immigration quotas were the "displaced persons" admitted after 1945 because they were relatives of people already in the United States; "war brides" from Germany, Japan, and other occupied countries; engineers and scientists who made up the "brain drain" of the fifties and early sixties from Britain and elsewhere; and exchange students and professors, often from Asia. Still, the census of 1970 revealed only 11 million immigrants, 4.6 percent of the total, as compared with 8.8 percent in 1940.

A declining number of Americans, moreover, even thought of themselves as possessing a "nationality" other than American. It was common enough prior to 1945 for someone with immigrant parents or grandparents to identify with an ethnic group and to bear the brunt of ethnic prejudices more or less often. By 1969, according to a census study, only about 75 million identified themselves as ethnic, and of those, more than two-thirds considered themselves as somehow German, English, or Irish, i.e., of the "older" immigration that abated by the 1890s. "Ethnicity" became in the 1950s and 1960s more a religious alignment than a national-origin one: a person was less apt to identify himself as Irish, Italian, or Russian, for example, than as Jewish, Catholic, or (usually a negative reference) WASP—White, Anglo-Saxon, and Protestant. With certain major exceptions—namely, blacks, Spanish-Americans, and Indians—ethnicity was on the wane as a divisive force in American life, as the era of mass immigration receded forty, then fifty, years into the past.

THE EMERGING METROPOLISES, 1900–1940

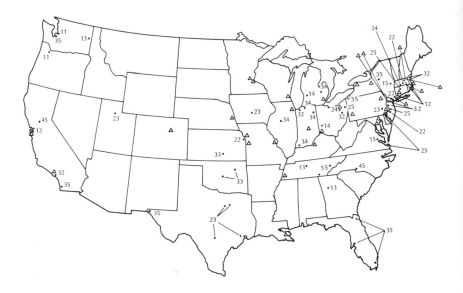

Each two-digit number represents a city. The first digit indicates the year of the federal census in which the city first had a 100,000+ population. The second digit indicates the chief reason why it reached that size. Triangles represent cities that had already reached 100,000+ by 1900.

First Digit

1 = City Reached 100,000+ by 1910
2 = City Reached 100,000+ by 1920
3 = City Reached 100,000+ by 1930
4 = City Reached 100,000+ by 1940

Second Digit

1 = Shipping and Commercial Center
2 = Satellite City
3 = Primary Processing Center and/or Regional Metropolis
4 = National Market Manufacturing Center
5 = Growth Based on Other or Mixed Reasons

Example: 23 = Regional Metropolis Emergent in 1920 Census
34 = Manufacturing Town Emergent in 1930 Census (i.e. During the 1920's)

Names of Cities:

11 Portland, Ore	22 New Bedford, Mass	25 Norfolk, Va	34 South Bend, Ind
11 Seattle, Wash	22 Camden, NJ	25 Wilmington, Del	34 Flint, Mich
12 Bridgeport, Conn	22 Kansas City, Kan		35 San Diego, Calif
12 Cambridge, Mass	22 Yonkers, NY	32 Long Beach, Calif	35 Jacksonville, Fla
12 Lowell, Mass	23 San Antonio, Tex	32 Gary, Ind	35 Miami, Fla
12 Oakland, Calif	23 Dallas, Tex	32 Lynn, Mass	35 Tampa, Fla
13 Atlanta, Ga	23 Houston, Tex	32 Somerville, Mass	35 Utica, NY
13 Nashville, Tenn	23 Fort Worth, Tex	32 Elizabeth, NJ	35 Erie, Pa
13 Spokane, Wash	23 Youngstown, Ohio	32 Paterson, NJ	35 Tacoma, Wash
14 Dayton, Ohio	23 Des Moines, Iowa	32 Canton, Ohio	35 Knoxville, Tenn
14 Grand Rapids, Mich	23 Salt Lake City, Utah	33 Wichita, Kan	35 Chattanooga, Tenn
15 Albany, NY	23 Reading, Pa	33 Oklahoma City, Okla	
15 Richmond, Va	24 Akron, Ohio	33 Tulsa, Okla	45 Sacramento, Calif
	24 Springfield, Mass	34 Peoria, Ill	45 Charlotte, NC
	25 Hartford, Conn	34 Evansville, Ind	
	25 Trenton, NJ	34 Fort Wayne, Ind	

The Metropolitan
Majority

In the hundred years from 1870 to 1970, American residential patterns reversed themselves, moving from about three-fourths rural to about three-fourths urban. After 1945, virtually all population increase was urban. The urban increase, moreover, was not evenly distributed, but was heavily concentrated in metropolitan areas, and, to be more precise, in suburbs rather than in central cities. In 1950 the Census Bureau redefined the term *urban* in order to recognize a new reality: for practical purposes, urban population included not only people who lived within incorporated limits of cities of 50,000 or more but also those in suburbs or unincorporated "fringe" areas adjacent to cities. Together they comprised the population of a "SMSA"—Standard Metropolitan Statistical Area—as, for example, those in the city of Chicago, in suburbs and satellites such as Evanston, Oak Park, and Gary, and in the unincorporated parts of several counties in northeast Illinois and northwest Indiana. The 243 SMSAs of 1970 grew 26 percent in the 1950s and 17 percent in the 1960s, accounting for the great bulk of post–World War II population growth.

But the increase was not in central cities. The number of million-plus cities remained steady at five from 1930 to 1970, when Houston joined the list, but each succeeding census has shown declines in the numbers living inside large cities. In the 1960s, twelve of the twenty-five largest cities and eight of the largest ten lost population. Yet all except one (Pittsburgh) of the twenty-five largest SMSAs gained. The real growth was suburban, and by 1970 more Americans lived in suburbs (76 million) than in central cities (64 million).

The tendency in almost every respect was for population, while concentrating in metropolises, to spread itself more evenly among them; for example, the six SMSAs over 3 million in 1970 had grown more slowly than the national average in the 1960s, and at half the rate of SMSAs between 1 million and 3 million, which grew 20 percent. New York continued to be the largest SMSA, with 11.4 million people in twenty-two counties in three states, but New York City gained only 1 percent in the sixties, and its Manhattan core lost over 10 percent, more than any county in the state. The New York metropolitan area, in turn, was at the center of a continuous string of SMSAs running from southern Maine and New Hampshire southward through the Boston area, Hartford, New Haven, New York, Philadelphia, Baltimore, and Washington to Norfolk in southeastern Virginia. By the early sixties, 20 percent of the American population lived in that "megalopolis." The most spectacular example of urban sprawl emerged after 1945 in southern California, as the amoeba-like Los Angeles became the country's third largest city, and its metropolitan area and contiguous SMSAs filled most of the land from Santa Barbara 150 miles to the Mexican border. Planless and centerless, with freeways and airports as its major reference points, southern California became the classic "slurb."

The causes and consequences of the new urbanization were immense and inseparable: new industries, widespread car and home ownership, freeways and interstate highways, the dream (and its frequent realization) of two cars in the garage and a swimming pool in the back yard, the spreading comprehension that California and Florida were more pleasant to live in than North Dakota or the Great Lakes area, and in many cases, a refusal to put up with the pollution, traffic jams, crimes, and general frenzy of central cities. Suburbanization rendered traditional forms of city government obsolete in many respects, but with rare exceptions, such as the incorporation of the surrounding county into city limits as Indianapolis and Jacksonville did in the sixties, broad municipal authorities were not created to provide efficient transportation, planning, or taxation.

At the Core of the Metropolis: The Black Migration

While suburbs and interurban areas grew planlessly, inner cities languished. The changes in the population of central cities in the fifties and sixties were much greater than the net figures indicate, and they were principally of two kinds, economic and racial. While higher-income urbanites fled to the suburbs, the center-city population became more and more a low-income one. Most of those who left were whites, and very often they were replaced by blacks. Central cities simultaneously underwent a lowering of their aggregate wealth and a marked increase in their nonwhite population. From the financial standpoint, their costs for education, welfare, and transportation rose at the same time that their tax bases declined.

The northern city nevertheless held strong attractions for southern blacks and others who moved into them after 1945. The exodus of blacks out of the South was well under way by World War I, was interrupted by the depression, and resumed after 1940 to involve millions through the fifties and, at a slightly slower rate, in the sixties. In 1940, 23 percent of the black population lived outside the

This graph shows the movement of whites away from core cities and into suburbs, and the movement of Negroes into metropolitan areas. In the 1960s, Negroes moved a little more often into suburbs than they did in the 1950s.

RESIDENTIAL CHANGES BY NEGROES AND WHITES, 1950–1970

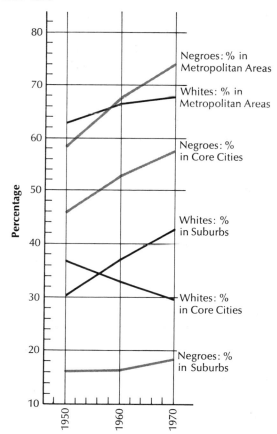

South; the proportion rose to 32 percent in 1950, 40 percent in 1960, and 47 percent in 1970, an increase augmented by the fact that, nationally, numbers of blacks rose faster than numbers of non-blacks, from 9.8 percent of the whole in 1940 to 11.2 percent in 1970. Because of higher birth rates and declining death rates, the black population jumped about 50 percent, from 15 to 22.7 million, between 1950 and 1970, while the nonblack population increased by less than a third. American blacks not only became less and less southern after 1940, but much less rural: a greater proportion of blacks than of nonblacks were urban dwellers by 1970, when half of the black population lived in fifty cities, a third in fifteen cities. The combination of the exit of whites to suburbs and the entry to blacks into core cities of metropolitan areas produced black majorities in six sizable cities, all but one northern, by 1970.

Black movement to the suburbs was by no means nonexistent; in the sixties, black suburban population increased at a faster rate than white in fifteen of the twenty largest metropolitan areas. But the numbers involved were small compared to the migration to core cities. There the man or the family that had become liberated from southern rural poverty found to some degree a wider range of opportunity than before, but also a wider range of problems. White racism, especially in the forms of discriminatory housing, discriminatory employment, and differential wage rates, depressed the lives of the new arrivals, and as a consequence blighted the northern cities they lived in. Many of the migrants were men in their late teens or early twenties, pushed from the South by poor rural conditions and farm mechanization; others were families in part attracted by higher welfare benefits; all of them found themselves in a more tightly segregated residential ghetto than most of the European and Asian immigrants of earlier decades. Ironically, groups that had been the recipients of racial and ethnic prejudice themselves, but had "made it" by the postwar period, became bearers of hostility. "White backlash" against black city-dwellers and more equal educational and economic opportunity was most virulent in city wards and suburbs peopled by whites of recent immigrant stock.

Despite his early arrival in the American colonies, the American Negro remained at the bottom of the status ladder while European and Asian immigrants made the difficult ascent. Differences in educational opportunities and achievements were one reason. Although

NEGROES MOVE NORTH AND WEST, 1940–1970

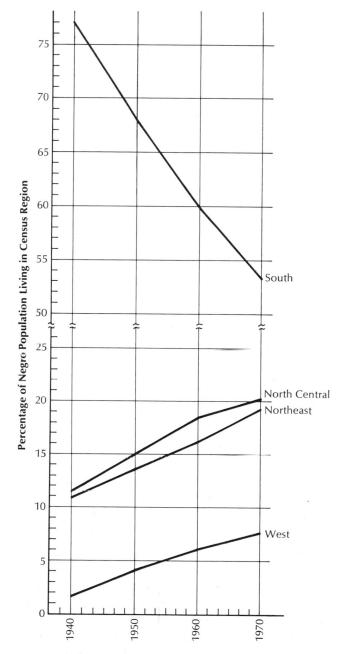

black young adults in 1970 had completed 12.1 years of schooling, on the average, they had still not caught up to the national average of 12.5 years, despite much improvement during the fifties and sixties. In part, the lag resulted from a weaker educational tradition among Negroes than among certain immigrant groups; the remarkable success of people of East European Jewish stock in making educational and occupational gains rested in part on their rabbinical tradition stretching back for centuries. The American Negro came from a very different social milieu: that of the southern rural or northern laboring subcultures with little time or place for books, and before that, the slave situation in which literacy was actually outlawed. Black Americans struggled for education and founded colleges during and after Reconstruction, and W. E. B. DuBois, early in the twentieth century, called for extensive education of the "talented tenth" of the black population. But social conditions precluded general success. Southern Italian and Slavic peasants had no intellectual tradition, yet their descendants eventually achieved education and upward mobility; why did blacks seem not to? The reasons were several.

One was a lack of economic stability. Other groups achieved sufficient income in the years after World War II to send their children to college at least at night or part-time, or to allow them to finish high school. The too-prevalent Negro pattern of job insecurity, frequent moves, low income, lack of low-cost public higher education, and exclusion from attractive jobs even with a high school diploma or a college degree served to discourage blacks from using the educational lever to wealth and status. Another factor was the need for and acceptability of unskilled jobs when the immigrants arrived in the late nineteenth and early twentieth centuries, and the phasing out and unacceptability of such jobs after 1945. Certain cultural barriers were more complex and forbidding. Residential segregation forced masses of black children into elementary and secondary schools whose substandard quality encouraged them to drop out or prepared them so inadequately that they had trouble staying in college even if they got there. Through the forties and fifties, the pattern of immigrant groups moving ahead generationally from peasant to worker to foreman or shopkeeper to politician or physician to professor or financier, a pattern begun by the Irish around 1860 and the Poles around 1900, was still too rare and slow among blacks to avoid a cultural hopelessness which fed poverty, urban riots, and more racism.

In one other respect the black migrants to northern cities underwent a different experience from the immigrants of a half-century before. Earlier minority groups were by no means wholly settled in ghettoes; many lived outside, and those inside mingled with each other and with the native-born poor. The ghetto dwellers also found doors leading out and "uptown." For the poorer black migrants of the forties and fifties, contrary to their expectations, the ghetto walls proved to be doorless and unscalable in the sixties. With the frustration of ghetto confinement compounded by the flooding evidence of increasing general affluence in society, riots broke out in black ghettoes in the 1960s. Race riots had happened before in the United States, such as in Chicago and other cities in 1919, and in Detroit in

Extremism in the early sixties: a representative of the white-supremacist, anti-Semitic American Nazi party. (Batzdorff from Monkmeyer Press Photo Service)

On the death of a friend: a member of the United States Navy Band at the funeral
of Franklin D. Roosevelt, 1945. (Ed Clark, LIFE magazine © Time, Inc.)

1943. But these began characteristically with an isolated black-
white scuffle and became bloody when white mobs invaded Negro
neighborhoods. Violence continued in the fifties: race-connected
dynamitings occurred many times in 1951, and in the first two
weeks of 1952 seven bombings took place in Georgia, Alabama, and
North Carolina alone. The riots of the sixties began differently,
often when white police attempted to arrest a ghetto resident for a
small offense; they were fed by Negro hatred of white storekeepers
who were, they felt, gouging them; and they blew up like spontane-
ous combustion throughout the resentment-saturated ghetto population. Dozens of deaths and millions in property damage resulted
from major riots in New York's Harlem in 1964, the Watts district
of Los Angeles in 1965, Chicago and other cities in 1966, and De-

troit and Newark in 1967. There were many other lesser conflagrations, and it seemed that no city would be spared, even one with "model race relations" as Detroit had been regarded. The riot wave abated after early 1968, but ghetto resentment and frustration still smoldered.

The Civil Rights Movement and the Black Social Structure

The Harlem riot of 1964, ironically, followed a decade of solid progress toward racial integration. Even after that event, the economic condition and standards of living of black Americans continued to improve. A "civil rights" movement, stressing the removal of political, educational, social, and economic disabilities and the assimilation of the black minority into the mainstream, took shape in the fifties and the early sixties. Integration of the armed services had already begun in the late forties, and in 1954 the United States Supreme Court cut down a crucial barrier to black advancement when it ruled, in the case of *Brown* v. *Board of Education of Topeka*, that school segregation was illegal and that the "separate but equal" dual school systems in the South had to be ended "with all deliberate speed."

The speed was all too deliberate in many cases, and coalitions of black integrationists and white liberals struggled through the late fifties and early sixties to end not only school segregation but other Jim Crow practices as well. Organizations such as the long-existent National Association for the Advancement of Colored People and Congress of Racial Equality (CORE), and the newly-formed Southern Christian Leadership Conference and Student Non-Violent Coordinating Committee (SNCC), and leaders such as Roy Wilkins, John Lewis, A. Philip Randolph, and above all Martin Luther King, Jr., fought to end racial discrimination. In 1955, when he was 27, King led a year-long boycott by Negroes of public buses in Montgomery, Alabama, to end the Jim Crow practice of segregating blacks in the back of the bus. The experience of the Montgomery boycott demonstrated that King's device of civil disobedience by nonviolent means would work and that the black community would follow it.

After the Montgomery episode, blacks together with thousands of sympathetic whites from North and South, many of them college students, employed nonviolent civil disobedience to dramatize and destroy southern statutes prohibiting equal Negro access to stores, restaurants, public accommodations, and the ballot box. The civil rights movement not only ended Jim Crow statutes on the state and local level but also massed support for federal laws prohibiting discrimination in voting (1957, 1960, 1965), in federally-financed housing (1962), in job opportunities (1964), and in residence (1968).

The movement was punctuated by dramatic confrontations. Several black children successfully entered Little Rock's Central High School in 1957, protected by federal troops sent by President Eisenhower to thwart the efforts of Arkansas Governor Orval E. Faubus to keep the school segregated. "Freedom riders" began in 1959 to end Jim Crow in intercity transportation, and in 1961 four black college students "sat in" at a segregated lunch counter in Greensboro, North Carolina, beginning several years of successful sit-ins. A young black student, James Meredith, enrolled at the University of Mississippi in 1962 with the aid of federal marshals over the intense opposition of Governor Ross Barnett and with the loss of two lives. King, Wilkins, and others led a nonviolent "March on Washington" in August of 1963, in which more than 100,000 Negroes and whites convincingly demonstrated mass support for stronger civil rights legislation. In April, 1965, King led another march, this time to Selma, Alabama, where thousands of civil-rights supporters protested anti-Negro voter registration practices.

These and many other episodes greatly improved the legal position, and in many ways the day-to-day living, of American Negroes to a degree unknown in American history save for the ending of slavery in the 1860s. The civil-rights victories did not come easily; the voter-registration drive of the mid-sixties met with gradual success, much of it due to the vigor of the Justice Department under Attorney General Robert F. Kennedy. School desegregation proceeded with maddening slowness against the intense and ingenious efforts, especially in Virginia, of White Citizens' Councils and the "white power structure" to frustrate the 1954 Brown decision and the many later Supreme Court decisions against educational discrimination.

Despite its many successes and the support of all three branches of the federal government, the integrationist, nonviolent civil rights movement began running aground about 1964. At that point the tide of its early, idealistic support receded, many blacks began taking a more militant stance and came to support various kinds of black separatism rather than integration, and the tactics of the sit-in and the mass march proved unable to wash away the hard rock of urban ghetto conditions. Disasters struck the movement in the form of murders: snipers killed Medgar Evers, the Mississippi NAACP leader, in 1963; a bomb killed four black girls in a Birmingham church that same year; Mrs. Viola Liuzzo, an Italian-American housewife from Detroit helping in the Selma march in 1965, was shot; several young black and white civil-rights workers were ambushed in Mississippi; and in Memphis, in April, 1968, Martin Luther King himself was assassinated.

Federal legislation and nonviolent demonstrations, by the mid-sixties, appeared unable to break down the combination of race hatred and urban poverty. Though nonviolence remained popular, at least while King was alive, other solutions to racial problems gained support among American blacks. "White backlash" was appearing in northern voting patterns; the integrationist coalition of blacks and white liberals was breaking down; and the "long hot summers" of ghetto riots began in 1964 in Harlem and continued to the spring of 1968, when violence broke out in many cities after King's murder. Beginning in 1963 and 1964, just when the integrationist, nonviolent movement apparently reached new peaks of success in the march on Washington and sweeping federal legislation, talk (and action) aiming at black separatism gained popularity as it had not done since the days of Marcus Garvey in the 1920s. King's "I have a Dream" of a racially integrated America was mocked by white backlash, by violence against civil rights workers, and by the ghetto riots themselves. Young black leaders in two of the most influential civil rights organizations, CORE and SNCC, made it clear that white support was no longer wanted. The best known of the new breed of non-integrationist leaders were Stokely Carmichael, who led SNCC in 1967 and popularized the term *Black Power*, Huey Newton and Bobby Seale, who formed the Black Panther Party in

Oakland in 1966, and the Panthers' Eldridge Cleaver (who subsequently immigrated to Algeria). Their message was very different from King's.

The variety of black programs, organizations, and leaders since the mid-sixties, and the variety of meanings attached to "Black Power," was very great. A major segment of this variety was the long-established separatist movement known as the Black Muslims. Its best-known exponent, Malcolm X, though he split away from Elijah Muhammad, the Muslims' founder, had many followers both before and after his assassination in New York in early 1965. Separatists of a more middle-class bent called for "black capitalism," which would create retail stores and industries run by blacks for blacks: a separate economy. Black Power meant for Carmichael a separate political effort by and for blacks, outside the structure of the existing major parties. For Eldridge Cleaver, as well as many Black Panthers and black ideologues on college campuses, Black Power carried an overt Marxian and Maoist theory of class struggle, and supported the alignment of American blacks with emerging third-world peoples, with Pan-Africanism, with the Vietnamese. All of these diverse groups had certain things in common, however: they first became prominent in 1963 and 1964, gained strength after the anti–Jim Crow work of the nonviolent civil rights movement was finished, were aided by the shift in emphasis from desegregation to voter registration and black political strength, and partly as a consequence of that shift, stressed black identity and participation and generally disdained the white support that characterized the civil rights movement. Many Black Power advocates took part in the protest in the late sixties against the Vietnam War and supported a more or less revolutionary view of foreign and domestic policy.

While black separatism undoubtedly enjoyed a large following among American blacks by the close of the sixties, the extreme militant versions were much less popular than those that called for larger numbers of black office-holders, businesses, and middle-class well-educated people. Many more blacks wanted to reform the whole American system, rather than overthrow it, in order to provide equal education, housing, income, medical care, and jobs for blacks, and to provide greater black political power in both North and South. The black-white coalition idea was by no means dead in the late sixties and early seventies. Both demographic and economic trends during the time of the civil rights movement, and later, suggested a complicated class structure and an improving economic situation in black America that might possibly bring about full black assimilation and equality—perhaps according to King's "dream," perhaps in some other way. There was no doubt that certain key black problems were also white problems and national problems: unemployment and crime were inherent in the bulge in the 15 to 25 age group, white as well as black; moreover, since almost half the black population became non-southern in residence, and the great majority urban, their problems were in some major respects simply a severe manifestation of traditional northern city problems. The degree of black residential segregation, for example, was great, but no greater than that of Puerto Ricans, and not much greater than that of certain ethnic groups. Quite possibly, residential segregation for blacks peaked in the 1960s. Given the fact that blacks, in large numbers, had very recently arrived in non-southern cities, as compared with other groups (the majority of other ethnic groups had arrived since 1945, and nearly all since 1915), and the fact that European immigrant groups required two or three generations to end enforced ghetto residence, the black ghettoes may well shrink in population, as Harlem already seemed to be doing by 1970.

Although it was still largely conjectural in the early seventies as to whether residential segregation was to decrease significantly, clear evidence did exist that the condition of the black minority had improved markedly in several major respects during the fifties and sixties. School desegregation, for example, proceeded, and when the trend toward racial mixture in public schools encountered the hurdle of residential segregation in the late sixties, many communities continued the process by busing white and black students across school-district lines—often, it must be said, despite loud legal and political protests. The proportion of blacks who had finished high school rose from 38 percent in 1960 to 58 percent in 1970 (as against 75 percent of whites). The annual income of the average black family rose in the same period from 51 percent to 61 percent of the white figure. This meant that, despite improvement during the sixties, a large gap still existed between black and white; but certain peculiarities of the minority group, especially the continued residence of many in the rural South and the large number of families without an adult male wage earner (27 percent for blacks, only 9 percent for whites in 1970), accounted for a large part of the gap.

Native racism, Albany, Georgia, September, 1962. The Grand Dragon said, "When we get through there'll be a lot of Negroes moving north." (Wide World Photos)

In contrast, the income of young black couples with children, who lived in northern cities, jumped from 75 percent of the figure for comparable whites in 1960 to full equality of income in 1970, thanks in large part to working wives. The job structure of black America changed radically during the 1960s, in the direction of congruence with national averages, and again as a product of the urban, non-southern demographic movement of blacks. Between 1960 and 1970, blacks *decreasingly* worked as blue-collar laborers (from 13.7 percent to 10.3 percent), as household domestics (from 14.2 percent to 7.7 percent), or as farm workers (from 12.1 percent to 3.9 percent); they *increasingly* were occupied as craftsmen and foremen (from 6.0 percent to 8.2 percent), as clerical workers (7.3 percent to 13.2 percent), and as professional and technical workers (from 4.8 percent to 9.1 percent).

The most dramatic changes among blacks were the decline in farming and the rise in white-collar jobs, especially professional ones (10 percent were white-collar workers in 1950, 16 percent in 1960, 28 percent in 1970), indicating the continuing development of black America in the direction of an urban middle class in education, income, occupation, and perhaps in residence. On the other hand, high unemployment or underemployment continued among many blacks, and about one-fifth of the black population (living in ghettoes in central cities) made little or no economic progress. Black America was evolving, in class structure, away from the long-time pattern of a lower class chiefly rural and southern and fractionally urban, to a pattern of a highly urban group dividing into a lower class at or below the "poverty line," a lower-middle class of blue-collar and white-collar workers, and a fast-growing middle or upper-middle class minority of professionals and managers.

The expansion of the black middle class, the improved levels of educational achievement, the emergence of black majorities in a number of cities, and the end of Jim Crow in voting increased black political power during and after the 1960s. Over 100 counties in the South, as of 1970, had black majorities, and with voter registration drives came the election of blacks to a number of county and city offices—though not, as of the early seventies, in numbers comparable to the proportion of black population. Outside the South, a new group of middle-class black leaders arose who were able to elicit electoral support in the core cities: increasing numbers of black congressmen were elected in the late sixties and in 1970, and in 1967 Richard Hatcher was elected mayor of Gary, Carl Stokes of Cleveland. Although Stokes' attempts to build a black-based political coalition apparently failed in the 1971 mayoralty election, that same election saw the defeat in Boston of a "white backlash" candidate. By the early seventies, it seemed probable, on the basis of events of the preceding twenty years, that black political power would increase; that income and educational gaps between blacks and whites would continue to narrow (though quite possibly not for the most disadvantaged 20 percent of the blacks; another gap was developing between that group and the growing black middle class); and that the black population would urbanize further and become still less southern, thus encountering more of the general social and economic problems, as well as prosperity, of the nation.

On the Fringe of the Metropolis: The Emerging Suburbs

By the early seventies, over 40 percent of white Americans and over 15 percent of black ones lived in suburban areas of one kind or another, surrounded by grass, TV antennas, and highways. The 76 million suburbanites of 1970—a number equal to the whole United States population in 1900—outnumbered those who lived in central cities by about 11 to 9. The suburb, as a new kind of urban living, was not yet prominent in the thirties, but after 1945 it became the hope, and then the reality, for millions. Many economic factors made suburbia possible: increasing family income, the "G.I. loan" and other federally-assisted mortgage plans to provide the credit necessary for returning war veterans and others to buy homes, a quick reconversion of the auto industry to peacetime production and the renewed availability of cars at "popular prices," a shortening work week and more leisure time, state and federal road-building to provide access to suburbs, and the mass production and assembly of homes. After 1945 suburban developers tossed up family dwellings by the thousands. The new suburbs often had a rickety quality; the story was told of a Soviet housing team which visited a Long Island development in the fifties and chatted with a happy young matron raking leaves in front of her "crackerbox." She and her husband, she said, had bought the house with a low down-payment and would own it outright in only twenty-five years. Driving away a few minutes later, the Russians asked their American guides how long those houses were built to last. The answer: "twenty-five years." Despite such impermanence, and despite fears that Americans were creating a wasteland of future "suburban slums," millions of people were happy to escape a lifetime sentence of rentals or cramped apartments. Life in Levittown or Park Forest was not magnificent, but those who were gaining footholds in such places found them improvements over the inner city.

By the mid-fifties suburbia was provoking a gloomy literature of social comment, which claimed that suburban life was mass-producing human zombies who rode commuter trains or drove on clogged expressways, worked as cogs in vast corporate machines, and existed with wives whose lives revolved around the coffee-Klatsch, the shopping center, and the bridge table—millions of people hypnotized by the "boob tube." But this was a caricature that ignored elements of social ferment responsible for suburban growth. Certainly the millions moving to suburbs did not agree with it, or at least they believed that the potential of suburban life outweighed the problems. The owners of development houses often regarded them as stepping-stones to something better, just as mobile Americans for 200 years had thought of real estate.

Because of rapid turnover, the actual average life of a home mortgage in the sixties was about eight years. The low down-payment, long-term mortgage home, something almost unknown in other countries, attached millions of people to private property, and presumably made them more socially stable (as Jefferson long ago claimed), but did not chain them to one piece of property like European peasants. As people bought cars on credit plans, traded them for new ones by renegotiating their payments, and sometimes "traded up" to higher-prestige makes, so they bought, mortgaged, sold, renegotiated, and often "moved up" in their housing. Around large cities, as suburbs spread, a hierarchy of prestige made suburbs more or less attractive according to how they fitted people's status aspirations and economic capabilities. The credit economy and the familiar American search for upward mobility underpinned the new suburbanization and made it a phenomenon without close counterpart in other countries, where credit and class lines were less fluid.

Suburbanization did have its negative aspects in addition to the cultural sterility that critics like William H. Whyte and David Riesman complained of; it also revealed flaws in American urban society. One was the weakness of public agencies in regulating development in the public interest, so that suburbs were provided with transportation, parks, schools, and other common facilities, as well as adequate zoning to prevent neon jungles from arising next to residential boulevards. Another was the tendency for the country, after 1940, to become visually homogenized, as suburban developments and even core cities looked more and more alike.

Metropolitan deficiencies were not restricted to suburbia. As crackerboxes dotted suburbia, high-rise apartments and boxy steel-and-glass office buildings appeared in centers of cities. Urban renewal projects, most of them financed with federal aid, began in the fifties to demolish slums and "substandard" city blocks with great abandon, eventually to replace them with outwardly neat high-rise apartments for low and middle income people. But little regard was given to the displaced slum dwellers, who often were simply forced to crowd into other slum areas. By 1970, some critics were convinced that the ill effects of urban renewal and the national highway program had outweighed the good, by destroying neighborhoods, forcing a rise in traffic and pollution, and devitalizing city centers. It was not clear whether the benefits of suburbia, urban renewal, and transportation networks were outweighing the disadvantages, and that lack of clarity reflected the growing inability of fragmented governmental institutions to define and serve the public need.

Metropolis, the Media, and Mobility

The expansion of metropolitan America after 1945 meant that people bumped into each other more than ever before—geographically, socially, and culturally. Some contacts increased understanding; other contacts were angry and belligerent. In 1940, four out of seven people in a population of 132 million lived in cities; in 1970, three-fourths of the much larger population of 205 million were urbanites, seven-tenths of the whole living in metropolises. The thirty-year process of metropolitan expansion reduced the spatial distance separating Americans; and the increasing commonness of travel, together with the relentlessly leveling effect of the mass media, especially TV, also reduced the differences in their experience.

Travel was not a prominent feature of the threadbare thirties, and auto production and sales slipped badly from the levels of the 1920s. During the war years of 1941–45, motor vehicle factories, busy producing weapons, made virtually nothing for the domestic private market. But as a by-product of the induction of millions into the armed services and the shifting of personnel around the country and overseas, vast numbers of people, especially young people, became familiar with cities and regions far from home; the Second World War accelerated the breakdown of localisms. When the war ended, the trend of the twenties toward wider family-car ownership and the use of cars, trucks, and buses for commercial purposes resumed. Demand for cars was so great in the first two or three years after the 1945 armistice that buyers gave car dealers substantial premiums to get their names at the top of the list for '46, '47, and '48 models. Even when the accumulated backlog of demand was satisfied, annual car production and sales pushed upward to 3, 5, and (by the early seventies) 10 million per year. Having achieved two-car status, thousands of families further indulged their lust for motion by buying motorboats or taking plane trips, often to Europe.

With mass ownership of cars came the interstate highway network, started in the mid-fifties with large federal expenditures and substantially finished by 1970; chains of motels, offering few of the traditional amenities of hotels but providing easy access and getaway for auto nomads; campsites and a camping equipment industry for those seeking more strenuous, or at least cheaper, vacations; shopping centers away from and sometimes larger than central business districts; suburban developments unreachable except by cars; air pollution; 50,000 road deaths a year; and finally, immense traffic congestion as expressways never caught up with (and indeed augmented) the stream of motor vehicles traveling on them.

Air travel increased after 1945 even faster, percentagewise, than motor vehicle travel. The airlines grew very rapidly as passenger carriers, especially after they introduced commercial jets in 1958. In the sixties commuter flights took people back and forth daily between cities as distant as New York and St. Louis. The largest airports became seriously overcrowded, commercial plane crashes (though there were few of them) resulted almost always from mid-air collisions rather than plane malfunction, and confusion was common enough to provoke the wisecrack "breakfast in London, lunch in New York, dinner in Los Angeles—and luggage in Buenos Aires." Indeed it became a peculiarly modern irony that people could travel hundreds of miles by air in less time than it took cars or buses to get to and from the airports at either end of the trip. As car and truck sales soared, and airline ticket agencies prospered, passenger traffic by railroad dwindled dismally, and commuter bus or train lines were in financial trouble almost everywhere. The nation's largest railroad, Penn-Central, went bankrupt in 1970, and railroad passenger service was dumped upon the federal government, whose new Amtrak agency was somehow supposed to rationalize and revitalize passenger trains.

Communications media contributed to the cultural extension of metropolitan America after 1945. Popular magazines and metropolitan newspapers rose in circulation with the growth of population, though sometimes not fast enough to offset rising costs and prevent liquidation; many metropolitan areas were reduced to a single daily paper, and even New York had only three general dailies by 1967. In contrast, commercial television expanded rapidly. Almost nobody in 1946 had ever seen TV; almost everybody had by 1952. Optimists who predicted that the new medium would bring a new spreading of high culture were quickly disappointed, and early in the sixties the chairman of the Federal Communications Commission called TV "a vast wasteland." But audiovisual soap operas, big-prize quiz shows (some rigged), situation comedies, cartoons, instantaneous visual coverage of news and athletic events, and by 1965 live broadcasting from Hawaii and Europe by communications satellites met general public acceptance. Whether baby-sitter, boob tube, or blessing, television became a standard part of American life, and a homogenizing force on American culture, from the late forties onward. Its effects on mass psychology and culture are yet to be measured.

Despite unprecedented ways and degrees of communicating with each other, Americans were still very far from harmonious by the early seventies. The forties, fifties, and sixties had brought riots and racism as well as split-level houses and color TV; mobility of class and status, as well as material prosperity, were abundantly visible among the majority, but certain groups (including some of the children of the affluent, post-depression middle class) were starkly disaffected, others mired in ghetto slums. The process of metropolization had left none untouched, for good or ill; demographic change had been inexorable.

10

THE ECONOMY SINCE 1940: FROM DEPRESSION TO AFFLUENCE

Still on its knees in 1940, the American economy reached the trillion-dollar level thirty years later, a level equal to two-thirds of the production of the rest of the world. While American rates of population increase, though large from 1945 to 1958, were lower than the world average and much lower than certain large underdeveloped countries, the American rate of economic growth was higher. The gap widened, and continues to widen unhealthily for all, between the living standards and national wealth of the United States and most other countries. America's historically unprecedented economic growth came as a delightful surprise during and immediately after World War II, when a return to depression was feared and predicted. Growth became an expectation and a major policy objective by business and government in the fifties and into the sixties, an objective generally achieved.

In the late sixties and early seventies an unaccustomed slackening in the rate of growth converged with demographic, cultural, and political factors—notably the recognition of environmental pollution as an unintended by-product of economic growth, and the Vietnam War as a wasteful expense—to produce a serious, widespread questioning of growth as a policy objective unless, like some intoxicating drug, its side-effects were better understood and controlled. Americans had reached the luxurious (and parochial) state of being able to be dissatisfied with their trillion-dollar economy on sociocultural grounds, so deeply had affluence permeated their thinking since the grim days before World War II.

In those three decades since the 1930s, economic life in America had changed in several major ways, aside from sheer increase in

From sea to shining sea in post–World War II America. (Elliott Erwitt, © Magnum Photos, Inc.)

size: it was largely recession-free; personal income had become more evenly distributed, particularly in the forties; consumption expenditures—"personal affluence"—dominated; the economic role of government had expanded vastly; the United States had assumed central responsibility for monetary stability and economic development in the non-Communist world.

The Economic Impact of World War II

All of the characteristics just mentioned, except for temporary restraints on consumption, had their beginning during the war years of 1940–45. In economic terms, World War II therefore functioned as the turning point between the economy of the depression and pre-depression years, and that of the postwar era.

During the thirties, the New Deal infused what were then considered massive amounts of federal funds into the economy to combat the depression. The disappointing success of that spending, and especially the unnerving recession of 1937, which occurred when the federal budget was nearly balanced, suggested to some conservatives that the New Deal had been wasteful and useless. But these observers stopped learning halfway through the lesson. The economy fully recovered only after federal spending for defense became huge, from late 1940 onward. That spending ultimately became ten times larger than the amount spent on World War I, and it transformed the greatly underemployed, underproducing economy of 1939 into a throbbing giant engine in two years. The real lesson of the time was that New Deal spending only partially succeeded in combating the depression, not because spending did not do any good, but because the New Deal did not do enough of it. From 1940 onward there was plenty. The only visible cost was a swiftly rising national debt; the main danger was that demand would so completely outrun supply that price inflation would destroy any semblance of real values. But the monetary, bonding, and enforcement powers of the federal government controlled the debt adequately, and neither the debt nor the degree of inflation ever approached the rates of those earlier postwar adjustment periods, 1865–68 and 1919–21. The major reasons for this success were the wartime agencies and policies that simultaneously controlled prices, limited excess individual

"Rosie the Riveter" at North American Aviation, Inglewood, California, 1942. World War II, among other things, expanded the female labor force. (Culver Pictures, Inc.)

and corporate incomes, made consumer durables scarce (thus building up a postwar backlog of demand), and provided jobs and good wages to millions.

By late 1940 the main economic indicators had climbed from depression to something approaching mid-twenties levels. At that point, in large part because of American willingness to sell war goods to the countries fighting the Axis powers (Germany, Italy, and Japan), and because of the Roosevelt administration's policy of supporting the anti-Axis countries by all means short of war, the great latent productive capacity of the United States began to be realized. Merchant ships, arms, ammunition, motor vehicles, electrical equipment, chemicals, and other war-related heavy-industry goods started flowing from American factories. Unemployment, still at 17 percent in 1939, dropped to 10 percent in 1941, under 5 percent in 1942, about 2 percent in 1943, and 1 percent in 1944. Investment dollars came out of hiding, personal incomes and buying power rose. The depression was over.

After a few false starts, the federal government in 1942 created several agencies to control the economy and inflation, among them the War Production Board and other boards to supervise transportation and manpower. In 1943 it combined these bodies into the Office of War Mobilization. In doing so, the government centralized economic control along lines similar to those of the Wilson administration during World War I. The wartime agencies were not as coordinated nor as comprehensively empowered as hindsight suggests that they could or should have been; often they were makeshift, inefficient, overlapped in authority, or lacked needed control over manpower or resources.

Nevertheless they surpassed in concept and execution the World War I mobilization. Unlike the situation in 1917–18, the War Labor Board during World War II supervised wage increases, limiting them to 15 percent, and extracted a pledge from unions not to strike during the emergency; labor generally kept its word. The Office of Price Administration governed rents, wages, prices, and the distribution of scarce consumer items such as butter, meat, sugar, and gasoline. Rationing books and ration stamps became as familiar to every adult as his driver's license or his paycheck, but though rationing meant more regimentation than Americans had dreamed they would put up with, it worked very well, and inflationary rises in the cost of consumer necessities were relatively slight. A certain amount of "black marketeering" did exist, especially in 1944 and 1945, but the public generally avoided it. Some items were not to be had; *Time* reported in May, 1945, that a dozen prewar golf balls that once sold for $10 were bringing $40 to $60. But reconversion to peacetime production soon brought back fresh golf balls (and inflation in the price of top-quality ones from 95 cents to $1.25 each).

Rationing, price controls, wage restraints, and central resource allocation were abolished by the end of 1946. But World War II did bring permanent changes in the national tax structure. Faced with the need to raise vast amounts of money to finance the war, the federal government, as in earlier wars, sought to raise money as much as it could by going to the people. Bond sales, a time-honored device, raised over $200 billion, from established capital markets and from small children who bought war stamps for ten cents. Taxes on the excess profits of corporations not only brought in large sums but also helped prevent the formation of a class of war profiteers, which had undermined national morale in earlier wars.

Most important, Congress raised personal income tax levels during the war to unprecedented heights—94 percent for incomes over $200,000 in 1944, with the lowest rate 23 percent on $2,000 incomes—and they have never returned to the low level of the thirties. The Sixteenth Amendment of thirty years earlier was being employed as a revenue producer and income leveler far more thoroughly than its progressive advocates had envisaged. In 1943 the government instituted a new mechanism for collecting income taxes, the "pay-as-you-go" plan, invented by Beardsley Ruml of Macy's (one of many businessmen in federal posts in wartime), by which a portion of expected annual income tax was withheld from each paycheck.

New taxes and bonds still did not meet expenses, and the national debt, about $43 billion ($325 per person) in 1940, soared to $259 billion (about $1,850 per person) in 1945. Businessmen, however, discovered that the national debt did not mean national disaster, and in fact—since much of it was in the form of negotiable circulating bonds—the debt greatly boosted the supply of money available for investment in new enterprises. By the fifties and sixties, nearly all observers considered a controlled federal debt to be an aid to growth, even though economists, businessmen, and bureaucrats alike realized that inflation had to be kept to a minimum and real growth maximized, which meant keeping debt increases and monetary values in check. Indebtedness had become, as Alexander Hamilton had claimed in a bygone day, a national blessing.

Postwar Business Cycles

Despite a 70 percent rise in the GNP since 1939, many economists feared in 1945 that the country might revert to depression conditions. Rapid demobilization would mean high unemployment, which together with the time lag presumably required for reconversion to peacetime production would bring stagnation again. But such fears did not materialize. Demobilization was slower, and reconversion faster, than after World War I; unemployment rose to only 3.9 percent in 1946. An estimated $250 billion in savings and other consumer assets were available for spending on goods such as cars, houses, and appliances whose purchase had been deferred during the war, and for many people, in fact, since early in the 1930s. Consequently, a considerable amount of inflation, rather than recession, characterized the years 1945 through 1948. The first postwar passenger car, a two-door '46 Mercury, rolled off the assembly line in Dearborn in June, 1945, on the same day that the last World War II bomber came off another assembly line a few miles away at Willow Run.

In addition, the federal government did not reduce expenditures to the levels of the thirties or the twenties. The exigencies of world politics required considerable outlays for defense and massive amounts of foreign aid, notably Marshall Plan aid for European recovery. Some welfare expenditures begun during the New Deal were continued and expanded, and veterans' benefits, whether for education, insurance, housing, or other purposes, amounted to several billion dollars per year. As a result of several factors—continued federal expenditure, rapid reconversion of the wartime industrial capacity, widely distributed disposable income, and new technology—the economy not only failed to slow down after 1945, but actually began to grow at a rate that quintupled it by the beginning of the 1970s, a quarter-century later. The gross national product doubled every ten or eleven years, from $214 billion in 1945 to $419 billion in 1956 to over one trillion dollars by 1971. Except for 1929 alone, the GNP in current dollars had never been one-tenth that size before 1940.

The economy was not recession-free during the postwar era. A downturn occurred in 1949, after the heavy postwar consumer demand had been met and before the military requirements of the Korean War restored the growth pattern. Federal expenditure leaped from about $40 billion in 1949 and 1950 to almost $75 billion in 1953, nearly all of the increase going for military expenses. The consumer price index rose a startling 8 percent in the first year of the Korean War but slackened to about 1 percent a year between 1952 and 1956. After Korea, in 1953 and 1954, a second postwar recession occurred, when a sudden drop of several billion dollars in defense spending set off a decline in GNP and employment. The downtrend could have spiraled toward depression, but instead it ended in 1955: consumer demand from the "baby boom," federal, state, and local spending, which continued or expanded as in the case of farm subsidies, and a rise in personal income made for a fundamentally more secure economy than existed in 1921 or 1929, when the primary and secondary postwar recessions of World War I began. Inflation returned, and the consumer price index rose almost 8 percent more from late 1955 until 1958. The classic response of tighter credit by the Federal Reserve and lending agencies only led to a third recession, marked by nearly 8 percent unemployment (the highest since 1940) while inflation mystifyingly continued. This recession lasted from 1958 to early 1961. The fifties, contrary to some popular impressions, were not a model decade of prosperity. Though growth continued, in the form of GNP, jobs, or income, the annual increase from 1953 to the close of the decade was only about 1 percent, much lower than the 5 percent of 1947–52.

The period from 1961 to 1968, in contrast, brought the longest unbroken peacetime growth spurt in history. With inflation holding at a minimal 1 percent in most of those years, real growth rates passed 5 percent per year. The federal government was closely linked to the general economy at so many points that federal expenditure, tax levels, bonding manipulation, and regulatory activity could be employed with some sensitivity to shore up soft spots and reduce inflationary overheating. The executive branch and a majority of the Congress accepted the Keynesian principle that deficit spending could be a positive instrument of economic growth, and that cuts in tax rates could stimulate growth, thus increasing the tax base, producing larger revenues for stimulatory uses. At the close of the sixties, however, inflation returned. The cost of living increased about 6 percent in 1969 and again in 1970, while a mini-recession, less severe than those of the 1950s but still disquieting, sent the unemployment rate to nearly 6 percent in 1970 and 1971. In certain industries, including high-skill ones such as aerospace, unemployment was twice as high. Historians remembered that the upward cycle of 1897–1929 ended in disaster, and realized that 1945–1970 was not a long enough period to allow the conclusion that depressions or serious recessions would never recur. Nonetheless the fact of a trillion-dollar economy, despite an unsatisfactorily slow growth rate for the GNP—again less than 1 percent—contradicted the idea of any imminent massive downturn.

Blue Collars:
Farmers and Workers

By the mid-thirties, the number of farms and farmers in America had started a long-term decline, which became more rapid after the depression ended. The peak number of farms in American history, 6.8 million, was reached in 1935. Thereafter the number dropped, to about 6 million in 1945, 4.5 million in 1955, and under 3.5 million in the mid-sixties, the lowest since before 1880. Farmers became America's disappearing workingmen. In the early 1930s more than 10 million people, about one-quarter of the labor force, worked in agriculture; by 1970, only one-twentieth.

At the same time, while fewer people lived and worked on the land, the land itself continued producing abundantly. A handful of other highly urbanized, highly industrialized countries (such as Britain and the Netherlands) also had very few farmers, but almost none of those countries fed themselves. In world terms, American farmers were a tiny band, but the United States continued to be so great an agricultural producer that it sent surplus crops in quantity to such giants as India and the Soviet Union. Never had so few produced so much for so many. Some economists remarked that the development of such huge agricultural production, and such high productivity per man-hour, was the really noteworthy fact of American economic history, more remarkable even than expansion of United States manufacturing or finance. Cultivated land rose to a peak of over a billion acres in 1950, and the average size of farms climbed while farmers disappeared. Except for purposely-controlled acreage reductions, in order to reduce surpluses, cultivated acreage remained steady from 1950 on.

Several factors underlay the decrease in number of farms and farmers and the rise in farm product. Better incomes and opportunities awaited farm youth in cities and suburbs. New machinery and chemical fertilizers brought hitherto incredible crop yields from intensively-farmed acreage. Surpluses (a problem since the twenties) and the resulting low crop and livestock prices relative to rising costs made the "family farm" unprofitable. Mechanization and technology rapidly reduced the man-hours needed to produce staple crops: the human labor needed to produce wheat in 1960 was one-seventh what it was in 1920; to produce corn, one-eighth; to produce cotton, one-fifth. In the meantime, the income of the dwindling troop of farm families running moderate-sized operations improved little, especially in comparison to nonfarm workers. The farmer's share of the ultimate retail price of food or clothing dropped through the period; farmers became annoyed at being blamed for high food prices when they got only one or two cents of the thirty-five or fifty cents a city-dweller had to pay for a loaf of bread. As one disgusted Oklahoma farmer said in the early fifties, running the farm had become a kind of expensive hobby for people who lived on what they earned in town. Technology, the ingenuity of agricultural technologists pouring out of land grant colleges, the mushrooming of producer cooperatives into quarter-billion-dollar corporate giants, and the coordination of crop and livestock production into national market industries, all helped make the word agri*culture* obsolescent, replacing it with the apt neologism agri*business.* Crop fields blossomed, meanwhile, amid abandoned homesteads and deserted country villages.

Technological obsolescence also began to thin the ranks of industrial workers, or at least the unskilled and semiskilled, after 1945. Industrial labor had been the noisy problem child of American social and economic life in the early twentieth century, struggling sometimes violently for a decent share of the worldly goods it helped produce. Many workers did not enjoy the right of collective bargaining, or wage rises commensurate with productivity rises, during the twenties. Their lack of buying power exacerbated the glide into depression. Part of the problem was insufficient unionization, especially in the auto, steel, and other mass-production industries. Not only did management resist unions, either in monarchical operations like the Ford Motor Company (which had a strong-arm antiunion security force) or corporate giants like the big steel companies, but leaders of the AFL craft unions also frowned on attempts to organize the millions of mass-production workers for fear of dividing and weakening the labor movement. That dangerous anomaly was ended in the thirties by the depression, tough new leaders like John L. Lewis and the Reuther brothers, and federal legislation, but only after monumental struggles.

The two early New Deal laws concerning labor, Section 7(a) of the 1933 National Industrial Recovery Act and the 1935 Wagner Act, asserted labor's right to bargain collectively, and the Wagner

Jim Barry appeared weekly in the *CIO News*, upholding the liberalism of big labor against threats from communists, crooks, and rapacious capitalists. (Courtesy of *The CIO News*, AFL-CIO)

Act set up a National Labor Relations Board to supervise unionization elections. Workers were no longer to be forced into company unions or fired for union organizing. Seizing on these two measures, John L. Lewis of the United Mine Workers led the fight for recognition of industrial unions within the AFL. Rebuffed in the 1935 AFL convention, Lewis punched "Big Bill" Hutcheson of the Carpenters' Union in the mouth, stalked out of the AFL, and formed the group known by 1938 as the Congress of Industrial Organizations, the CIO.

The epic time of American industrial unionism was 1936 and 1937. Strikes, pitched battles, and propaganda filled the newspapers; managements fought unionization by almost every kind of device, from the brutal to the free-enterprising: *Newsweek* reported in July, 1937, that the United Mine Workers had filed a complaint against the Clover Fork Coal Company of Cincinnati for enticing miners away from union meetings by sponsoring striptease shows at the same hour. "Big Steel," the United States Steel holding company, responding to pressure but avoiding strikes, signed a recognition pact with the Steel Workers' Organizing Committee. Other steel companies learned the hard way: Tom Girdler of Republic Steel and other leaders of "Little Steel" adamantly refused to settle with the union. The union struck the companies, and despite the vicious opposition of management and some public authorities—such as when Chicago police fired on a steelworkers' rally, killing ten and injuring many others, in the "Memorial Day Massacre" of 1937—the steel industry was unionized by the time World War II began. Meanwhile, the United Auto Workers moved in on the car manufacturers. The crucial turning point was the UAW's successful sit-down strikes, in the Chevrolet and Fisher Body factories of General Motors in the early weeks of 1937. The auto workers occupied the machines, so that strike-breakers could not be used to deprive them of their jobs. Benefiting tremendously from the refusal of Frank Murphy, the Democratic governor of Michigan, to move them out with militia, they brought General Motors to the bargaining table and a contract. Chrysler, the smaller companies, and ultimately Ford made their peace, and the CIO-affiliated United Auto Workers had unionized the auto industry. Industrial unions conquered the electrical, rubber, and other industries in the late thirties also, and by Pearl Harbor Day, the CIO had 5 million members.

World War II, with its urgent demands for defense production, spurred unionization, and by 1945 nearly 15 million American workers were organized into unions, about 36 percent of the non-agricultural working force. But although total union membership rose to over 18 million in the late fifties, it declined thereafter in total numbers, and in fact declined since 1945 as a percentage of all workers. Like the farmer, the factory worker was beginning to disappear. The increasing automation of factories made blue-collar workers, except for the highly skilled, less necessary. Jobs for service workers and white-collar workers of all kinds opened up much faster. It was as though the vast struggle to unionize industrial workers and to legitimize the place of industrial unions in the capitalist structure had been won just in time—in the final decade before the blue collar itself began to become obsolescent.

Consumer Orientation in Manufacturing and Services

After 1945, the trend, which began to be visible in the 1920s, of increasing expenditures for consumer goods accelerated so greatly that by the late fifties more workers held jobs to provide services than jobs to produce goods. The driveshafts of the manufacturing sector were consumer durables, especially cars and houses, and the producer durables, such as steel and electrical equipment, needed to make consumer durables. New housing starts and new auto production became, more than in the twenties, prime indicators of how well the economy was performing.

Industries not directed to home and personal consumption did appear. The growth industries of the fifties and sixties were offshoots of advanced technology and were often tied to national defense or to services—planes, missiles, computers, electronic equipment, office machinery such as calculators and photoduplicators. As manufacturing companies reached out to expand their markets and profits, a new form of consolidated firm emerged, the conglomerate, linking under one financially powerful management several companies producing relatively unrelated items. Where "natural monopoly" existed, as in telephone communications, a single dominant corporation (American Telephone and Telegraph) reached the size of $50 billion in assets by 1971. The largest bank held over $25 billion in deposits, and fully 115 manufacturing firms enjoyed sales of over a billion dollars in 1970—while in the entire world only 64 other companies were that large. Reflecting the consumer orientation of the economy, nearly all of the top twenty industrial corporations produced either motor vehicles, steel (much of it used to make cars), petroleum products (including gas and oil for cars), or items connected with personal services such as aircraft, computers, and office equipment. The market for phonograph equipment (stereos, tape recorders), for mobile homes, for boats, televisions, and sporting goods boomed during the sixties; in view of the facts of the age structure, the enormous "youth market" was not surprising.

Services, particularly those involving money and finance, formed an essential lubricant to the consumption economy. The checking account, the credit card, the auto loan, and the home mortgage were easily understandable credit instruments involving fairly small transactions on an individual or family basis. Taken collectively across the economy, however, the sum of such transactions added up to a mighty arsenal of devices for the rapid circulation of money. Unquestionably the sale of new cars by the millions and new homes by the hundreds of thousands per year could never have occurred, and certainly did not occur in other countries, without such widespread and relatively easy installment credit. Exemplary though American manufacturing expansion was, the availability of credit for nearly any kind of purchase was an achievement of economic technology that set the United States apart. Although consumer credit spread as incomes and consumption demands arose—from half a billion dollars in 1945 to ten times as much in the mid-sixties, three-quarters of it in the form of installment debt—credit did not outrun incomes and assets; credit supported the economy rather than shook it.

Big and Little Spenders: Changes in Income Distribution

One of the key weaknesses in the economy during the 1920s was a distribution of income too unbalanced in favor of wealthier groups to sustain the levels of consumption needed to keep the economy moving. Also, rises in real wages during the twenties did not keep pace with rises in newly-produced wealth. After 1945 these two

FAMILY INCOME, 1950–1969 (IN CONSTANT 1969 DOLLARS)

(A) with Less than $3,000
(B) with $3,000 to $4,999
(C) with $5,000 to $9,999
(D) with $10,000 to $14,999
(E) with $15,000 or More

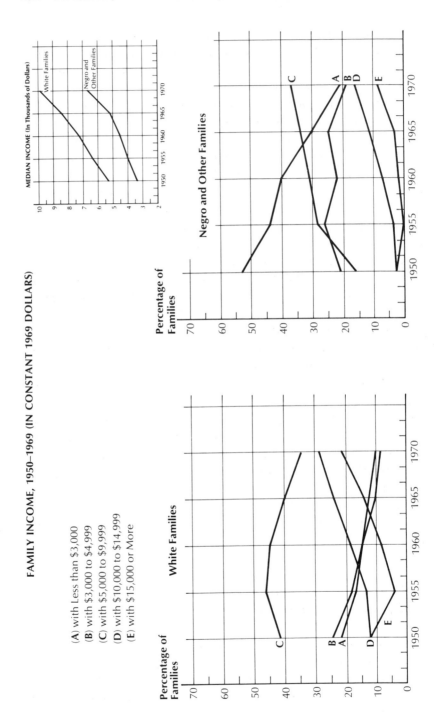

flaws were not fully eliminated, but they were substantially reduced. Measurably, though not completely, income distribution in America became democratized beginning with the World War II years.

Average real income rose substantially during World War II and again during most of the 1960s, kept pace with the cost of living even during brief periods of above-average inflation such as the late forties and late sixties, and fell back only in a few high-inflation years such as 1951. Average family income, in current dollars, was about $1,200 in 1939. By 1945 it doubled, and gradually rose thereafter to about $10,000 at the beginning of the 1970s. In general, unionized blue-collar workers benefited more than salaried people. Average weekly paychecks for union workers, stable at about $24 through the twenties, crept upward to about $30 at the outbreak of World War II. After a rapid rise during the war, weekly wages kept climbing, and were well over $100 a week in the sixties. At the same time, the average work-week shrank to a norm of forty hours after the war, while for white-collar workers the thirty-five hour week became common.

Increases in average real income were important, but certain changes in the distribution of income were even more significant. The highest-paid few received more money, but a smaller share of all money earned, while middle-income people, and to a lesser extent the poor, received a larger share. But the changes in the direction of more equitable income distribution did not take place steadily across the whole period: they occurred to a moderate degree during the New Deal years and in the late 1940s, to a marked degree during World War II, and to a very slight degree, if at all, between 1950 and 1970.

These figures are corrected for inflation; actual numbers of earned dollars were larger in later years. Among white families, the "C" group rose during the early 1950s through gains from the (poorer) "A" and "B" groups, and fell thereafter through losses to the wealthier "D" and "E" groups. The steepest decline of any group was among the non-white poor ("A") group, as Negro families in general moved into the "B" and especially the "C" groups, and in the sixties, though slowly, into the "D" and "E" groups. Despite these improvements in the family income of Negroes, the median for them remained significantly and steadily below the median for white families.

The democratization of income was caused in large part by two factors: rises in rates of personal income taxes, moderately during the thirties and steeply during the war; and the end of widespread unemployment, coupled with marked wage and salary increases for blue- and white-collar workers, in the early 1940s. Neither tax rates nor employment rates changed drastically after 1950, and neither did income distribution. To take a few examples: in the late 1920s, just before the crash of 1929, the 5 percent of the population receiving the highest incomes creamed off about 34 percent of all income earned. During the depression and the New Deal, the highest-paid 5 percent received gradually smaller shares, until in 1940 they took in about 25 percent of all income. During World War II their share fell more quickly, to about 18 percent. But after 1950 it rose again slightly, and remained steady at 21 percent to 23 percent into the early 1970s. Similarly, the highest-paid 20 percent of the population underwent a significant drop in income during World War II and immediately afterwards, falling to just over 50 percent in 1950. But thereafter they steadily received 51 percent to 56 percent.

At the other end of the scale, the 20 percent of the population receiving the least income did not benefit from the decreased share of the wealthy, but consistently received only about 5 percent of total income from the end of World War II through the 1960s. The real beneficiaries were the people who can be called the "middle class." About half the population—not the poorest and not the wealthiest —enjoyed a substantial rise in their share of real income during and shortly after World War II, and their share remained generally steady from then on. The *economic* consequences of this redistribution included an increase nationally in what economists call the marginal propensity to consume, since the high-income few, having more than enough to meet consumption desires, tended to save or invest rather than spend. Redistribution to middle-income people meant expanded markets for homes, cars, appliances, and services, providing the economy with a large and steady consumption underpinning. The *social* consequences of income redistribution were, above all, the broadening of the "affluent society" and bourgeois mores and attitudes among the middle class, together with persistent frustration and a sense of hopelessness among the poorest 20 percent because of their lack of relative improvement in income and their inability to share in middle-class affluence.

The lack of improvement in the relative position of the lowest-income 20 percent since 1950 has had serious impact, perpetuating "pockets of poverty" in certain rural areas such as Appalachia and in core cities. The contrast between high- and middle-income people on the one hand and the poor on the other hand was especially visible in the sixties, and occasionally (when coupled with race tension) resulted in urban rioting. Income disparities might have been more serious yet, even revolutionary, had not the static position of the poorest 20 percent, in terms of their share of income, been masked to a considerable extent by increases in their actual dollar income. In 1947, about 48 percent of white families and about 81 percent of nonwhite families had incomes of $3,000 or less. For

The "highest income 5%" is part of the "highest income 20%" in this graph. Note that in 1929, the highest-income 5% received more income (salaries, rents, dividends, interest) than 80% of the rest of the population; by 1969 the share of the upper 5% had declined greatly, but that group still received more income than almost half the rest of the population. Note also that shifts in income distribution have been inconsequential since the early 1950s: the lines are almost level from that time on.

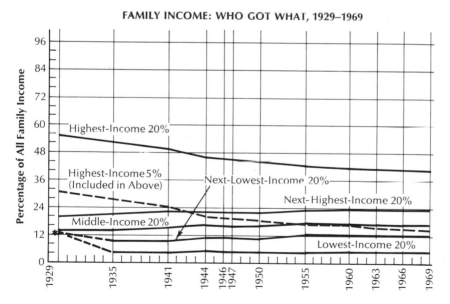

FAMILY INCOME: WHO GOT WHAT, 1929–1969

*In 1929, Combined Figure For Lowest-Income 20% and
Next-Lowest-Income 20%.

blacks and whites alike, rises in dollar income in the late forties and early fifties removed large numbers of people from the under-$3,000 category, and by 1966, only about 14 percent of white families and 30 percent of black ones had incomes that low. More than a fifth of the black families in the country joined the $3,000–$6,000 income group between 1950 and 1955, and another fifth (many of them the same people) arrived at the $6,000–$10,000 category between 1955 and 1966. Among white families, one-fifth joined the $6,000–$10,000 group during the 1950s, and one-fifth crossed the $10,000 income mark during the 1960s. The "poverty line," if we define it as the maximum dollar income of the poorest-paid 20 percent of the nation's families, gradually rose to about $3,800 at the beginning of the 1970s. In short, the relative position of low-income Americans changed little, though their actual dollar earnings went up; for the middle-income group, both relative and actual earnings improved; for the high-income 20 percent, its proportionate share of all income held fairly steady after 1950, but its actual dollar income rose. For everybody, dollar earnings have risen substantially since 1950, even after discounting inflation, but the distribution of earnings among income groups has changed very little. Income trends since 1940 produced above all a strengthening, economically and socially, of the middle class.

The Strengthened Spring of Government

Beginning with the New Deal in the thirties, expanding during World War II, and continuing thereafter, the role of the federal government as a stimulator and underwriter of economic growth was much larger in recent decades than it historically had been. Despite the complaints of economic traditionalists in the fifties against "creeping socialism," and the complaints of *both* self-styled conservatives and liberals about bureaucracy by the late sixties, the federal government became so entwined with the economy after 1933 that the economy could no longer be called "capitalistic" in any traditional, government-free sense. There has never been an era of true *laissez faire* in American history. But prior to the New Deal and World War II, federal activity as a stimulator or regulator had been confined chiefly to tariffs and banking laws, federal taxes had been low except in wartime, federal payrolls were relatively small, and the public sector—federal, state, and local governments—generated but a small fraction of the GNP. The public-sector share of national income, which held steady at 4 percent to 6 percent between the Civil War and World War I, rose to about 8 percent during the twenties. After that it jumped to a permanent level of 20 percent to 25 percent. Federal employees, not counting the armed services, numbered over 1 million in 1940 and rose after World War II to between 2 and 3 million, many cushioned by civil service from sudden unemployment. State and local governments each had payrolls (not including millions of public school and college teachers) about as large as the federal government. Personal income-tax rates, though they dropped in the late forties from wartime highs, never again fell to the level of the thirties or earlier, and higher taxes on corporate profits brought tens of billions to the Treasury annually.

Chief Justice Marshall was correct when he wrote in 1819, in *McCulloch* v. *Maryland*, that "the power to tax . . . involves the power to destroy." He failed to note that the power to spend was power to create. The federal government used its creative power in many areas from the thirties onward, and one of the most socially consequential was the underwriting and expansion of business and consumer credit. This was true of both Republican and Democratic administrations. The Reconstruction Finance Corporation, which Hoover began in 1932 and which Roosevelt and Truman relied on heavily as a stimulator, lent billions for the rebuilding and expansion of businesses until Eisenhower liquidated it in the mid-fifties. Federal deposit insurance was one of the less heralded New Deal measures when it was created in 1933, but the protecting of accounts in banks, savings-and-loan associations, and credit unions benefited inestimably by assuring depositors that their money was safe, and by the economy effectively ended banking panics, runs on banks, and the fears preventing many people from employing money productively in the form of savings. Government loans at low interest rates financed hospital construction under the Hill-Burton Act of 1943. The "G.I. loan," the low-interest home-mortgage plan for World War II and later veterans, both stimulated the home-building industry and made home ownership a reality for millions. Government-established financial guarantors such as the Federal National Mortgage Association supported mortgage loans for large numbers for whom conventional bank credit would have been too scarce or expensive and down payments too high; the FNMA supplemented the resources of banks and also created a pool of negotiable mortgage securities that further lubricated the national money and credit system. Successive educational aid acts in the fifties and sixties allowed colleges and universities to borrow at low rates to build dormitories and libraries.

After 1940 the federal government spent most copiously for national security. War and defense costs were high not only during World War II, the Korean War of 1950–53, and the Vietnam War, but also during technical peacetime. In only a few budget years after 1945 did the federal government manage to keep defense and military costs below half or even two-thirds of its total operating budget. Defense spending was not entirely an economic waste; it stimulated production, accelerated the growth of high-technology industries (aircraft, computers, miniaturized electronic devices for the space program, for example), provided employment, and maintained an aggregate demand, which kept the economy moving. But few things were more useless than an obsolete warplane or rocket. With good reason, many people lamented the waste inherent in huge defense expenditures, and some complained in the late sixties about the $24 billion spent to put men on the moon. Would the economy plunge into depression if defense spending dropped drastically? The past offered few models. By the late sixties, however, alternatives to military spending were apparent, as estimates were made that it would take one trillion dollars to revamp the nation's cities, or hundreds of millions to improve education, to erase the poverty line, or to end environmental pollution.

The enormous defense outlays of the federal government generated another concern, which was more directly political than economic: the connections between the Pentagon and the several dozen multi-billion-dollar corporations from which the Pentagon did the bulk of its buying. Some corporations producing aircraft and rocketry did most of their business with the federal government. Thousands of people in California, Washington, Georgia, Texas, and other states depended on these companies—and on the federal government's contracts with them—for their jobs. Thousands of others (families, landlords, grocers, car dealers, etc.) depended on those defense employees' paychecks. The government, for political reasons, was unable to abruptly stop buying defense goods from

The commuter hassle, already a bore in 1950. (Brown Brothers)

these companies. Indeed when Lockheed, which enjoyed nearly $2 billion in defense contracts in 1968 alone, almost went bankrupt in 1971, Congress rescued it by authorizing a $250 million loan. Many political commentators worried about the power of the "military-industrial complex"—the term first became prominent in the Farewell Address of President (and former General) Eisenhower in January, 1961—of Pentagon officials and large defense contractors, most of which employed dozens of retired army and naval officers. Though a group so large was hardly a malign conspiracy, and though civilian and elected officials (especially in Congress) supported this nexus instead of controlling it, the community of interest and common purpose (and, often, common military background) of Defense Department and corporation executives sometimes enabled corporations to avoid competitive bidding for contracts or to secure funds for billion-dollar cost overruns, such as on Lockheed's C-5 transport plane. Taxpayers had little control over these practices. But in an economy where by 1970 only 1,300 companies did 45 percent of the nation's business and the government accounted for over 20 percent of the GNP, such a community of interest was hardly surprising. The "military-industrial complex" was but one case, though a major one, of a government–private-enterprise power nexus in a post-capitalist economy. Its power rested equally on the military's desire for the strongest defense posture, the companies' profit motive, the economic welfare of their localities, and the political requirements of their congressmen.

The federal budget also included billions after World War II for foreign aid ($143 billion in the twenty-six years after 1945), veterans' benefits, farm price supports, interstate highways, and education and welfare. About 3 percent of the GNP, much of it from federal sources, went for research and development. Some funds came from the Defense Department or the Office of Education, some from semi-autonomous agencies such as the National Science Foundation, the National Institutes of Health, the National Aeronautics and Space Administration (NASA), and the Public Health Service, mostly for basic research in the physical, biological, and medical sciences. In no other country was "R and D" such a large part of national outlay, and it was contributing to the growing gap in economic level between the United States and the rest of the world, even after cuts in government-financed research programs after 1968.

The United States in the World Economy

As in the past, foreign trade played a smaller role in the American economy than it did in West European countries or Japan. Exports and imports formed a smaller part of the GNP after 1945 than they had before—5 percent or less for exports, 2 percent to 4 percent for imports. Throughout most of the postwar period, the American balance of trade was favorable, and despite continued heavy demand elsewhere for American agricultural products, well over half of the value of total exports were in finished manufactured goods by the 1960s. Toward the close of that decade, however, the trade surplus disappeared: Americans showed a great predilection for efficient, low-priced cars, cameras, stereo equipment, and other goods made abroad, especially from Germany and Japan. At the same time, the dollar had become overpriced relative to many foreign currencies, and American goods were not selling competitively on foreign markets. In 1971 the United States balance of trade was in the red for the first time since 1895.

Even before the reversal of the trade balance, the balance of all international payments was unfavorable. In almost every year after 1945, the United States spent more overseas from public and private sources than other people spent in the United States. The major reasons were corporate investment, foreign aid, military spending, and foreign travel. So much investment capital was generated in the United States after 1945 that corporations and private individuals placed billions in foreign enterprises—over $12 billion in Europe alone by the mid-sixties. The "Big Three" auto makers had European subsidiaries; American oil companies had extensive foreign holdings; IBM captured 70 percent of the world computer market; private investors bought the bonds of foreign governments and private companies. Europeans worried about the American challenge to European business, while South Americans and people in other developing areas feared an augmentation of American economic imperialism. The complaints sounded much like those that Americans themselves made in the late nineteenth century, when the United States was a heavy borrower of British and European investment capital. But after 1945, America was the lender and the suspected imperialist.

Foreign aid began flowing outward *en masse* immediately after World War II. It included armaments, economic and technical assistance, low-interest development loans, and outright grants, depending on the apparent needs of the moment and the country concerned. Of the $50 billion in economic aid distributed between 1948 and 1970, Western Europe was the major beneficiary ($15 billion), especially in the early postwar period; considerable amounts went to Southeast Asia, especially in the sixties ($4 billion to Vietnam alone), and to India and Pakistan ($6 billion), East Asia ($7.6 billion), Latin America ($5 billion), the Middle East ($5 billion), and Africa ($2.4 billion). The initial foreign-aid effort, except for refugee relief, was the European Recovery Program, or the Marshall Plan, which began in 1947. American funds poured into Western

Europe to restore war-wrecked economies. The expenditure was largely motivated by enlightened self-interest; if Europe remained economically supine she would also remain militarily and politically supine, a prey to Communist takeovers. Policy-makers remembered the vengeful and self-defeating reparations policy that helped keep European economies unstable after World War I and that contributed to the rise of Hitler; this bit of history suggested that it would be practical to be more generous after World War II. After Europe recovered, American foreign aid flowed elsewhere, following the principle that socially, economically, and militarily stable nations would be better able to resist the influence of Moscow and Peking. Part of the motivation for foreign aid was altruistic—simply to help less fortunate peoples—but national security played the major role. Nor was the profit motive neglected; much of the aid had strings attached, requiring it to be spent on American products.

Military costs, particularly for the two wars since 1950 on the Asian mainland, as well as the maintaining of sizable garrisons in Germany and elsewhere, pushed the balance of payments further into the red. So did tourism; the millions of affluent Americans who traveled to Europe and other parts of the world far outnumbered, and spent far more money, than the European, Latin American, and Japanese tourists who came to the United States to be amazed by its great distances and appalled by its high prices.

For all these reasons, the American economy, which was so internally affluent, steadily deteriorated as a factor in the world monetary system. In 1945 the United States was preeminent within that system. It held the bulk of free-world gold reserves and had just led in the setting up of new international monetary machinery to avoid the economic nationalism and chain-reaction financial panics that had done much to bring on the Great Depression and World War II. Treaties signed at Bretton Woods, New Hampshire, in 1944, set up an International Monetary Fund and an international bank for development and recovery loans to governments. The dollar and the British pound sterling became, with gold, the bases of most nations' monetary reserves, and efforts to keep the international financial channels from drying up because of a lack of funds or imbalances in currency exchange rates were remarkably successful through the fifties and into the sixties. Governments and central bankers developed gold substitutes, such as "Euro-dollars" and "special drawing rights," to provide international liquidity. But the

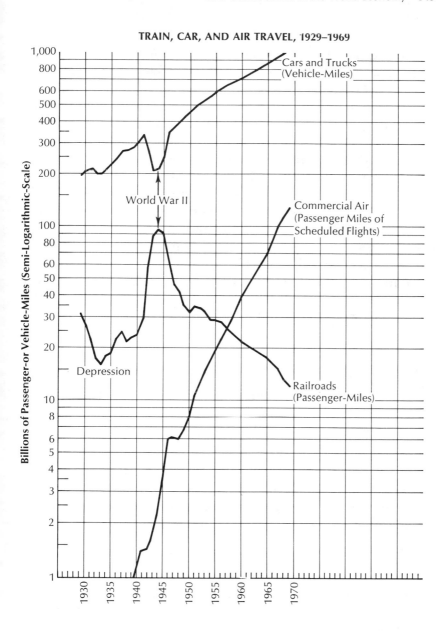

TRAIN, CAR, AND AIR TRAVEL, 1929–1969

The figures for cars and trucks represent the numbers of miles traveled by these vehicles, regardless of how many passengers they carried; the figures for trains and planes are for the number of passengers carried times the number of miles traveled. The lines indicate the restrictions on private cars, and also the great use of railroads, during World War II; the increase in motor vehicles and drop in passenger train travel since 1946; and of course the exceptional increase in commercial air travel after World War II.

chronic imbalance in the United States' international payments caused a steady drain on American gold reserves, and by the late sixties more than half of the $24 billion in gold held at the end of the war had dribbled away to Europe and Japan. The British were in similar trouble, and were forced after several crises to devalue the pound sterling in 1967. In 1971 the Nixon administration abruptly revised the Bretton Woods system by terminating the dollar's convertibility with gold, and the major trading currencies of the world (the German mark, the pound, the yen, and others) floated upward in relation to the dollar, amounting to a devaluation of the dollar to make American goods more competitive. Congress changed the gold price from $35 an ounce to $38, but inconvertibility remained. Congress also reduced foreign aid programs in 1971–72. The quarter-century after World War II had been noteworthy for international monetary cooperation. In 1971 some signs began to point to a resurgence of competitive economic nationalism unseen since the 1920s and 1930s.

The Lessons of the Recent Past

Between 1940 and the early 1970s, the American economy had proved to be unprecedentedly successful in reviving from the Great Depression and in setting historic levels of production, wealth, and income. The depression receded into history, millions of people with no memory of it grew to adulthood, and the majority assumed that the upward cycle operating since 1945 was permanent. Even by the early seventies, however, the time had not yet come when anyone could say with certainty that increasing affluence and an economy free of depressions was to be the permanent norm. The post-1968 recession showed again that setbacks still happened. Nevertheless, that recession, though sobering, was mild in contrast with past ones, even those of the fifties. Threats of disaster had been greatly reduced in several critical ways, making the economy distinctly more sound than it had been during the long prosperity cycle from 1897 to 1929. Personal income was distributed more evenly than before the depression. Even though millions were still below the "poverty line," and these millions were a major social as well as economic problem, median income and the size of the middle-income group had increased.

A second critical difference between the pre- and post-depression economies flowed from the conjunction of the consumer orientation of goods and services with a vast public, including the large body of young people, in a position to buy these goods and services. Another difference, at least from before 1940, was the relatively serene labor picture; the enormous problem of how to integrate the working class successfully into the economy, the full recognition of labor unions, the "labor question" that was so thorny in 1900 or even 1930, had been fairly well solved. Strikes still occurred, non-union areas still existed, black workers were too often unemployed or underemployed, but labor relations were not such a critical national problem as in earlier decades. The fourth difference was the activity of government, especially the federal government, in many sectors of the economy, creating a highly complicated "mix" between the public sector and private enterprise. Patches of socialism balanced patches of old-line capitalism, and most of the economic fabric interwove public and private threads. Nagging doubts remained as to whether prosperity could survive a big reduction in the huge and essentially wasteful federal spending for military purposes, but the Vietnam War demonstrated that even the enormous economy of the late sixties was hard put to produce guns and butter at the same time. Education, urban problems, health and welfare, pollution reduction, public transportation, and research and development still cried for funds; there was plenty of butter left to churn, if the gun-buying stopped. In world terms, the American economy was larger than that of other nations overall, individual Americans were more affluent on the average than anybody else, and the gap between the United States and the poorer nations was widening, not closing. The economy had greatly improved the overall quality of American life, but by 1971 it was also endangering it, especially by atmospheric pollution, from ubiquitous cars, trucks, and planes, and industrial pollution of rivers and lakes with chemical wastes. Utopia, as always, was still some distance off.

Youth at war: an Army sergeant comes upon a wounded Viet Cong soldier near Dalat, February, 1970. (U.S. Army Photograph)

11

SINCE 1953: THE HIGH TIDE AND EBB TIDE OF LIBERAL POLITICS

American domestic and foreign politics since 1953 have generated an enormous jumble of evocative names and dates. Some, like the several civil rights acts, stir pride, while others, like the aborted summit meeting of 1960 or the Bay of Pigs disaster of 1961, Americans prefer to forget. Four very different men inhabited the White House, and from Eisenhower to Kennedy to Johnson to Nixon the thrust of politics moved in no single, clear direction. Though there was a tendency to move toward the left, as from a Joe McCarthy to a Gene McCarthy, various kinds of "right" persisted, as in Taft, Goldwater, and even George Wallace. Political decisions raised men triumphantly to the moon, but in the meantime, the lack of such decisions allowed further pollution of lakes and oceans. Despite the confusion, however, a pattern began to emerge by the early seventies. In foreign affairs, the years since 1953 were the time of the later Cold War: a national preoccupation with "world communism" pervaded the fifties, reached the height of its concrete expression in the Vietnam War, and largely as a result of that war began to give way after about 1967 to neo-isolationism or to a more realistic appraisal of communist polycentrism, or both. In domestic affairs, the Republican administration led by Eisenhower did not repeal, and in fact extended, the welfarish federal activism of the New Deal and Fair Deal; Kennedy and especially Johnson brought such activism to its zenith; by 1970 many former sympathizers were expressing deep doubts about the very worthwhileness of it all. And the definitions of *liberal* and *conservative* changed, while self-described radicalism waxed and waned on Left and Right.

"Dynamic Conservatism" at Home

As Eisenhower took office in January, 1953, a businesslike, no-nonsense attitude emanated from the corridors of Washington. When his new Defense Secretary, former General Motors chairman Charles E. Wilson, averred that "what was good for the country was good for General Motors, and vice-versa," the pro-Democratic press howled, but many nodded in assent, as they had in the mid-twenties when Coolidge barked that the business of America was business. Yet in important ways, the Republican accession of 1953 differed in fact and context from that of 1921. When the voters chose Eisenhower, they selected a man far more versed in international problems than Harding or Coolidge had been. The new president was to prove a soothing leader of the people, responsive to their hope of ending the acrimony and uncertainty of the late Truman years. In this, Eisenhower was greatly aided by three events: Stalin's sudden death on March 5, 1953; an immediate thaw in North Korean peace negotiators' attitudes, and on July 27, armistice and the end of the Korean War; and on August 12, the successful explosion of a hydrogen bomb by the Soviet Union. The thermonuclear gap had closed, and the balance of terror, the third phase of the Cold War, began.

By the time of his election, Eisenhower was in his early sixties, a national hero, an eminently successful army leader who excelled as a coordinator and manager of vast operations such as D-Day in Normandy. He was, however, almost entirely innocent of civilian life and politics. As president, the upright, optimistic ex-soldier proved to be no reactionary, but no great innovator either. He performed excellently a key role of the presidency, that of chief of state; however, he was less able to broaden the G.O.P.'s voting base. Truman had been vigorous but partisan; Eisenhower was benign but a unifier of the people. He tried to remain "above the fray," and delegated executive authority. Since he had been elected as a Republican, the advisers and cabinet officers to whom he delegated responsibility represented the philosophy of the Republican party at that time—particularly John Foster Dulles, the secretary of state, a Presbyterian leader and Wall Street lawyer; George M. Humphrey, the secretary of the Treasury, former head of a Cleveland steel company; and General Motors' Wilson at the Defense Department.

The cabinet, the National Security Council, and the White House staff blended the various Republican constituencies of eastern banks and law firms, big manufacturing companies, and midwestern and western smaller cities. Wealthy, WASP, predominantly Protestant, the country's new leaders talked of ending "creeping socialism," "throwing out the New Dealers," restoring "states' rights," renewing the "spirit of free enterprise," and "cleaning up the mess in Washington." The realities of office and the good sense of many Republican leaders in Congress and, in the executive branch soon muted these slogans.

Eisenhower's first term, from 1953 to 1957, started with a strong right-wing Republican, pro-business conservatism in domestic policy but moved steadily after 1953 toward a less doctrinaire "dynamic conservatism," as "Ike" called it. The initial pro-business attitude was evident in budget-cutting and lower taxes, and in three instances where federally-controlled natural resources were turned over to private enterprise for development. The first anti-conservationist action also affirmed "states' rights"; the Submerged Lands Act of 1953 transferred nationally-owned crude oil deposits off the shores of California, Louisiana, and Texas to the states, which leased them to private oil companies. In the second and third instances, also in 1953, private companies benefited directly, when they received the rights to build hydroelectric projects in Idaho's Hell's Canyon and, in the later notorious Dixon-Yates contract, to supply power to the Atomic Energy Commission despite the local availability of the Tennessee Valley Authority.

The furore over the Dixon-Yates contract in 1954, together with the onset of a business recession embarrassing to a "businessmen's government," signaled a decline in anti–Fair Deal conservatism. The death of Senator Taft on July 31, 1953, deprived the responsible Republican right wing of its greatest leader, and Eisenhower's own internationalism—a bent not shared by the Right—was manifested when in December, 1953, he presented the United Nations with his "Atoms for Peace" program for international cooperation in finding peaceable uses for atomic energy. In 1954, Congress approved that idea, and also defeated by a 50–42 vote a constitutional amendment offered by Ohio's Senator John W. Bricker to require all international agreements to be "legislated by Congress," which would have prevented executive agreements like Yalta, then a *bête noire* of Republican neo-isolationists. The extreme Right suffered an even more severe blow in the spring of 1954, when Senator McCarthy provoked a congressional investigation of Communist subversion allegedly rampant in the United States Army—and over-reached himself. Eisenhower had refused "to get in the gutter with that guy," but the president's hands-off attitude allowed McCarthy and his allies to snoop for "security risks" in the State Department, the Foreign Service, and other agencies. A large national TV audience watched the Army-McCarthy hearings for six rollicking weeks. The hearings showed that the Department of the Army harbored some incompetents—no surprise to a country full of ex-G.I.'s—but no Communists. The result was not to purge the army, but to reveal McCarthy for the mud-slinging demagogue that he was. His large popular support dwindled. A year later the Senate censured him, 67–22, for tarnishing its image, and the thrust of the Second Red Scare was broken. Before that happened, however, many government workers had lost their jobs and, as "security risks," could not get new ones. In academia, it was not wise to speak of Marx or the Russians or communism without a tone of sober denunciation. The Cincinnati National League baseball team was referred to in the press, suddenly and consistently, as the "Redlegs," almost never as the "Reds," their traditional name for many decades. And the president of a state teachers' college in Massachusetts was quoted as saying, "I know of no Reds or Communist-minded persons either among the faculty or the students here. . . . The type of students who go here are not of the highly intellectual type among which [sic] such tendencies exist." To some, like the atomic physicist J. Robert Oppenheimer or the veteran foreign service officer John Carter Vincent, who lost their security clearances after McCarthyite attacks, the effects were more serious and more lasting. The country did not benefit from the episode.

The Eisenhower administration continued to move away from the doctrinaire slogans of 1953. The Atomic Energy Commission canceled the Dixon-Yates contract in 1955, after the press showed that an expert who recommended it to the government was involved in selling Dixon-Yates securities. In the same year, Eisenhower asked Congress for several measures that were almost Fair-Dealish, and in 1956 Congress extended social security and federal public housing, and authorized the $33 billion, sixteen-year interstate highway program. Republican loss of control of Congress by a narrow margin to the Democrats in 1954, plus the 1954 recession,

President and Mrs. Eisenhower and Vice President and Mrs. Nixon celebrating their
reelection in Washington, November, 1956. (United Press International Photo)

no doubt aided the shift from right to center. The election results of
1956 showed further that the voters wanted centrist politics. Tired
and suspicious of doctrinaire partisanship, whether right-wing Republican or left-wing Democratic, people voted more than ever for
"the man, not the party," and re-elected Eisenhower by 9½ million
votes over Adlai Stevenson while returning Democratic majorities
to both houses of Congress, an unprecedented division. Leaving Eisenhower's personal popularity aside as an important but short-
term variable, the election results showed that the G.O.P. had made
only one significant inroad on the F.D.R. coalition of labor, city-
dwellers, blacks, Jews, and other ethnics. The exception was the
South, where Republicans chipped away at traditional Democratic

solidity while the Democrats, though their 1956 civil rights plank was weaker than that of the Republicans, took an increasingly active lead in civil rights legislation under Speaker Sam Rayburn and Senate Majority Leader Lyndon B. Johnson, both Texans.

Rayburn and Johnson were instrumental in the passage of the two outstanding measures of the second Eisenhower administration, the Civil Rights Acts of 1957 and 1960. The first mandated voting rights by giving federal courts the power to hold in criminal contempt persons interfering with the voting of others; it set up the Civil Rights Division of the Justice Department and a national Civil Rights Commission. The 1960 act provided stronger penalties for interfering with voting, voter registration, or school desegregation. These were the first civil rights acts since the Reconstruction.

In other areas, the second Eisenhower administration feinted to the left and right, keeping its general direction along the center. Moving along New Deal pathways, it extended social security, raised the minimum wage, and continued reciprocal trade. After the Soviet Union launched the first earth satellite, Sputnik, in 1957, Congress acted out of concern for both security and welfare to create the National Aeronautics and Space Administration and the National Defense Education Act (for secondary, graduate, and teacher education) in 1958. And it moved to the right when it passed the Landrum-Griffin labor law of 1959, which was intended to control labor racketeering and big-union bureaucracies. But even Landrum-Griffin did not reflect the intense anti-union feeling evident twelve years before in Taft-Hartley. The Eisenhower administration had not rolled back the New Deal and Fair Deal, but instead mildly extended them.

Dulles, Diplomacy, and Cold War Demons

In foreign affairs also, Eisenhower and Dulles worked within the broad framework of the Truman-Acheson policies. Despite some distaste for the containment policy and some sloganeering in 1953–56 about "liberation" of Eastern Europe or "unleashing Chiang Kai-shek" upon mainland China, the Eisenhower administration continued the policy of containment. After Stalin's death, Soviet intransigence lessened, and the United States, while extending containment through bilateral and multilateral defense treaties, also grew to accept coexistence with an unfriendly nation as established fact. A large part of the world had become a "Communist bloc," but as long as that area did not expand significantly, and it did not after 1949, the United States would learn to live with it. Also, though Western Europe remained the chief concern of American foreign policy, Asia received more attention because of the rapid end of colonialism in the fifties, Europe's successful recovery, and disturbing power vacuums elsewhere. Finally, the Russians' successful explosion of a thermonuclear bomb in 1953, only months after the first American blast at Eniwetok Atoll on November 1, 1952, followed by such weaponry developments as rockets, ballistics missiles, and nuclear-powered warships in both the United States and the U.S.S.R., brought about the "nuclear stalemate" of the later Cold War.

The chief architect and executor of American foreign policy from early 1953 until his retirement with fatal cancer early in 1959 was Secretary of State John Foster Dulles. No less a Cold Warrior than Acheson, Dulles's utterances carried the added element of black-or-white, Calvinistic zeal against "world Communism." In January, 1954, he declared that the United States would depend for its security primarily upon "a capability for massive retaliation without delay," using "both conventional and atomic weapons." But the emphasis was to be on air-deliverable atomic weapons rather than conventional ground forces. The announcement of "massive retaliation" raised some hard questions. Did it mean a substantial reduction in ground forces? It did. Was that a product less of State Department diplomatic concerns than of Treasury Department budget-cutting? Very likely. Was the United States actually increasing the possibility of nuclear war by depending so much more on nuclear response? Probably it was, or so thought many in the United States and around the world for whom a clear line separated nuclear from non-nuclear weapons. To use even a small, "short-range" atomic cannon to protect, say, West Germany from a ground attack from the East would invite immediate escalation up to the level of thermonuclear bombs. But to Dulles and his supporters, this clear line was not clear at all.

As it happened, nuclear responses never took place, and "massive retaliation" remained more a slogan than a reality. As a slogan it may have had the practical virtue during the heyday of McCarthyism of mollifying the vocal neo-isolationists in the Republican party, such as California's Senator William F. Knowland. To others, however, easy words were apparently being substituted for realistic analysis—and realism meant at that time, to many Democrats and Republicans alike, a flexible containment of Soviet expansiveness.

Although Dulles had criticized containment during the 1952 campaign as a spineless policy, he came to realize that a policy of attempting to reverse post-1945 Communist entrenchments in East Europe or Asia ran an unacceptable risk of general war. Since he refused to shed his basic analysis of world politics, that peace was being threatened by aggressive Communism, he had to become a practitioner of containment himself. With one exception, when the United States supported dissident Guatemalans and Hondurans in the overthrow of the Communist-oriented Arbenz government in Guatemala in the spring of 1954, containment in the Eisenhower-Dulles version consisted of building up (but not using) armaments, plus conference-table diplomacy. In the spring and summer of 1954, for example, a peace conference at Geneva effected the exit of the French from Indochina. Some Americans, including members of the administration, urged that American troops be sent to replace the French. Eisenhower refused to become involved in another Asian land war one year after Korea, and the American response was instead a mutual defense treaty in the Truman-Acheson tradition. In September, 1954, the Southeast Asia Treaty Organization (SEATO) linked the United States, Britain, France, Australia, New Zealand, Pakistan, Thailand, and the Philippines by common defense pledges, though not a common defense force like NATO's. A few months later, when the Red Chinese bombarded Quemoy, Matsu, and other Nationalist-held islands just off the mainland, the United States signed a defense treaty with the Taiwan government; but the American commitment did not include the offshore islands.

For almost three more years, both the American and Soviet protagonists in the Cold War seemed chiefly preoccupied in consolidating their positions and, in 1955 at least, in reducing tensions that might escalate into war. On one side, Germany became a member of NATO in early 1955; on the other, the Russians created, in response, the Warsaw Pact in May. The occupying powers made Austria a neutral country that same month. Then in July came the greatest thaw in the Cold War since 1945: a summit conference at Geneva, bringing together Eisenhower and Premiers Bulganin of Russia, Eden of Britain, and Faure of France. The Geneva meeting was one of many during the Eisenhower years that tried to come to grips with disarmament, nuclear arms control, East-West cultural contacts, and a German peace treaty including Berlin; thus, the summit conference was more unusual for its participants than for its agenda. And little concrete came out of it; details were passed along to a nonproductive Foreign Ministers' meeting. However, an elusive but real "Spirit of Geneva," easing tensions and producing at least the hope that problems were cooperatively soluble, was a welcome if momentary relief after nearly a decade of Cold War.

Three disruptive events in 1956 dispelled the "spirit of Geneva," but their net effect on the Cold War power balance was to confirm the status quo. In June, workers in Poland rioted for improved living conditions and religious freedom and the end of Soviet occupation. Nationalists within the Communist party assumed power and faced down Soviet leaders attempting to reestablish control. The Russians accepted a Poland with ideas of its own, since the new government remained thoroughly Communist and a member of the Warsaw Pact.

Just as the Soviets worked out their compromise with Poland in October, a more severe threat to the satellite system erupted in Hungary. There nationalism went farther: revolutionaries demanded Hungary's withdrawal from the Warsaw Pact and the end of the Communist party's political monopoly. These changes the Soviets would not tolerate, and in early November, Russian forces rolled into Hungary, crushed the popular uprising, and installed a puppet government. The United States government cheered on the Polish and Hungarian rebels but found that liberating the Iron Curtain peoples was only a slogan after all; Western forces could no more have supported the Hungarian nationalists without a general war breaking out than the Russians could have invaded West Germany without war.

The third event of 1956 that confirmed the status quo even made temporary bedfellows of the United States and the Soviet Union:

when Britain, France, and Israel invaded Egypt in October in an attempt to re-take the Suez Canal, which Egyptian President Gamal Abdel Nasser had recently nationalized, both superpowers denounced the invasion as "colonialism." The invading armies withdrew under American pressure without reaching the canal or overthrowing Nasser. The divergence between rhetoric and action, characteristic of Dulles's foreign policy, was manifest; American policy continued to rely on containment and deterrence.

No territory changed hands permanently after the shooting died down on the Nile and the Danube, but neither the United States nor the Soviet Union could regard their alliance systems with complacency. Poland, Hungary, and the Suez had wiped away not only the "Spirit of Geneva" but also the illusion of two opposing monoliths. Around the world, more talk was heard of neutralism, Europe as a "third force," the "third world" of Asia and Africa. The British successfully tested their own hydrogen bomb, or "independent deterrent"—independent of the United States—in 1957, and in March of that year six West European nations signed the Treaty of Rome, establishing the European Common Market.

The Common Market was a satisfying development for the United States, since it was the culmination of the American postwar effort to support European economic (and hence political) recovery. But although long-term policy had worked in Western Europe, the United States had few grounds for satisfaction elsewhere from 1957 to 1961. The Russians announced in 1957 that they had an operational Inter-Continental Ballistic Missile (ICBM), and in October and November, they proved it by launching the first two *Sputniks*. The United States managed, after several "flopniks," to orbit a satellite weighing about 3 percent as much as Sputnik II in January, 1958. Abruptly shaken out of complacency about American superiority in Cold War weaponry and in science and engineering, the government set up the National Aeronautics and Space Administration (NASA) and began appropriating billions for rocketry, an expenditure continued in the space program of the sixties. Instability in the Middle East, and Dulles's fear that the area would fall into the Soviet orbit, was not wholly solved either by the congressionally-supported "Eisenhower Doctrine" of 1957, promising aid to any Middle Eastern country requesting it, or by a brief landing of marines in Lebanon, which did request aid the next year to ward off a Nasser-style coup. In East Asia, the Chinese bombarded Quemoy and Matsu again in 1958, and in Latin America, a "goodwill mission" by Vice-President Nixon was marred by a torrent of harsh words and rotten fruit in Lima and Caracas. Finally, on November 27, 1958, Premier Nikita Khrushchev of the Soviet Union gave the Western powers an ultimatum over Berlin: in six months he would turn Soviet Berlin and its access routes over to the East Germans, and the West had better make arrangements with the diplomatically unrecognized satellite. The United States, Britain, and France firmly rejected Khrushchev's ultimatum and reiterated their rights to Berlin under the Yalta and Potsdam agreements. The Western view did prevail, but in general, 1957 and 1958 had produced few Western successes, and at the same time there was a

Soviet Premier Nikita Khrushchev inspects an American meat market, September, 1959. (Dennis Stock, © Magnum Photos, Inc.)

marked upturn in Soviet prestige and self-confidence, because of Sputnik and because of Khrushchev's blustering.

The seriousness of the Berlin crisis sobered both sides. In mid-1959 Khrushchev and Eisenhower agreed to an exchange of state visits to discuss a German settlement and other problems. The tough, stubby ex-machinist arrived in Washington on September 15 and bounced around the country giving startled Americans a view of the world's top Bolshevik. Khrushchev came across not as an abstract Cold War demon but as a robust Red politician. Preaching "peaceful coexistence" as the only sane alternative to nuclear destruction, Khrushchev then spent hours with Eisenhower at the latter's retreat at Camp David, Maryland. The resulting "Spirit of Camp David" promised no more Berlin ultimatums; instead, there would be a summit conference in 1960. Two months later Eisenhower made a peace-seeking tour of his own, to India and other countries, and won an enthusiastic response, reminiscent of Wilson's reception in Europe in 1919. He was ready to go to the summit.

The rosy climate of late 1959 quickly proved to be only a brief lull in the Cold War. The time came for the summit meeting at Paris in May of 1960. As the summiteers arrived, Khrushchev indignantly announced that the Russians had shot down an American U-2 high-altitude spy plane and captured the pilot. Eisenhower denied, then admitted the flight; he refused to apologize, so Khrushchev stalked out of Paris and withdrew his invitation of a return state visit to Eisenhower. In the fall of 1960, he issued another Berlin ultimatum. By then, the Congo was split by civil war, with one faction supported by the Soviets. At the same time, a Soviet satellite was developing in the Caribbean, where the government of Fidel Castro, which had overthrown the rightist dictatorship of Fulgencio Batista on New Years' Day of 1959, shook hands with Russia. In eight years. Eisenhower had avoided war, but he had only marginally stabilized the peace. The Cold War still wore on. Inclined in his first term-and-a-half to "let Foster do it," Eisenhower played the peacemaker's role much more vigorously in 1959. Unlike the more hard-nosed Truman, he rested great confidence in good will and warm feelings, as at Geneva or Camp David or his trip to India and Europe. The fragile warmth he conveyed was quickly dissipated each time—in 1960 by the U-2 episode, Cuba, and Berlin—but a measure of it always persisted. Eisenhower, however fatuous he appeared to "realists," always struck a responsive chord.

The Warren Court

7

Though the Eisenhower administration was not innovative in any broad sense either in domestic or in foreign policy, the chief justice of the Supreme Court whom Eisenhower appointed in 1953 proved to be as vigorous and innovative as any since John Marshall. Earl Warren and the majority of the Supreme Court for the next sixteen years made that body into an agent of change very much in contrast to its role as a bastion against change from Reconstruction days down to the late thirties. The Warren Court became the glory of liberals and the despair of reactionaries as it changed the course of American law and life by asserting the civil rights of minority groups and of individuals, and by restoring electoral democracy to state government. In so doing, it matched the more innovative political mood of the sixties better than that of the fifties.

Public reaction to the Warren Court's activism was by no means wholly favorable. Segregationists, repressive "law-and-order" advocates, and far-rightist groups like the John Birch Society were infuriated by the Court's civil rights and civil liberties decisions. For years during the sixties, motorists driving along US 40 outside of Columbia, Missouri, and other places were suddenly greeted by an enormous billboard shrieking "Impeach Earl Warren." And the criticism was not restricted to the frantic Right. Some responsible constitutionalists, among them Felix Frankfurter, himself a justice and usually regarded as a liberal one (he was appointed by F.D.R. after the court-packing fight), objected to the lack of "judicial restraint" in some decisions and urged that the Court was producing an excess of judge-made law through a too-literal application of the Bill of Rights; as a result, minorities were being protected to the harm of the majority. But the majority of the Court, and many observers, felt that it was about time for minorities to be protected and that Court action was necessary in the absence of action by Congress and the states.

The major contributions of the Warren Court began in May, 1954, when it unanimously overthrew the "separate but equal" doctrine of 1896 and declared public school segregation to be inherently discriminatory, in *Brown* v. *Board of Education.* In dozens of subsequent decisions, the Court struck down other infringements of civil rights. In 1955 it ruled that the University of Alabama had to admit two Negro women seeking admission since 1952. The Court also banned segregation in tax-supported playgrounds, golf courses, and parks. In 1956 it ordered three Negroes admitted to the University of South Carolina, and another to the law school of the University of Florida, and it outlawed segregation on intra-state buses. In 1959 the Court threw out a Louisiana law forbidding interracial boxing matches, and affirmed that no black could be tried for any crime in counties lacking black voters (and thus black jurors). In 1960 it upheld the 1957 and 1960 Civil Rights Acts and reversed the conviction of Daisy Bates, the head of the Arkansas NAACP, for refusing to hand over its membership list to the state. After many other desegregation decisions, the Court seemed to hedge in 1964 and 1965 when it said that though it forbade segregation, it was not commanding integration; school boards did not have to take positive steps to stop "racial imbalance resulting from housing patterns." But the Court was refining the law, not reversing it, and in 1967 it threw out a recently-passed constitutional amendment in California that allowed racial discrimination in the sale or rental of housing. In the late sixties and early seventies, the main desegregation effort was in busing school children to achieve racial balance; the Court also upheld busing, despite widespread public objections.

The Warren Court struck down not only racial discrimination but also infringements of individual rights by local, state, or federal governments—a position very much in contrast to the McCarthyism prevalent at the time Warren was appointed. In the late fifties, the Court severely restricted federal and state subversive-control devices; in 1958 it stopped the State Department from refusing to issue passports to people alleged, without due process, to be "subversives"; in 1960 and 1961 it upheld parts of state and federal anti-subversive laws but ended the use of illegally-obtained evidence in state courts. It reaffirmed safeguards against double jeopardy and self-incrimination, and the right to confront accusers, including the FBI. In the case of *Miranda* v. *Arizona*, in 1966, it upheld the right of an accused person to be represented by a lawyer during police questioning, and required police to warn the accused of his rights—decisions that brought the Court much censure on the grounds that it was hamstringing law enforcement agencies and legally underwriting a national crime wave. In another area of the law, however, Warren and the other justices were on the side of simple demography: they ended rural domination of long-unredistricted state legislatures in *Baker* v. *Carr* (1962), and in two other decisions in 1964 they required that United States congressional districts had to be as nearly equal as possible in population and that both houses of state legislatures had to be apportioned on the basis of population—the "one man, one vote" doctrine. Warren, on his retirement in 1969, said that he considered the reinvigoration of electoral democracy in the states to have been his greatest achievement. The Constitution had proved again, as Chief Justice Hughes had remarked in 1926, to be what the Supreme Court said it was, and while Earl Warren was chief justice, the ancient document was revealed as a far more potent defender of the rights of individuals, black and white, than many people ever suspected.

Kennedy and the New Frontier

Eisenhower, despite his remarkable personal popularity, brought no permanent gains to the G.O.P. voting coalition. In the congressional election of 1958, as the sharp recession of that year reminded many voters of the link between Hoover and the depression, the Democrats gained enormously, moving ahead 283 to 153 in the House and 64 to 34 in the Senate. Labor, Negroes, Jews, and other ethnics voted Democratic as firmly as ever, and while central cities remained Democratic, the rapidly growing suburban rings did not behave as Republicans hoped. Many suburbanites had large mortgages and expensive commuting costs; they had grown up during the Roosevelt and Truman administrations; they lacked the Republican traditions of small-town or rural residents. The solid G.O.P. base remained the small towns and farms of the Midwest, other demographically stagnant areas, many small businessmen, and parts of the once-solid South; the base was not growing (Nixon, for example, won 49.5 percent of the popular vote when he ran in 1960, but only 43 percent in 1968).

The Democratic party was benefiting from several middle- and long-term factors. Voters born under the sign of Roosevelt were coming of age. The three Eisenhower recessions still evoked memories of 1929. The right-wing nationalistic and economic rhetoric used by many Republicans—"liberal Republicans" were not yet a powerful wing—did not resonate well in an increasingly affluent, mobile, and internationally-aware society. The Democrats were taking over the civil rights issue. In 1960 these trends were basic to Democratic victory.

Meeting at Los Angeles in June, the Democrats gave a first-ballot nomination to the forty-two-year-old Massachusetts Senator, John F. Kennedy, whose political organization and victories in primaries overcame misgivings that he could not be elected because he was Catholic. The Republican nomination went with little debate to Vice-President Nixon. Nixon made some headway by criticizing Kennedy's "inexperience," until a series of four TV "debates" in September and October scotched that issue when the telegenic Kennedy more than held his own. Successfully claiming that the United States had fallen behind the U.S.S.R. in strategic weapons —"missile gap" was the phrase—Kennedy spoke to the uncertainties of many voters about the Cold War. (The missile gap seemed to disappear after Kennedy took office, but the infatuation of Americans with rockets and missiles continued, and Kennedy was widely applauded when he announced a program to put a man on the moon in the sixties.) Kennedy also faced the "Catholic issue" squarely, promising not to succumb to Catholic lobbying for federal aid to parochial schools. Kennedy's religion still lost him votes among some non-Catholic Democrats, but those were probably offset by gains among Catholics who had fallen under the spell of the Eisenhower personality or who had been leaning Republican because of Cold War issues (the "loss" of Poland, the apparent march of Communism). In the last four days of the campaign, when Martin Luther King, Jr. was jailed in Atlanta, Kennedy and his brother Robert interceded to get King freed, an effort successfully publicized in big-city black precincts. By the narrowest margin since 1888, just over 100,000 popular votes, Kennedy won and carried slightly reduced Democratic majorities into Congress. Despite some defections by non-Catholic Democrats, some Republican Catholics voted for Kennedy, and the liberal-labor-urban-ethnic coalition held.

In its roughly 1,000 days of existence, Kennedy and his New Frontiersmen produced a record generally along these lines: in domestic affairs, very substantial success at the beginning, deteriorating into grave difficulties with Congress especially after the death of Speaker Sam Rayburn in late 1961; in foreign affairs, a miserable start, followed by real *détente* in the Cold War after Kennedy led the country through the Cuban missile crisis of October, 1962. The domestic legislation can be ticked off quickly. Several laws in the

Attorney General Robert Kennedy and President John F. Kennedy outside the White House at the time of the Cuban missiles crisis, October 1, 1962. (Wide World Photos)

New-Deal–Fair-Deal tradition were passed in 1961, including social security extension, the n.inimum wage increase to $1.25, $4.9 billion for public housing over four years, various urban development authorizations, and more federal aid to education. New departures in legislation were not forthcoming. Kennedy wanted, and did not get during his term, a civil rights law, a tax reform act, and medicare. In 1962, after Rayburn died, Congress gave him a Trade Expansion Act extending trade reciprocity, a law creating a communications satellite corporation, and little else except military and space appropriations. Kennedy's domestic achievements were mainly administrative rather than legislative, such as Justice Department vigor in enforcing black voting rights, a fight in April, 1962, against inflationary price hikes by the nation's steel companies, and the first anti-poverty expenditures. Despite this thin record, Kennedy managed to convey to the public in America and elsewhere a sense of youthful motion, progress, and prosperity, creating a progressive mood that lasted long after him, somewhat like that other popular young president of sixty years before, Theodore Roosevelt.

Congress did cooperate with Kennedy in two new international programs, the Peace Corps and the Alliance for Progress, both begun in 1961. The first provided volunteers in teaching, medicine, and technical assistance in underdeveloped areas of the world, and the second was to be a cooperative development policy for Latin America. Their success was considerable in view of their slender funding. Otherwise, Kennedy's first efforts in foreign affairs were unsettling. His first positive act was in fact a disaster: the American-supported invasion of Cuba, at the Bay of Pigs on the south coast, in April, 1961. Plans for an invasion by CIA-trained Cuban refugees were far advanced when Kennedy took office. He could have stopped the invasion but was told it had to take place then or never. He let it proceed. Tactical blunders together with gross underestimates of Castro's military and popular strength doomed it as soon as it struck the beach. Another damaging episode soon followed: Kennedy wanted to get a personal estimate of Khrushchev and perhaps ease Russian-American tensions as Eisenhower seemed to have done in 1955 and 1959. The two met in Vienna in June, but nothing was resolved, and Khrushchev apparently gained the dangerous impression that Kennedy was an insubstantial, indecisive youth.

From that nadir, Kennedy's handling of foreign affairs had to improve. He firmly rejected in July another Khrushchev threat to turn Berlin over to the East Germans, and the Communists could find no better way to stop the mass exodus of East Germans than to erect the Berlin Wall in August. He increased American advisory forces in South Vietnam but refused to commit ground troops either there or in Laos. Instead, he worked successfully for Laotian neutrality at the Geneva conference of 1962, a settlement that the Pathet Lao and other Communists failed to honor. American prestige in Latin America was briefly repaired early in 1962 when the Organization of American States ostracized Castro, and prestige improved generally in February when, ten months after the Russians, the United

States put a man in space—the three-orbit Mercury VI mission of John Glenn.

The crucial event in foreign affairs during the Kennedy years, more critical than any since 1945, occurred in October, 1962. American reconnaissance flights in September and October photographed what proved to be Russian-built offensive missile installations in Cuba, missiles with a range extending from the Panama Canal to Washington. The president called in Soviet Ambassador Andrei Gromyko, who denied that any such missiles existed. But the evidence was clear. Kennedy went before national television on October 22 and uttered the strongest words of the Cold War: an attack by Cuban-based missiles on the United States or any hemisphere ally would be regarded as an attack by the Soviet Union itself upon the United States and would be met by the full retaliatory arsenal. Furthermore, Kennedy placed a naval "quarantine" on any vessels bringing offensive missiles to Cuba, and he demanded that the existing bases be dismantled.

The obvious courses of action in the face of the missile threat were, on the one hand, an air strike and invasion of Cuba; on the other, stern protests but little else. An invasion "upheld" the Monroe Doctrine but would have violated Cuban sovereignty and killed Cubans and Russians. Protests would have been ineffective. Kennedy and his advisers found a middle way, which gave the Soviets time to think and maneuver. Official Soviet messages were not encouraging, but a private letter from a deeply shaken Khrushchev was, and Kennedy chose to respond to it rather than to the official dispatches. Soviet ships bound for Cuba began turning back; American naval crews boarded others and let them proceed when they discovered no "contraband," and the Soviet Union backed down. Slowly the existing bases in Cuba were dismantled. The threat of offensive nuclear missiles within easy range of the United States subsided, while Castro found he had been only a pawn on the chessboard of the two superpowers. Kennedy had won a clearcut victory in the most direct and nightmarish confrontation between the United States and the Soviet Union since the Cold War began, and many commentators believed that his handling of the Cuban missile crisis was the finest American exercise in crisis diplomacy in the twentieth century.

Critics at the time, such as Walter Lippmann, argued that Kennedy might better have offered the Russians a swap—to close American bases, obsolescent anyway, in Turkey and Italy, in return for the Soviets' dismantling the Cuban sites. And some commentators later in the sixties criticized Kennedy for going to the brink of nuclear war over the installation of missiles that they believed not especially dangerous considering the availability of the American Polaris fleet and land-based missiles. But generally the verdict was heavily for Kennedy.

The missile crisis marked the end of a stage in the Cold War as it had developed since the death of Stalin, because the Soviets could not then doubt that the United States would defend itself and its commitments. Also, the Soviet Union accepted at least for a time the need to continue the thermonuclear balance of power that had developed since 1950. Another key factor pushing the Soviet Union toward *détente* was the severe rift between Russian and Communist China, a rift that had become a gulf by 1963. The Cold War cliché, "Soviet bloc," no longer held much meaning, and though the myth of a monolithic world Communism still bemused parts of the American press and public, and recurred from time to time in political speeches, American policy-makers knew that it was very much in America's interest to widen the Sino-Soviet split. The East-West *détente* paid a real dividend in August and September of 1963, when nuclear tests in the atmosphere—resumed suddenly by the Russians in September, 1961, and by the United States in March, 1962— were ended by a United States–Soviet test-ban treaty, also signed by many other countries. Though France and China did not sign it, the test-ban treaty deeply impressed world opinion by greatly reducing the pollution of the earth's atmosphere by radioactive fallout and by offering renewed hope for negotiated settlement of disagreements.

By the fall of 1963, the Kennedy administration was achieving a noteworthy record in foreign policy, while New Frontiersmen were still working with a stubborn Congress to get progressive legislation. Then came the sudden, tragic end. On November 22, a sunny Friday afternoon in Dallas, where he had gone to make a speech, John Kennedy was assassinated. The apparent killer was Lee Harvey Oswald, acting upon motivations never clearly unraveled. After Kennedy died, Lyndon Johnson was rushed to the presidential plane, Air Force One, was sworn in by a lady federal judge, and returned immediately to Washington. Two days later, Oswald himself was fatally shot while in the custody of the Dallas police by a local restaurant owner, Jack Ruby, as 15 million people watched aghast on television. Violence had made its way from the southern country-side, where black and white civil rights workers had been killed during the preceding several years, and from northern cities, where the summers of riots were just beginning, to the White House itself.

The Rise and Eclipse of the Great Society

A month of national mourning ended just before Christmas. As Congress reconvened, the country's mood remained one of shock, self-doubt, and the desire somehow to expiate the Kennedy murder. President Johnson quickly channeled these feelings into a drive to enact into law the measures Kennedy had sought in 1963, and which Congress had balked at. Tax reform sped through Congress, lowering rates in order to stimulate investment and consumer spending, and to continue the non-inflationary growth of those years. The Civil Rights Act of 1964 passed after the Senate voted to close off debate, for the first time on a civil rights bill; it enforced the right to vote, gave federal district judges the power of injunction to prevent discrimination in public accommodations, and set up a Commission on Equal Employment Opportunity. The Economic Opportunity Act of 1964 established a Job Corps and a Youth Corps to train and employ young people, especially from minority groups.

Johnson's experience as Senate majority leader, and his remarkable force of character, were making the Kennedy program a reality. He was shortly to enlarge upon it and preside over the greatest flurry of new welfare legislation since the thirties. Johnson, who once said that Franklin D. Roosevelt "was like a daddy to me," was ideally equipped by background, inclination, and training to direct his larger-than-life energies to carrying out the unfinished welfare measures of the New Deal and Fair Deal. In two ways, however, his background and experience bequeathed him tragic flaws. First, he was as obviously southern-rural as Kennedy had been northeastern-metropolitan; little empathy grew up between Johnson and the growing mass of suburbanites and megalopolitans. Second, he lacked experience and, basically, interest, in international affairs; but the same bitter irony befell him that had befallen those two

"YOU ABSOLUTELY SURE YOU'RE AN ELEPHANT?"

Herblock of the *Washington Post* comments on Republican problems before the Goldwater nomination in 1964. "You Absolutely Sure You're An Elephant?"—from *The Herblock Gallery* (Simon and Schuster 1968).

other progressive Democrats, Wilson and F.D.R.: despite his primary concern with domestic reform, international problems were going to occupy his presidency with terrible urgency. Ultimately they scuttled it.

Johnson was driven by the desire to be "president of all the people," and in his first three years in the White House, from late 1963 well into 1966, he achieved that aim very well. After wresting a stack of stalled legislation from Congress early in 1964, he concerned himself with the election. He was nominated without opposition at the Democratic convention at Atlantic City and chose as his running-mate Senator Hubert Humphrey of Minnesota, for fifteen years a favorite of the northern liberal Democrats and of labor and farmers. The Republicans, already the odds-on favorites to lose, made their defeat certain by succumbing to a masochistic urge to test a theory.

Since the days of Senator Taft, a vocal segment within the G.O.P. had claimed that their party's failure since 1928, except for the almost nonpartisan Eisenhower, was caused by nominating pale quasi-liberal reflections of the Democrats' candidates on quasi-liberal platforms. If the Republican party would only nominate a "real alternative," a true conservative, so the theory went, it would draw millions of disgusted voters who had sat out elections for years rather than vote for either "liberal" candidate. This theory was put to the test in 1964. The Republicans nominated an attractive, often muddle-mouthed Arizona senator, Barry Goldwater, who had published a book in 1960 called *The Conscience of a Conservative*. The book summed up the platform of the Republican right wing at that time: drastically limit federal power and spending; reassert the power of the states, including the decision of whether or not to desegregate schools; stop federal farm subsidies and restore agriculture to free-market conditions; restrict the power of big labor unions by ending industry-wide collective bargaining and by making union membership voluntary; fight the Cold War to "win," not simply contain. The book sold well, and in one respect the conservatives were correct—no one was sure how many voters might agree with its philosophy.

Goldwater attempted honestly to discuss issues in 1964 but started losing votes immediately. In his acceptance speech he declared that "extremism in defense of liberty is no vice," and many people in that nervous summer of the Harlem riot remembered the word "extremism" rather than the word "liberty." He gave signs of wanting to repeal social security, a position not popular with the growing number of older Americans, an otherwise Republican-leaning group. He seemed to believe that nuclear weapons and defoliating the jungle would win in Vietnam. A joke made the rounds to the effect that Roosevelt proved somebody could be president forever; Truman proved that anybody could be president; Eisenhower proved you didn't need a president; and Goldwater proved you'd better not have a president. Johnson, meanwhile, made every effort to broaden the Democratic coalition, achieve national consensus, and publicize his welfarish Great Society program.

Johnson was reelected in a landslide, with 61 percent of the popular vote, a larger percentage than F.D.R.'s in 1936. Right-wing Republicanism, and rightist organizations, such as the John Birch Society or the Christian Anti-Communist Crusade, were demonstrated to have been shrill, small minorities. Goldwater carried only Arizona and five deep-South states. On civil rights, foreign policy, and welfare issues, the mass of voters preferred Johnson. With the support of huge Democratic majorities in Congress, many of them first-term liberals, Johnson began to sign the Great Society into law. The Voting Rights Act of 1965 outlawed literacy tests where fewer than 50 percent of the voting-age population was registered, and provided federal registrars for those areas. Medical care for the elderly became part of the social security system. Federal aid to elementary, secondary, and higher education reached new heights. Another bill provided $1.1 billion for highways, industries, and jobs in Appalachia. A new immigration law abolished the national origins quota system of the twenties and gave priority to immigrants who were refugees, artists, or professionals, or relatives of Americans, without regard to nationality. A host of other bills extended existing programs dealing with air and water pollution, job training, public housing, public transportation, and the "war on poverty." In that first session of the Eighty-Ninth Congress, more progressive measures became law than in any session since 1935.

While Congress was rolling up this impressive record, an ominous series of events elsewhere foretold a distinct change in the national mood between the early sixties and the late sixties. The Chinese Communists exploded an atomic bomb in 1964; Nehru of India died in May, 1964; at home the summers of urban race riots had begun; Khrushchev was deposed on October 15, 1964, creating uncertainty about Russian actions; Johnson's forceful reactions to the apparent shelling of two destroyers in the Gulf of Tonkin in August, 1964, and the developments in the Dominican Republic in the spring of 1965 disturbed many Americans. Johnson became increasingly preoccupied with foreign affairs and increasingly sensitive to criticism. No dramatic list of new laws tumbled down from Capitol Hill in 1966—only a Truth-in-Packaging Act to protect consumers, a "model cities" act, and a federal auto safety act. The fall elections reduced Democratic majorities to their lowest level since 1956 and removed many of the welfarish freshmen elected in 1964. The more conservative Congress passed an air pollution act in 1967, and in 1968 a Crime Control Act (allowing wiretapping), a tax surcharge, and the last Great Society measure, the 1968 open housing law.

The Vietnam Quagmire

Congress and the country cooled on Lyndon Johnson, and he on them, before 1968. Domestic unrest, both in urban ghettoes and in middle-class universities, gave rise to demands for "law and order" which Johnson did not seem to provide. In foreign affairs, the administration seemed to many Democrats and young independents repressive and imperialistic, reverting to Cold War attitudes that compared invidiously with the "liberalism" of Kennedy's Alliance for Progress and nuclear test-ban treaty.

Johnson's first foreign crisis occurred when a military coup overthrew an American-supported, middle-of-the-road government in the Dominican Republic on April 24–25, 1965. The military claimed it wanted only to restore a former president, Juan Bosch, who had been a client of the United States during Kennedy's time. By 1965, however, Bosch and his supporters were suspected of Castroism. Johnson sent more than 4,000 marines, first to evacuate Americans, then to restore order. On May 2, Johnson claimed that Communists were leading the coup, an assertion denied by its leader, Colonel Francisco Caamano, when he became president on May 4. An OAS truce of May 5 was immediately broken by a

rightist attack, which was effectually supported by the 20,000 supposedly neutral American troops present. The rightists took over by
the end of May. Many Americans, and millions around the world,
were sorely troubled by Washington's quick intervention and apparent regression to the Bay of Pigs mentality of responding to suspected Castroism with overwhelming military force. Dismay grew
into vocal opposition and general distrust of the federal government
over the following three years, when the Dominican pattern was repeated on a much broader scale in Southeast Asia.

The chronology of America's involvement in Vietnam really begins with the defeat of Japan in 1945, and the simultaneous refusal
of the Asian colonies of European countries to resume their prewar
status. French Indochina was one of these colonies. A charismatic
local leader named Ho Chi Minh, who had helped found the
French Communist party in 1920, declared Vietnam independent
in September, 1945. France recognized Vietnam as "a free state
within the French Union" in March, 1946, but this was not enough
independence for Ho, and fighting began between Ho's forces (the
Viet Minh) and the French in December, 1946. In mid-1949 a native government formed with French approval, led by the Emperor
Bao Dai, was established in Saigon, and the United States, as usual
trying to reconcile its own anti-colonialism with the need to support
its European allies, recognized this Saigon government in February,
1950. Four months later, just as war was breaking out in Korea, the
Americans sent a Military Assistance Advisory Group, thirty-five
men, to Saigon. In December, 1950, a mutual defense agreement
was signed between the United States and the Saigon government.

Fighting grew ever more bitter between the French and the Viet
Minh. In an effort to end it and to settle the future of Indochina,
the French, the Vietnamese insurgents, and representatives of other
countries met for a peace conference in Geneva in the spring of
1954. Not long after the conference began, news arrived of the
definitive French defeat at Dien Bien Phu by the Ho Chi Minh
forces. The Geneva settlement reflected this military fact, fixing the
seventeenth parallel as a truce line between North and South Vietnam, the North under Ho and the South under the Bao Dai government. Additional troop commitments or new bases on either side
were banned. Free elections, to decide which government would re-
unite the North and the South, were scheduled for no later than
July, 1956, and an international control commission composed of

India, Canada, and Poland was to supervise the truce. The United States was not a signer of the Geneva agreement but acquiesced in it because Dien Bien Phu left no real alternative.

By 1955, it had long been clear that Ho and the Hanoi government had strong ties, ideological and military, with Russia and China, while the Saigon government was tied to the West. In October, 1955, the Saigon government changed: Bao Dai's "Empire" was defeated in a referendum in South Vietnam and was succeeded by a republic, with Ngo Dinh Diem as president. In the following year, Diem refused, with Dulles's approval, to hold the reunification elections scheduled at Geneva, on the ground that the North was intimidating voters; indeed, it was likely that the Ho government would have won control over, or at least an important place in, an elected government for both Vietnams.

Through the late fifties Communist-led guerillas supported by Hanoi fought in the South. The small group of American advisers were still there, and the first American battle death occurred on July 8, 1959. In May, 1960, the advisory group was enlarged from 327 to 685 at Diem's request, and in October, Eisenhower promised to continue American support. The fighting intensified. In December, 1960, insurgents in the South united as the National Liberation Front, and the American advisers multiplied under Kennedy, numbering 4,000 by the end of 1962. In November, 1963, Diem was overthrown by the South Vietnamese, with American acquiescence because of fears that he would make a deal with Hanoi. He was immediately assassinated (without American foreknowledge). A succession of unpopular, unstable military juntas succeeded Diem, while the American advisory group, which grew to 15,000 by the end of 1963, reported that South Vietnam was in danger of collapse. In January, 1964, the Joint Chiefs of Staff recommended to Secretary of Defense Robert McNamara that full American force be brought to bear.

Early the following August, the Navy reported that North Vietnamese torpedo boats had fired on two destroyers, the *Maddox* and *C. Turner Joy*, in the Gulf of Tonkin. Three days later, a virtually unanimous Congress passed a resolution—which had already been put into draft form by the National Security Council in late May—authorizing the president to use whatever force he deemed necessary to stop "aggression" from the North against the South in Vietnam. The Tonkin Gulf Resolution was Congress's quick response to

Johnson's request, and it became the major warrant for massive expansion of American involvement. Even before it passed, Johnson had authorized retaliatory bombing of North Vietnamese naval forces; Congress was well aware of that. Congress was not aware, nor was the president or the public, how deeply the involvement would become.

The Vietnam action must be understood within the context of Cold War and containment. For twenty years before 1965, through the administrations of Truman, Eisenhower, and Kennedy, American policy had sought at first the removal of French colonialism, and after that the establishment of an independent national government. With regard to that government, the United States was caught in the fifties between a preference and a requirement: it preferred that the government of Vietnam should be popularly elected and democratic; it required that it be anti-Communist. Ho Chi Minh was and always had been a Communist, and the United States could therefore not tolerate his rule in the South. Diem and his successors did not observe the niceties of Western democratic procedure, but they were not Communist; therefore they were supported by United States economic aid and military advice against Communist insurgency.

American policy-makers were concerned not only with Vietnam. President Eisenhower had compared the area to "a row of dominoes"—if one domino, such as South Vietnam, fell to the Reds, it would inevitably knock over the next domino and the next and the next; all would be absorbed into "the Communist bloc." Laos and Cambodia, the other two parts of French Indochina that became independent countries under the Geneva agreement of 1954, would fall, then Malaya, Thailand, Burma, Indonesia. The domino theory was not unrealistic in the fifties, if one accepted the basic assumption that the overriding aim of American foreign policy was to contain communism, in Southeast Asia or anywhere else. In the mid-sixties, by which time Thailand and Malaya were relatively stable and pro-Western, when a measure of neutrality existed in Laos and Cambodia, and when the Communist Party of Indonesia had been wiped out in a bloody purge, many thought the "domino theory" no longer reflected Southeast Asian realities. Moreover, containment itself and the very notion of a communist bloc had been overtaken by events, particularly the widening split between China and the Soviet Union.

Yet in South Vietnam the battle went on. By the end of 1964, the American advisory force of 23,000 was not sufficient to sustain the Saigon government against insurgency. President Johnson was profoundly convinced that "freedom" had to be preserved against "aggression." To him, South Vietnam was the plug of Southeast Asia; if the plug got pulled, the whole region would go down the drain, and the Pacific would become a "Red Sea"—a prospect even more threatening than Japanese control of the same area in 1941. The United States therefore had to preserve South Vietnam for the sake of America's own security. Besides that, the administration argument ran, we had promised our ally Diem that we would stand by him; not only would it be immoral to break that promise, but it would also be dangerous, since our other allies would no longer be willing to trust our promises to aid them. This "credibility argument" was given by a Defense Department official in April, 1965, as 70 percent of the reason for American involvement.

Chiefly on those grounds, the struggle in Vietnam took on a wholly new dimension in 1965. American bombing raids over the North began in February, in an attempt to prevent Ho Chi Minh from supporting his own forces and the insurgents in the South. On April 1, Johnson authorized 3,500 Marines at Danang to take an offensive combat position, the first direct use of ground troops. More American combat troops arrived in the summer reaching the 125,000 level in July. The war escalated in 1966, as Johnson and Nguyen Cao Ky, who was then premier of South Vietnam, agreed at Honolulu in February to stand together to resist aggression; as American planes dropped bombs on military targets near the main North Vietnamese cities of Hanoi and Haiphong in June; as they bombed the demilitarized zone around the seventeenth parallel in July, seeking to destroy North Vietnamese forces; and as the size of the American contingent climbed toward the half-million mark.

But the massive intervention did not stop the Viet Cong and their North Vietnamese supporters. For Americans, the war in Vietnam was like no war they had ever experienced. The enemy was not a uniformed force, as in the Korean stalemate, and nothing like a modern mechanized army, as in World War II. The Americans and the South Vietnamese faced instead an elusive, tenacious, highly motivated foe who slid back into villages and countryside almost as soon as those areas seemed to have been "pacified." General William Westmoreland, the American commander, claimed to see "light at the end of the tunnel," but the tunnel kept stretching and the light receding. Substantial progress was apparently reached in September, 1967, when elections were held successfully in over 80 percent of South Vietnam, stabilizing the Saigon government and giving it a claim to legitimacy. But illusions of imminent victory were shattered when the Viet Cong launched an all-out offensive on January 30, 1968, the lunar new year, successfully raiding many bases and cities that the Americans and South Vietnamese believed to be most secure. The "Tet offensive" was a turning point in the war: though the Viet Cong suffered heavy losses, their offensive produced a destructive effect upon sagging American morale.

Domestic criticism of the American involvement in Vietnam mounted through 1966 and 1967, in proportion to the rising commitment and the rising awareness of its lack of success. A considerable part of the criticism rested on moral grounds—sometimes traditional pacifism on religious or secular principles, sometimes revulsion at the weaponry and tactics (napalm, the bombing of the North) which the United States was employing. Others criticized the involvement not as a moral, but as a strategic, mistake. Senator J. William Fulbright of Arkansas, the chairman of the Senate Foreign Relations Committee, said in 1966 that American postwar hostility to communism in any form had blinded the country to the possibility, present in Vietnam, that communism and national aspirations could be united in the same movement and leaders, which the United States could oppose only at unacceptable cost. A few outspoken generals objected to the war as a tactical impossibility. Commentators on foreign policy pointed out that the Vietnam involvement was myopic, focusing American eyes on one small part of the world while ignoring the rest. What about Africa, where the Ghanaian leader Kwame Nkrumah was deposed, or Europe, where de Gaulle was leading France out of NATO, in early 1966? But the Vietnam involvement preoccupied Americans. When Soviet Premier Aleksei Kosygin visited the United Nations in June, 1967, President Johnson met him for a cordial summit meeting at Glassboro, New Jersey. The two leaders had serious and promising talks. But significant improvements in Soviet-American problems were crippled by the divisive involvement in Vietnam.

Caught up in an Asian land war despite years of advice from most State Department and Pentagon policy planners, the Johnson administration found itself unable to pull out of Vietnam, unwilling to invade North Vietnam not only because of the huge involvement that step would mean but also because of the great risk of triggering full-scale Chinese intervention as happened in Korea, and unable to stop sending troops and materiél to help Saigon. By mid-1968, the Vietnam War had become the longest war the United States had ever engaged in, dated from the first casualties in 1959, and it had involved more killed and wounded than the Korean War. It was also, by then, the least popular.

Other events reinforced dissatisfaction in 1967. In Newark, 26 died and 1,500 were injured in a race riot in mid-July; a week later, 40 died and 2,000 were hurt in Detroit. Cries for "law and order," police repression, and the restoration of American dignity at home and abroad grew ever louder. The Great Society had become a term of derision by early 1968. Racial violence, opposition to the war, its dismal progress especially after the Tet offensive, unrest on college campuses, all coalesced to make a mockery of Johnson's noble dream.

On March 31, 1968, Johnson appeared on national television. He talked mostly about the impasse in Vietnam. He realized that his tactic of trying to bomb the North Vietnamese into surrender, or even into peace talks, had failed. He therefore announced that the United States was stopping the bombing of the North except for tactical bombing near the seventeenth parallel. This was news enough. But then he announced that, in view of the deep division in the country over the Vietnamese War, he would not seek, and would not accept, the Democratic presidential nomination in 1968. Exhausted and frustrated, done in by the Vietnam crisis, which he could neither avoid nor explain, Lyndon Johnson was getting out. Insofar as the American system of government allowed, the chief of state had abdicated.

The Nixon
Years

Six weeks later, on May 10, preliminary peace talks including North and South Vietnam and the United States opened at Paris. About 550,000 American troops were in South Vietnam at that time, and peace was far off—some people remembered that the Korean War dragged on for two years after peace talks began—but the fighting, though it did not stop, lost some of its vicious intensity.

At home, however, violence and tensions increased. Columbia University was wracked by radical student protest in April and May. On April 4, Martin Luther King was shot dead on a hotel balcony in Memphis. Riots, fires, and looting sprang forth upon King's assassination; Washington and other major cities seemed at a distance to be raging in flames. In April and May, Senator Robert F. Kennedy, the heir to the Kennedy mystique, ran for the Democratic nomination that Johnson had left open. On the night of June 5, he too was assassinated in Los Angeles, minutes after winning the California primary. In late July a pitched battle between police and black militants in Cleveland brought death to a dozen people.

Campus unrest, racial troubles, and the Vietnam War combined to give the politics of 1968 a fragmented, unstable quality. Many Americans were puzzled about national problems and uncertain about how to solve them; others, on both Left and Right, were very certain about what to do. Small but visible minorities at either end of the political spectrum each had authoritarian answers: the revolutionary Left, such as the Weathermen faction of Students for a Democratic Society and the few extreme black militants, advocated (and occasionally practiced) violence to overthrow a social and political system that to them was beyond redemption. The radical Right, represented by a renascent Ku Klux Klan and underground paramilitary groups, readied themselves for repressive counterattack on threats to white America. Neither Left nor Right regarded conventional politics as a satisfactory means to the end they sought; they were true radicals, rejecting the political system.

Within the political system itself, however, polarization also occurred. Two other groups, much larger than the true radicals but, like them, motivated much more by ideology than by economic concerns, stood to the Left and the Right. The latter included unrepentant ex-Goldwaterites seeking a "tougher" foreign policy, more free enterprise, and above all "law and order" in cities and on campuses, and also many northern workers as well as southerners unhappy with "favoritism" toward blacks. This group either remained within the Republican right wing or supported the third-party candidacy of Alabama Governor George C. Wallace. Another sizable and diverse group, the New Left, had been emerging in the mid-sixties, and insofar as it was a political bloc (it had broader concerns than electoral politics), it stood at the fringe of the Democratic party. To a greater or lesser degree, the New Left was frustrated by unresponsive bureaucracy, whether on campuses, in government, or in large corporations or unions. It was distressed by what it saw as the failure of democracy to function on behalf of the people, in such areas as the escalating Asian war, the brutal way it was being fought by the United States, selective service, pollution by irresponsible and selfish businesses, the continued oppression of blacks, women, students, and others. The New Left was much more vague about its positive program than about what it disliked, but no one could doubt that it was a sizable group, especially among the young.

Closer to the center of the political spectrum were several groups who together were certainly still a majority—the "Old Left" liberals who had constituted a majority of the Democratic party for a generation, the "liberal Republicans" (a minority of that party), the middle-of-the-roaders in both parties. All of them agreed, despite clear differences over specific issues, with the tradition of federal activism for social and economic betterment. There were many more subtleties in the politics of 1968 than this sketch suggests, but out of all the complexities, two things stand out: a fragmentation of political opinion not seen since at least 1948 and a dissatisfaction with the pace of social-political change—too slow for the Left, too fast for the Right.

The Republican nominating convention in August selected Richard Nixon on the first ballot, rejecting a bid from New York's Governor Nelson Rockefeller, who was too liberal for the delegates despite favorable public opinion polls. Nixon, considered politically dead after his 1960 loss to Kennedy and a 1962 defeat for governor of California, had worked hard for delegate votes in 1967 and 1968, and as a middle-of-the roader, he promised to restore party unity after the Goldwater debacle of 1964. His choice of a running mate, Spiro T. Agnew of Maryland, who was acceptable to South Carolina's Strom Thurmond and other southern archconservatives, revealed a key element in Republican strategy: to make major inroads in the once Democratic South.

The Democratic convention at Chicago reminded many of the old remark of the humorist Will Rogers—"I belong to no organized political party. I am a Democrat." By convention time the race for

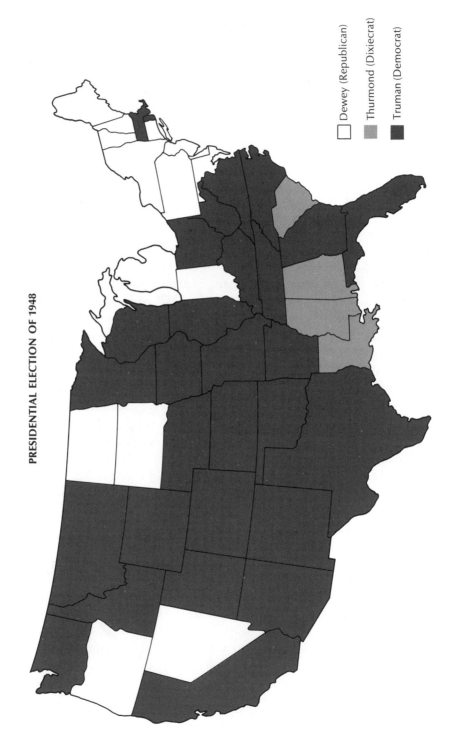

PRESIDENTIAL ELECTION OF 1948

☐ Dewey (Republican)

▨ Thurmond (Dixiecrat)

■ Truman (Democrat)

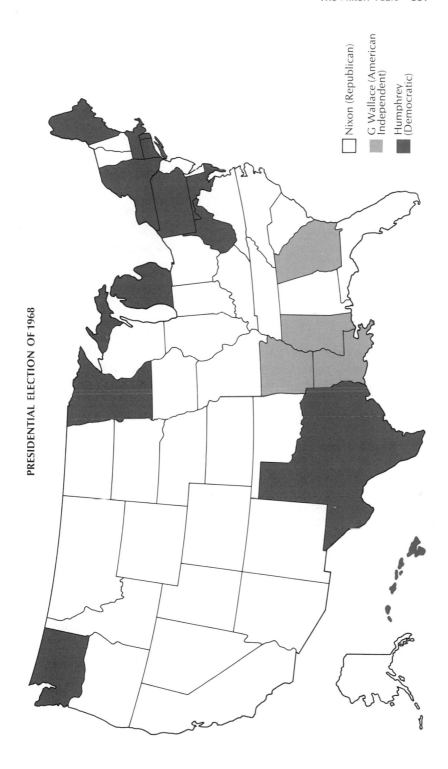

PRESIDENTIAL ELECTION OF 1968

Nixon (Republican)

G Wallace (American Independent)

Humphrey (Democratic)

the nomination narrowed down to two Minnesotans, Vice-President Hubert H. Humphrey and Senator Eugene McCarthy. McCarthy, prior to Johnson's withdrawal on March 31, won surprising support in primaries and public opinion polls in an apparently quixotic effort to dramatize opposition to the Vietnam War. As the "peace candidate," he was naturally attractive to the New Left. After the June 5 assassination of Robert Kennedy, some of Kennedy's support went to McCarthy, some to Humphrey. The vice-president had been a contender for Democratic nominations before but had always been dismissed as too outspokenly liberal compared to men like Stevenson or John Kennedy. In 1968, ironically, he was cast as the Establishment "heavy," the loyal defender for the past several years of Johnson's Vietnam policy. Enthusiasm for McCarthy could not overcome solid organizational support for Humphrey, however, and the vice-president was duly nominated. By then, however, the convention had become a shambles. For several days, radicals and McCarthy partisans battled in parks and outside of Michigan Boulevard's hotels with Chicago police. Strict security measures inside the convention hall infuriated many delegates, and Chicago's Mayor Richard J. Daley, directing the police, the security guards, and the tightest political machine in the country, became a symbol of repression. Humphrey, nominated with Daley's help, could neither bring the McCarthy group back into the Democratic fold, nor get rid of the tarnish his once-liberal image had acquired.

Humphrey struggled through the campaign as the underdog, and in its closing days gathered strong support from disgruntled liberal Democrats and others who suddenly realized that the country was about to elect a Republican president. The late Humphrey surge was not enough: Richard Nixon was elected by a margin only slightly larger than the one by which he had lost to Kennedy in 1960. Except for the South, the main elements of the old Democratic coalition—blacks, Jews, Catholics, workers, and newly-voting ethnics such as Puerto Ricans and Mexicans—voted for Humphrey rather than Nixon, to the extent that they voted. But many normally Democratic voters stayed home. The black vote outside the South was down 11 percent from 1964; those voters plus others opposed to Vietnam could have given Humphrey a winning margin. The South, except for Texas, voted for Wallace or Nixon. Wallace's threat to throw the election into the House of Representatives by depriving either major-party candidate of an electoral college majority did not materialize, but he won five southern states and nearly 10 million votes, many of them from younger (aged 21 to 34) and working-class people. Nixon, winning with 43 percent of the popular vote and over 2 million fewer than he received when he lost in 1960, had not broadened the Republican base except in a few southern states. He had simply solidified the "law and order" tendencies of the Republican center. To political analysts, the chief lesson of the 1968 election was a declining commitment to *either* of the major parties, and the expansion of an independent, fluid voting mass drawn less along economic and ethnic lines than along ideological ones.

Nixon stepped carefully through his first year as president, seeking to escape and if possible defuse the explosive tensions of 1968. Vietnam and economic recession were his major problems through much of his first term. He wound down the Asian conflict with some difficulty; he attacked with less success the twin problems of rising unemployment and rising inflation. He also reversed post-1949 policy toward mainland China, and his Supreme Court appointments gave that body a decidedly more conservative cast than it had under Earl Warren.

Public opinion polls in 1969 revealed a majority in favor of rapid or gradual withdrawal from Vietnam, and Nixon responded by announcing successive cuts in American troop levels. The announced American policy was "Vietnamization," removing American forces as the Saigon government progressively controlled South Vietnam. American combat units were gradually sent home and not replaced. The process was not smooth; after the neutralist ruler of Cambodia, Prince Norodom Sihanouk, was deposed by a military group in March, 1970, South Vietnamese and American forces invaded the country in order, as Nixon said, to destroy the enemy "nerve center" there and give Vietnamization more time to succeed. The Cambodian invasion touched off another wave of anti-war demonstrations on campuses and elsewhere, one by-product being the shooting of four students at Kent State University by national guardsmen. But American ground forces did leave Cambodia by July 1, and troop withdrawals from Vietnam continued through 1971.

Meanwhile, in another move to lessen international tension, Nixon unilaterally renounced American use of chemical and biological weapons. Negotiations proceeded with the Soviet Union to limit strategic arms. In the summer of 1971, Nixon announced that he had arranged to visit China within the following year, and the United States finally acceded to the admission of the People's Republic of China to the United Nations, an event that generated thunder on Nixon's right when, in accord with Peking's requirements, the United Nations at the same time expelled the Taiwan government of Chiang Kai-shek. The Peking visit went on as scheduled, in February, 1972, and public opinion polls showed popular confidence that it was a step toward world peace—though not the greatest thing since 1945, as Nixon made out. Concrete results were few, except that Nixon apparently agreed that Taiwan was really part of China, as Chou En-lai said, and the American garrison in Taiwan would ultimately depart, as tensions in "the area" (including Indochina?) lessened. In May, Nixon visited the Soviet Union, and after several days of talks with Communist Party Secretary Leonid Brezhnev and other Soviet leaders, the president came home with signed agreements on scientific exchanges, cooperation in space programs, and most important, a strategic arms limitation treaty outlawing anti-ballistic missile (ABM) systems and setting lids on offensive nuclear weapons. Despite a step-up in the Vietnam War in April, when Nixon ordered strategic bombing and the mining of Haiphong and other North Vietnamese ports to prevent the arrival of Soviet-made weapons, which fed a new Hanoi offensive, he and the Soviet leaders preferred to sidestep the Vietnam issue and anxiously pursue *détente*.

At home, the Nixon administration sought economic stabilization first through the traditional medicine of higher interest rates and restricted federal spending, especially for educational and social programs (though defense spending and federal deficits increased). He did continue the Model Cities program, supervised tax reform bills in 1969 and 1971 intended to benefit low and middle income families and to stimulate business investment, and asked Congress for a federal welfare act to provide a minimum family income and vocational training. The recession of 1969–70 eased somewhat in 1971, but unemployment and inflation rose to rates of about 6 percent. With a bevy of potential Democratic presidential contenders looking for an issue for 1972, Nixon was under pressure and made a

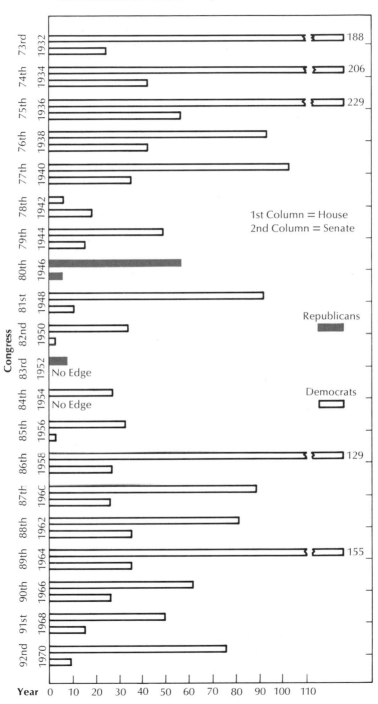

CONGRESSIONAL MAJORITIES, 1932–1968 ELECTIONS

1st Column = House
2nd Column = Senate

Republicans

Democrats

No Edge

No Edge

Congress

Year

Number of Members Over Combined Opposition

dramatic move in August, 1971, by announcing a "New Economic Policy" involving dollar devaluation and a several-phase federal system of price and income controls unlike anything since Truman reinstituted price stabilization during the Korean War.

Nixon's New Economic Policy manifested a federal activism untypical of historic Republican philosophy, and his new departures with regard to Southeast Asia and China were more congenial to those on the liberal side of the political spectrum than to those on the right. In the area of civil rights, however, he shifted markedly from the Kennedy-Johnson policies, slowing down the drive for continued desegregation and the registering of southern black voters. This, some analysts conjectured, was intended both to hold the gradual Republican voting gains in the South as well as to help prevent a resurgence of Wallace strength in 1972. Attentive also to the "law and order" issue, the Nixon administration through Attorney General John Mitchell dealt harshly with thousands of anti-war demonstrators who descended on Washington early in May, 1971. Quite possibly, however, the most far-reaching of Nixon's efforts would prove to be his Supreme Court appointments: given the unusual opportunity to appoint four new justices between 1969 and 1971, Nixon nominated several men too conservative or unqualified for the Senate to accept, and others whom the Senate accepted but who were predicted to be less vigorous seekers after civil liberties and civil rights than Warren and others whom they replaced. It was almost as if Nixon was assuring a Republican judiciary, no matter what happened at the polls, as John Adams did for the Federalist party in 1801 when he appointed the long-lived John Marshall and others. Nixon was undoubtedly aware that the Democrats gained seats in Congress in the 1970 election, and that labor, blacks, Jews, and Spanish-Americans still voted Democratic while higher-income people and business-minded conservatives voted Republican. He also was aware of what that meant: that the ethnic and economic voting patterns of forty years had not basically changed; that moderately liberal Democrats were beginning to be elected in the South; and that Republican slippage in membership continued as it had since 1940. A Gallup poll in 1971 showed that fewer people, especially that growing group of people in their twenties, identified themselves as Republicans than as "independents." Democratic identification, meanwhile, remained steady overall and increased during the sixties among blacks.

"Oh, you're very, very funny . . . So,
   you wouldn't 'Send a knight out on a dog like this'"

Hugh Haynie of the Louisville *Courier-Journal* comments on Democratic problems,
1972. (Reprinted by permission of Hugh Haynie and the Louisville *Courier-Journal*)

As the seventies opened, the prognosis was guarded for the future success of the Grand Old Party. The voters had never warmed to the anti-labor conservatism of Taft in the late forties or the "dynamic conservatism" of the Eisenhower administration, and certainly not to Goldwater, nor, visibly, to Nixon's brand of Republicanism. While the definition and content of "Right" or "conservative" changed substantially over twenty-five years, it had never won a secure national majority at the polls. At the same time, however, the Democratic party and the kinds of liberalism it portrayed itself as representing from Roosevelt through Johnson had no grounds for over-confidence. For over thirty years, the "liberal" voter was for the most part a person with ethnic and economic concerns. Liberalism was cast in terms which appealed to ethnic and economic identifications. But in the late sixties and early seventies, new groups of voters appeared—the young (especially numerous after the voting age was lowered to eighteen in 1971), the highly-educated, the affluent middle-class. These people were much less sensitive to economic and ethnic liberalism than the voting mass of the forties and fifties. At the same time, new issues were generated that were less directly economic or ethnic than broadly social—issues such as the environment, the abolition of poverty, the ending of military involvements, and the general quality of life. Certain leading political commentators who had solid histories of liberalism through the fifties and sixties openly wondered by 1970—given the obvious distrust of government on the part of many citizens and the many sorry side-effects of governmental activism—whether further extensions of federal actions would carry either the credibility or the astuteness necessary to make them work. The widespread desire for new approaches and new solutions to national problems, and the instability (perhaps even disintegration) of the post-F.D.R. Democratic coalition, was evident in the 1972 Democratic primaries. Then Senator George McGovern of South Dakota, appealing to suburbanites and others motivated more by ideology than economics with a vaguely "New Leftish" program, defeated the middle-of-the-road Senator Edmund Muskie of Maine and the Old Left hero, Hubert Humphrey. Yet the biggest vote-getter in many primaries was Alabama's George Wallace, until he was nearly killed by an assassin in May. The Democratic party, the majority party since 1930, was in flux.

It was clear by the early seventies that American politics—the ways in which government operated at home and overseas, the ways in which the voters responded, the ways in which new issues were generated, sharpened, and dealt with—were shifting into patterns that were in important respects dissimilar to the politics of the middle third of the century, from Franklin Roosevelt to the late 1960s.

12

CULTURE AND SOCIETY
SINCE THE FORTIES

The quality of American culture changed as much between World War II and the seventies as its demographic structure, economy, and politics. Cultural changes were varied and elusive; as always, they did not admit of the precise measurement possible with population, GNP, or votes. Nevertheless a distinctive American culture undeniably existed, tying Detroit closer to Los Angeles, 2,000 miles away, than to Windsor, just across the river, and the tie was more than representation in the National Football League. The changes that took place in that culture in the three decades after the Great Depression were legion. Some were as superficial (or, at their most heartfelt, "symbolic") as the rises and declines of women's hemlines or men's hair length. Others were pervasive but not often, in their content, profound, such as the developing universality of television after 1945. Still others constituted variations on older American cultural themes, such as the practically universal faith in democracy, and resentment when democracy was frustrated. Individual achievement in the arts and sciences flourished, and so also, consistently, did mediocrity. The great majority of Americans maintained a pride of nationality as strongly as in the past, a pride unconsciously evident among some of the most vociferous internal critics, especially young ones in the sixties: their dissatisfactions often stemmed from comparisons of the actual America with what they thought, on the basis of American-generated ideals, America ought to be, rather than from comparisons with existing cultures and nations elsewhere.

Youth at home: at the Harvard strike of 1969. (Constantine Manos, © 1970 Magnum Photos, Inc.)

At first it was a relief to be out of the enervation of the depression; the Second World War, ghastly though it was, at least channeled and concentrated individual energies on the common cause of winning. The whiff of coming affluence and the uncertainty about economic relapse, the fear that the new prosperity might go out of style, marked the late forties; the best-seller lists in 1948 were crowded with evidence of a search for stability. Then came the "new normalcy" of the fifties. That superficially somnolent decade brought an end to the terrifying instability of the early Cold War, and an end, mostly by peaceful means, to European colonialism. At home the "Age of Eisenhower" meant self-flagellation over suburbia, freeways, and life as a cog in a corporation, together with a frequently fruitful search for the new house, the new car, and the high salary; Americans beat their breasts about materialism, and at the same time delighted in it. By 1959, sociologists argued about the meaning and merits of suburbia and the "beat generation," the anti-affluence youth movement of that decade, whose bards were Allan Ginsberg, Jack Kerouac, and Lawrence Ferlinghetti; Walter Reuther of the UAW declared that "complacency" was America's number-one problem. But public opinion polls measuring the national self-image reported that the majority viewed the changes of the fifties as social progress.

Another poll in 1964 reported similarly. By then the country had basked in the glow of Camelot, with John Kennedy as king; the early sixties were a new "era of good feelings," undergirded by the measurable diffusion of civil rights and of affluence. The climate of the late sixties was markedly different: ghetto riots, assassinations, the Vietnam War, the New Left youth movement, each contributed to a fragmentation of culture, a frightening sense of internal division. In 1971 a Roper poll revealed that 64 percent of Americans felt that the "United States has lost its proper sense of direction," and only 23 percent felt that the country was on the right track; opinion divided on just what that was. At the same time, however, an apparently irrepressible and timeless American characteristic prevailed despite the cultural confusion: the press also reported a remarkable optimism about the future, and the general expectation that the 1980s, if not the seventies, would be richer, better-fed, and more helpfully technological than ever. Despite the cultural crisis of the late sixties, and all the changes since the early forties, American culture retained some identifying qualities that gave it continuity with its own past, and distinctiveness from the cultures of other peoples.

The Sciences,
Hard and Soft

One of those continuing features was scientific and humanistic achievement. As befitted a society with a strong technological background, large size, and substantial world involvements, the United States had a highly advanced "knowledge industry" in science and technology, stimulated in part by World War II and then by the postwar defense establishment. The most spectacular application of scientific theory was in nuclear physics with the creation by the Manhattan Project of World War II of a sustained nuclear chain reaction in 1942; from that creation came the atomic bomb in 1945. Since then, research into the behavior of subatomic particles, with the aid of cyclotrons and other accelerators, became the most glamorous branch of physics. Peacetime applications of atomic energy proceeded much less vigorously; twenty-five years after the first atomic bombs, only a small fraction of the power generated for homes or businesses came from atomic reactors; most power still came from oil, coal, and running water. Theoretical advances in chemistry and biology, such as the identification of isotopes or the components of genetics were common but attracted less attention than plastics, vaccines, and other examples of applied chemistry or biomedicine.

Scientific inquiry, inside and outside of universities, became more of a group undertaking. Individuals might be credited with some scientific or technical discovery. Individual Americans won their share of Nobel prizes, many of the winners being European or Asian emigrants such as C. N. Yang and E. Segre in physics, and Selman Waksman and Severo Ochoa in physiology, as well as the native-born Herman Muller, Willard Libby, Linus Pauling, and James Watson. But most scientific work was done by laboratory teams. Much of it after 1945 was funded generously by private foundations and government agencies, which supported everything from the most abstract mathematics to pestkillers. For over a decade, beginning in the late fifties, the government undertook substantial research and development projects through its own agencies, especially NASA, which spent $24 billion through the sixties developing solid fuels, miniaturized circuitry, and the Saturn rocket to put Neil Armstrong and Edwin Aldrin on the moon in the summer of 1969, and other astronauts there later. By that time several hundred satellites had orbited the earth, some American, some Russian, serving purposes that included military reconnaissance, weather tracking and prediction, and the intercontinental televising of football and soccer games.

The most revolutionary technological invention of the age was the electronic computer. The first became operational in the forties and early fifties, and second and third generation computers, ever faster and smaller, were developed in the sixties. By then they were standard equipment in hundreds of thousands of factories, offices, university research institutes, and government agencies. The social effects of these machines were immense. To point out just a few: their application in factory automation, beginning in some quantity in the late fifties, brought about substantial increases in productivity per worker and a marked and apparently permanent decline in national needs for unskilled and semi-skilled labor; and, at the same time, they brought about a corresponding need, by no means met during the sixties, to raise millions to a much higher level of education and job training than was previously necessary. Computers also facilitated the spread of the economy's consumer orientation, by such devices as nationwide credit card systems (e.g., BankAmericard, Master Charge, and others that became operational in the middle and late sixties) and the ability to make plane reservations almost anywhere in the world within seconds (if you stood in line long enough) through computerized telecommunications. The federal government used computers to store and retrieve information about taxes, vital statistics, intelligence, and internal security—with ominous and frequently noted implications, by the late sixties, for individual civil liberties. By that time few people still feared the machine itself—nervous jokes about "mechanical brains" taking over the world were common enough in the fifties—but some doubted whether the people who had access to computer-stored data on income taxes, criminal records, or consumer credit would always use the data with responsible regard for the privacy of individuals.

Funds for research and development, from private foundations and from the government, underwrote science and technology during the fifties and sixties to an unprecedented degree. But scientists and engineers, though the most affluent groups, were not the only beneficiaries from philanthropy. As the value of foundation assets boomed with the rest of the economy after World War II, philanthropy surpassed the scale even of the library-building and university-endowing of the Rockefellers, Stanfords, and Carnegies of the late nineteenth century. In a typical manifestation of the postwar trend toward corporate bureaucracy, the grand patron of former days was replaced as a philanthropist by the boards of directors and the program officers of private foundations like Ford, Rockefeller, Carnegie, Kellogg, Lilly, or Sloan. The foundations functioned not only in the time-honored role of patrons of arts and letters, supporting graduate fellowships, amateur theater groups, or scholarly monographs, but also as social engineers, funding antipoverty programs and international development projects. Ford, the largest foundation with assets of over $2.5 billion by 1970, made what was probably the biggest donation of modern times in the mid-fifties when it gave one-half billion dollars on a matching basis to colleges and universities to raise faculty salaries, which were abnormally depressed at that time.

Government-funded research and development also expanded greatly in scope and scale after 1945. Much of it was related to national security, and helped provide weapons, attack detection systems, or intelligence gathering by the CIA and National Security Administration. But the tradition of government-sponsored research that was not immediately "mission-oriented" was a long one, going back to Thomas Jefferson's support of the Lewis and Clark expedition of 1804–06. Hundreds of millions came from the National Science Foundation, the Department of Health, Education, and Welfare, the Defense Department, and other federal agencies to colleges and universities for research in the physical, biological, and social sciences. Some of it was classified and defense-related, but many projects were not mission-oriented, as when the Pentagon sponsored linguistic research into the structure of exotic languages or the State Department helped fund overseas study programs for

American undergraduates. Congress passed an International Education Act in 1966 and created a National Endowment for the Humanities in 1965, and though it provided neither act with funds remotely comparable to those which supported "hard" and "soft" science, it did demonstrate that only part of federal philanthropy was related to national security.

The social sciences, whose intellectual content was still suspect in many quarters before World War II, flourished after 1945. Anthropology, economics, political science, sociology, and other fields had a growing number of practitioners on university faculties, greatly expanded student enrollments, and a wide general audience. Like research in the natural sciences, social science was increasingly performed by research teams, and was increasingly quantitative, mathematical, and computer-dependent. Scholarly journals such as the *American Political Science Review* or the *Quarterly Journal of Economics*, whose contents were once accessible to any "literate person," became so mathematical and statistical by the early sixties that literacy in many social science areas included "numeracy"—i.e., mathematical literacy—at least through basic calculus. Most of the important breakthroughs emanated from universities—developments such as Wassily Leontief's invention of input-output analysis in macroeconomics at Harvard in the forties and early fifties; the development of econometrics by Paul Samuelson of M.I.T. and Simon Kuznets of Harvard (especially the latter's concept and measurement of gross national product) in the forties, which won them two of the early Nobel prizes in economics; the investigations of Theodore Adorno's research team at Stanford into authoritarian personality (around 1950); Guttmann's scaling theory, at Cornell in the early fifties; Noam Chomsky's theories in structural linguistics at M.I.T. from 1957 on; or Anatol Rapoport's theories of conflict resolution, developed at Michigan in the late fifties and the sixties. Most of these exceptional contributions, and others not mentioned, escaped popular notice. But a few social scientists with literary gifts, like David Riesman and C. Wright Mills in sociology, John Kenneth Galbraith in economics, and Henry Kissinger in international relations, reached a wide audience in the fifties and sixties, telling Americans what was going on in their society and in the world. Anyone who read newspapers became familiar with the results of opinion polls conducted by George Gallup, Elmo Roper, Louis Harris, and others. Social scientists became policy-makers, or at least bureaucrats, from New Deal days onward. The Bureau of the Budget and, from 1946, the Council of Economic Advisers, helped close the gap between academic economics and policy formulation, especially as professional economists succeeded to some degree in devising predictive theories to control business cycles and promote economic growth.

The fascination of Americans with numbers, machines, and science itself was nothing new in the postwar period; it could be traced back at least as far as Benjamin Franklin and his kite and key (and near-electrocution). But after 1945, the national confidence in science and technology was confirmed more strongly than ever by computers, telecommunications, rocketry, the space program, and a more "scientific" social science. If you can't count it, it doesn't exist, thought many. Despite the occasional worries of scientists that they would be under-funded, the postwar years were a heyday for science and technology, as massive amounts of money helped produce remarkable results, to the near-unanimous applause of the science-enthralled American public.

The Arts, Fine or Coarse

In contrast to the "hard" and "soft" sciences, where invention, theory, and measurement abounded, literature did not flourish as it had done in the past. Fiction, poetry, and the theater had their devotees, and statistics concerning sales of novels or theater tickets seemed to show a healthy level of popular support. But the quality of literary output did not, on balance, reach the heights of the mid-nineteenth century, the days of Hawthorne and Melville, or of the late Gilded Age, when Clemens and James were active, or of the twenties. The giants who began publishing in the twenties—notably Hemingway, Faulkner, Fitzgerald, Sinclair Lewis, and Eugene O'Neill—produced some of their best work in the thirties and, except for Fitzgerald who died in 1940, into the forties. Their powers declined thereafter, and they died off in the fifties and early sixties. Critics and literary historians have yet to identify postwar writers who have filled their shoes.

The postwar years were not a Golden Age in literature; there is some doubt as to whether they were even a Silver Age. There were several likely reasons why that was so. One had to do with style and structure, and what social or individual function literature (novels or plays) was supposed to perform. The writers of the 1880–1930 period had already explored, sometimes magnificently, the limits of realism and naturalism. Their successors frequently practiced social realism very well indeed—witness John Steinbeck's *The Grapes of Wrath* (1939), the single great novel of the depression, describing the trek of Tom Joad's family of "Okies" from dustbowl despair to near-peonage in California, or Robert Penn Warren's fictional description of the Huey Long regime in Louisiana, *All the King's Men* (1946). But most realistic novels, however excellent, were not innovative except in two relatively minor ways: they described an increasing number of segments of American life—the small-town upper-status groups of James Gould Cozzens and John O'Hara, John Updike's eastern milltowns, J. D. Salinger's puzzled youth in the cities, Edna Ferber's Texas, James Jones's and Norman Mailer's battlefields of World War II—and they described whatever they were concerned about with an increasing degree of sexual explicitness.

In short, the naturalism and realism of postwar fiction, though often well done, was not innovative. When writers attempted to depart sharply from description and embark on experimental forms of fiction, the popular response was too slight to encourage publishers to put them into print. Experimental fiction together with electronic or serial music or abstract expressionism in painting may have been the finest theoretical innovations in art in the mid-twentieth century, but they fared poorly in America's mass market. The spread of television inhibited book-reading, and no doubt would have done so even further had it not been for the "paperback revolution," which began putting cheap editions into airports, drugstores, and supermarkets as well as bookstores from the late forties onward. The murder mysteries of Agatha Christie and Erle Stanley Gardner, the James Bond spy fantasies of Ian Fleming, sex spoofs like Terry Southern's *Candy*, and thousands of other stories of crime, spies, sex, and the Old West sold by the carload. American literature after 1945 was by no means devoid of the good; some wrote vividly of minority groups—notably Philip Roth, Bernard Malamud, and Saul Bellow (especially *Herzog*, 1965) about American-Jewish life; and Richard Wright, Ralph Ellison, Willard Motley, and James Baldwin, about the black experience. Also, playwrights such as Arthur Miller (*Death of a Salesman*, 1948, and other plays) and Edward Albee (notably *Who's Afraid of Virginia Woolf*, 1960) described persistent tensions of American middle-class life with power and accuracy. But the good was not the best.

Postwar architecture also demonstrated that America was not a society that placed its highest priority on artistic excellence. The development of pre-stressed concrete freed architects from linear constraints, and some of them produced remarkable new forms with it, such as Frank Lloyd Wright's muffin-like Guggenheim Museum in New York (1958) and Eero Saarinen's TWA terminal at Kennedy Airport (1959). Edward Durrell Stone endowed his American embassies and other buildings with lightness and warmth, and even the blocky "international style" invented in the twenties by Walter Gropius and others could reach excellence in the hands of masters; see for example New York's Seagram Building (1958) by Ludwig Mies van der Rohe and Philip Johnson. These and other highly able architects produced bridges, homes, and office buildings of lasting merit. As in the past, Americans acquitted themselves well in architecture, perhaps because it is the art form most dependent on technology. With some important exceptions, however, the architecture of postwar America reflected a society that valued or respected utility, massiveness, power and rapid expansion, more than ornament, elegance, or the human scale. Ubiquitous tall boxes gave a visual sameness to Boston, Chicago, Atlanta, Houston, and other large cities. A particularly grotesque example, in the opinion of many critics, was the enormous Pan-Am building built in the late fifties next to, and dwarfing, New York's ornate old Grand Central Station. The Pan-Am building disregarded human scale and inten sified mid-town traffic problems; in the context of the needs of its area, choking on cars and people, it was not even efficient. Neither were rubber-stamp suburban developments tossed up without adequate concern for traffic patterns. Government buildings in Washington and elsewhere were often massive and faceless. The concern of governments and corporations to build the most square footage for the least cost resulted in a prevailing architectural style that represented visually the increasing power of large organizations.

Painting flourished in the postwar period, so much so that in many respects the center of the art world shifted from Paris to New

The situating of the massive John Hancock Building next to Boston's Trinity Church, a Gilded Age gem designed by Henry H. Richardson in the 1870s, was a typical architectural nightmare of the 1960s. (Michael Dobo)

York after 1945. A large part of the reason was economic: the subsidizing of painters and sculptors by private patrons and by educational institutions, together with the growth in the numbers of affluent, upper-middle-class buyers. Though the content of works of art may have mystified their buyers, as it certainly did the mass of Americans, the market flourished. Realistic painting, dominant in the thirties and into the forties, had fewer practitioners afterwards—the best-known was Andrew Wyeth—and the dominant style of the fifties was abstract expressionism, the completely nonrepresentational arrangement of color and space, by Jackson Pollock, Mark Rothko, Robert Motherwell, and hundreds of others. In the early sixties some younger painters departed from abstraction and re-introduced social criticism into painting and sculpture in the form of "pop art." Outstanding and famous examples were Andy Warhol's *One Hundred Campbell Soup Cans* (1962) and Claes Oldenburg's *Hamburger with Pickle and Onion* (1963), which were celebrations of contemporary vulgarity. Other styles and other artists abounded in the sixties; American painting was diverse and comparatively rich.

Classical music fared less well, for despite the development of the long-playing phonograph record in the late forties, and hundreds of symphony orchestras in the fifties, audiences preferred harmony, melody, and rhythm to the atonalism that became orthodox. Contemporary music any more avant-garde than that of Igor Stravinsky or Béla Bartók seldom got played, and was practically unknown except to professional musicians. Despite the work of several very able composers such as Aaron Copland, Roy Harris, Wallingford Riegger, or John Cage, the main thrust of American music was non-classical. Styles in popular music changed, but it was indeed popular, whether the big-band "swing" of the thirties or the "bop" of Dizzy Gillespie, Charlie Parker, and others in the forties or the "cool jazz" of Stan Kenton, George Shearing, Gerry Mulligan, and others in the fifties. Then came "rock" in the sixties, together with troubadours of youth protest such as Joan Baez and Bob Dylan. The rock festival became the most heavily populated musical event of the late sixties, drawing at times up to 300,000. Rock spoke to many more people than either the classical idiom or musicals, despite the great distance that musicals had traveled from Rodgers' and Hammerstein's *Oklahoma* of 1943 to *Hair* in 1967.

Affluence, leisure, and the media had not produced, despite some critics' hopes in the early days of TV, a broad dissemination of high culture (i.e., classical music, "serious" drama, and the like). Perhaps it was true after all that such artistic efforts could be enjoyed only by intellectual (or social) elites; if so, the democratization of the social structure was reason enough for the democratization of musical and artistic taste in the direction (downward) of "mass taste."

Booze, Sex, and Other Kicks

In many areas of the arts, a trend was evident in the late sixties toward a new dadaism, a celebration of the freak-out. Wider drug use, psychedelic experience, and the general availability of pornography in print or on film, contributed to a youthful "counter-culture" that rejected the values of the "straight society" in the arts and politics, and adopted a mode of discourse that was anti-rational. But this movement, like the hippie movement of the early sixties, the "beat generation" of the fifties, and earlier bohemias, involved only a small if raucous minority. After 1945, the great majority of Americans, young, middle-aged, or old, were not remarkably innovative in their pleasure-seeking. In each month of 1945, Americans bought 9,263,000 pulp magazines (love and adventure stories), 7,976,000 true confessions magazines, 3,223,000 detective-story magazines, 10,755,000 movie magazines, and 25,215,000 comic books. Popular entertainment changed in certain respects as a consequence of the spread of affluence; with more leisure time and more disposable income, the middle-class mass worked harder at enjoying itself, but it did so generally in "middle-class" ways. The movies, which occupied vast amounts of leisure time in the twenties and thirties, gave way to TV from the late forties onward; blockbuster films flopped magnificently, even when they displayed liberal expanses of Elizabeth Taylor as Cleopatra. Film distributors, however, made a financially rewarding discovery in the early fifties: "art theaters," showing mainly foreign-made films, were profitable even though the cavernous cinema palaces built in the twenties stood empty. The trend in films from the epic to the epidermic continued through the sixties. While television drew away the mass film audience, foreign films drew viewers, partly because the Bergman or Fellini film was dramatically superior to TV and partly because foreign movies were often more sexually explicit. With the liberalizing of obscenity laws in the sixties, the "X"-rated film became a staple of some movie-houses. By then frontal nudity and explicit sexual acts were to be found in domestically-produced films as well as in the theater or on bookstands. Contrary to conservative expectations, however, the occasional display of genitalia did not plunge the nation into wholesale debauchery. Though movie houses closed by the hundreds in the fifties, new ones opened in the sixties, accompanying the expansion of the youth market. The film-goer sought out "X"-rated films less often than films about World War II (*Patton, The Longest Day*), war spoofs (*Dr. Strangelove, MASH*), or problems of the young (*The Graduate, Midnight Cowboy*).

Back in 1919, H. L. Mencken, who hated censorship as much as prohibition, averred that censors banned books and movies "on the theory that the enforcement of chastity by a huge force of spies, stool pigeons and police would convert the republic into a nation of incomparable uplifters, forward-lookers and artists." The "huge force" even included corporate enterprise: in September, 1936, a man shot some movie film inside a nudist colony, according to the *New Yorker*, and sent the film to Eastman Kodak to be developed. Eastman refused to return the film on the ground that it was obscene. When the photographer sued, the judge upheld Eastman. But the elaborate censorship apparatus withered away after 1945, and sexual candor increased greatly, most noticeably in the 1960s. On the other hand, such sexual behavior as premarital intercourse, adultery, or homosexuality, though more openly discussed, was probably no more common than around World War I. A few signs of a "second sexual revolution" appeared in the middle and late sixties; group sex merited several sociological surveys by 1971 and was found to be practiced by a small number of non-religious people, mostly over twenty-five, either as a form of "marriage therapy" or just "swinging" or as better exercise than tennis or jogging. But there was no hard evidence that such practices, including premarital intercourse among the young, were any more common than they had been since the twenties, to judge from surveys of high school and college students. The new sexual revolution was evidently more talk than action.

Attitudes toward liquor changed little after the repeal of prohibition in 1933, except for dwindling support for state and local prohibition, and increased consumption in suburbia. In most states,

The Old Tavern

Dinner Theatre

SPECIAL REDUCED
EASTER RATES
7⁰⁰

Per Person

**Tues., Wed.
& Thurs.**

Open Easter Sunday

**DAMES
AT SEA**

One of post-Christian America's Easter celebrations.

consumption of alcohol was forbidden to people under twenty-one, and in most states the young flouted the law to about the same extent, apparently, that they always had.

By the sixties, many more people—in medicine, education, law, the churches, and government—were concerned about the extent and effects of tobacco and narcotics. After the Surgeon General's report of 1964 linked smoking with respiratory and heart diseases, campaigns began in the public schools and the media to warn the young against smoking—not, as in the progressive era or the twenties, because it was "immoral," but because it was physically dangerous. Consumption of marijuana undoubtedly increased, and hard drugs like heroin and the hallucinogens apparently spread in use from members of urban minorities to others, especially in the fifteen-to-thirty age group, but unbiased statistics were scarce. On the other hand, a survey of thousands of high-school student leaders in 1971 revealed that more than nine-tenths had never used hard drugs, and more than three-fourths had never used marijuana, despite the admission by the great majority that drugs were easily available.

As with pornography, the availability of liquor and narcotics by no means led inevitably to mass corruption; young and old alike, or most of them, preferred the more socially acceptable forms of affluent hedonism such as the trip to Florida or Europe, the new car, the football game. American culture was far more "permissive" in 1970 than it was in 1945, but permissiveness did not mean a collapse of values, even at the time of the much-discussed "cultural crisis" of the late sixties. Mores varied among age, income, and ethnic groups, but the media-propagated values of the middle class were more pervasive, more the norm, than in the forties.

Institutions and Behavior: Churches and Bureaucracies

While the media played a key role in homogenizing cultural values, major social institutions reinforced this homogenization. Among those institutions, the educational system, corporations and other bureaucracies, and the churches were most influential. Church attendance reached new peaks in the fifties, inspirational books by ministers, monsignors, and rabbis sold well, evangelists (especially Billy Graham) reached large audiences, and astronauts read prayers from outer space. Pentecostal chapels flourished in the Midwest and South while urban blacks crowded store-front churches, and on weekends the cars of worshippers filled the parking lots of suburban Catholic and Protestant churches and Jewish Reform temples. Critics, many from within the churches, complained that the postwar rise in church-going indicated religiosity, not real religion, and perceptive theologians and other citizens disapproved of the linking of religion with nationalism—the syndrome of "piety on the Potomac," as the writer William Lee Miller termed the Eisenhower administration's propensity for stressing the religious purpose of American life or of holy war against "atheistic Communism," a popular phrase in the conservative and some of the Catholic press. But religion in the fifties also included serious theology; Reinhold Niebuhr's neo-orthodoxy and the theistic existentialism of the Swiss theologian Paul Tillich influenced many Protestants, while the neo-scholasticism of Jacques Maritain and others dominated Catholic seminaries and colleges until the sixties.

In the mid-sixties, church attendance stabilized. American Catholicism, heavily tinged with an Irish-American Jansenism, which was theologically conservative as compared with Catholicism in northern Europe, was profoundly shaken by the Second Vatican Council of 1962–65. Vatican II ushered in a democratic spirit involving the substitution of English for Latin in the liturgy, ecumenical activities of wide scope, criticism of ecclesiastical authority, and, late in the decade, a severe decline in religious vocations and in Catholic school enrollments. Protestant theology became less concerned with neo-orthodoxy as increasing numbers of Protestants worried more about urban and racial discord in secular society, and some theologians announced that God was dead. The influence of religion on society was evidently less potent than the influence of society on religion; American culture, like the cultures of industrialized countries generally, was secular and post-Christian. Nonetheless, an amalgam between the "Judeo-Christian tradition" and "the American way of life," noted by the sociologist Will Herberg in 1955, persisted, at least for white Christians; secular and religious values continued to reinforce each other.

Bureaucratic institutions were a homogenizing influence of greater impact than the churches. Large organizations, whether governmental, corporate, political, educational, or voluntary, touched the lives of nearly all Americans with increasing frequency. Bureaucratization was not new in the postwar period; it had been going on for many decades. But after 1945 the process of working in, or relating to, large organizations became increasingly common. The bureaucratic experience inevitably stressed the efficient performance of a defined, segmented social or economic role, rather than the personal relationships of the "whole individual"; it emphasized how somebody functioned, not "who he was." At the same time, incidentally, social institutions came to involve increasingly personal rather than formal relationships, especially in the family, which became less extended, with several generations living together, and more nuclear, with only one generation of parents and children living together. The trend toward bureaucracy, and the impersonal behavioral aspects of it, increased after 1945 as governments became larger and their functions expanded, as more and more people were employed by large firms, and as the size of producing, retailing, or servicing units became greater.

As bureaucratization took place, it was often poorly understood. In particular, it seemed to threaten the dignity of the individual. Jokes about the proliferation of numbers—zip codes, area codes, social security numbers—for all sorts of identifying purposes poured through the various mass media; to young people especially, it seemed that in contemporary society there was no god but the government, and the computer was its prophet. The ancient American distrust of monopolies became newly focused on a distrust of government, especially as the Johnson administration's "credibility gap" widened over the Vietnam War. Individualism, that deeply cherished American value, seemed to be disappearing. College students accordingly carried signs reading "I am a person; do not fold, staple, or mutilate." In certain parts of the country, notably the western and midwestern regions only six or eight decades removed from the raw frontier, the individualistic "Code of the West" stiffened resistance to twentieth-century bureaucratization with appeals to Goldwaterish conservatism. Right-wing fears of the decline of individualism were shared by the "New Left," both of them opposed to an apparently inexorable bureaucratic trend. The mass of Americans had no quarrel with the security, abundance, and high incomes that their social and economic organizations brought them, but this did not prevent some on the Left and the Right from complaining about being homogenized in the pervasive bureaucratic centrifuge. But complaining about bureaucracy did not solve it, anymore than rejecting it or "copping out" did; the problem remained of how to cope with the reality of it—and that, in large part, was a job for education.

Institutions and Behavior:
Education and Youth

The educational system was another homogenizer. Elementary education expanded greatly between 1945 and the late sixties in order to accommodate the bulge at that time in the five-to-fourteen age group. Secondary schooling became common. While less than a third of the seventeen-year-olds of 1930 graduated from high school, three-quarters did so by 1965, and by 1970 the average American had finished between twelve and thirteen years of school. A large jump in the proportion of high-school graduates occurred in the thirties, from 29 percent in 1930 to 51 percent in 1940, no doubt because there was little point in leaving school only to join the unemployed during the depression. The high-school population dipped slightly in the early forties, as much of it went off to fight World War II, but after 1945 high-school attendance and graduation became normal. Compared to developed countries in Europe and elsewhere, in which the usual age for leaving school was fourteen or fifteen, American youths were already, by 1950, prolonging their social adolescence and delaying their entry into the job market much longer than their counterparts elsewhere.

In the postwar period, elementary and secondary education in the United States had acquired a standardized set of characteristics and functions. Although education through the high-school level was paid for and operated by state and local governments, there existed a national pattern in curricula, teacher-training requirements, textbooks, and expected social function, with only minor variations. Great differences of many kinds did exist, as for example between the schools of high-income suburbs and those of inner cities; however, it was not until the sixties that these differences began to be studied seriously and dealt with programmatically, but even then, incompletely. In the meantime, the public school as a social institution was generally expected to provide a young person with enough skills to make him employable in a blue- or white-collar job, or to proceed to college; to wean the child away from infantile dependence on the family and, over a period of twelve years, train him to function with his peers and in the general society; to imbue in him the general values of American society; to make him a good and loyal citizen.

However, the actual functions of the schools were not quite the same as the expected functions, especially through the early or middle sixties. They did provide skills; they also kept a number of people occupied and out of the job market through their late teens (and colleges and professional schools kept many of them well into their twenties); they made students patriotic or at least in some sense nationalistic; and by stressing the values of democracy, individualism, and peaceful social interaction, they raised in students expectations

Jackson State College, Mississippi, May 15, 1970: a girls' dormitory after police fired on it. They were returning sniper shots, they said. (Wide World Photos)

that those values would exist in the larger society. They did not prepare students to be calmly disappointed when those values were thwarted; they did a poor job of explaining other cultures or the place of the United States in the world, and thereby did little to dispel the myth of American omnipotence; they failed to explain the bureaucratic, complex nature of the society into which the young were about to move. A major consequence of these failures was a disturbing gap, in the minds of many young people, between the values they learned and the realities they met, leading to dysfunction and alienation for considerable numbers, expressed most vividly in higher education later, particularly in the campus unrest of 1964–70.

College and graduate education boomed after 1945, not only because of the demographic bulge in the eighteen-to-twenty-five age
group in the late fifties and the sixties, but also because of a spectacular rise in the proportion of that age group that went to college. In
1940 about 16 percent of the eighteen-to-twenty-one-year-olds did
so; by 1960 the proportion had doubled; by 1970 it had nearly tripled, to about 45 percent. The reasons for the increase included successive G.I. bills after 1945; increasing family and personal income,
and foundation and institutional support; diminishing opportunities for those with only high-school training; and increased opportunities for those with college degrees. Postgraduate education expanded even faster than undergraduate. While the number of
college graduates tripled after 1945, the number of master's and
doctor's degrees that were awarded quadrupled or quintupled. By
the late sixties, the number of American faculty members—over
half a million—exceeded the number of college students in many
other highly-developed countries. The married student became a
common phenomenon after World War II, as did barrack-type
housing on many university campuses. The veterans of that war,
and then the Korean War, became, first, a new breed of serious, up-
wardly-mobile student interested less in campus capers than in good
grades and good recommendations, and then, the gray-flannel, but-
ton-down-collar business and professional men of the fifties. By the
sixties that group was well on its way to suburbia, and the college
population was again predominantly the less worldly-wise, more
idealistic post-adolescent. That group quickly gained worldly experience, but in the civil rights movement rather than on World War
II battlefields or in Korean trenches.

When the civil rights movement went "black" and the Vietnam
involvement deepened in the mid-sixites, the pro-democratic, anti-
bureaucratic ideals of many college students became expressed in
"the student movement." Only a tiny minority, like the Weathermen in 1968–70, were revolutionaries who would use violence to
overthrow what they believed was a rotten society. A much larger
group—still only about 10 percent of the young but including many
of the more gifted college students—constituted the "New Left"
campus protesters and demonstrators at Berkeley in 1964, San
Francisco State and Columbia in 1968, Harvard in 1969, Kent
State in 1970, and hundreds of other campuses. Demonstrations

were noisy but mostly nonviolent during 1964–67, and they usually focused on a combination of national issues (the escalating Vietnam War, the draft, a faster pace to civil rights) and campus problems (disciplinary regulations, bureaucratic red tape, unresponsiveness of the university to "relevant" social problems). Tactics were usually derived from the successes of the civil rights movement of 1959– 63—the mass march, the exhortatory songs and long speeches, and the sit-in—but deans' and presidents' offices were being sat-in, instead of lunch counters. When administrators called in police to quell the disturbances, the result frequently was to enlarge the disturbances substantially, provoking previously uninvolved faculty and students to join the demonstrators.

In this early and generally nonviolent period, the major activist organization was Students for a Democratic Society (SDS), whose manifesto, the 1962 "Port Huron Statement," called for "participatory democracy" in higher education and society generally. The SDS cooperated with SNCC, the civil-rights organization, until SNCC divested itself of white membership in 1966. As SNCC and other black rights groups became more militant, the SDS radicalized and divided. Its 1969 national convention was taken over by the revolutionary and terrorist Weatherman faction. Few joined it. But although the SDS fell apart, campus unrest continued in 1968 and 1969 over issues such as ROTC, university involvement in defense contracts, on-campus recruiting by government agencies, and the draft. In this phase, protest episodes were studded with incidents of arson, scuffles between police, demonstrators, faculty, and administrators, disruption of classes, and "trashing" of offices.

The Cambodian invasion of 1970 triggered a rash of demonstrations, and the climax of five and a half years of unrest occurred at Kent State on May 4, 1970, when Ohio national guardsmen killed four students and injured eleven others. In August a terrorist bomb wrecked a laboratory and killed a graduate student at the University of Wisconsin. Meanwhile, several black students had been killed at South Carolina State College at Orangeburg in 1966 and at Jackson State in Mississippi in 1970; these were less widely publicized and commemorated than the Kent affair. But the mood of alienation and militance was deeper and broader on the campuses of black colleges than anywhere else. The killings of 1970 had a chilling effect, and the next two academic years were almost free

Cheesecake in 1945: Jane Russell. (Culver Pictures, Inc.)

of the many violent protests and demonstrations of 1964–70. The winding down of the Vietnam War, the conversion of the draft to a lottery system in 1970, and suitable campus changes (ending defense contracts and ROTC credit, starting black studies programs,

Cheesecake in 1970: Raquel Welch. (Culver Pictures, Inc.)

liberalizing the curriculum) also contributed to a quiet atmosphere unknown since the late fifties.

Undoubtedly a substantial proportion of college students after 1970 retained their suspicions of bureaucratic structures and their disillusion at failures in the democratic ideal. There was strong evidence, however, that only a minority of the young were of the New Left persuasion. A survey of youth made in 1969 revealed that three-fourths believed that American political and business institutions were basically sound, while 72 percent of those in college and 82 percent of others agreed with the principle that "competition encourages excellence." Evidently the rumors of the death of the "work ethic" were, to paraphrase Mark Twain, greatly exaggerated. Considerable numbers of students and the non-college young, in fact, supported George Wallace in 1968; while the New Left developed on campuses, a New Right developed among other young people, some conservative middle-class, many from non-mobile working-class backgrounds. Yet the majority of college-age Americans in the early seventies, white or black, evidently belonged to neither extreme: they were guided by aspirations of academic and, later, professional achievement that were more realistic, but also less immediate, ways of expressing social concern than those attempted by students in the sixties.

Mobility, Affluence, and the Constraints of the Outside World

Occupational mobility increased after 1940, pushing millions whose grandparents had been non-English-speaking immigrant workers into the professional and white-collar ranks. People of Slavic, Italian, or East European Jewish stock, descendants of immigrants who, according to the racist restrictionists of the early twentieth century, would never be assimilated into American democratic society fought their way upward, taking advantage of night schools, public education, and veterans' educational benefits. By the forties, the doctor or lawyer or engineer of newer-immigrant stock was already fairly common in northeastern and north central cities. College and university faculties, once a WASP preserve, opened to Jewish, Japanese, Italian, Slavic, black, and Puerto Rican Americans in the fifties and sixties. Despite the continuing scar of racism, manifested not only in traditional anti-black discriminations but also in episodes such as the forced internment of over 100,000 Japanese-Americans, two-thirds of them citizens, during World War II because of hysterical suspicions that they might be "disloyal," the United States was a more open society, with greater opportunity, than in the past.

Recruitment into the top ranks of business leadership was only marginally easier than it had been earlier; most business leaders still came from business backgrounds and families already well up the status ladder. But after 1945, with the expansion of education and government as well as business, and the increasing need for trained professionals of all kinds, career options were less limited to business. Government and academic life appeared to many college graduates, by the mid-sixties, to be "where the action is," and the growing social concern among the young and others for the abolition of poverty, discrimination, and environmental problems engendered a new breed of public servants and public-service lawyers, physicians, and social workers. The traditional American folktheme of individualistic achievement and material accumulation still prevailed, but as it became easier to realize through the fifties and sixties, and was indeed realized by a larger proportion of society than ever before, it was becoming tempered by the deep desire to accomplish truly and fully another traditional ideal—democracy.

The effects of affluence in the America of 1945–70 were vast and often surprising. In October, 1936, an advertisement for Camels in the *New Yorker* named a bevy of society women with names like Biddle, Byrd, Cabot, du Pont, and Rockefeller as "a few of the distinguished women who prefer Camels' costlier tobaccos," along with "casual house parties . . . the amusing new dinner jackets . . . charity work . . . gathering a gay crowd for a midnight snack from the chafing dish." Thirty years later Camels were being touted as the smoke for the unpretentious common man, who would walk a mile (in blue jeans and a pullover) for one, and who left the fancy filters and ovals for social climbers. Nobody cared about the distinguished women, *gay* meant something very different, and every suburban housewife had her chafing dish. Affluence certainly provided a better standard of living for most people, bringing cars, color TV, and air conditioning into their experience and often into their possession. It provided a substantial broadening of the availability of higher education, and, in turn, more affluence. It also helped produce a homogenized sameness in many areas of American life: in 1971 the *New York Times* quoted an IBM executive's complaint that "with the cars, the roads, the road signs, you can't really tell whether you're driving from the airport downtown in Memphis or in Minneapolis. Hell, I can't tell whether I'm in Houston or Des Moines." The same article noted the existence of 3,600 Kentucky Fried Chickens, 1,850 McDonald's, 855 Howard Johnson restaurants and 445 Howard Johnson Motor Lodges, 1,358 Holiday Inns, 1,137 Burger Chefs, 4,253 Dairy Queens, 2,300 A & W rootbeer stands, 1,935 Tastee Freez's, 352 Pizza Huts, 387 Taco Bells, 1,200 Seven/Elevens, 485 Chicken Delights, 3,000 One-Hour Martinizing cleaners, 4,000 Western Autos, 4,500 Hertz offices, and so on *ad infinitum*—the bulk of them developed after 1955 and each with its own display sign, usually large. The affluent life of metropolitan America was short on artistic quality, long on bureaucracy and homogeneity. But few emigrated; if America was not entirely lovable, it was hardly leavable. And there were some signs by the early seventies, especially in the attitudes of many younger people, that the extension of affluence to the 20 percent below the poverty line and the improvement of the quality of American life generally were to be the main national priorities in the closing decades of the twentieth century.

As affluence and mobility worked their changes in society, and as individualism and democracy continued to be valued, international events forced changes in attitudes about nationalism and the role of America in the outside world. The isolationism of 1919–39 did not continue, except briefly and among a right-wing minority, after 1945; the atomic bomb and the Cold War could not be ignored. Throughout much of the postwar period, however, Americans usually saw their country through the same ideological prisms as in the past: the providential destiny of the United States, its innate moral superiority, its duty to protect "freedom." But the thermonuclear Sword of Damocles and the Southeast Asian quagmire of the sixties had a sobering effect. By the early seventies, the tendency to identify everything disturbing in the outside world as a product of "the international Communist conspiracy" had greatly dwindled. Domestic crises during the turbulent sixties also helped destroy national overconfidence. Possibly a new maturity was to pervade America's world relations in the seventies, while a concern for humanistic values seemed to be creeping into the conduct of domestic problems. Only the future would tell—a future seen as a *tabula rasa*—its record yet to be etched. But if the first seven decades of the century were any guide, new crises would occur, be overcome, and be resolved into new social forms in which the good mixed ambivalently with the bad—but in which democratic values would continue to be cherished.

Appendix

Population Characteristics, 1860–1970

(All Numbers in Millions)

	1860	1870	1880	1890	1900	1910	1920	1930	1940	1950	1960	1970
Total Pop.	31.4	39.8	50.2	62.9	76.0	92.0	105.7	122.8	131.7	150.7	180.0	204.8
Rural	25.2	28.7	36.0	40.8	45.8	50.0	51.6	53.8	57.2	54.5 * 61.8	54.0	53.9
%	80.3	72.0	71.7	65.0	60.4	54.4	48.8	43.8	43.4	36.3 41.0	29.9	25.7
Urban	6.2	9.9	14.1	22.1	30.2	42.0	54.2	69.0	74.4	96.8 88.9	125.3	149.3
%	19.7	28.0	28.3	35.0	39.6	45.6	51.2	56.2	56.6	63.7 59.0	70.1	74.3
White	26.9	33.6	43.4	55.1	66.8	81.7	94.8	110.3	118.2	134.9	158.8	177.6
%	85.8	84.5	86.5	87.8	88.0	88.8	89.7	89.9	89.9	89.5	88.3	86.7
Nonwhite	4.5	5.0	6.8	7.8	9.2	10.2	10.9	12.5	13.5	15.8	20.5	25.6
%	14.2	15.5	13.5	12.2	12.0	11.2	10.3	10.1	10.1	10.5	11.7	13.3
Male	16.1	19.5	25.5	32.2	38.8	47.3	53.9	62.1	66.1	74.8	88.3	98.9
%	51.3	50.7	50.9	51.3	51.0	51.5	51.0	50.6	50.2	49.7	49.2	47.8
Female	15.4	19.0	24.6	30.7	37.2	44.6	51.8	60.6	65.6	75.9	91.0	104.3
%	48.7	49.3	49.1	48.7	49.0	48.5	49.0	49.4	49.8	50.3	50.8	52.2
Foreign-Born	4.0	5.5	6.5	9.1	10.2	13.3	13.7	13.0	11.4	10.1	9.7	NA
%	12.8	13.8	12.9	14.5	13.4	14.5	12.9	10.6	8.7	6.7	5.4	—
Foreign-Stock	NA	5.3	8.3	11.5	15.6	18.9	22.6	25.9	23.0	23.6	23.8	NA
%	—	13.3	16.5	18.3	20.6	20.6	21.4	21.1	17.4	15.7	13.2	—

* First number reflects old census definition of *urban*; second number reflects revised definition (see page 297).

419

POPULATION CHARACTERISTICS, 1860–1970 (Continued)

(All Numbers in Millions)

	1860	1870	1880	1890	1900	1910	1920	1930	1940	1950	1960	1970
New England	3.1	3.5	4.0	4.7	5.6	6.6	7.4	8.2	8.4	9.3	10.5	11.8
%	9.9	8.8	8.0	7.5	7.4	7.2	7.0	6.7	6.4	6.2	5.8	5.8
Middle-Atlantic	7.5	8.8	10.5	12.7	15.5	19.3	22.3	26.3	27.5	30.2	34.2	37.2
%	23.9	22.1	21.0	20.2	20.4	21.0	21.1	21.4	20.9	20.0	19.0	17.7
East North Central	6.9	9.1	11.2	13.5	16.0	18.3	21.5	25.3	26.6	30.4	36.2	40.3
%	22.0	22.8	22.4	21.5	21.1	20.0	20.2	20.6	20.2	20.1	20.0	19.7
West North Central	2.2	3.9	6.2	8.9	10.3	11.6	12.5	13.3	13.5	14.1	15.4	16.3
%	7.0	9.8	12.4	14.2	13.6	12.6	11.8	10.8	10.3	9.4	8.6	7.9
South Atlantic	5.4	5.9	7.6	8.9	10.4	12.2	14.0	15.8	17.8	21.2	26.0	30.7
%	17.2	14.8	15.2	14.2	13.7	13.3	13.2	12.9	13.6	14.1	14.5	15.0
East South Central	4.0	4.4	5.6	6.4	7.5	8.4	8.9	9.9	10.8	11.5	12.1	12.8
%	12.7	10.8	11.2	10.4	9.9	9.1	8.4	8.1	8.2	7.6	6.7	6.2
West South Central	1.7	2.0	3.3	4.7	6.5	8.8	10.2	12.2	13.1	14.5	17.0	19.3
%	5.4	5.0	6.6	7.5	8.6	9.6	9.7	9.9	10.0	9.6	9.5	9.4
Mountain	0.2	0.3	0.7	1.2	1.7	2.6	3.3	3.7	4.2	5.1	6.9	8.3
%	0.6	0.8	1.4	1.9	2.2	2.8	3.1	3.0	3.2	3.4	3.8	4.0
Pacific	0.4	0.7	1.1	1.9	2.4	4.2	5.6	8.2	9.7	14.5	21.2	26.5
%	1.3	1.8	2.2	3.0	3.2	4.6	5.3	6.7	7.4	9.6	11.8	12.9

Suggestions for Further Reading

The books and articles mentioned below constitute only a fraction of the available literature on recent American history. They do not form a bibliography for specialists or advanced students, but rather a series of suggestions for probing more deeply into certain topics that have been touched upon in this brief text. A few items, because of their breadth, should be listed at this point. An interpretation of American development, written before postwar affluence fully bloomed but no less intriguing because of that, is David Potter's *People of Plenty: Economic Abundance and the American Character* (1954). Another book no longer new but still informative and highly readable, especially as a survey of the interaction of ideas and reform politics, is *Rendezvous with Destiny: American Reform from Tilden to Truman* (1952) by Eric F. Goldman. A delightful and provocative social history, by Gilman M. Ostrander, appeared in 1970, with the accurate title of *American Civilization in the First Machine Age, 1890–1940: A Cultural History of America's First Age of Technological Revolution and "Rule by the Young."* For a highly compendious survey of twentieth century American history emphasizing politics and foreign affairs, see Arthur S. Link and William B. Catton, *American Epoch* (2d ed., 1963). Ross M. Robertson's *History of the American Economy* (2d ed., 1964) is probably the liveliest and most intelligent book on its subject. Much of the statistical material in this book came from the invaluable *Historical Statistics of the United States, Colonial Times to 1957*, and the handy *Pocket Data Book 1971*, both published by the Bureau of the Census. For an extended and vigorous treatment of foreign affairs, see Robert H. Ferrell, *American Diplomacy*, and for constitutional history see Alfred H. Kelly and Winfred A. Harbison, *The American Constitution*; each has recent editions current through the late 1960s.

Chapter 1: The Eclipse of the Old America, 1865–1897

The most useful survey of American development from Reconstruction to World War I is Robert Wiebe's *The Search for Order*; though occasionally too abstract, it perceptively relates a great deal of information to its main thesis—that through a process called "bureaucratization" American society changed in fifty years from an array of isolated local communities to a cohesive entity. The book also has an excellent bibliography current to 1966. Another survey, highly colorful and emphasizing society rather than politics, is *The Age of Excess* (1965) by Ray Ginger. An older book, centering on politics, is Matthew Josephson's *The Politicos 1865–1896* (1938), whose mine of information, attractively presented, remains valuable despite its now quaint Marxian rhetoric. A series of essays on the politics and culture of the late nineteenth century, generally quite up to date, is *The Gilded Age* (2d ed., 1970), edited by H. Wayne Morgan. Surveys of two decades, with emphasis on politics, are John A. Garraty, *The New Commonwealth 1877–1890* (1968) and Harold U. Faulkner, *Politics, Reform, and Expansion 1890–1900* (1959).

Much more work has appeared on the political history of the late nineteenth century than on the social, but some excellent treatments of certain aspects of social development have appeared recently, notably Stephan Thernstrom's *Poverty and Progress: Social Mobility in a Nineteenth Century City* (1964), detailing the slow mobility changes in Newburyport between 1850 and 1880; Thernstrom and Richard Sennett published in 1969 a fascinating collection called *Nineteenth Century Cities: Essays in the New Urban History.* Robert Dykstra's *Cattle Towns* (1968) analyzes social structure in frontier communities. For a comprehensive treatment of urban developments see Blake McKelvey, *The Urbanization of America 1860–1915* (1963), and for an elegant treatment of the relation of transportation changes and urban growth see Sam B. Warner, *Streetcar Suburbs* (1962), on the Boston area. A fine delineation of the character and values of the Gilded Age small businessman is William Dean Howells' novel of 1885, *The Rise of Silas Lapham.*

Economic developments have been accurately summarized by Edward C. Kirkland in *Industry Comes of Age* (1967); the same author described what made entrepreneurs tick in *Dream and Thought in the Business Community* (1956). Surveys of special economic topics include Henry Pelling, *American Labor* (1960); Milton Friedman and Anna J. Schwartz, *Monetary History of the United States* (1963); John Stover, *American Railroads* (1961); Gilbert C. Fite, *The Farmers' Frontier 1865–1900* (1966); Rodman W. Paul, *Mining Frontiers of the Far West* (1962). Governmental economic policy and the interaction of economics and politics have had many historians; among their best works are the seminal essay by Wallace D. Farnham, " 'The Weakened Spring of Government': A Study in Nineteenth Century American History," in the *American Historical Review*, April, 1963; Clifton K. Yearley's monumental study of taxation, social values, and political organizations, *The Money Machines: The Breakdown and Reform of Governmental and Party Finance in the North 1860–1920* (1970); Lee Benson's pathbreaking *Merchants, Farmers and Railroads: Railroad Regulation and New York Politics 1850–1887* (1955); Harold D. Woodman, "Chicago Businessmen and the 'Granger Laws'," in *Agricultural History*, April, 1962; Edward A. Purcell, Jr., "Ideas and Interests: Businessmen and the Interstate Commerce Act," in *Journal of American History*, December, 1967. On the social, economic, and political aspects of the "money question," see Irwin Unger, *The Greenback Era* (1964), and Walter T. K. Nugent, *Money and American Society 1865–1880* (1968).

National politics are discussed in the surveys mentioned above and in H. Wayne Morgan, *From Hayes to McKinley* (1969). Two of the most exciting books on the late nineteenth century published in recent years concentrate on the Midwest, but their thesis—that local, cultural, ethnic, and religious issues were frequently more important than economic ones in influencing political behavior—makes them significant: Paul Kleppner, *The Cross of Culture: A Social Analysis of Midwestern Politics 1850–1900* (1970), and Richard Jensen, *The Winning of the Midwest: Social and Political Conflict 1888–96* (1971). Carl Degler's essay, "American Political Parties and the Rise of the City," in the *Journal of American History* (1964), contains many good ideas. Changes in political philosophy are the main concerns of Sidney Fine in his excellent *Laissez-Faire and the General Welfare State* (1956). On Reconstruction, the best treatments are John Hope Franklin's brief *Reconstruction after the Civil War* (1961) and Kenneth Stampp, *The Era of Reconstruction* (1965); for detailed examinations see John and LaWanda Cox, *Politics, Principle, and Prejudice 1865–1866* (1963), Eric McKitrick, *Andrew Johnson and Reconstruction* (1960), and Robert P. Sharkey, *Money, Class and Party* (1959). The best treatment of civil service reform is Ari Hoogenboom's *Outlawing the Spoils* (1961). Robert D. Marcus has examined the organizational structure of the Republican party and found there was not much of that, but there were many other things, in *Grand Old Party* (1971). Biographies of political figures of this period abound; among the best recent ones are Paolo Coletta, *William Jennings Bryan* (3v., 1964, 1969), Martin Ridge, *Ignatius Donnelly* (1962), and John A. Carpenter, *Ulysses S. Grant* (1970). On Populism and the election of 1896, John D. Hicks' *The Populist Revolt* (1931) is still standard, and Paul Glad's *McKinley, Bryan, and the People* (1964) and J. Rogers Hollingsworth's *The Whirligig of Politics: The Democracy of Cleveland and Bryan* (1963) are very good. State-level studies for this period are numerous and good; see for example W. I. Hair, *Bourbonism and Agrarian Protest: Louisiana Politics 1877–1900* (1969). State-level studies on Populism, with implications for the regional and national scenes, include Walter T. K. Nugent, *The Tolerant Populists: Kansas Populism and Nativism* (1963) and Sheldon Hackney, *Populism to Progressivism in Alabama* (1969). Hackney's book is also a discussion of the continuity (actually the lack of it) between Populism and progressivism, a subject dealt with in another state by David Thelen in *The New Citizenship: Origins of Progressivism in Wisconsin 1885–1900* (1972). On old-style city machine politics, *Lords of the Levee: The Story of Bathhouse John and Hinky Dink*, by Lloyd Wendt and Herman Kogan (1943), is delightful.

The best introductions to black history for the period are the appropriate chapters in John Hope Franklin's general history, *From Slavery to Freedom* (1967), Rayford Logan's *The Negro in American Life and Thought: The Nadir 1877–1901* (1954), and C. Vann Woodward's *The Strange Career of Jim*

Crow (1955). For other minorities see Oscar Handlin's exceptionally fine *The Uprooted* (1951), on immigrants, and for a particular group, Moses Rischin's *The Promised City: New York's Jews* (1962). John Higham's *Strangers in the Land* (1954) is the standard treatment of nativism.

There are many cultural and intellectual histories. Among the best: Richard Hofstadter, *Social Darwinism in American Thought* (rev. ed., 1955); Paul Carter, *The Spiritual Crisis of the Gilded Age* (1971), on the conflict of religion and science; Robert Kelley, *The Transatlantic Persuasion: The Liberal-Democratic Mind in the Age of Gladstone* (1969), on parallels between British, Canadian, and American "liberals"; Elting Morison, *Men, Machines, and Modern Times* (1966), on technology; Henry May, *Protestant Churches and Industrial America* (1949) and Thomas T. McAvoy, *The Great Crisis in American Catholic History* (1957), on religion.

Chapter 2: Demography, 1897–1930: A Truly Continental Society

Mobility for some, the lack of it for others, were pervasive trends in the early twentieth century. Much remains for historians to do in explaining mobility patterns, but some reliable studies do exist. Frederick Lewis Allen sees mobility in the period to have been deeply intertwined with the spread of motor vehicles in *The Big Change* (1952). A collection of essays edited by John Braeman, entitled *Change and Continuity in Twentieth Century America* (1964), examines aspects of mobility and other matters. Two extremes of American society are discussed in Robert Bremner's *From the Depths* (1956), on how the country awoke to poverty problems, and E. Digby Baltzell's *Philadelphia Gentlemen* (1958), on an urban elite. A classic on mobility and other ways of life in a small city (specifically, Muncie, Indiana) is *Middletown* (1929), by Robert S. and Helen M. Lynd.

Three recent studies have clarified the migration of southern Negroes to northern cities: Seth Scheiner's *Negro Mecca: A History of the Negro in New York City* (1965); Gilbert Osofsky's *Harlem: The Making of a Ghetto* (1966), and Allan Spear's *Black Chicago* (1967). Francis Broderick, *W. E. B. DuBois* (1959) and E. David Cronon, *Black Moses: The Story of Marcus Garvey and the Universal Negro Improvement Association* (1955) are leading biographies of two outstanding Negro reformers. Race ideas, from inside and outside, are the subject of *Black Exodus: Black Nationalist and Back-to-Africa Movements* (1969) by Edwin S. Redkey, and *Race: The History of an Idea in America* (1963) by Thomas F. Gossett. See also August Meier, *Negro Thought in America 1880–1915* (1963); Charles Flint Kellogg, *NAACP: A History of the National Association for the Advancement of Colored People 1909–1920* (1967); S. P. Fullinwider, *The Mind and Mood of Black America: Twentieth Century Thought* (1969), and Nathan I. Huggins, *Harlem Renaissance* (1971).

The most comprehensive survey of urbanism is Blake McKelvey's *Ur-*

banization of America, of which volume I (1963) stops at 1915 and volume II (1968) continues into the sixties. But in many ways the most interesting description of urbanism in the early twentieth century, at least urban politics, is the pioneer muckraking work by Lincoln Steffens, *The Shame of the Cities* (1904).

On immigration in general, read Milton M. Gordon, *Assimilation in American Life: The Role of Race, Religion, and National Origins* (1964). A good general survey is Maldwyn A. Jones, *American Immigration* (1960). The condition of urban immigrants was described calmly but vividly by I. S. Hourwitch in *Immigration and Labor* (1912). There are many studies on particular immigrant groups; in addition to Rischin's, mentioned above, the most thoughtful include *The Tragedy of German-America* (1940) by John Hawgood; *The Greeks in the United States* (1963) by Theodore Saloutos; *The Slavic Community on Strike* (1968) by Victor R. Greene; and *The Immigrant Upraised: Italian Adventurers and Colonists in an Expanding America* (1968) by Andrew F. Rollé.

The best books on the history of the South are *The Origins of the New South 1877–1913* by C. Vann Woodward (1951), and *The Emergence of the New South 1913–1945* by George B. Tindall (1967). A more strictly social, but very able, study is John Dollard's *Caste and Class in a Southern Town* (1937). An elusive but important aspect of southern, and national, history is beginning to come to light, thanks to David Chalmers' *Hooded Americanism: The First Century of the Ku Klux Klan* (1965).

On women, see Eleanor Flexner, *Century of Struggle: The Woman's Rights Movement in the United States* (1959); Alan P. Grimes, *The Puritan Ethic and Woman Suffrage* (1967); Aileen Kraditor, *The Ideas of the Woman Suffrage Movement* (1965); and William L. O'Neill, *Everyone Was Brave* (1969). Also good is O'Neill's *Divorce in the Progressive Era* (1967).

Chapter 3: The Economy, 1897–1929: The Sunshine of Prosperity

The size and complexity of the American economy and of particular businesses became almost unmanageable in the early twentieth century, and so did the task of historians trying to analyze and describe them. Two recent studies have dealt admirably with size and complexity, and although neither of them makes easy reading, they are well worth the effort. Alfred D. Chandler's *Strategy and Structure* (1962) takes several large enterprises (Sears Roebuck, General Motors, DuPont) as case studies of the evolution of modern management devices without which sheer size would have immobilized giant firms. Morton Keller's *The Life Insurance Enterprise 1885–1910: A Study in the Limits of Corporate Power* (1963) deals with a similar problem in a single vast industry. The problems involved in the separation of ownership from management, which arose as big businesses went "public" in the twentieth century, and how these businesses therefore needed to be made publicly responsible, are explored in *The Modern Corporation and Private Property* (1932) by A. A. Berle and Gaston C. Means. An interesting and readable thesis on the limits of corporate power and how management and labor interrelate is John K. Galbraith's *American Capitalism: The Concept of Countervailing Power* (1952). Two contemporary accounts of the role of finance capital in business concentration provide fascinating reading: the report of the "Pujo Committee" which investigated the "money trust" (*Investigation of Financial and Monetary Conditions in the United States*; 3 vols., 1911–13); and the story of the leader of the congressional investigation of Wall Street after the 1929 crash, Ferdinand Pecora's *Wall Street Under Oath* (1936). Albro Martin's *Enterprise Denied: Origins of the Decline of American Railroads 1897–1917* (1971) suggests that progressive regulation was misguided and harmful. An excellent and critical view of the "Fed" is Elmus R. Wicker's *Federal Reserve Monetary Policy 1917–1933* (1966). For quantitative studies, see appropriate essays in Robert W. Fogel and Stanley L. Engerman, eds., *The Reinterpretation of American Economic History* (1971).

For labor history and unrest, see two books by David Brody: *Labor in Crisis 1919* (1965), a survey of a violent year, and *Steelworkers in America* (1960), describing labor problems in a single industry. For a general overview see Selig Perlman's *History of Trade Unionism in the United States* (1922) or Foster R. Dulles' *Labor in America* (1949). Melvyn Dubofsky described a leading radical labor group in *We Shall Be All: A History of the Industrial Workers of the World* (1969). A unique attempt to let workers tell their own story, through transcripts of personal interviews, has been done by Eli Ginzberg and Hyman Berman, *The American Worker in the Twentieth Century* (1963). On standards of living, Paul Douglas' *Real Wages in the United States 1890–1926* remains valuable (1930).

For a description of the Federal Reserve in its early years, see E. W. Kemmerer's *The ABC of the Federal Reserve System* (1918). Hans Thorelli, *Federal Antitrust Policy* (1955) is authoritative on its subject. Robert Wiebe's *Businessmen and Reform* (1962) explores the input of businessmen themselves on regulatory legislation in the early twentieth century; Gabriel Kolko's *The Triumph of Conservatism* (1963) deals with the same problem in a somewhat radical and ultimately less convincing way.

The stock market in the twenties has been described very vividly and successfully by Robert Sobel in *The Great Bull Market* (1968), while the most lucid single volume on the debacle of 1929 is *The Great Crash* (1955) by John K. Galbraith.

Chapter 4: Ideas and Attitudes in the Early Twentieth Century

Progressivism, because of its variety, has been a favorite subject for debate ever since it happened. General surveys include Harold U. Faulkner's

Quest for Social Justice (1931), which concentrates on social aspects; portions of Richard Hofstadter's *Age of Reform* (1955) and Goldman's *Rendezvous with Destiny* (1952), which relate ideas to social and political currents; and studies of groups of reformers such as Daniel Aaron's *Men of Good Hope* (1951), Daniel Levine's *Varieties of Reform Thought* (1964), David Noble's *The Paradox of Progressive Thought* (1958), and Charles Forcey's *Crossroads of Liberalism* (1961); these mostly discuss leaders and publicists. Louis Filler analyzed the muckrakers outstandingly in *Crusaders for American Liberalism* (1939). The social-reform strain in progressivism is Allen Davis' subject in *Spearheads for Reform: The Social Settlements and the Progressive Movement 1890–1914* (1967). Samuel Haber discussed the obsession of some progressives with efficiency in society and business in *Efficiency and Uplift* (1964). A fine essay is "Social Tensions and the Origins of Progressivism" (*Journal of American History*, 1969), by David Thelen.

Progressives were never loath to speak for themselves, and several key progressive statements were originally published as tracts for the times; for example, Herbert Croly, *The Promise of American Life* (1909), and Walter Lippmann, *Drift and Mastery* (1914). E. A. Ross, the Wisconsin sociologist, also wrote a muckraking tract called *Sin and Society* (1907); his autobiography, *Seventy Years of It* (1936), is one of the best. Jane Addams' *Twenty Years at Hull House* (1911) is an important document. *The Autobiography of Lincoln Steffens* (1931) stands as one of the finest autobiographies ever written by an American.

The intellectual life of the time was in ferment, and the best approach to pragmatism, according to taste, is either William James' *Pragmatism* (1907), a series of readable essays, or Ralph Barton Perry's biography, *The Thought and Character of William James* (1935). A strikingly fine book, which finds common themes in the intellectual upheavals which took place in history, law, economics, philosophy, and the general thought of the period, is *Social Thought in America: The Revolt Against Formalism* (1949), by Morton G. White; it is required reading. Historians have not neglected themselves, either; changes in historical thought are described in John Higham, *History* (1965), and Richard Hofstadter, *The Progressive Historians* (1968). August Meier's *Negro Thought in America 1880–1915: Radical Ideologies in the Age of Booker T. Washington* (1969) is valuable.

Mark Schorer's *Sinclair Lewis* (1961), W. A. Swanberg's unsympathetic *Dreiser* (1965), and Arthur Mizener's *The Far Side of Paradise* (1951), on F. Scott Fitzgerald, are outstanding among literary biographies.

Good histories of education are available. Rush Welter's *Popular Education and Democratic Thought in America* (1962) and Lawrence Veysey's *The Emergence of the American University* (1965) are partly devoted to this period. *The American College and University* (1962), by Frederick Rudolph, is a very good general treatment. For progressivism in education, see Lawrence A.

Cremin, *The Transformation of the School* (1961), and Patricia A. Graham, *Progressive Education* (1967).

Studies of woman suffrage are mentioned above (Chapter 2). On other progressive interests, see David M. Kennedy, *Birth Control in America: The Career of Margaret Sanger* (1970); Mark Haller, *Eugenics* (1963) or Donald K. Pickens, *Eugenics and the Progressives* (1968); and Edwin T. Layton, Jr., *The Revolt of the Engineers: Social Responsibility and the American Engineering Profession* (1971). On psychoanalysis, see John C. Burnham, *Psychoanalysis and American Medicine 1894–1918* (1967), and Nathan G. Hale, Jr., *Freud and the Americans: The Beginnings of Psychoanalysis in the United States 1876–1917* (1971).

The popular mood of the early twentieth century has been captured in the most direct fashion by the multivolume "headline history" by Mark Sullivan, *Our Times*. Van Wyck Brooks' *The Confident Years* (1955) concentrates on popular moods and literature. Frederick Lewis Allen's *Only Yesterday* (1931) is a vivid portrait of public preoccupations during the "roaring twenties." Perhaps the most compelling and thoughtful book on changes in social mores and self-images, as expressed in literature and elsewhere, is Henry F. May's *The End of American Innocence* (1959), which makes the case that the foundations of contemporary attitudes came not during the twenties but in the years 1912–1917.

Chapter 5: Politics and Empire in the Progressive Period, 1897–1916

America's muscle-flexing as a world power, which marked the McKinley years, has been well attended to by historians. Ernest May's *Imperial Democracy* (1961) is a good general treatment; recent and useful is David Healy's *U.S. Expansionism: The Imperialist Urge in the 1890s* (1970). *American Diplomacy 1900–1950* (1951), by George Kennan, is a provocative interpretation by a noted diplomat of how foreign policy decisions made around 1900 affected events down to World War II and beyond. For a solid explanation of how the United States became involved in the Spanish-American War and subsequent imperial adventures, Julius Pratt's *Expansionists of 1898* (1936), though in places superseded, remains useful. Opposition to these adventures is explained intelligently in Robert L. Beisner's *Twelve Against Empire: The Anti-Imperialists 1898–1900* (1968). On Caribbean policy, Dexter Perkins' *The Monroe Doctrine* (1938) is authoritative, with special aspects dealt with by Allan R. Millett in *The Politics of Intervention: The Military Occupation of Cuba 1906–1909* (1968). China policy has been clarified by Charles Campbell's fine monograph, *Special Business Interests and the Open Door* (1951). William L. Neumann's *America Encounters Japan: From Perry to MacArthur* (1968) takes in much historical territory.

The political history of the progressive period has been given its most effective brief survey in George Mowry's *The Era of Theodore Roosevelt* (1958), but Russel Nye's *Midwestern Progressive Politics* (1951) deals in more depth with a crucial phase of the movement. On certain national leaders, see H. S. and M. G. Merrill, *The Republican Command 1897–1913* (1971). For progressivism in the West, see George Mowry, *The California Progressives* (1952). The field is studded with good biographies of progressive leaders; a few of them are Richard Leopold's brief *Elihu Root and the Conservative Tradition* (1954) or Philip C. Jessup's more exhaustive *Elihu Root* (1938); Claude Bowers' *Beveridge and the Progressive Era* (1932) on the Indiana Senator; Robert M. La Follette's *Autobiography* (1919); Melvin G. Holli's *Reform in Detroit: Hazen S. Pingree and Urban Politics* (1969), on the untypical Detroit mayor; John Semonche's *Ray Stannard Baker* (1969); Robert Crunden's *A Hero in Spite of Himself: Brand Whitlock in Art, Politics and War* (1969); John Garraty's *Righthand Man* (1960), on George Perkins; Alpheus T. Mason's magisterial *Brandeis* (1946); and Dewey Grantham's *Hoke Smith and the Politics of the New South* (1958).

State and regional studies, in addition to those by Nye, Mowry, and Thelen mentioned already, are led by Richard Abrams' *Conservatism in a Progressive Era: Massachusetts Politics 1900–1912* (1964); A. D. Kirwan's *Revolt of the Rednecks* (1951), on Mississippi; Sheldon Hackney's *Populism to Progressivism in Alabama* (1969); and Hoyt Landon Warner's *Progressivism in Ohio* (1964). For a critical view, see Stanley P. Caine, *The Myth of a Progressive Reform: Railroad Regulation in Wisconsin 1903–1910* (1970). For radical politics, *The Socialist Party of America* (1955), by David A. Shannon, and *The Roots of American Communism* (1957), by Theodore Draper, will serve well. There is a growing literature on progressive issues; urban social reform and welfare found its historian in Roy Lubove, whose *The Progressives and the Slums: Tenement House Reform in New York City* appeared in 1962. On the prohibition drive, one can read the fervently favorable biography of *Frances Willard* (1944) by Mary Earhart, or the trustworthy monograph, *Prohibition and the Progressive Movement* (1963), by James Timberlake. On the progressives' unhappy proclivity toward certain forms of repression, see William Preston's *Aliens and Dissenters* (1963). The best history of agrarian problems for this and subsequent periods is *Agricultural Discontent in the Middle West 1900–1939* (1951), by Theodore Saloutos and John D. Hicks.

The first President Roosevelt has been biographized several times. The reader can choose among the readable and anecdotal *Theodore Roosevelt* (1931), by Henry F. Pringle, or the scholarly, well-written *Power and Responsibility: The Life and Times of Theodore Roosevelt* (1961), by William F. Harbaugh, or the short and penetrating analysis by John M. Blum, *The Republican Roosevelt* (1954). Howard K. Beale's *Theodore Roosevelt and America's Rise to World Power* (1956) emphasizes foreign affairs.

Henry F. Pringle, *The Life and Times of William Howard Taft* (1939), is a useful biography, while the revolt in Republican ranks against "stand-pat-tism" during the Taft administration is described by Kenneth Hechler in *Insurgency* (1940). The best brief survey of the Taft and Wilson years up to World War I is Arthur S. Link's *Woodrow Wilson and the Progressive Era* (1954). Link has been writing the standard multivolume biography of Wilson; several volumes have appeared since 1947. A critical incident in Wilson's Mexican policy is the subject of Robert E. Quirk's *Affair of Honor* (1961).

On the early civil rights movement, Louis E. Lomax's *The Negro Revolt* (1963) is very helpful.

Local government was of major concern to progressive reformers; for an unsympathetic view of them as a self-seeking interest group read Samuel P. Hays, "The Politics of Reform in Municipal Government in the Progressive Era" (*Pacific Northwest Quarterly*, October, 1964). A recent and excellent treatment of a key aspect of local politics is John M. Allswang's *A House for All Peoples: Ethnic Politics in Chicago 1890–1936* (1971).

Chapter 6: Progressive Foreign Policies, the "Great War," and the Twenties

In addition to several of the books suggested at the end of Chapter 5, the foreign policies of the teens and twenties are illuminated by studies such as *The Inquiry: American Preparations for Peace 1917–1919* (1963) by Lawrence Gelfand; *Wilson the Diplomatist* (1957) by Arthur S. Link; *The Diplomacy of the Dollar* (1950) by Herbert Feis, on economic influences on the foreign policy of the twenties; Thomas H. Buckley's *The United States and the Washington Conference* (1970); and Robert H. Ferrell's books, *Peace in Their Time* (1952), on the Kellogg-Briand pact and surrounding events, and *American Diplomacy in the Great Depression* (1957). For a study of the literature, read Daniel M. Smith, "National Interest and American Intervention 1917: An Historiographical Appraisal," in *Journal of American History* (1965). Elting Morison's *Turmoil and Tradition* (1960) is the standard and excellent biography of Henry M. Stimson.

The domestic politics of the twenties are being studied with some care by historians, and books on particular phases are becoming more abundant. Some of the best are Robert Murray's *Red Scare: a Study in National Hysteria* (1955), and Stanley Coben's biography of that event's leader, *A. Mitchell Palmer* (1963); William M. Tuttle, Jr.'s *Race Riot: Chicago in the Red Summer of 1919* (1970); Daniel Bell's essay on "Marxian Socialism" in *Socialism in American Life* (1952), edited by Stow Persons, delineating the inner history of socialist and communist politics in the twenties; Burl Noggle's *Teapot Dome: Oil and Politics in the Twenties* (1962); and David Burner's *Politics of Provincialism: The Democratic Party in Transition 1918–1932* (1968). Albert U. Romasco has written an excellent study of the politics of the Hoover Administration, *The Poverty of Abundance* (1965).

Several fine books deal with states and regions. George Tindall, *The Emergence of the New South 1913–1945* (1967) is standard. J. J. Huthmacher's *Massachusetts People and Politics 1919–1933* (1959) has ramifications well beyond a single state. Biographies of statesmen are led by Huthmacher's *Senator Robert F. Wagner and the Rise of Urban Liberalism* (1968); John A. Garraty, *Henry Cabot Lodge* (1953); Richard Lowitt, *George Norris* (1963); Lawrence W. Levine, *Defender of the Faith: William Jennings Bryan, the Last Decade 1915–1925* (1965); Oscar Handlin, *Al Smith and His America* (1958); Joel Seidler, *Norman Thomas* (1961); Donald R. McCoy, *Calvin Coolidge, the Quiet President* (1967); and the first volume of Frank Freidel's biography, *Franklin D. Roosevelt: The Apprenticeship* (1952).

General treatments of the late teens, the twenties, and the early thirties, all readable and reliable, are William Leuchtenberg, *The Perils of Prosperity 1914–32* (1958); Arthur M. Schlesinger, Jr., *The Age of Roosevelt: The Crisis of the Old Order 1919–1933* (1957); and John D. Hicks, *The Republican Ascendancy 1921–1933* (1960). Two provocative interpretive essays are Henry F. May's "Shifting Perspectives on the 1920's" (*Mississippi Valley Historical Review*, 1956), and Arthur S. Link's "What Happened to Progressivism in the Twenties?" (*American Historical Review*, 1959).

Chapter 7: The Great Depression, 1929–1940

The depression experience, Roosevelt, and the New Deal combined to produce intense feelings, and for many years after the thirties, dispassionate histories of the period were lacking. The New Deal had its severe critics, and more often, its ardent defenders. With the publication in 1963 of William E. Leuchtenberg's *Franklin D. Roosevelt and the New Deal 1932–1940*, which gave the New Deal credit for many changes and recognized the centrality of F.D.R. in the story, yet pointed out that the New Deal did not really "cure" the Depression, and benefited middle-class groups much more than others, scholarship on the period has become more detached. When recent scholars have been critical, they have usually suggested that the New Deal did not go far enough; critics in the thirties and forties, on the other hand, usually said it had gone too far. Leuchtenberg also wrote a survey of the years leading up to the New Deal: *The Perils of Prosperity 1914–32* (1958), which was followed in the same series by Dexter Perkins' *The New Age of Franklin D. Roosevelt 1932–45* (1957); both are brief, good treatments.

On the Depression, several books mentioned for chapter 6 are important; see also Broadus Mitchell, *Depression Decade: From the New Era through the New Deal 1919–1941* (1947); Dixon Wecter, *The Age of the Great Depression*

1919–1941 (1948), a pair of fortyish surveys; Daniel M. Smith, *War and Depression: America 1914–1939* (1972), which contains current interpretations and bibliography; John Shover, *Cornbelt Rebellion* (1965), on Midwestern agrarian unrest; Irving Bernstein, *Turbulent Years: A History of the American Worker 1933–1941* (1969); and Sidney Fine, *Sit-Down: The General Motors Strike of 1936–1937* (1969). A very important contemporary document is Robert and Helen Lynd's *Middletown in Transition* (1937), a follow-up of their book on Muncie during the twenties, drawing many comparisons between the twenties and the thirties.

Several excellent biographies of Roosevelt now exist. The most elaborate one is incomplete: Frank Freidel's *Franklin D. Roosevelt*, three volumes (1952, 1954, 1956) of which are now in print. Arthur Schlesinger, Jr., has also yet to finish his *The Age of Roosevelt*; three volumes (1957, 1959, 1960) exist covering from 1919 through the early New Deal. The best shorter biography is by James McGregor Burns, *Roosevelt: The Lion and the Fox* (1956), on the Depression and New Deal years, and *Roosevelt: The Soldier of Freedom* (1970). Views by contemporaries and associates of F.D.R include Frances Perkins, *The Roosevelt I Knew* (1946); Robert E. Sherwood, *Roosevelt and Hopkins* (1946); *The Secret Diary of Harold L. Ickes* (1953–54); Eleanor Roosevelt, *This I Remember* (1949); and Rexford G. Tugwell, *The Democratic Roosevelt* (1957).

Relevant biographies deal with various key figures of the period; the Roosevelts themselves are dissected in Joseph P. Lash's compassionate *Eleanor and Franklin* (1971). For the man who was probably F.D.R.'s greatest threat for a time, read T. Harry Williams' beautifully written *Huey Long* (1969). On the diplomat and statesman once called "the last of the American Genro," Henry L. Stimson, Elting Morison's *Turmoil and Tradition* (1960) is definitive and absorbing. Arthur Mann's two volumes on the "Little Flower," *Mayor Fiorello LaGuardia of New York* (1959, 1965) are excellent, as are J. J. Huthmacher's *Senator Robert F. Wagner and the Rise of Urban Liberalism* (1968) and John M. Blum's *From the Morgenthau Diaries* (1959). Donald R. McCoy, *Landon of Kansas* (1966) deals with the progressive Republican whom F.D.R. defeated in 1936. Edward L. and Frederick H. Schapsmeier have described the life of the unusual man who was Secretary of Agriculture in the New Deal, vice-president during the War, and Progressive (anti–Cold War) candidate for president in 1948, in *Henry A. Wallace of Iowa: The Agrarian Years 1910–1940* (1968) and *Prophet in Politics: Henry A. Wallace and the War Years* (1970).

On various aspects of the New Deal, the following are dependable and thoughtful: Harry Millis and E. C. Brown, *From the Wagner Act to Taft–Hartley* (1950), on federal labor legislation; Donald R. McCoy, *Angry Decade* (1958), on radical opponents of the New Deal; George Wolfskill, *Revolt of the Conservatives: A History of the American Liberty League* (1962); James T.

Patterson, *Congressional Conservatism and the New Deal: The Growth of the Conservative Coalition in Congress 1933–1939* (1967), an excellent study whose implications for national politics carry down nearly to the present; Patterson, *The New Deal and the States: Federalism in Transition* (1969); Otis L. Graham, *Encore for Reform: The Old Progressives and the New Deal* (1967); George Q. Flynn, *American Catholics and the Roosevelt Candidacy* (1968); Raymond Wolters, *Negroes and the Great Depression* (1970); David Green, *The Containment of Latin America: A History of the Myths and Realities of the Good Neighbor Policy* (1971), which is critical. For an historiographical critique read Richard Kirkendall, "The New Deal as Watershed: The Recent Literature," in *Journal of American History* (1968).

Chapter 8: World War and Cold War, 1938–1953

For years the historical questions concerning the entry of the United States into World War II were extremely vexed. Although the controversy has not subsided completely, it is now at a stage of rationally argued interpretive differences rather than of bitter recrimination. The leading works that are generally sympathetic to Roosevelt and his administration in foreign policy before the War, and that have found wide acceptance among historians, are Herbert Feis, *The Road to Pearl Harbor* (1950), and the lengthier *Challenge to Isolation* (1952) and *The Undeclared War* (1953) by William L. Langer and Everett Gleason. Generally unsympathetic, but also respectable, reasonable, and well-regarded, is Paul Schroeder's *The Axis Alliance and Japanese-American Relations 1941* (1958). Roberta Wohlstetter, *Pearl Harbor: Warning and Decision* (1962) is the best account of that episode. A good collection of all viewpoints is Robert Dallek, ed., *The Roosevelt Diplomacy and World War II* (1970). On domestic opposition to foreign involvements in the thirties, the events that led to the Neutrality acts, see John E. Wiltz' penetrating *In Search of Peace: the Senate Munitions Inquiry 1934–35* (1962). Wiltz' *From Isolation to War 1931–1941* (1968) is the best brief survey of the events, and the historical writing about them, of its period. Dorothy Borg's *The United States and the Far Eastern Crisis of 1933–38* (1964) is thorough and well-balanced. Robert Divine, *The Illusion of Neutrality* (1962) is a good overall account of the foreign policies of the prewar years; see also Divine's useful *Roosevelt and World War II* (1969). On China, Paul Holbo's *United States Policies Toward China* (1969) deals effectively with the whole twentieth century, with a chapter on World War II; on a key episode, see Barbara Tuchman's *Stilwell and the American Experience in China* (1971).

The most useful general history of World War II is the two-volume work by A. Russell Buchanan, *The United States in World War II* (1964). On the last stages of the European struggle, read Stephen Ambrose's *Eisenhower and Berlin* (1967). Kent Roberts Greenfield, *American Strategy in World War II* (1963) is authoritative, and John Snell's *Illusion and Necessity: The Diplomacy of Global War* (1963) is a good survey of its subject. For detailed, accurate, and highly readable accounts of grand strategy and wartime diplomacy, consult the several books by Herbert Feis entitled *The China Tangle* (1953), *Japan Subdued* (1960), *Between War and Peace* (1960), and especially *Churchill, Roosevelt, Stalin* (1957).

James McGregor Burns' *Roosevelt: Soldier of Freedom* (1970) is best on the war leader.

A full-scale biography of Harry S Truman has not yet seen print, but when it does it will not supplant the valuable and highly readable *Memoirs* (1955, 1956) of the former president. For the Truman years, Eric F. Goldman's *Crucial Decade—And After* (1960) is a delightful survey of trends both political and popular. Domestic affairs are dealt with by Stephen K. Bailey, *Congress Makes a Law* (1950), on the Employment Act of 1946; Harry Millis and E. C. Brown's *From the Wagner Act to Taft-Hartley* (1950); Richard S. Kirkendall, *The Truman Period as a Research Field* (1967); Allen J. Matusow, *Farm Policies and Politics of the Truman Years* (1967); Theodore Draper, *The Roots of American Communism* (1957); Michael Rogin's fine *The Intellectuals and McCarthy* (1967); Robert Griffith, *The Politics of Fear: Joseph R. McCarthy and the Senate* (1970); and the vigorously critical biography by Richard Rovere, *Senator Joe McCarthy* (1959). Alistair Cooke's *Generation on Trial* (1950) deals with the Hiss-Chambers episode.

Biographies and memoirs are more plentiful concerning military and diplomatic leaders. Among the best and most recent are *Memoirs, 1925–1950* (1967) by George F. Kennan, and *Present at the Creation* (1969) by Dean Acheson. *The Forrestal Diaries* (1951), edited by Walter Millis, is a valuable personal statement, as are *The Private Papers of Senator Vandenberg* (1952), and James F. Byrnes' *Speaking Frankly* (1947) and *All in One Lifetime* (1958). Robert H. Ferrell's *Marshall* (1967) deals with General George C. Marshall's years as Secretary of State, while Forrest Pogue has so far published two volumes of his *George C. Marshall* (1963, 1966), complete to 1942. Recent and excellent is James T. Patterson's *Mr. Republican* (1972) on Robert A. Taft.

A useful and balanced book on the Yalta Conference and the postwar settlements is by John L. Snell *et al.*, *The Meaning of Yalta* (1956). On the Potsdam Conference see Herbert Feis' *Between War and Peace* (1960). A dissenting view on the origins of the Cold War, carrying the idea that the atomic bomb was used on Japan in order to soften up the Russians, is *Atomic Diplomacy: Hiroshima and Potsdam* (1965), by Gar Alperovitz. George F. Kennan, *American Diplomacy 1900–1950* (1951) discusses the immediate postwar world in historical context. Asian policy is described well in *America's Failure in China 1941–1950* (1963) by Tang Tsou.

The Cold War and its origins has recently become one of the most hotly debated topics among American historians. The prevailing view through the fifties and into the sixties was sympathetic to the Truman administration, and assumed basically that the Marshall Plan, the Berlin airlift, NATO, and other security treaties were undertaken in an effort to "contain" a real threat of Soviet expansion, especially in Europe. That view began to be criticized heavily in the late sixties, as Vietnam policy eroded credibility in the government's conduct of foreign policy, retrospectively as well as currently; the new, "revisionist," view finds that the United States was as much, or more, responsible for the Cold War confrontation as the Soviet Union was. Though Chapter 8 of this book does not reflect this new viewpoint to any marked degree, I have taken it seriously and have taken account of its more considered points. Among the more prominent statements of the new viewpoint are two books by Gabriel Kolko: *The Politics of War: The World and United States Foreign Policy 1943–1945* (1968) and *The Roots of American Foreign Policy* (1969), which find American intransigence to the Soviet Union, and thus the beginnings of the (American-inspired) Cold War, to have begun as early as the middle of World War II. Another book representing the new view is Lloyd C. Gardner's *Architects of Illusion: Men and Ideas in American Foreign Policy 1941–1949* (1970). Two collections of essays representing various points of view are Thomas G. Paterson, ed., *Cold War Critics* (1971), and Barton J. Bernstein, ed., *Politics and Policies of the Truman Administration* (1970). A very handy book, which carries three distinct and comparable essays, is *The Origins of the Cold War* (1970), by Lloyd C. Gardner, Arthur Schlesinger, Jr., and Hans Morgenthau.

Chapter 9: Demography, 1940–1971: Youth, Suburbs, and Civil Rights

Basic demographic changes in the United States during the first half of the century have been described technically by Donald Bogue in *The Population of the United States* (1959). A preliminary but helpful summary of the 1970 census, by Philip Hauser, appeared in *Scientific American* in September, 1971. The growth and sprawl of metropolises is discussed in *Megalopolis* (1961), by Jean Gottmann, which treats of the merging of metropolitan areas in the Northeast; in a group of essays edited by *Fortune* magazine, *The Exploding Metropolis* (1958); in Raymond Vernon's *Metropolis 1985* (1960), the concluding and prognosticating volume in a series on the New York area; and in *The Death and Life of Great American Cities* (1962), a stimulating diatribe against city planning practice and urban trends, by Jane Jacobs. The growth of suburbs and their problems is Robert Woods' subject in *Suburbia* (1959). Two case studies of very different examples of urbanism are the Lynds' *Middletown in Transition* (1937) and Herbert Gans' *The Urban Villagers* (1962), on an urban-renewable Italian neighborhood in Boston.

Gans' *The Levittowners* (1967) is excellent; so is *The Ghetto* (1928), on Jewish immigrant neighborhoods, by Louis Wirth.

Two differing books on social mobility, both sociological, are *Big Business Leaders in America* (1955), by W. Lloyd Warner and James Abegglen, and *The Power Elite* (1956), by C. Wright Mills. On the South, including racial demography and problems, see Thomas D. Clark, *The Emerging South* (1961); James Agee and Walker Evans, *Let Us Now Praise Famous Men* (1941); George Tindall's *Emergence of the New South 1913–1945* (1967); and Dan T. Carter, *Scottsboro: A Tragedy of the American South* (1969). Nathan Glazer and Daniel P. Moynihan trenchantly commented on latter-day immigration and assimilation in *Beyond the Melting Pot* (1963).

On the Negro migration and the civil rights movement, see the several books mentioned in the bibliography for Chapter 2, as well as the following: August Meier and Elliott Rudwick, *From Plantation to Ghetto: An Interpretive History of American Negroes* (1969); Ralph Ellison's novel, *The Invisible Man* (1952); James W. Silver, *Mississippi: The Closed Society* (1964); Howard Zinn, *SNCC: The New Abolitionists* (1964); and *The Autobiography of Malcolm X* (1966), by the assassinated Black Muslim leader. For government policy, consult William C. Berman, *The Politics of Civil Rights in the Truman Administration* (1970). A careful and well-written treatment of an ugly episode is Roger Daniels' *Concentration Camps USA: Japanese Americans and World War II* (1971).

Popular moods and the impact of mass media and mass society in the fifties were explored with intelligence and style in *The Lonely Crowd* (1950) by David Riesman, and *The Organization Man* (1956) by William H. Whyte. John K. Galbraith told of life in an increasingly prosperous United States in *The Affluent Society* (1958), but the story of the many who were not prosperous was told by Michael Harrington in *The Other America* (1963).

Chapter 10: The Economy since 1940: From Depression to Affluence

For a sound study of the domestic economy during and immediately after World War II, see Joel Seidman, *American Labor from Defense to Reconversion* (1953). Measurements of the distribution of income, and how it became more democratic in the mid-twentieth century, abound in Simon Kuznets' *Shares of Upper Income Groups in Income and Savings* (1953). The best summary of economic developments during the Eisenhower period is in Harold Vatter, *The U.S. Economy in the 1950s* (1963), and of the period immediately following, in Seymour Harris' *The Economics of the Kennedy Years* (1964).

Economic thought had to change before economic practice could change, and both are theorized upon and described in several highly useful books. Thurman Arnold, a New Dealer, produced a book influential in the thirties in breaking down myths, *The Folklore of Capitalism* (1937). For changes in the relations between management and ownership, and their implications for society, see James Burnham, *The Managerial Revolution* (1941), and Adolf A. Berle, *The Twentieth Century Capitalist Revolution* (1954), the latter being an especially fine little book on modern big business and social responsibility. The influence of the British economic theorist, John Maynard Keynes, which was pronounced in the Kennedy administration, is better understood after reading Robert Lekachman's *The Age of Keynes* (1966). For a sociological analysis of changes in the labor force after World War II, see C. Wright Mills' *White Collar* (1951). For recent statistics, the Census Bureau's *Pocket Data Book 1971* is a handy reference source.

Chapter 11: Since 1953: The High Tide and Ebb Tide of Liberal Politics

Eisenhower is too recent a figure to be as yet the subject of a full-scale biography, but some of his associates have provided memoirs. Sherman Adams, *Firsthand Report* (1962) is that of President Eisenhower's chief aide. Emmett J. Hughes presents an unflattering portrait of the White House operation in the fifties in *Ordeal of Power* (1963). A highly useful examination of the Eisenhower presidency, as well as those of Hoover, Roosevelt, and Truman, is Walter Johnson, *1600 Pennsylvania Avenue* (1960). On domestic events during the Eisenhower years, see also Archibald Cox's *The Warren Court: Constitutional Decision as an Instrument of Reform* (1968), and on the civil liberties decisions, Anthony Lewis' *Gideon's Trumpet* (1964). Robert Dahl, *Who Governs?* (1961) is a political scientist's analysis of urban politics.

Short biographies of Eisenhower's two-time electoral opponent are Stuart G. Brown's *Conscience in Politics* (1961) and Herbert J. Muller's appreciative *Adlai Stevenson: A Study in Values* (1967). The enigmatic and powerful figure of John Foster Dulles awaits a biographer; Herman Finer's *Dulles over Suez* (1964) is critical of American policy of 1956. Tad Szulc, *Winds of Revolution* (1963) is a survey of Latin America and the United States' relations with it. *Nuclear Weapons and Foreign Policy* (1956) by Henry Kissinger, is a fifty-ish analysis of general strategy by the scholar who later became President Nixon's foreign policy adviser.

Although John F. Kennedy did not live to write his memoirs, it has been said that two massive books by close associates have come near to doing that job. Theodore Sorenson's *Kennedy* (1965), by JFK's "alter ego," is remarkably objective, and Arthur M. Schlesinger, Jr.'s *A Thousand Days* (1965) is a highly readable history of the Kennedy administration. An excellent and well-informed analysis of the campaign and election of 1960, leaning a bit more toward Kennedy than toward Nixon, is *The Making of the President 1960* (1961) by Theodore F. White. The anthology by the editors of *Fortune* called *America in the Sixties* (1960) has interesting material on politics and society. Two books dealing with aspects of domestic affairs during the Kennedy years are Jim F. Heath's *John F. Kennedy and the Business Community* (1969) and Eugene B. Skolnikoff's *Science, Technology, and American Foreign Policy* (1967) by a participant-observer. For a view of the Bay of Pigs episode read Karl Meyer and Tad Szulc, *The Cuban Invasion* (1962); on the missile crisis of 1962, a perceptive and dramatic narrative is Elie Abel's *The Missile Crisis* (1966). A bibliographical statement is James T. Crown, *The Kennedy Literature* (1968).

Two biographies of Lyndon B. Johnson are useful: Rowland Evans and Robert Novak, *Lyndon B. Johnson* (1966), and the more sympathetic *The Professional* (1964) by William S. White. On the presidential years, a private but poignant and informed viewpoint is provided by Eric F. Goldman in *The Tragedy of Lyndon Johnson* (1968). John Bartlow Martin, the ambassador to the Dominican Republic, reported on the 1965 American involvement there in *Overtaken by Events* (1966). The elections of 1964 and 1968 have had many commentators, but perhaps the most thorough has been Theodore F. White in *The Making of the President 1964* (1965) and *The Making of the President 1968* (1969). The American involvement in Vietnam has been discussed with perhaps the greatest candor and objectivity by a French journalist, Bernard Fall, in *Two Vietnams* (1964) and *Vietnam Witness* (1966), the latter a series of Fall's articles written over many years in Southeast Asia. J. William Fulbright's *The Arrogance of Power* (1966) is the statement critical of American involvement by the Chairman of the Senate Foreign Relations Committee.

On broad political and electoral trends, *The Real Majority*, by political analysts Richard Scammon and Ben J. Wattenberg (1970), is stimulating. Right-wing politics are assessed by James McEvoy III in *Radicals or Conservatives: The Contemporary American Right* (1971), and the complexities of politics in the largest state are analyzed historically by Michael P. Rogin and John L. Shover in *Political Change in California: Critical Elections and Social Movements 1890–1896* (1970).

Chapter 12: Culture and Society since the Forties

National moods and mores are not easy for contemporaries to capture accurately. Occasionally, as in David Riesman's *The Lonely Crowd* (1950), it happens. Another good attempt is *Coming Apart: An Informal History of America in the 1960s* (1971), by William L. O'Neill. One of the best books ever written on the flaws in American race relations was done by a foreign observer, the Swedish sociologist Gunnar Myrdal, whose *American Dilemma* appeared in 1944. Religious patterns in the postwar period were discussed by Will Herberg in *Protestant-Catholic-Jew* (1955), and by Samuel A. Mueller and Angela V. Lane in "Tabulations from the 1957 Current Population Survey on Religion: a Contribution to the Demography of American

Religion," in *The Journal for the Scientific Study of Religion*, March, 1972, who refine and revise Herberg's views. Popular culture was surveyed in a series of essays edited by Bernard Rosenberg and D. M. White, *Mass Culture: The Popular Arts in America* (1957). One of the most thorough social-science research projects on American society was led by Alfred Kinsey and published as *Sexual Behavior in the Human Male* (1948) and *Sexual Behavior in the Human Female* (1953)—the famous Kinsey Reports. Frederick Lewis Allen wrote in a very different way, but valuably, about American society in the thirties in *Since Yesterday* (1940).

Except for Carlos Baker's *Hemingway* (1969), few biographies of recent leading writers have appeared, but novels by these writers often provide excellent descriptions of parts of American society. The "Studs Lonigan" trilogy by James T. Farrell provides a realistic insight into Chicago street life in the thirties; John Updike's *Rabbit, Run* (1960) is a penetrating treatment of youth in a drab Eastern city in the fifties. The depression and its impact are clearly seen in John Steinbeck's *The Grapes of Wrath* (1939).

Problems in education have been surveyed by James B. Conant in *Slums and Suburbs* (1964), and, for the sixties, in Jonathan Kozol's *Death at an Early Age* (1967). Martin Mayer's *The Schools* (1961) is a highly readable look at elementary and secondary education. The great changes in universities and their social function were examined by Clark Kerr in *The Uses of the University* (1963). Philanthropy, the foundations, and research and development need more historical treatment, but Robert Bremner's *American Philanthropy* (1960) is a broad-scale beginning. On attitudes of youth in the middle and late sixties, Seymour Martin Lipset and Earl Raab presented a balanced view in "The Non-Generation Gap" (*Commentary*, August, 1970).

Index